HARVARD ECONOMIC STUDIES

VOLUME C

The studies in this series are published by the Department of Economics of Harvard University. The Department does not assume responsibility for the views expressed.

ECONOMIC

CONCENTRATION

AND THE

MONOPOLY

31467

PROBLEM

Edward S. Mason

HARVARD UNIVERSITY PRESS
Cambridge, Massachusetts
1 9 5 7

HD 2785
M39e

The Harvard Economic Studies
1906 to 1956, Volumes I to C

By John Kenneth Galbraith

With this volume Harvard Economic Studies celebrate a double anniversary. It is now fifty years since the series was first established. This is the hundredth volume. Even in economics a fifty-year life span establishes no great claim to antiquity, but this series is, almost certainly, the oldest as well as the largest of its kind. It also, in a small way, mirrors the fashions and, one hopes too, the progress of economic science during this century. The fiftieth anniversary and the century volume provide an occasion for reflecting briefly on these changes. But first a word on the Harvard Economic Studies themselves.

At a meeting of the Department of Economics on January 23, 1906, Professors Frank W. Taussig and Thomas Nixon Carver were appointed a committee to consider the possibility of publishing a series of volumes on economics. They so recommended, and on February 10 their recommendation was accepted. The present name of the series was settled upon at the same meeting. Professor Carver was nominated to be in charge and remained principally in charge for more than two decades. If a scholarly enterprise, like a country, is blessed by being without history, the Harvard Economic Studies are fortunate indeed.

In a sense, however, the decision to found the series was merely the last link in an earlier and more interesting chain of events and one that sought to insure that the Harvard Economic Studies would be sound as to subject matter and which at least succeeded in insuring that they would be soundly financed. These events had their origin in the career of David A. Wells, one of the most engaging public figures of the nineteenth century. Born in 1828, Wells by the end of the Civil War had had a considerable career as a newspaper publisher, inventor, and entrepreneur. In 1864 he published his notable pamphlet, *Our Burden and Our Strength,* in which he came powerfully to the defense of the greenbacks. (They could be regarded and held with confidence for, behind them, lay the wealth and bur-geoning industrial strength of the North.) This timely document, which was given a vast circulation, brought Wells to the attention of Lincoln who made him Chairman of the National Revenue Commission. Wells's interest in economics, especially in taxation and international trade, developed rapidly, and although he was discharged by Grant for acquiring excessively free trade views — then as in our own time the device was to abolish his post — economic policy continued to be his central preoccupation until his death in 1898. His faith was that of his century. He believed in individualism, sound money, laissez-faire, free trade, honest government, and the social rewards of enlightenment. He did not doubt that these values were immutable, and in pursuit of this conviction he willed one-third of his estate to Harvard — there was a similar bequest to Williams College — with the following instruction:

They [the President and Fellows of Harvard College] shall hold and invest the same in such manner as will afford the largest annual income consistent with reasonable security.

2nd. They shall offer annually a prize of five hundred dollars, to be competed for by any undergraduate of the senior class in such College or University, respectively, or by any graduate of the same of not more than three years standing for the best essay, or detailed result of personal investigation in . . . [a lengthy list of economic topics]

3rd. The prizes when awarded shall be known as the David A. Wells Prizes and shall be paid in gold coin of standard weight and fineness, or in the form of a medal of gold of corresponding value, suitably inscribed, at the option of the recipient.

4th. No subject shall be selected for competitive writing or investigation and no essay shall be considered which in any way advocates or defends the spoliation of property under form of process of law; or the restriction of commerce in times of peace by Legislation, except for moral or sanitary purposes; or the enactment of usury laws, or the impairment of contracts by the debasement of coin; or the issue and use by Government of irredeemable notes or promises to pay intended to be used as currency and as a substitute for money; or which defends the endowment of such 'paper,' 'notes' and 'promises to pay' with the legal tender quality.

5th. The remainder of the income of said fund shall be respectively by said corporations devoted each year to the publication and distribution of the essay for which the prize may be awarded, including all legitimate expenses incident to the management of the fund and the use of the income, and the several prize essays shall be free to any one to reprint and circulate.

In our sensitive age Wells' proscriptions in Clause 4 would be counted an assault on freedom of inquiry. With a regret functionally related to the sum involved, Harvard would now be required to refuse a gift so restricted. Fifty years ago, however, attitudes were more easygoing. In any case, Wells was only excluding conclusions which presumably no reputable scholar would reach in the first place. And, in fact, no manuscript has been offered against which the prohibition has seemed to run too remorselessly. The far more serious problem was the implication in the will that the results of the permissible scholarship might be given away free.

On this point, according to plausible legend, President Eliot intervened. He stated vigorously his belief that anyone who received an economic monograph for nothing would value it at precisely nothing. But if the essays were to be sold what should be done with the money? The Harvard Economic Studies were the answer. The Wells bequest would be used to publish the Wells Prize essays. And the revenues from their sale would be used to publish yet other books by faculty members or graduates of the University. This involved a liberal construction of Wells's intent but one of which he most likely would have approved.

In the years since 1906, Wells Prize essays have been published at the rate of rather less than one a year. The competition has been confined in practice to Ph.D. theses. In some years no prize has been awarded because there was no worthy competitor. In other cases individuals have been awarded the prize but have never submitted their manuscripts in final form for publication. All this means that rather fewer than half of the volumes in the series have been prize essays. Since the proceeds from the sale of the Wells Prize essays become available to finance the publication of the other volumes, every prize essay adds to revenues but not to costs. Not surprisingly, the Studies have been admirably solvent throughout their life. In 1922, in response to a query from Professor Leonard White of the University of Chicago about the series, Professor Carver observed, "We have not yet had to refuse publication, on account of lack of funds, of any volume we were really anxious to publish."

This has continued to be the case. It does not mean, however, that financial stringency has never been pleaded as an excuse to anxious but otherwise unqualified authors.

The first volume in the series, by William Hyde Price, was a history of the internal grants of monopoly (on mining, mechanical inventions, glass) in sixteenth- and seventeenth-century England. (The volume of 261 pages was published at $1.50. Though still in print, the price was at some point raised to $2.00.) That the series should have begun with a volume on economic history was appropriate, for nothing so sharply distinguishes the early years of the series as the concentration of titles in this field. A volume can presumably be classified as history if it deals with events remote in time from the writing and if the author's primary concern is with the period of which he treats and not the use of its evidence to illuminate some contemporary problem. By this standard no fewer than fifteen of the first twenty-five volumes — those published up to 1923 — were devoted to economic history. Of the last twenty-five volumes — those published since 1944 — not more than five are concerned with history.

The change came in the second half of the thirties. Then there was a great increase in titles of contemporary import: monetary policy, market regulation, antitrust policy, foreign exchange, and the economic experiments of Germany and Italy. The postwar volumes reflect a similar interest.

Quite clearly, the series owes a good part of such distinction as it enjoys to its economic historians. Among these there have been two — Professors N. S. B. Gras and Earl J. Hamilton — who have each contributed three distinguished volumes. Two more have come from Professor Abbott Payson Usher, for a total of eight from these three scholars. Professor Usher was also for many years the devoted and conscientious editor of the series. Sharing honors with Professors Gras and Hamilton as the most prolific contributor to the series is Professor Seymour Harris. He is the author of three works in the series and quite possibly he should be given a decision over his competitors, for one of the works — his sternly orthodox plea for hard money, *Twenty Years of Federal Reserve Policy* — runs to two volumes.

The volume here introduced is the second contribution by Professor Mason. His earlier one, published in 1932, was on the decline and impending fall of the street railway industry in Massachusetts (*The Street Railway in Massachusetts*). It is tempting to cite from this serious and competent study what can perhaps be regarded as the most remarkable example of wishful thinking in the history of economic analysis. "The theory has been current in street railway circles for the last two or three years," Professor Mason notes in summing up his findings, "that the registration of privately owned motor cars has about reached its maximum." It must quickly be added that the author himself declined to accept this hypothesis.

Economic theory entered the series very gradually. In the first twenty-five volumes, there was no work devoted exclusively to economic theory. The nearest approach were the theoretical chapters of Taussig's *Some Aspects of the Tariff Question,* published in 1915, and Z. C. Dickinson's mainly psychological study, *Economic Motives,* which appeared in 1922. The theory of international trade was substantially enriched by Volume XXVI, Professor Viner's *Canada's Balance of International Indebtedness, 1900–1913,* in which an excursion into economic history provided the occasion for investigation of the theory of international capital movements. An avowedly theoretical contribution came two years later in 1926 with James W. Angell's *The Theory of International Prices.* At intervals thereafter came the further theoretical contributions by which the series is perhaps best known. These latter include Professor E. H. Chamberlin's *The Theory of Monopolistic Competition* which, now in its seventh edition, is by a wide margin the series' best seller; Paul A. Samuelson's *Foundations of Economic Analysis,* the series' most formidable exercise in mathematical economics; and James S. Duesenberry's influential *Income, Saving, and the Theory of Consumer Behavior.* All three of these studies, incidentally, were originally submitted as Ph.D. theses. The first two were Wells Prize essays at Harvard; Professor Duesenberry's was submitted at the University of Michigan.

The very earliest volumes of the Harvard Economic Studies were published by Houghton Mifflin Company. Since Volume VI, however, they have appeared under the imprint of the Harvard University Press. A word should be said about the role of the Press. Among university people there is a nearly universal conviction that all university presses are inefficient and unbusinesslike, lacking in initiative, and otherwise incompetent. This feeling is evidently based on the deep-seated belief that no enterprise connected with an institution of higher learning can be operated with intelligence. It would be hard to justify these beliefs so far as the Harvard Economic Studies are concerned. Nearly every author has had a deep, if often unacknowledged, debt to the patient and skillful editorial assistance of the Harvard University Press. Books pass through the Press in rather less time than is common with commercial publishers. In appearance the volumes are urbane and to some tastes possibly handsome. The distribution is prompt and efficient. In a scientific series, it is doubtful if more can be asked.

The sales of the volumes in the Harvard Economic Studies are not large. The first volume in the series in the first fifty years has sold 309 copies; the second (*The Lodging-House Problem in Boston,* by A. B. Wolfe) appears from what may be deficient records to have so far sold only 102 copies. Another early volume has a recorded sale of only fifty-nine copies. The rate of publication in the series has accelerated moderately with the passage of time: it took twenty-nine years to publish the first fifty volumes and only twenty-one years to publish the second fifty, despite the important interruption of World War II. Sales of the more recent volumes have been considerably greater than the early ones. The typical volume now sells from five hundred to a thousand copies, and about one in ten runs to several times these figures. If a sale of, say, seven hundred copies seems small, it should be inquired how many people need to read about the application of linear programming to refinery operations or go into the technical aspects of crop forecasting. While a good publisher will make all who are concerned aware of the existence of such books, he will never try to unload them on an unsuspecting public.

Mention of sales brings this note properly to its concluding point, namely, the standards which should rule in the selection of volumes for a series such as this. These are simple to state, even though they are less simple to practice: the critical test is not the subject-matter or the extent of the interest in the subject, but the quality of the workmanship. The book of general topical interest and importance will normally find a publisher. For a series like this to search for such books and to make their publication a measure of its success is to duplicate what is already being done. But the work of high scientific or scholarly value with a limited or highly specialized audience presents a very different publishing problem. For these it is not easy to find a publisher because such books cannot — within the framework of conventional attitudes on book prices — be published at a profit. The subsidy which the Harvard Economic Studies enjoys is specifically to insure that scholarly and scientific merit are not sacrificed to the inconsistent or hostile criteria of the market.

No one would want to argue that all of the one hundred books so far published in the Harvard Economic Studies would still survive the critical scrutiny of a highly qualified jury concerned only with their scientific and scholarly merit. There have been mistakes; in particular, it has, on occasion, been too tempting to award the Wells Prize to the best of a meagre crop. Nonetheless the criterion that the quality of the work and no other criterion should rule is well established. And it will be worth holding to. Our task must be to publish the very best of the Harvard contributions to economics, on occasion for the many, but more often for the few.

October 1956

Acknowledgments

The author is indebted to the following publications, publishers, individuals, and organizations for permission to republish certain of the papers included in this volume:

American Economic Review; Chamber of Commerce of the United States, Washington, D. C.; *Harvard Law Review;* Industrial Relations Research Association, *Proceedings; Journal of Industrial Economics;* McGraw-Hill Co., *Explorations in Economics: Notes and Essays Contributed in Honor of F. W. Taussig;* McGraw-Hill Co., and Seymour Harris, ed., *Economic Reconstruction;* National Planning Association, Washington, D. C.; *Quarterly Journal of Economics; Review of Economics and Statistics; Trade Regulation Committee of the Association of the Bar of New York City; World Politics;* David McCord Wright, ed., *Money, Trade, and Economic Growth, in Honor of J. H. Williams; Yale Law Journal; Yale Review.*

Contents

General Introduction   1

PART I. THE LARGE FIRM AND THE STRUCTURE OF INDUSTRIAL MARKETS

Introduction   13
Chapter 1 Economic Concentration and the Monopoly
            Problem: A Review of Recent Literature   16
Chapter 2 Industrial Concentration and the Decline of Com-
            petition   44
Chapter 3 Price and Production Policies of Large-Scale
            Enterprise   55
Chapter 4 International Commodity Controls   73
Chapter 5 Schumpeter on Monopoly and the Large Firm   91

PART II. WAGE-PRICE PROBLEMS

Introduction   105
Chapter 6 Price Inflexibility   109
Chapter 7 Price Policies and Full Employment   134
Chapter 8 Competition, Price Policy, and High-Level Sta-
            bility   168
Chapter 9 Prices, Costs, and Profits   181
Chapter 10 Labor Monopoly and All That   196

PART III. RAW MATERIALS, SECURITY, AND ECONOMIC GROWTH

Introduction   221
Chapter 11 American Security and Access to Raw Materials   224
Chapter 12 Raw Materials, Rearmament, and Economic De-
            velopment   237
Chapter 13 An American View of Raw-Material Problems:
            The Report of the President's Materials Policy
            Commission   253
Chapter 14 Energy Requirements and Economic Growth   276

PART IV. ANTITRUST POLICY

Introduction   327
Chapter 15   Monopoly in Law and Economics   332
Chapter 16   The Current Status of the Monopoly Problem
             in the United States   351
Chapter 17   The New Competition   371
Chapter 18   Workable Competition Versus Workable Mo-
             nopoly   382
Chapter 19   Market Power and Business Conduct: Some
             Comments on the Report of the Attorney Gen-
             eral's Committee on Antitrust Policy   389
Index   403

ECONOMIC CONCENTRATION
AND THE MONOPOLY PROBLEM

General Introduction

The papers included in this volume relate mainly to problems of monopoly and the large firm and cover the period of the last fifteen to twenty years. It is a period with a definite beginning, but the end is not yet in sight. A re-examination of the position of large firms in the American and other industrial economies, and the monopolistic and other consequences thereof, may be said to have begun with the almost simultaneous appearance in 1932–33 of Chamberlin's *Theory of Monopolistic Competition*, Robinson's *The Economics of Imperfect Competition*, and Berle and Means' *The Modern Corporation and Private Property*. These studies not only have initiated subsequent inquiry, but also serve to point out fairly clearly the area with which we are concerned. On one side is a re-examination of market "models" and the theory of the firm; on the other, factual and statistical studies of economic concentration, market structure, and business policies. Both sides have contributed, moreover, to a reformulation of the central issues of public policy in the field of business organization.

Our present investigations have been by no means the exclusive product of private enterprise. Beginning in 1939 with the impressive *The Structure of the American Economy*, by the National Resources Committee, both the executive and the legislative branches of the American government have contributed extensively to these studies. The Temporary National Economic Committee in the late 1930's was as fecund in literary output as it was abortive in action. No less than 39 monographs and 44 volumes of hearings emanated from the Committee. During the second world war, the Special Senate Committee investigating the National Defense Program (Truman Committee) and a subcommittee of the Committee on Military Affairs (Kilgore Committee) laid bare the foreign cartel connections of American firms. Since the war, both House and Senate committees have poured out a Niagara of hearings on economic concentration, mergers, price discrimination, fair trade, and the fate of small business. The Federal Trade Commission has contributed a series of studies on the question of mergers and concentration. Finally, the Antitrust Division, revitalized early in the Roosevelt administration, has established an extensive record and has persuaded the Supreme Court to broaden substantially its interpretation of antitrust policy.

It would be a pleasure to report that these voluminous studies and investigations in academic halls, in business, and in government have brought lawyers, economists, and the general public to substantial agreement on the relation of bigness to monopoly and what should be done about it. In fact, the movement has been from a position of relative certainty to one of relative uncertainty in both professional and lay circles. In the 1920's, economists were confident that they had in the competitive market "model" a useful analytical tool applicable to the greater part of the economy. Monopoly was considered to be a distinct though less important phenomenon, and duopoly (or oligopoly) a textbook curiosity. Furthermore, both lawyers and economists substantially agreed concerning the meaning and extent of monopoly, and the relevance of economic analysis to antitrust policy. The sharp distinction in economics between competition and monopoly was adapted to the pro or con requirements of legal action and of public policy. Monopoly either existed or it did not. And if it existed, the remedy was clear; either a restoration of competition through appropriate antitrust action or public regulation.

The relative certainty regarding both diagnosis and prescription has long since given way to a rather fumbling uncertainty. The study of imperfect competition revealed to Mrs. Robinson a "world of monopolies." To the followers of Chamberlin, on the other hand, both competition and monopoly became delimiting concepts between which lay market reality in diffuse and various blend, of different sizes, shapes, and kinds. In reaction against this apparently unmanageable diversity of market types, some students have attempted to rescue the competitive model and to refurbish it for modern usage. Others, insisting that most industrial markets are oligopolies, have sought, by adding considerations neglected by earlier theorists, to "determine" business policies in situations treated by their predecessors as indeterminate.

The lack of agreement among economists has spread to the general public and to legal practitioners in the field of public policy. One common reaction to the precise statement of the requirements of pure competition is that monopoly is everywhere and something must be done about it. Another, even more common, is that since monopoly is everywhere, and we seem to be getting along, nothing need be done about it. Recent judicial interpretation of antitrust policy has been welcomed in certain legal quarters as a bringing of legal thinking into touch with economic reality. Elsewhere these ventures have been deplored as departures from the traditional and firm ground of jurisprudence into the morass of speculative economic theorizing. And, though various pundits in slick-paper magazines have aligned the general public firmly on the side of big business, the evidence indicates doubt and lack of faith in earlier idols rather than a confident conviction of the virtue of new ones.

The fact that relative certainty concerning both the size and shape of the monopoly problem and what to do about it has given way to relative uncertainty obviously does not mean that we know less about the structure of the American economy than we knew twenty years ago. Quite the contrary; though it would have to be said that the delineation of what we do not know has been a contribution of the last two decades fully as important as the development of what we do. In fact progress — if it may be called that — in this area has largely been the development of striking theses that have later disintegrated under the corrosive action of factual criticism. The resulting synthesis has usually been much less striking but much more realistic.

Thus the principal inference drawn from the original study of the 200 largest corporations was that control is separated from ownership and that this must be considered as a phenomenon of great portent to the functioning of the economy. Later investigators have questioned whether ownership in the large corporation is as impotent as supposed and, more important, what difference it makes in any case. An assiduous reader of the voluminous literature on the organization of the large firm that has appeared since the discovery of the separation of ownerships from control may, perhaps, be excused if he vouchsafes a pertinent — though inelegant — "so what"? The arresting thesis proffered in the 1930's about the growing "rigidity" of prices and what this was doing to output and employment in the economy has suffered a similar attenuation. So likewise has the view, nurtured in recent years by the Federal Trade Commission, that the

American economy is on a one-way street toward ever-increasing concentration. May we not also expect to find, when research has been given time to catch up, that "countervailing power" is not as countervailing as sometimes supposed?

No one who is other than eclectic, methodologically speaking, has any business in the field of business organization. The price theorist is, sooner or later, sure to became lonesome in the exclusive company of his market models. The collector and classifier of census data and price statistics will, at some stage, begin to wonder about the relevance of his aggregates and averages. The assiduous devisor of questionnaires, having drawn the secret of the "full-cost principle" from the conscious and the subconscious of his business subjects, may discover ultimately that there is less inconsistency between this principle and profit maximization than he had once supposed. All of these people have, nevertheless, something to contribute to each other and to the subject under study and, consequently, it is unwise to don prematurely the old school tie of a particular orthodoxy.

Twenty years ago, when the theories of monopolistic and imperfect competition burst upon the world, there was some reason to believe that a new basis had been laid for the systematic investigation of what it has become fashionable to call "micro economics." Unfortunately, things have not worked out that way. The theory came into the world remarkably full-blown and it has so remained. It has provided a beautifully logical and consistent set of propositions without direct operational applicability.

This is not to say that the theory is irrelevant; far from it. Its essential contribution has been to open our eyes to the fact that firms typically have a scope of action with respect to prices and price structures, outputs and product mix, advertising and selling, investment, research, and other economic dimensions that require examination. Moreover, such an examination must make use, on the one hand, of market structures that typically include only a limited number of firms and, on the other, of facts regarding the internal organization of businesses that may be thought to lie altogether outside the purview of economics.

The "real" theorists, of course, do not like this, and one of the familiar reactions is a retreat to Marshall. In certain respects, indeed, a retreat to Marshall seems appropriate. The Chamberlinian "large number case" does not appear to be sufficiently different from the Marshallian competitive market to justify an abandonment of the competitive analysis. It is questionable, however, to what size segment of manufacture and distribution this analysis is applicable. To date, the answers to this question are the product of what in Friedman's phrase can only be described as "casual empiricism." The data relating to percentages of product and industry output accounted for by relatively few firms suggest to me that the economic area not adapted to a competitive analysis is large, but I would have to admit that the proposition is still debatable.

Whatever the magnitude of the industrial segment adapted to a competitive analysis, that part that is not so adapted cannot, in the main, be usefully analyzed as monopoly. The Marshallian dichotomy between monopoly and competition is irretrievably broken and no one can put it together again. This is to say that in many — I would say most — industrial markets some type of oligopoly holds the field. From the point of view of a satisfactory theoretical analysis this is unfortunate. But it does not necessarily drive us into "sheer empiricism," "rank institutionalism," or some other like fate.

It must be admitted, however, that valid generalizations usable as a basis for prediction or for public action in their field are hard to come by. The nature of some of the difficulties and our progress — or lack of progress — in handling them can be seen by directing attention to certain of the central problems. What will be the effect of an increase or decrease in national income on prices and quantities in a market? How are differences in business practices among different markets explained? Under what circumstances can a market situation be judged sufficiently competitive to pass muster under a sensible antitrust policy?

When the term "market" is used, a Marshallian industry is meant; that is, a census industry appropriately adjusted for product and spatial considerations. Unless we can use the conception of the market and, with it, properly rectified industry data, the field of industrial organization is a wilderness. Triffin, with his general equilibrium of the firm, has attempted to lead us up the garden path, and if we expect to retain our virtue, we had better retreat as rapidly as possible to the shelter of the Marshallian industry.[1] As Andrews has emphasized, "Governments insist on administering in terms of industries, businessmen persist in thinking against an industrial background, and our official statistics continue to be collected on the basis of definitions of industries which, although they vary from source to source, nevertheless agree in significant details." [2]

The industry so conceived is a grouping of firms on the basis of a similarity both of products and of production processes. The products have to be sufficiently substitutable to permit some rough estimate of price and income elasticity of demand. Let those who refuse to conceive of a demand function except on the assumption of a perfect substitutability of products follow their interests elsewhere. As Yntema has suggested, what concerns us in this area is a distinction between five per cent and fifty per cent "causes." The production processes should be sufficiently similar to permit us to make reliable inferences regarding the structure of costs, i.e., the relation of overhead to variable costs, and the responsiveness of variable costs to changes in factor prices. Given the industry so defined we have at least the beginnings of an analysis that may tell us something interesting concerning the three questions previously raised.

One fairly obvious distinction that emerges from an examination of the behavior of prices and quantities in different industries, in response to changes in national income (a distinction central to O.P.A. experience), is between industries that roughly conform to Marshallian competitive requirements, such as textiles and lumber, and those that do not. The former group of industries shows a characteristically sensitive price as well as output response: the latter typically exhibits an output response without much short-range alteration of price. A good deal of attention has been paid in recent years to this industrial phenomenon of relative price stability in the face of sizeable quantity variations, and some plausible hypotheses have been developed to explain it. The firms in these industries are considered to be confronted by a demand function that, at least in the short run, is more elastic above the prevailing price than below it.

---

[1] Robert Triffin, *Monopolistic Competition and General Equilibrium Theory* (Cambridge, Mass., 1940).

[2] P. W. S. Andrews, "Industrial Analysis in Economics," *Oxford Studies in the Price Mechanism,* edited by T. Wilson and P. W. S. Andrews (Oxford, 1951), p. 140.

Moreover, firms in these industries are regarded as possessing excess capacity — except perhaps at the top of the business cycle — and operating at constant average and marginal cost. These hypotheses provide *an* explanation of observed short-run price and quantity behavior and, for many markets, that explanation may be adequate.

It is obvious, however, that the hypotheses do not tell us much of what we should like to know about price and quantity responses to sizeable variations in income, or to changes in factor prices that persist over time. In order to go further we need to know more about the interrelation of firms in the group, about the scope of action open to the firm in other areas than price and quantity changes, and about the conditions of entry of new firms. These elements show sizeable differences among industries, differences that not only help to explain price and quantity behavior but are relevant to the problems confronting public action in this field.

In analyzing these differences it is useful to distinguish between elements that lie outside the control of an individual firm and those that are within control. A basing-point system, despite various attempts to show that it is an inevitable natural phenomenon, usually depends upon the deliberate action of firms. The conditions that make a basing-point system practicable, however, having to do with numbers and cost structures of firms together with characteristics of the product, lie outside the control of firms. Fundamentally, the relevant conditions, internal to the market but external to the firm, involve technological considerations affecting scale, numbers, conditions of entry, and cost-structures as well as product characteristics that assume economic significance in relation to consumers' tastes. The responses of firms to their underlying conditions in the shape of product variations, product structures, selling behavior, pricing techniques, and the like are various but not infinitely variable. Both the external conditions and the discernible pattern of competitive behavior constitute a structure of the market that is relevant both to price-quantity predictions and to issues of public action.

It is an open question to what extent a recognition of the scope and coverage of oligopoly markets forces us into "sheer empiricism" via an institutional study of particular industries. My own view is that the principle types of competitive behavior to be found in the industrial sector of the economy can be related to conditions of the

sort noted above and that a not unmanageable number of characteristic market structures may be thereby derived that can be useful for
assisting prediction and also for informing public policy.

What we are interested in "predicting" is not only price and quantity behavior but the performance of firms and groups of firms in a
much fuller sense, including cost-price relations, capacity-output relations, the role of product variation and selling outlays, and profit
rates. Only to the extent that we can infer or predict, however
roughly, the performance of firms from observed elements of market
structure, can we proceed to any sort of judgment relevant to public
action in this area. Let us by all means use the Marshallian competitive model where we can, recognizing that to depart from it leaves
us with successive linkages between market conditions, patterns of
competitive behavior, business performance, and ultimate judgments
regarding the efficiency of resource use that at every point are brittle
and insecure. But depart from this model we must, if we are to pay
any productive attention to a large segment of the economy.

It is in this muddy but not uninteresting field that most of the
papers in this volume wallow. Part I, after a summary statement of
our current knowledge — and ignorance — concerning economic concentration in relation to monopoly, begins with some reflections on
a subject indicated by the title of an important work of the late
1930's: Arthur R. Burns' *Decline of Competition.* These reflections
suggest a view frequently expressed about this book, that what was
most clearly shown was rather a decline in economists' belief in competition than a decline in competition itself. To date, no very convincing proof has been advanced that American industry is any more
or any less monopolistic than it was fifty years ago. The section
appropriately ends with reflections on the views of a friend and colleague, the late Professor Schumpeter, who essentially held that the
competition "that counts" is the product of innovation and change
having little, if anything, to do with numbers of firms or other elements of market structure. As the intervening essays indicate, my
view is that both the Burns and the Schumpeter positions are exaggerated.

Part II is concerned with that remarkable and remarkably unsatisfactory controversy that may be said to have begun in the 1930's

with Gardiner Means' thesis concerning administered versus market prices and that continues today under the general heading of "the wage-price problem." In the main, the argument deals with the behavior of prices and wage rates and its consequences in the cycle. The problems in brief are: what are rigid prices?; why are prices rigid?; and what of it? We have made more progress toward answering the first two questions than we have toward the third.

Part III represents, in a sense, a digression from the main theme of the book and is concerned with raw-material problems. It is not that questions of monopoly and competition are less important in this area. But my interest in raw materials has been primarily in relation to the conditions of continued economic growth and national security rather than to problems of monopoly and competition.

Part IV centers on the question of monopoly and public policy. It is said that a concern for antitrust policy is bred in the bone of all loyal Americans, and certainly American economists have tended to give a disproportionate amount of attention to antitrust problems. In this field, economics mingles indissolubly with the law, and perhaps the lawyer-like qualities of the American citizenry, so often remarked by foreigners, have something to do with this preoccupation. The twin concerns of public policy here are with private power and with efficiency. We seek a structure and practice of business that on the one hand limits private economic power and, on the other, promotes efficiency in the use of resources. Economic theory presents us with a market model in which both objectives became possible in static equilibrium. Unfortunately, the model does not tell us what to do with change nor, when technology decrees a market structure markedly dissimilar to the model, is it easy to tell how much private power it is necessary to tolerate in order to achieve a given level of efficiency. Hence our woe.

Lawyers, dealing with concrete cases, like to think of the law as an "action science." But when efficiency and market power are the desiderata, the standards of action are primarily economic. Lawyers also describe themselves as "specialists in relevance." But logical relevance makes no distinction between magnitudes, and unless the relevant variables are somehow quantified, action may depart far from agreed objectives. Thus law and economics are joined; lawyers pressing for reasonable decision are forced to draw on economic "generalities," while economists find themselves plying their trade in the unforeseen and cramping quarters of concrete cases.

The result to public policy in terms of distinction between acceptable and unacceptable market structures and business practices bears only a remote relation to the strictures of welfare theory. Unfortunately, this is not the only field of applied economics characterized by such remoteness.

PART I

THE LARGE FIRM AND THE STRUCTURE OF INDUSTRIAL MARKETS

Introduction

The papers in Part I mainly relate to the large firm in the American economy and to various alleged effects of economic concentration on competition. Chapters 1 and 2 represent my reactions in the 1930's and the 1950's to the constantly reiterated charge that concentration is increasing and competition declining in the United States. Since, despite a flood of publications on the subject in the intervening period, my current views are remarkably similar to those expressed in 1938, there is a certain amount of duplication between these chapters. Chapter 3, on the "Price and Production Policies of Large-Scale Enterprise," dates from a period when I was sanguine — perhaps too sanguine — concerning the possibility of explaining differences in business practices and certain types of business policies in terms of observable and measurable differences in the structure of the markets in which firms operate. Although some useful work has since been accomplished in this area, an earlier attempt at an elaborate market classification has long since been abandoned for want of data, want of time, and the intrusion of other preoccupations. Chapter 4, on "Cartels and Commodity Agreements," is in part a contemporary reaction to a peculiar wartime aberration in the Antitrust Division and various committees of Congress, whereby an important explanation of this country's lack of preparedness for war was sought in the foreign business connections of American firms. My views on international cartel and commodity agreements were shaped mainly from 1944 to 1946, when I was chairman of a government interdepartmental committee established to prepare a United States position for the abortive discussions on the proposed International Trade Organization. Chapter 5 is concerned with the late Professor Schumpeter's views on the large firm and the monopoly problem. Almost everything that has been and can be said in praise of the "new competition" was said first — and much better — by Schumpeter.

The task of delineating the role of the large firm in the American economy is partly one of removing the rubbish that surrounds the discussion of this subject. Almost everywhere abroad the United States is considered to be *par excellence* the country of "monopoly capitalism," whatever that means. If this allegation has anything to do with the relative importance of large firms in their particular industries or with the relation between large firms and industry in general, the available statistics do not support the allegation. Recent studies have shown by various measures that in Canada and England the share of economic activity accounted for by the largest firms tends to be greater, industry by industry, than in the United States. Since there is a great variation among industries in degree of concentration, the position of large firms with respect to industry as a whole will be strongly influenced by the composition of industrial output. Although data are not avaliable for other industrial countries in as great detail, it may be surmised that a similar situation prevails elsewhere. The largest American firms are very large indeed, but what is forgotten is that American industries and industry in general are also very extensive.

This does not mean, of course, that large-scale enterprise does not play an important role in the American economy. The fact that in 1946 the 113 manufacturing firms with assets over $100 million held 46 per cent of all the assets of manufacturing firms must be set beside the fact that there are 4 million independent business units in the American economy and if agriculture is included, about 8 million. The fact of the matter seems to be that any industrial economy is highly concentrated. In India, with two-thirds of the labor force in agriculture, economic concentration in the economy as a whole is low, but it should be noted that even in India the Tatta Steel Works accounts for a larger percentage of total iron and steel output and for a larger share of total industrial output than does the United States Steel Corporation in this country.

Nor does it appear to be true that, in any general sense, economic concentration is increasing in the United States. Despite much oratory to the contrary, the number of independent business units seems to be increasing at about the same rate as the population, and, despite the paucity of data earlier than about 1931, there is some reason to believe that the position of the largest firms in relation to non-agricultural activity is substantially what it was at the turn of the century.

I would claim to be as aware as most that the statistics on concentration do not tell the whole story. There is the question what the process of industrialization and urbanization, in which the emergence of the large firm is an essential part, does to political behavior in a democracy. There is the problem of absentee ownership and the withering of community enterprise and independence. There is finally and perhaps most importantly the changing role of the individual in relation to the corporate giant that employs him and the giant trade-union of which he is a member. Industrialization and the concomitant rise of big corporations, large-scale unions, and pressure-group government have certainly played havoc with the ideals and possibilities of Jeffersonian democracy. But this development is not limited to the United States and in any case presents a range of problems to which techniques of economic analysis are not particularly relevant.

I

Economic Concentration and the Monopoly Problem: A Review of Recent Literature

The question-asking titles of various recent publications, such as "How Big is Big Business?"; "How Did Big Business Get Big?"; "How Big is Too Big?"; "Is Big Business Getting Bigger?"; suggest a number of issues concerning the measurement and the significance of the size of firms in relation to markets and to the economy.[1] These issues are all relevant to what has become known as economic concentration, a subject of increasing interest to American economists.

The measures of concentration that have been principally used are of two general types. The first, hereafter called general concentration, purports to measure the share of some economic activity accounted for by large firms, i.e. firms over a certain size, in the economy as a whole or in some large segment thereof. Gardiner Means, in the publications that initiated the current study of economic concentration in the United States, attempted to measure the share of the assets of all non-financial corporations accounted for by the assets of the two hundred largest corporations.[2] For his purposes, a corporation was large if it controlled assets of $80 to $100 million or more. The Federal Trade Commission in its *Report on the Concentration of Productive Facilities,* 1947 (published in 1949), purported to show the percentage of the various assets of all manufacturing corporations held by manufacturing corporations with total assets of $100 million and over. The Commission found that 113 manufactur-

---

[1] Edwin George, "How Big is Big Business?" *Dun's Review,* March 1939; "How Did Big Business Get Big?" *Dun's Review,* Sept. 1939. Peter Drucker, "How Big is Too Big?" *Harpers,* July 1950. M. A. Adelman, "Is Big Business Getting Bigger?" *Fortune,* March 1950.

[2] "The Large Corporation in American Economic Life," *American Economic Review,* 1931. With A. A. Berle, *The Modern Corporation and Private Property* (New York, 1932).

ing corporations, in 1947, held assets of over $100 million and that these large corporations held 46 per cent of the total assets held by manufacturing firms. Adelman, in a recent study that has received substantial attention, reports that of the total of 36.4 million workers in private, non-agricultural industry in 1948, firms employing more than 10,000 accounted for 22.7 per cent of the employment. There were 260 such firms, and they employed 8.2 million workers. He also found that in this same large segment of the economy, the 287 corporations with assets of over $100 million accounted for 42.9 per cent of the assets of all corporations in this segment.[3]

These are all general measures of concentration. The large firm is alternatively defined as a firm with assets of $100 million or over or with 10,000 workers or over. The size of the firm could also be measured in terms of value of product, value added, total sales, total shipments and in various other ways. The universes of which these large firms are a part are variously conceived as all non-financial corporations, all manufacturing corporations, all non-agricultural firms, etc. The universe could also be understood as the total economy or some large segment other than those mentioned above. To the significance of these general measures of concentration we shall return presently.

The second type of concentration measure purports to indicate the share of an industry or product accounted for by the largest firms in the industry or producing the product. The 1939 Report of the National Resources Committee measured the percentage of output and employment of various census industries accounted for by the four and the eight largest firms in these industries.[4] A British study measures the percentage of output and employment in various British industries accounted for by the three largest firms.[5] A recent Canadian investigation is concerned with the share of employment in Canadian industries accounted for by the largest employers.[6] An im-

[3] "The Measurement of Industrial Concentration," *Review of Economics and Statistics*, Nov. 1951, pp. 275, 277.

[4] *The Structure of the American Economy*, 1939.

[5] H. Leak and A. Maizels, "The Structure of British Industry," *Journal of the Royal Statistical Society*, 1945.

[6] Gideon Rosenbluth, "Industrial Concentration in Canada and the United States," *Canadian Journal of Economics and Political Science*, 22 (1954).

portant monograph published by the Temporary National Economic Committee indicated for 1807 census products the percentage of output accounted for by the four largest producers of each product.[7]

Similar measures are available for establishments as well as firms. In addition to employment and output, the dimensions of the firms' (or the establishments') activity in relation to all firms (or establishments) in an industry or product grouping could be indicated in terms of sales, value added, assets, shipments, and in various other ways. This type of concentration we shall call market concentration for reasons to be discussed presently.

SIZE VERSUS MONOPOLY

General measures of concentration professing to indicate the share of the economic activity of some large segment of the economy, say manufacturing, controlled by the largest firms, have no *necessary* connection with monopoly, a market phenomenon. The largest firms may invariably — or generally — operate in large markets. If, despite their size, the share of the various markets occupied by these firms is relatively small, if collusions among these firms are absent, and if various other elements of market structure are favorable, it is conceivable that a high degree of general concentration in manufacturing industries as a whole could be compatible with a high degree of competition in each manufacturing market.

Market measures of concentration, on the other hand, may have some relation to monopoly — a question to be examined presently — but have no *necessary* connection with size of firms. A local market may be occupied by only two or three grocery stores each enjoying a substantial degree of monopoly power. But none of the stores qualifies as a large firm. The shoe-string or dish-mop industry may be highly concentrated, but not in the hands of huge corporations. Local brick markets are in fact highly concentrated, but brick companies are not among our industrial giants. It is conceivable that the economy, or the manufacturing sector, might be shot through with strong positions of monopoly, even though the degree of general concentration is relatively small.

In fact, as everyone knows, the American economy and in particular the manufacturing and public utility sectors, are highly con-

[7] W. L. Thorp and W. F. Crowder, *The Structure of Industry*, T. N. E. C. Monograph No. 27.

centrated.[8] Firms that are large by any test account for a substantial percentage (by any measure) of total activity. And there is reason to believe that in many cases large manufacturing firms are not devoid of monopoly power. In the case of public utilities it is presumably their "natural" monopoly position that has put them in the category of regulated enterprises. Moreover, the combination of size with monopoly is commonly understood to create the problem frequently indicated by the phrase "concentration of economic power." If large firms invariably bought and sold in competitive markets, their ability to influence economic activity would be sufficiently circumscribed to make the problem of "economic power" of little importance. On the other hand, if monopoly power, though existing throughout the economy, were invariably in the hands of small firms, this power would certainly not be concentrated.

Nevertheless, while it is size in combination with monopoly that constitutes one aspect — perhaps the most important aspect — of economic concentration, it is advisable to keep these elements separate in any analysis of the total problem of concentration. Failure to do so has converted much of the discussion of this subject into argument at cross purposes. Many facets of business size that are important to the structure and functioning of the economy have little to do with the extent of monopoly. And clearly monopoly may constitute a serious problem irrespective of size.

SOME NON-MARKET ASPECTS OF BUSINESS SIZE

If the significance of large firms is to be considered independently of market phenomena, it is necessary not only to justify the importance of some non-market aspect of economic structure or behavior but also to show that this aspect is different from what it would be in the absence of large firms. Thus Berle and Means, in their pioneering study, were primarily interested in ownership rights and responsibilities and the relation of business ownership to control. They contended that the aggregation of assets into large holdings

---

[8] According to Adelman's calculations ("The Measurement of Industrial Concentration," p. 275), firms employing over 10,000 which accounted, in 1948, for 22.7 per cent of private, non-agricultural employment, accounted for 30.8 per cent of manufacturing employment, and 55 per cent of employment in public utilities other than transportation.

with the attendant dispersal of stock ownership tends to "separate" ownership from control. For their purposes some financial measure of size was obviously appropriate, and it may well be that, for the period covered by their observations, $80 to $100 million in assets provides a fairly good dividing line between the "small" corporation in which control tends to rest in the hands of its owners and the "large" corporation in which ownership passes into other hands.

If, on the other hand, we take another much discussed non-market aspect of size which relates to the area of administration and decision making, we may require both a different measure of size and a different conception of large and small. It is commonly urged that the large firm creates a managerial problem to which "bureaucracy" is the only answer. The consequences for business administration and the operation of the firm are variously reported to be the development of a hierarchical structure, a professionalization of management attitudes and interests, expansion of the area covered by operating standards or routines, growth of record-keeping, development of group decisions, and the like. Schumpeter speaks of the emergence of a "trustified" economy in which innovation, formerly the characteristic of the individual entrepreneur, becomes a quasi-automatic product of large-scale business organization.[9] Other writers have stressed different aspects of "corporate bureaucracy."

We are not concerned here with an evaluation of the economic or political significance of these phenomena but rather with their relation to general measures of concentration. If the emphasis is on the "bureaucratic" aspects of size, what is the best measure of size? It seems possible that financial measures apropriate to the question of control versus ownership should here give way to number of employees. And at what size does a firm become large enough to exhibit these supposed characteristics?

These are two of the non-market attributes of size much discussed in the literature on concentration; but there are others. Justice Douglas of the Supreme Court is eloquent on the deleterious effects of business size (in the form of chain-store or multiplant corporations)

---

[9] Cf. "The Instability of Capitalism," *Economic Journal*, Sept. 1928, p. 384; and "Der Unternehmer in der Volkswirtschaft von Heute," in *Structur Wandlungen der Deutschen Volkswirtschaft*, 1 (1928).

on the independence and vigor of local community life in America.[10] Some writers point to the growth of large firms as the primary explanation and justification of big labor unions. This juxtaposition, which has recently been examined as a type of "countervailing power," has non-market aspects that are relevant to any examination of the consequences of general concentration.[11] Large firms have also, and contradictorily, been alleged to have exceptional influence on governmental policies and actions and to be exceptionally vulnerable to political attack. Over and above all these relatively specific non-market attributes of size are certain vague and undifferentiated supposed consequences for the "class structure of society" and the "functioning of the democratic process."

No one supposes that in this welter of reported non-market aspects of big business there are not important consequences for the functioning of the economy and of society that merit careful study and examination. But it must be said that to date the literature on economic concentration has not been very successful in relating these consequences to business size or to measures of general concentration. It is, perhaps, partly through this combination of conviction of the importance of general concentration with the difficulty of specification that attention has turned to the question of whether concentration is increasing or decreasing and away from the analysis of the results of any particular level of concentration. Before we cope with this question, however, a word needs to be said concerning the relation of concentration measures to the division of industrial organization between firms and markets.

These are the two major forms of business organization. The study of industrial or business organization is essentially the study of the structure and functioning of markets and the study of the structure and behavior of firms. The market, as John R. Commons emphasized decades ago, encompasses bargaining transactions among legal equals. The firm, on the other hand, encompasses managerial or rationing transactions involving the relations between administrative superiors

[10] Cf. the dissenting opinion in Standard Oil Company of California v. U. S. (337 U. S. 293, 1948); also the dissenting opinion of Justice Douglas in U. S. v. Columbia Steel Co. (334 U. S. 495, 1947).

[11] Cf. J. K. Galbraith, *American Capitalism: The Concept of Countervailing Power* (Boston, 1952).

and inferiors. As a firm grows, transactions that could conceivably be organized through the market's price mechanism are transferred to the administrative organization of the firm.[12] The number of firms and their size distribution gives some indication of the extent to which the economy, or some sector of it, is subject to an administrative as against a market organization of its resources.

It is possible to imagine an economy characterized by an extensive division of labor in which business firms are both very numerous and very small. Such an economy would show a very low index of concentration. The chief organizing device would be competitively determined prices indicating to each business unit relative scarcities of supplies and the direction of consumer wants. The number of purchase and sales transactions that would be required to assemble materials and parts into finished products and to get these finished products into the hands of consumers would be very large. And, despite a common impression that the market is a costless institution, the transfer of products from one hand to another is expensive. It is the avoidance of such "transfer costs," through the integration and combination of conceivably separable operations, together with the "indivisibility" of efficient technical and administrative ways of using resources, that account, on the cost side, for the size of firms.[13]

It is also possible, if we wish to exercise our imagination in the opposite direction, to conceive of the economy as one firm with the only transfers those of labor services from independent workers to the firm and of finished products from the firm to ultimate consumers. Such an economy would exhibit the highest possible index of concentration. It is, however, generally and rightly considered that such a form of organization would lack the basic data required for a rational allocation and use of resources, i.e., prices for materials, labor sources, semi-finished and finished goods provided by the bidding of independent suppliers and users in free markets.

Thus, although the administrative-managerial and the bargaining-market devices are alternative ways of organizing resources, a substitution of one for the other is compatible with efficient use of re-

---

[12] Cf. R. H. Coase, "The Nature of the Firm," *Economica*, 1937.

[13] As Chamberlin has shown, even if all factors are "infinitely divisible," it does not follow that the optimum size of firms will be very small. E. H. Chamberlin, "Proportionality, Divisibility and Economics of Scale," *Quarterly Journal of Economics*, Feb. 1948, p. 229.

sources only within limits. Some of the most difficult and important problems of analysis and public policy in the field of industrial organization have to do with the relation of size to efficiency, the effect of size on the structure and functioning of markets and what to do in situations in which an efficient organization of resources requires managerial units of a size incompatible with a competitive functioning of the market.

Measures of general concentration throw little or no light on these problems. But, as between economies or sectors, or between different periods of time in the same economy or sector, differences in concentration ratios can serve to indicate the relative importance of administrative-managerial as against market-bargaining transactions. And data on the size distribution of firms are a useful supplement to mere numbers. It is important to know that there are 8 million "decision making units" in the American economy. But it is also important to know that the largest 260 of them account for roughly 13 per cent of private employment; the largest 1000 for, perhaps, 20 per cent; and that the smallest 8 million of these units account for less than 30 per cent of total employment or value added.

IS CONCENTRATION INCREASING?

The discussion of trends in concentration has from the beginning been subject to a strong ideological slant, and this slant is not altogether absent from current discussion. To Marx it was clear that "one capitalist kills many" and his "laws" of concentration and centralization, which may be interpreted as tendencies toward reinvestment of earnings and toward amalgamation, were central to his vision of the development of capitalism. The direction of these tendencies was toward one firm in an industry, and, ultimately, one firm for the whole economy. Marx, however, attempted no quantitative assessment of the strength of these tendencies, and the best that Engels could do, in completing and editing Volume III of *Capital* which appeared in 1890, was to introduce some portentous observations concerning the growth of cartels and combines.

Whether or not one capitalist kills many, the rate of growth in the number of business firms, in the United States at least, has tended to approximate the rate of growth of the natural population. There were in this country in 1929 some 3.1 million non-agricultural business enterprises and in 1952 approximately 4 million. The number per thousand of population was 25.5 in 1929 and was also 25.5 in 1952. It is unnecessary, to say, however, that these figures throw no light on what has happened to the position of the largest firms.

If we think of concentration in terms of the share of aggregate national income, employment, or wealth accounted for by the largest private enterprises, it is obvious that there must be an increase in concentration in any industrializing economy. The shift from the agrarian economy of the United States in 1820, when 80 per cent of the gainfully employed were in agriculture, to the highly industrialized economy of the present, when the comparable figure is about 12 per cent, is, among other things, a shift from areas in which the typical economic unit is *relatively* small, then and now, to areas in which the typical business unit has always been *relatively* large. So far as this country is concerned, we know enough about the facts of economic history to be able to say with some confidence that the most important explanation of changes in general concentration lies in shifts in economic activity among sectors with different degrees of concentration, rather than in changes in the degree of concentration in these sectors. This has been true in the past and may well continue to be true in the future. But whereas in the past the shifts among sectors have persistently worked in the direction of increasing general concentration, it is by no means clear that they well continue to do so.

The overwhelmingly important impulse to increasing concentration, the industrialization of the American economy at the expense of agriculture, has, after all, about reached its limit. The share of the gainfully employed in agriculture will, no doubt, decline somewhat from its present 12 per cent but it cannot decline much further.[14] The per cent employed in manufacture — and this is also true of other mature industrial economies — has remained relatively stable for the last three decades. As the table indicates, the areas showing substantial relative gains in employment during the last few decades are trade, private services, and government.

[14] For conflicting views on what may happen to U. S. agricultural employment, see Colin Clark, "Afterthoughts on Paley," and Edward S. Mason, "Comment," in *Review of Economics and Statistics,* August 1954.

Percentage Distribution of the Gainfully Occupied by Industries, 1900–1940[a]

	1900	1910	1920	1930	1940
Agriculture	37.9	31.6	27.4	22.1	18.0
Manufacturing	21.6	22.5	26.1	23.0	23.9
Trade	8.9	9.6	9.9	12.7	14.4
Government	2.7	3.6	4.5	5.0	6.1
Private services	12.2	13.0	11.7	15.1	17.3

[a] Adapted from Table 8, p. 34, in George J. Stigler, *Trends in Output and Employment* (National Bureau of Economic Research, 1947).

The figure for manufacturing, it is true, rose to 26 per cent in 1950, which approximately restored that sector to its position in 1920. But unless the future brings a marked increase in the per cent of employment in arms production, the share of manufactures in total employment is not apt to increase further. The expansion of trade and private services, on the other hand, represents growth in areas in which concentration is relatively low. Consequently it is a fair guess that for the economy as a whole, any substantial future increase in concentration will have to depend on increasing concentration within, rather than shifts among, sectors.

Although we know most about the trend of concentration in manufacture, some information is available concerning trends in other sectors. In retail distribution there seems to have been no increase in concentration since 1929. According to Adelman the sales of chain stores and mail-order houses were 21.5 per cent of total retail sales in 1929 and 20.7 per cent in 1950.[15] In the field of public utilities concentration was very high in the 1920's and early 1930's (railways and public utilities represented 103 of Means' 200 largest corporations in 1928) and was apparently increasing rapidly until 1935 when the Public Utilities Holding Company Act appeared in the statute books. But from 1935 until 1950, public utility holding companies divested themselves of some $16 billion in assets.[16] There is evidence that concentration in American agriculture has somewhat increased, but census figures indicate that in 1950 it still required

[15] "The Measurement of Industrial Concentration," p. 293.
[16] Adelman, quoting the Securities and Exchange Commission, *Fifteenth Annual Report*, pp. 62–63.

103,000 farms to account for 26.7 per cent of the value of farm products sold.[17]

As with so many other aspects of concentration, interest in the quantitative study of historical trends was first awakened through a paper by Gardiner Means in 1931, the results of which were later published in *Modern Corporation and Private Property*.[18] Means found that the assets of the 200 largest non-financial corporations grew faster during the period 1909–1929 than the assets of all non-financial corporations and that the discrepancy in rates of growth was particularly marked in the period 1924–1929.

The data on which these estimates were based were, of necessity, published corporate capitalization figures, and the period in question was one in which corporate financial practice was squeezing the water out of inflated capital structures. Later critics have raised the unanswerable question of who was squeezing harder — the 200 largest or all non-financial corporations? [19] If the former were more effective, the trend toward concentration was underestimated by Means; if the latter, the trend was overestimated. The critics appear to agree, however, that for the period 1924–1929 the trend is unmistakable.[20] In the first place, the shortness of the period lessens the probability that changes in corporate accounting practice could markedly affect the results. Second, the discrepancy between the rate of growth of the 200 largest and of all financial corporations is too large to be explained by probable differences in accounting practice. And in the third place, the period coincides with the second great merger movement in American industry, which was characterized in particular by the consolidation of local properties into the great public utility holding companies.

Later, using Bureau of Internal Revenue data, Means calculated trends in concentration for the period 1929–1933.[21] The increase in

---

[17] Ronald L. Mighell, *American Agriculture: Its Structure and Place in the Economy* (Census Monograph Series, 1955).

[18] Gardiner C. Means, "The Large Corporation in American Economic Life," *American Economic Review*, March 1931.

[19] Cf. Edwin B. George, "Is Big Business Getting Bigger?" *Dun's Review*, May 1939.

[20] George, "Is Big Business Getting Bigger?"; and Adelman, "The Measurement of Economic Concentration," p. 285.

[21] National Resources Committee, *The Structure of the American Economy*, Appendix 2.

the percentage of assets of all non-financial corporations accounted for by the target 200 was marked, and a breakdown of the data indicates that increased concentration during this period was unmistakable both for manufacture and for public utilities. The increase in concentration, however, was limited to the period 1929–1931, and there are reasons having to do with the greater financial stability of large corporations why a sharp decrease in general business activity should produce this temporary — and reversible — result.

The results of these investigations were striking and were, in many circles, considered ominous. At least as impressive as the calculated rates of increase in concentration in the corporate sector were the estimates of what *would* happen if these rates continued for any considerable length of time (though prediction was eschewed). Berle and Means pointed out that if the 1909–1929 rate of increase were projected forward, "then 70 per cent of all corporate activity would be carried on by two hundred corporations by 1950. If the more rapid rates of growth from 1924 to 1929 were maintained for the next twenty years, 85 per cent of the corporate wealth would be held by two hundred huge units." [22]

Despite the fact that 1950 has come and gone without these dire consequences, much of the literature on concentration continues to exude an ominous presentiment of catastrophe. This is particularly true of two postwar studies, the *Report of the Smaller War Plants Corporation on Economic Concentration in World War II*, and the reports of the Federal Trade Commission on mergers.[23] In none of these documents, in fact, do the statistical data indicate clearly increasing concentration, but the reference and suggestions emanating therefrom, together with some forthright statements, strongly imply such an increase. For example, according to the F.T.C. Report on Mergers, "The importance of external expansion in promoting concentration has never been more clearly revealed than in the acquisition movement that is taking place at the present time — a movement which is strengthening the position of big business in several ways." The Report also holds that "No great stretch of the imagination is

[22] *The Modern Corporation and Private Property*, p. 40.
[23] 79th Congress, 2nd session, Document No. 206; and *The Present Trend of Corporate Mergers and Acquisitions*, 1947, and *Report of the Federal Trade Commission on the Merger Movement, A Summary Report*, 1948.

required to foresee that if nothing is done to check the growth in concentration either the giant corporations will ultimately take over the country, or the government will be compelled to step in.[24]

The principal author of this report later declared, however, that, "A careful reading of the Commission's Merger Report will reveal that in no place did the Commission state that the merger movement has *substantially* increased concentration in manufacturing as a whole." And he goes on to state, "Indeed, if the Commission had made any general statement on this point, it would probably have concluded, based on its own data, that the recent mergers have *not* 'substantially' increased concentration in manufacturing as a whole." [25]

Since we are concerned here with trends in general concentration and since it now appears clear, despite widespread interpretation to the contrary, that neither the S.W.P.C. or the Federal Trade Commission reports concern themselves with these trends, we shall move on to a study that admittedly does so.

M. A. Adelman's paper "The Measurement of Industrial Concentration" is by far the most illuminating study of trends in concentration that has appeared to date. The paper presents two statistical estimates of trends in concentration. The first involves a comparison of the per cent of total corporate assets in manufacture held by the 139 largest manufacturing corporations in 1931 with the per cent held by the 139 largest in 1947. The second estimate, based on data collected by Nutter[26] on the extent of concentration at the turn of the century, attempts to compare the per cent of value added accounted for by "concentrated" [27] industries in 1901 with the per cent accounted for by such industries in 1947. Since the second comparison uses what we have agreed to call market measures of concentration, discussion is postponed to the next section. We are here concerned only with the trend in general concentration evidenced by the change in the position of the largest corporations.

[24] *The Merger Movement, A Summary Report,* pp. 25, 68.

[25] John M. Blair and Harrison F. Houghton, "The Lintner-Butters Analysis of the Effect of Mergers on Industrial Concentration," *Review of Economics and Statistics,* Feb. 1951, p. 67 and footnote 12.

[26] G. Warren Nutter, *The Extent of Enterprise Monopoly in the United States, 1899–1939* (Chicago, 1951).

[27] A concentrated industry is defined as one in which the four largest firms account for 50 per cent or more value added in the industry.

The number is 139 because in 1931 — the first year the *Statistics of Income* presented balance-sheet data in size groups — there were that many manufacturing corporations with assets over $50 million. These corporations held 46.5 per cent of the assets of all manufacturing corporations. Data compiled in 1946 by the Department of Commerce on the assets of the 1000 largest manufacturing corporations, together with Federal Trade Commission and Security and Exchange Commission collections of consolidated balance-sheet data by size groups, permit an estimate of the per cent of total corporate manufacturing assets held by the 139 largest in 1947. After correcting for the effects of wartime accelerated amortization and abnormally high inventories, Adelman estimates that these large corporations held, at the end of 1947, 45 per cent of total assets.

The figures for 1947, however, are on a consolidated basis whereas those for 1931 are not. Applying a correction to the 1931 data based on the 1947 relationship between consolidated and unconsolidated assets raises the 1931 percentage of total manufacturing assets held by the largest 139 to 49 per cent. The net conclusion is, then, that concentration in American manufacture as increased by the percentage of total assets held by the largest companies fell during these 16 years from 49 to 45.

The corrections and adjustments in the original data undertaken by Adelman are reasonable and have not been seriously questioned by later critics. A more difficult question is whether the estimates for 1931 and 1947 can fairly be said to fall on or near a trend line representing changing concentration. As we have indicated, the greater financial stability of large corporations tends to produce a swing above such a trend line in depression and a swing below it in prosperity. The economy has witnessed an almost continuous upswing since 1931. The inventory and amortization adjustments introduced by Adelman accomplish a partial but perhaps not an adequate correction of this tendency. To put it another way: the period as a whole from 1931 to 1947 might be considered abnormally favorable to the establishment of new — and the growth of small — firms, with the result that the largest firms in manufacture tended to show an abnormally low percentage of total assets at the end of the period.

A second difficulty arises from a phenomenon that has plagued earlier estimates of trends in concentration, a change in corporate practice regarding capitalization. There is reason to believe that this was a much less important factor during the period covered by Adelman's study than in the 1909–1929 period covered by Means' first study, but there is some evidence, noted by Adelman,[28] that large corporations more actively "wrote down" the value of their assets during the 1930's than did small corporations. Both of these influences work in the direction of overstating a downward trend in concentration (or understating an upward trend), and there may be other — though minor — reinforcing factors.[29] It is altogether improbable, however, that their total effect destroys the validity of Adelman's carefully stated conclusions:

> If there has been any strong and continuing tendency since 1931 to greater concentration in manufacturing, it must be detectable in the corporate balance-sheet statistics for that period. These statistics do not show it. Therefore the tendency probably does not exist.[30]

This is an important, though negative, conclusion. There are tendencies toward dispersion as well as concentration in manufacture as in other sectors of the economy, and it cannot be assumed that, for any extended period of time, the *net* effect is an inevitable increase in concentration.

An attempt to push back a measurement of the trend in concentration to the beginning of the century yields much less satisfactory results. In the first place, it makes a great deal of difference from what year the trend is to be measured. The period 1897–1903 was the focus of a merger movement so large as to dwarf all previous and subsequent experience.[31] An estimate of change in concentration from a year before 1900 might show a large measure, whereas an estimate of the change after 1903 might produce rather different results. In the second place, data relevant to concentration, however

[28] P. 290. See also Edwin B. George's "Comment" in "Four Comments on 'The Measurement of Industrial Concentration': with A Rejoinder by Professor Adelman," *Review of Economics and Statistics,* May 1952, p. 169.

[29] Cf. George, "Comment."

[30] "The Measurement of Industrial Concentration," p. 290.

[31] On the importance of the first merger movement, see George W. Stocking's "Comment" on Adelman's paper in "Four Comments," *Review of Economics and Statistics;* and his "Comment" on "Survey of the Evidence and Findings on Mergers" by Jesse W. Markham, in *Business Concentration and Price Policy* (National Bureau of Economic Research, 1955), p. 191.

measured, are more scanty and of lower quality the farther back inquiry is pushed.

Adelman's comparison of the per cent of value added by manufacture that is represented by industries in which the concentration rate is 50 per cent or over, in 1901 and 1947, reveals that 33 per cent of total value added came from such industries at the earlier date and 24 per cent in 1947. The data on the earlier period, however, do not all relate to the year 1901 and, to repeat, what year is chosen may make an appreciable difference. It should also be noted that the measure of concentration used here is quite different. Whatever way it is measured, the percentage of manufacturing activity controlled by the largest firms could increase appreciably, or decrease, with negligible change in the per cent of value added coming from concentrated industries. Measures of industry concentration have an importance of their own that will be examined presently; but they have no necessary relevance to the share of the economy, or some important sector of it, occupied by the largest firms.

In summary, it is clear that a relatively small number of large firms own a relatively large per cent of total assets and account for a relatively large per cent of economic activity (however measured) in manufacture and in the total area of corporate enterprise. Concentration is particularly marked in manufacture, mining, public utilities, and — though no data are presented here — among financial institutions. The areas of wholesale and retail distribution, service activities, agricultural, and, needless to say, professional self-employment, are much less concentrated. If all areas are lumped together, some sense of the position of the largest private enterprises in the economy is given by the fact that in 1948, the 260 largest accounted for 13.2 per cent of the employment of the total labor force. The differences in concentration among the various large sectors of the economy are so great that any sizeable shift in economic activity between areas of high and low concentration is bound to change overall concentration substantially. This, in fact, is what has happened in the United States and other industrializing countries as the relative importance of the agricultural sector has declined. Although we have no measure of the trend of general concentration in the United States, we are probably warranted in saying that concentration has increased considerably and that the principal reason for this increase is the change in the relative importance of industry and agriculture. There seems good reason for believing that this particular shift has about reached its limit in this country. The relative importance of agriculture is not going to decline much further and the sectors of economic activity now apparently on the increase are areas of relatively low concentration. Consequently, it seems probable that if over-all concentration in the United States is to increase, it will be the result of increase within large sectors rather than of shifts among them. There is little evidence of any such increase within important sectors of economic activity during the last two or three decades but, of course, this situation could change.

CONCENTRATION AND MONOPOLY

The principal intent of those concentration studies that purport to measure the per cents of industry or product output produced or sold by the largest firms is to throw light on the existence or nonexistence, or degree of, monopoly. Attention is focused not on size as such but on size in relation to a market. There have been several such studies in recent years, and our purpose in the next few pages is to assess the relevance of industry or product measures of concentration to the extent of monopoly and to its increase or decrease over time.

The two basic questions confronting all these studies are first, whether the available industry or product data conform closely enough to meaningful market data to be used as effective substitutes; and second, assuming a rough equivalence of industry and market, what is the monopolistic or competitive significance of market shares?

The basic information has to do with the national output (shipments, sales, value added) of census products or of any one of the variously defined census industries. The central problems encountered in forming a judgment on the degree of conformity of the product or industry to a market involve geographical space and product grouping. The figures available are on a national basis; markets may be local or international. Stigler has effectively shown that for a number of products the introduction of import data significantly reduces the calculated concentration ratio.[32] On the other hand, it has been

[32] G. Stigler, "The Extent and Bases of Monopoly," *American Economic Review*, Supplement, June 1942.

commonly assumed that product or industry concentration data on a national basis tend to understate actual market concentration in that many markets are local or regional. Nutter points out, however, that, "It is not clear in the absence of concrete data that regional ratios would be consistently higher than national ratios. Many might be lower."[33] He goes on to say, "The important question is whether the changes would be large enough to affect judgments about the monopolistic character of an industry." We must infer from his subsequent analysis that Nutter thinks these changes would not be large enough. There is, however, a real possibility that they would be.

The second problem involves assembling commodities into groups so as to permit a reasonable inference of high substitutability within the group and a significantly lower substitutability among products inside and outside the group. What we are offered is a choice among a series of industry classifications ranging from a relatively narrow classification of census products on the one hand to broad industry groups on the other. The notable study by Thorp and Crowder calculated concentration ratios for 1807 census products and found, not unexpectedly, high ratios for a large percentage of these products.[34] For many of the products, however, it would not be difficult to find close substitutes. Indeed, Crowder does not claim that high concentration ratios with respect to a census product necessarily have any monopoly significance. The National Resources Committee study, under the direction of Gardiner C. Means, used census industries that in many cases group products which are quite clearly not very close substitutes. Concentration ratios were, of course, much lower than those found by Crowder.[35]

Nutter, in commenting on these studies, remarks that "Crowder's definition of the industries is not clearly an improvement over the approach in the Means study."[36] He shows that in some industries there is a prima facie case for thinking that the product definition gives a closer approach to the relevant market considerations, but in others the census industry definition is to be preferred. Yet these two

[33] Nutter, p. 15.
[34] W. L. Thorp and W. F. Crowder, *The Structure of Industry*, T.N.E.C. Monograph No. 27.
[35] *The Structure of the American Economy*, Ch. VII and Appendices 7 and 8.
[36] Nutter, p. 11.

definitions yield decidedly different concentration ratios, which means that the consistent use of either one of them will necessarily produce some rather large departures from acceptable market concepts.

Both area and product considerations cast substantial doubt on the validity of using uncorrected census product and industry data in calculating *market* shares of large firms. Such industry data must be used as a starting point in any empirical study of monopoly and competition, but in many cases, it is necessary to combine or subdivide in order to obtain data usable in effective market analysis. Before commenting further on these studies, we must look at our second basic question: What is the monopolistic or competitive significance of market share?

Let us assume that the per cent of sales or output of a census product or industry sold or produced by the largest firm or firms is in fact a per cent of "the market." What is the monopoly significance if the number of firms is small and the per cent is large? Various studies of market concentration calculate shares for the largest firm, the three largest, four largest, or eight largest. What is the relative virtue of the different numbers? Given a high degree of concentration, is eight better than four, or four better than one? A recent important study has brought out the significant fact of a high degree of correlation among the various measures. "An industry with a 'high' percentage of assets (or output) concentrated in the largest firm, in comparison with other industries, does not in general have a 'low' percentage of assets concentrated in the largest two, three or four firms." [37]

If this is accepted, what conclusions are we to draw, say, from the fact that in a particular market 50 per cent of the sales are made by the 4 largest firms? In particular can we assume, either for purposes of analysis and prediction or for public policy, that this market can be treated as monopolized? Admittedly market concentration has an important relevance to monopoly. Some substantial degree of concentration is a necessary condition to the exercise of monopoly power but it is not a sufficient condition. Furthermore, monopoly comes in various sizes and shapes. Recent attempts to relate con-

[37] Gideon Rosenbluth, "Measures of Concentration," *Business Concentration and Price Policy*, p. 64.

centration data directly to monopoly either implicitly or explicitly divide markets into monopolistic *or* competitive markets.

This is not an acceptable procedure either for analysis and prediction or for public-policy prescription. For instance, given 50 per cent of sales in the hands of four firms, can it be assumed for the purpose of predicting price and quantity response to some outside disturbance that the firms in question will act in a way sufficiently similar to the action of one firm facing this external disturbance to justify the introduction of such a simplifying assumption? Or, if we reverse the procedure, can we usefully assume, given a concentration rate of less than 50 per cent, that the market in question will behave sufficiently like the Marshallian competitive market would behave to justify treating it as such? The answer to both these questions must, I think, be no.

Nor can we conclude from an inspection of concentration ratios that antitrust action is or is not justified. This is true not only with respect to existing antitrust policy but would be true for any reasonable antimonopoly policy. Such assumptions and judgments would be invalid even if we could accept commodity and industry data as satisfactorily defining and economic market. They must be considered much less valid when the inadequacies of commodity and industry data are taken into account. This does not mean that industry data and the calculation of concentration ratios are not important to the study of monopoly. They are, however, the beginning and not the end of such a study.[38]

[38] There have been in recent years two interesting studies purporting to estimate the respective shares of monopolistic and competitive markets in the United States in the late 1930's. Cf. George J. Stigler, "Competition in the United States" in *Five Lectures on Economic Problems,* London, 1949, and G. Warren Nutter, *The Extent of Enterprise Monopoly in the United States 1899–1939.* Both studies draw heavily on Clair Wilcox, *Competition and Monopoly in American Industry,* T.N.E.C. Monograph No. 21.

Wilcox's careful study led him to the conclusion that, "No sort of an estimate concerning the comparative extent of competition and monopoly in American markets is justified by the available evidence" (p. 308). Stigler and Nutter, however, are not so inhibited. Nutter, referring to 1937 and 1939, finds that in these two years (1) the effectively monopolistic industries accounted for between 20 and 21 per cent of national income; (2) workably competitive industries, between 55 and 56 per cent; (3) the governmental and "regulated" sector, between 19 and 20 per cent; and (4) households and

HOW CONCENTRATED IS THE U. S. ECONOMY?

The available data on concentration make it clear that a large per cent of value added by manufacture in the United States comes from industries in which a few firms account for a large share of the

---

non-profit enterprises, about 4 per cent (p. 20). Stigler finds that, in 1939, in terms of national income produced, competition accounted for 55.2 per cent, compulsory cartels for 2.5, monopoly for 24.4 per cent, while 17.9 per cent was unallocable (p. 50).

Both Stigler and Nutter are fully aware of the definitional and measurement difficulties involved in such estimates. For their rather limited purpose, which appears to be mainly the refutation of ill-considered assertions that monopoly either now "dominates" or inevitably must "dominate" the economy, these difficulties may not be too serious. Such estimates, however, can obviously not be used (nor, presumably, are they so intended) to indicate what segments of the economy justify the application of antimonopoly measures.

The initial basis of the estimates is a selection of industries to be called "monopolistic." The "competitive" sectors are residual. Nutter indicates (p. 19) that his list of monopolistic industries is drawn mainly from Wilcox. To this list he has added "any manufacturing census industries with concentration ratios in 1935 of ½ or larger and any census products of major value with concentration ratios in 1937 of ¾ or larger. . . ." The basis of Stigler's selection is not very clear though he indicates (p. 48) that he finds "it easy to follow the classification of Clair Wilcox. . . ."

Both authorities use competition in its "workable" rather than "pure" sense and both assume — and I would agree — that a large number of buyers and sellers is, in the absence of collusion, a sufficient, though not a necessary, condition of workable competition. There is, however, in neither study any examination of numbers or conditions of entry in the so-called competitive sectors. These are merely markets that are "left over" when the monopolistic sectors have been identified.

Neither Nutter nor Stigler make a distinction among various forms of private monopoly. Single-firm monopolies, various types of oligopolies, and cartels of different sizes and shapes are lumped together. The most important desideratum appears to be fewness of buyers or sellers, i.e., some considerable degree of market concentration. But fewness is neither a necessary nor a sufficient condition of monopoly in any public-policy sense of the term.

Finally, the single figure estimate of the per cent of economic activity characterized as competitive or monopolistic is derived from an estimate of national income generated in various industries and sectors characterized as monopolistic or competitive. Markets in different sectors of the economy, however, or in different stages of the productive process, are likely to have different strategic leverages with respect to the behavior of the economy as a whole. As Stigler recognizes, "There is little presumption that an economy which is 40 per cent monopolized will be more unstable or inefficient or slower of growth than another economy which is 25 per cent monopolized; the industrial distribution of the monopolies and their strength and patterns of behavior are also important variables" (p. 46).

product. Although Stigler and Nutter conclude that income generated in what they would call monopolized markets may not be more than 20–25 per cent of income generated in the economy as a whole, the per cent in manufacture is much higher. According to Nutter's estimate, it may have been as high as 40 per cent in 1937–1939.[39] Do American manufacturing industries tend to be more highly concentrated than the same industries in other countries, and is the share of economic activity accounted for by large firms in manufacture in general and in the economy as a whole comparatively high?

There seems to be a general impression abroad that this is so. We have been accustomed for decades now to descriptions from beyond the iron curtain of the United States as the land of "monopoly capitalism," whatever that means. And it has been the author's experience in so-called underdeveloped areas that even to raise a doubt whether this country is in all respects the most highly concentrated economy in the world is to provoke expressions of derision.

Yet what evidence we have indicates that industry by industry the American economy is less concentrated than many other economies, and there appears to be some reason to believe that in terms of general concentration the share of economic activity accounted for by large firms may be less than that in other countries with a similar degree of industrialization.

Rosenbluth's careful study, "Industrial Concentration in Canada and the United States," concludes, "that in 50 of the 56 industries for which a comparison of firm concentration can be made, concentration is higher in Canada than in the United States. . . . If we eliminate industries with separate regional markets and those in which exports or imports are important (in Canada), it is found that, of a total of 34 industries that can be compared 30 exhibit higher concentration in Canada."[40] The information supplied by Leak and Maizels' study of concentration in British industry makes it clear that industry concentration is also higher in Britain than in the United States.[41]

[39] Nutter, *The Extent of Enterprise Monopoly,* Table 2, p. 21.

[40] Gideon Rosenbluth, "Industrial Concentration in Canada and the United States," *Canadian Journal of Economics,* August 1954, p. 335.

[41] H. Leak and A. Maizels, "The Structure of British Industry," *Journal of the Royal Statistical Society* (1945). As Rosenbluth points out in his "Measures of Concentration," pp. 71–72, "The percentage of manufacturing industries with concentration ratios above any given level is higher in the United King-

Although we have no statistical comparisons of general concentration in manufactures, i.e., the per cent of value added (or some other measure of economic activity) accounted for by firms over a certain size, it is highly probable that general concentration is higher in Canadian and British manufactures than in the United States.[42] It is also probable that general concentration is higher in the manufacturing sectors of many economies.

The reasons for this are not far to seek. Despite large differences in factor proportions in different countries, techniques of production tend to be similar industry by industry in at least large sectors of these industries. In India and Pakistan, hand looms exist side by side with large-scale textile plants. But technology in the large-scale plants is very similar to that in the textile plants of the United States, United Kingdom, and Japan. And in most of the growing industries of underdeveloped areas, there is no technological equivalent to the hand loom. Such is the spread of machine technology that, insofar as the size of firms is governed by technological considerations, firms in a given industry will tend to grow to similar sizes even though the size of the industry is primarily determined by the national incomes of countries; in other words, the size of firms is heavily influenced by a technology that knows no national boundaries.

Thus it is that even in the undeveloped countries of the world, concentration in particular industries may well be strikingly higher than in the United States. Although the United States Steel Corporation is frequently considered to dominate the iron and steel industry in this country, its *relative* position does not approach that of the Tatta complex in the iron and steel industry of India. And Pakistan's one large paper mill clearly represents a higher degree of industry concentration than is found in the paper industry in the United States.

---

dom than in the United States, and the same relation holds for the percentage of employment. It is clear, therefore, that the general level of concentration is higher in the British industries."

[42] According to Rosenbluth, "Industrial Concentration in Canada and the United States," p. 337, "If . . . the Canadian economy consisted chiefly of industries with low concentration, one might well conclude that the general level of concentration is lower in Canada, even though each industry is more concentrated than in the U. S." On the contrary, "industries with low concentration are somewhat more important in Canada than in the U. S., but the difference is not great" (p. 338).

Whether general concentration in manufacture or in the broader industrial sector of the economy is higher in one country than in another will depend not only on differences in concentration in particular industries but on the composition of industrial output. There are very large differences in the degree of concentration industry by industry, and those industries which are highly concentrated in one country tend to be highly concentrated in another. Taking both considerations into account, it seems probable that there are many countries in which general manufacturing or industrial concentration may be higher than in the United States, but the analysis that would either support or refute this conclusion has not yet been undertaken.

The degree of concentration in an economy as a whole, i.e., the share of economic activity accounted for by the largest enterprises, will be mainly determined by the extent of industrialization. Since the per cent of the labor force engaged in manufacture is higher in Britain than in the United States; and since it may well be that by certain measures British manufactures are more concentrated than American, it is distinctly possible that Britain can be described as a more concentrated economy in general than the United States. In India and Pakistan, on the other hand, where half to two-thirds of the national income comes from, and three-quarters to four-fifths of the labor force are employed in, agriculture, general concentration is low. But we may be sure that, as these countries industrialize, general concentration will increase.

IS MONOPOLY INCREASING?

Finally, let us consider the question whether there exists a pronounced trend towards monopoly in American manufacture. Since this is the subject of Chapter 2, which represents the author's views in the late thirties, and since these views have not substantially changed, this section will be brief. The answer in a nutshell is — we do not know. The difficulties of formulating an "operational" definition of monopoly and of assembling relevant and comparable data over a long period of time are such as to make attempts at measurement relatively fruitless. Qualitative arguments supporting the decline-of-competition thesis stress the growing size of firms, the substitution of price quoting and various pricing formulas for "open" markets,[43] the concentration of research (and presumably innovation) in a few firms, the declining importance of import competition in manufactures, and other factors. Those who argue that monopoly is not increasing and may be declining point out that markets as well as firms are growing in size, that improved transportation facilities have converted local and regional markets into national, that, with the proliferation of products, "gaps in the chain of substitutes" are becoming narrower, and that innovation is performing with increasing effectiveness its rate of "creative destruction." All this is mostly sound and fury signifying little.

Nutter's painstaking and important study, which purports to give a quantitive estimate of the trend of monopoly from 1899 to 1937–1939, deals substantially, in fact, with changes in concentration ratios.[44] His starting point is "a list of highly concentrated industries in the period 1895–1904." Examination of this period centers on 1899 in order to utilize the census data of that year on value added and income originating in industries.[45] The *indicium* of monopoly is a concentration ratio of 50 per cent or more. Nutter finds (p. 45), "In 1899, monopolistic industries accounted for 32.0 per cent of manufacturing income."

He develops for 1937 a "narrow" and a "broad" indicator of monopoly. The narrow indicator is, again, a concentration ratio of 50 per cent or more. By this test, monopoly declined from 32 per cent to 28 per cent of income originating in American manufacture between 1899 and 1937. The broad indicator consists of all manufacturing industries classified as monopolistic by Wilcox[46] "plus any additional manufacturing census industries with concentration ratios

---

[43] Cf. Vernon A. Mund, *Open Markets: an Essential of Free Enterprise* (New York, 1948).

[44] *The Extent of Enterprise Monopoly.*

[45] The fact that the over-all figure of income originating in concentrated industries refers to 1899, even though the data on concentration in particular industries may come from any one of the years between 1895 and 1904, does not seem to be objectionable. Nutter's sources were presumably concerned mainly with concentration produced by mergers and consequently quoted figures representing the highest degree of concentration attained by mergers. The study, therefore, would appear to measure changes in the degree of concentration *after* the first great merger movement. It seems probable that, were data available from the mid-nineties, the comparison with 1937 would show a substantial increase in concentration.

[46] *Competition and Monopoly in American Industry.*

of ½ or larger and census products of major value with concentration ratios of ¾ or larger." By this test the per cent of manufacturing income originating in monopolized industries increased from 32 to 38.3 between 1899 and 1937.

Nutter points out, "These conclusions are all subject to serious qualification, which result from probable inaccuracies in measurement and from the arbitrary nature of definitions of monopoly" (p. 46). I should prefer to consider this a study of changing concentration (involving one measure of concentration) based on an exhaustive examination of some rather unreliable data.

Adelman's comparison of concentration ratios in American manufacturing industries "around 1901" with concentration ratios in 1947 does not pretend to answer the question whether monopoly is increasing or decreasing.[47] The earlier figures are taken from Nutter's study and weighted in terms of value added in various industries in 1901. The later year is chosen to take advantage of the concentration ratios calculated by the Department of Commerce from 1947 census data. The comparison indicates that 32.9 per cent of value added by manufacture was produced, around 1901, in industries in which the largest 4 firms accounted for 50 per cent or more of value added, while in 1947 the comparable figure was 24 per cent.

Adelman points out various weaknesses of the data and the arbitrary character of the concentration measurement and concludes: "The odds are better than even that there has actually been *some* decline in concentration. It is a good bet that there has at least been no actual increase; and the odds do seem high against any substantial increase."[48]

I should be prepared to accept this cautiously stated conclusion but would insist — as indeed Adelman does himself — that a comparison of concentration ratios, even based on reliable data, cannot tell us whether American manufactures are more or less monopolized than 50 years ago.

CONCLUSIONS

Various measures of general concentration show that a substantial share of total economic activity is carried on in a relatively small

[47] "The Measurement of Industrial Concentration."
[48] "The Measurement of Industrial Concentration," pp. 292, 293.

number of large corporations. This is a useful estimate to put beside estimates of the large number of independent firms operating in the economy. Concentration is uneven among the large sectors of the economy and is particularly high in public utilities, manufacture and mining. Differences in degree of concentration among various sectors probably give a rough indication of the relative importance of market versus managerial activity in these sectors. The high degree noted in certain areas is presumably the basic fact from which much of the recent literature on "managerial economics" takes shape. It must be noted, however, that to date no very clear-cut relationships have been established between size of firms and the process of business decision-making. The same negative statement must also be made with respect to alleged social and political consequences of size.

Market measures of concentration are, in general, higher for census products than for the various classes of census industry. For either products or industries there is a wide range of concentration ratios in American manufacture. In Adelman's phrase, "concentration is highly concentrated." Neither uncorrected-census-product or census-industry data offer a very good approximation to economic markets. Even if they did, we should not usually be entitled to infer clear-cut conclusions concerning monopoly or competition from data on market shares alone. The information on industries and firms used in calculating market concentration ratios is relevant but partial.

The available information appears to suggest that although many U. S. manufacturing industries are largely concentrated and although the largest firms in the economy account for a significant per cent of economic activity, American industries are less concentrated than similar industries in many other countries, and general concentration is no higher — it may even be somewhat lower — than in countries showing a comparable degree of industrialization. Since the degree of general concentration depends fundamentally on the extent of industrialization, general concentration tends to be low in under-developed countries. We may be sure, however, that it will increase as these countries industrialize.

The studies of trends of both general and market concentration have yielded useful negative conclusions. It is clear now, as it was not clear before, that there is no inevitable historical force at work that must produce, over any extended period of time, an increase in the per cent of economic activity accounted for by the largest firms either in American manufacture or in the economy as a whole. I think it has been demonstrated that between 1931 and 1947 there was no substantial increase in concentration in manufacture, and at least serious doubts have been cast on the existence of any such tendency over the last fifty years. But I think it impossible to draw from these data conclusions regarding the trend of monopoly.

2

Industrial Concentration and the Decline of Competition[1]

A series of writers from the time of Marx to this have looked upon the process of industrial concentration and pronounced the end of competition. "One capitalist kills many"; with the eventual and not too remote consequence being the emergence of some form of monopoly as the characteristic market situation. Until comparatively recently such conclusions were the almost exclusive property of the socialists. As a recent writer has put it, "bourgeois" economists have "denied this development until the phenomena apparently became so overwhelming as to be familiar to anybody but the professional economist who was always the last to recognize its existence." [2] Now, however, as so often happens in the social sciences, the pendulum has swung in the other direction, and the economist's "world of competition" is giving way to a "world of monopolies."

It would be foolhardy indeed to assert that many markets in this or any other country are "purely" competitive. Whether there are many or few, however, is irrelevant not only to the question whether control is becoming more concentrated and monopoly power more important but also to the question whether the economy functions very differently than it would if markets were purely competitive. The latter question, concerned with the "degree" of monopoly control, obviously is not only important but, as we shall see, relevant to the problem of concentration of control. Though it has been theoretically considered,[3] it is, however, usually ignored by those who attempt to

[1] Reprinted from *Explorations in Economics; Notes and Essays Contributed in Honor of F. W. Taussig* (New York, 1936).

[2] O. Lange, "Marxian Economics and Modern Economic Theory," *Review of Economic Studies,* June 1935, p. 190.

[3] One of the few papers dealing directly with this question is A. P. Lerner's "The Concept of Monopoly and the Measurement of Monopoly Power," *Review of Economic Studies,* June 1934, p. 157. The degree or extent of monopoly power must presumably be calculated with reference to some standard,

make out a statistical case for concentration of control. It is with the nature of the statistical case that this paper is primarily concerned.

Writers on the concentration of control ordinarily use the term in two different but related senses. The first, having to do with the internal organization of a business enterprise, usually the corporation, signifies the observed tendency of the power of decision on business issues to pass into the hands of the owners of an increasingly smaller percentage of the firm's assets. Although in a sense it is true to say that the "divorce" of control from ownership is inherent in the nature of the corporate form of organization and is at least as old as the corporation itself, there is no doubt that, by reason of the increasing number of stockholders, their geographical distribution, and the series of legal changes strengthening "control" against "ownership," this divorce has tended to become more complete. It is an important phenomenon and merits all the attention it has been given in recent years.

There is, however, a second and more important sense in which concentration of control is used relative to the structure and functioning of markets. Here control is dependent on a firm's possession of some degree of monopoly power. Given pure competition in all the relations with which an enterprise becomes involved in its purchase of materials, the services of factors of production, and the sale of its products, control in this sense of the word would be absent. We may note in passing that the importance of the first type of concentration of control depends in part on the importance of the second. The influence of a controlling group in a corporation on the disposition of income, for example, has increased significance if this income is enhanced by a position of monopoly power.

Most of the literature on the concentration of control, though vague

---

which might be pure competition or some one of a number of "ideal" arrangements of resources. The variables whose divergence from the standard constitutes the degree or extent of monopoly power might be volume of output, price, profits, or any one of a number of other possibilities. The results are likely to differ with the type of equilibrium situation chosen for the purpose of comparing the standard with the monopolistic arrangement. For example, a short-run monopolistic adjustment of price or output may differ from a comparable competitive situation by more or less than the long-run equilibrium adjustments. The problem is a very complicated one, and it seems probable that any measurement of the degree of monopoly power must be specifically related to the particular purpose in view.

on the meaning of this concept, is concerned with some or all aspects of the problem of market control. What evidence is there that monopoly power is an important and increasingly significant phenomenon in American economic life? When it is maintained that competition is on the decline, what is meant is certainly not that purely competitive markets are now less numerous or less important than at some previous time. Pure or perfect competition is a concept that has never accurately described a large sector of economic reality. Markets in which the demand for the products of an individual firm is perfectly elastic have probably never existed outside of agriculture and, at times, the organized produce and security exchanges. Although it may be said that with the decline in the relative importance of agriculture the importance of purely competitive markets has also declined, against this dictum may be set the fact that with rapid improvements in transportation the area within which these markets might justly be described as purely competitive has increased. The same improvement in transportation has, moreover, frequently weakened a position of local monopoly by bringing its market into contact with alternative sellers of the same or similar products.

Nor does the thesis that the competitive market is on the decline ordinarily have reference to the phenomena treated by the theory of monopolistic competition. This theory has taught us to see some degree of monopolistic control in the possession of every enterprise whose product, or the services connected with its sale, are to some extent differentiated from the products and services of rival enterprises. If we define a commodity or the market for a commodity as one "bounded on all sides by a gap in the chain of substitutes," [4] we may envisage many markets in which each of a large number of sellers, no one of preponderant size, enjoys some degree of monopoly control because of slight product or service differentiation. This type of monopoly power, however, has no necessary connection with large-scale enterprise or fewness of sellers in the market, nor does it disturb the writers on concentration of control.

What they appear to mean by the decline of competition is that at some critical point in the development of many if not most industrial markets a decline in the number of sellers, the growth in the size of

---

[4] Cf. Joan Robinson, *The Economics of Imperfect Competition* (London, 1933), p. 5.

some of them, or collusion between them has led to the substitution of some one of a variety of monopolistic responses for a competitive response of firms to the market situation. Markets in which buyers and sellers customarily act without too much regard for the results of their action on the market situation or on the actions of their rivals have given way to markets in which at least some sellers, by reason of their size, are forced to take account of the probable effects of their action.

The evidence presented to substantiate this thesis is usually of two sorts: (1) data on the size of firms, on the share of business wealth or of output controlled by particular firms, and on agreements, understandings, or conventions between firms; and (2) data on the behavior of prices of particular commodities.

The most striking evidence of the importance of large-scale enterprise in the American economy is that presented by Gardiner Means in his statistics concerning the assets of the 200 largest corporations in this country. He interprets the statistics to indicate control by these non-banking corporations of 38 per cent (in 1930) of the non-banking "business wealth" of the country.[5] Although Means was not primarily concerned with market control, these figures have been widely used to indicate concentration of control in this sense. It would be interesting to know how the percentage of business wealth controlled by the 5, 50, 100, and 200 largest business enterprises in 1930 compared with the percentages controlled by the largest enterprises forty or fifty years ago. It must be remembered that if enterprises were smaller then, so also was business wealth a fraction of its present magnitude. Granted the change has been considerable, how relevant is it to the concentration of control? If control means power to vary within wide limits the use of these assets and, by inference, use of the labor resources associated with them, obviously changes in the conditions imposed on this power by government regulation are pertinent. For certain uses of the term control, then, large-scale enterprises in the public-utility industries belong in a separate category.

Other strictures on the significance of these data for the problem of concentration of control are, however, more important. The 200 largest business enterprises are in many instances financial and

[5] A. A. Berle and G. C. Means, *The Modern Corporation and Private Property* (New York, 1932), p. 32.

marketing but not operating units. Without a study of the internal organization of these business enterprises and the extent to which decentralization has transferred the power of decision to subordinate units, it is difficult to assess the importance of this material. If a merger between hitherto competing concerns brings former operating units into a rather loose federation, by how much has the concentration of control progressed through such a merger? All too little is known of the internal organization of large-scale business enterprises, but clearly this is a consideration relevant to the problem of concentration of control.

Equally relevant and of decisive importance is the question of the structure of the markets in which large-scale concerns or their subordinate operating units buy materials and the services of the factors and sell their products. Ordinarily enterprises of this size are not one-product firms; for instance, the United States Steel Corporation or the Allied Chemical Company manufactures and sells hundreds of products. The gross size of the concern, though possibly determining the monopoly position and control of the firm in one market or one set of economic relations, may be without significance in other markets. Before such data as the increasing ownership of assets, in dollars or percentages, of the 200 largest corporations can be used as an indication of concentration of control in any very significant sense, both the market relations and the internal organization of these firms must be studied. And if such a study is to throw light on the growth of concentration of control, it must not only analyze the existing situation but must be directed to changes in these aspects of the problem over time.[6]

In addition to data on size of business enterprises or of central office groups, material concerning the share of the market or percentage of the volume of output of particular commodities or groups of commodities possessed by a firm or a small number of firms is frequently offered as evidence of concentration of control. This sort of evidence is collected in greatest detail and most definitely stressed

[6] The central office group, marked by the operating control of two or more plants, used by Willard Thorp in his study on *Integration in American Industry* (Washington, 1924), is possibly a unit of greater significance for the problem of concentration of control than is the business enterprise. Without an examination of the market relations of central office groups, however, little could be made of his statistics as an indication of concentration of control.

in Laidler's book, *Concentration of Control in American Industry* (New York, 1931). Unfortunately this and other studies of the same phenomena give a very unprecise idea of the position of the large American firms in the markets in which they buy and sell. Nor is it possible from available statistical sources to measure in many industries the share of the market possessed by particular firms or to trace the development of the market situation. The importance of a firm in an industry might be measured in terms of physical output, sales, or total assets — to take the most significant and available indices. For most purposes physical output is perhaps the best unit. Although the automobile, steel, and mining industries publish such data and although fragmentary material is available in Federal Trade Commission and other industry studies, no comprehensive statistics are at hand for this purpose.

Statistics of gross sales and gross incomes have been reported for major industrial groups for the past ten years, but this helps us little in the analysis of particular markets. The gross sales or income figures for individual firms frequently cover a multitude of commodities. The Treasury Department has reported balance-sheet totals for major manufacturing groups since 1926, but again the statistics of assets of individual firms and industrial groups do not lend themselves to an analysis of the share of the market possessed by the large firms.

Insofar as material concerning percentages of national output of products or related groups of products possessed by one or a few firms can be collected, it is, of course, likely to underestimate the importance of a firm or firms in particular markets. There is nothing like a national market in any useful sense of the term for most commodities but rather a series of regional markets between which transport costs offer a certain amount of protection to any control that local enterprises may enjoy. The Standard Oil Company of New York marketed in 1930 less than 10 per cent of the total national sales of gasoline, but in New England the sales of this company were well over 30 per cent of the whole. The 15 refiners of imported cane sugar who formed the Sugar Institute sold in 1930 something less than 85 per cent of the total national sales of sugar, but in a number of the states on the eastern seaboard they were the only sellers of sugar. The importance of this consideration, influenced by the location of production centers, the marketing areas of different firms, and transport cost between centers of consumption, varies greatly among different commodities and is in any case difficult to assess without more knowledge of the geographical flow of commodities than we now possess.

Granted, however, information now inaccessible concerning the share of local markets possessed by individual firms, or the more important of them, how significant would these data be for an analysis of the concentration of control or monopoly power? It is clear one cannot pass immediately from statistics of share of output produced by individual firms to conclusions regarding the production and price policies of these firms. Admitting that the existence of one or a few large firms in a market produces a situation in which some or all of them attempt to take account of the effect of their own policies on the market situation or on the policies of their rivals, does this lead to a serious departure from competitive standards in the determination of price, output, and investment policies? If we are to rely on facts rather than a highly abstract theory for the answer to this question, it is astonishing how inadequate that answer must be.

Industries dominated by one or a few large firms are sometimes said to show the influence of small numbers on concentration of control through the phenomenon of price leadership. One firm, the leader, formulates its price and production policies with due regard to the probable effect of these policies, if followed by its rivals, on the market situation as a whole. Such a policy insofar as it exists certainly indicates some degree of control; how much depends on the extent to which the leader, in order to preserve its position, is forced to take account of and accommodate itself to the possibly divergent interests of its rivals. One of the most illuminating recent treatments of this practice mentions as industries in which price leadership has been most notable, steel, petroleum, agricultural implements, and anthracite coal.[7] In two of these industries, steel and petroleum, the power of the leader today is certainly considerably less than it was thirty years ago. All the evidence of price leadership in the other two industries dates from prewar times. Many other examples of price leadership may be and are given, but one cannot read careful accounts of this practice without realizing how very tentative and unsatisfactory is the available evidence. There seems little doubt

[7] A. R. Burns, *The Decline of Competition* (New York, 1936).

that at certain times in a number of industries prices have been set by a leader, but it is equally clear that in periods of depression or other rapid change in the market situation the followers have broken away from the leader.

Monopolistic control in a market dominated by a few firms does not need to take the form of price leadership. All the firms setting their prices with due regard for the effect of their price policies on each other may succeed in eliminating price competition altogether. A striking example of the price uniformity and stability that such a situation may produce is presented by the cigarette industry, in which the four large firms producing 80 to 90 per cent of the total volume of output quote prices that move together without apparent collusion. Here again, however, the example is badly chosen for the purpose of indicating increased concentration of control, since dispersion rather than concentration has been the fate of the tobacco industry as compared with prewar days.

Evidence of collusion between sellers and buyers, agreement for price fixing or sharing the market, and the effects of such collusion on prices and outputs is even more inadequate than that concerning price leadership. The pooling arrangements of the seventies, eighties, and nineties were clearly illegal after the 1899 decision in the Addyston pipe case. It is commonplace that the interpretation of the antitrust laws, while extremely lenient toward mergers, was clearly opposed to arrangements for united action among independent firms. Writers on industrial organization and trust policy differ markedly in their opinions as to how successfully the law against agreements has been evaded. Certainly undercover agreements for fixing prices and sharing the market have continued to exist as well as conventional arrangements that have served the same purpose. There is no doubt, furthermore, that on occasion the statistical and price-reporting services of trade associations have been used to promote united action on price and output. In how many industries collusion has been possible, how successfully agreements have been maintained, and in what ways and to what extent prices, output, and investment have been affected by agreement remain, however, nearly a closed book. One can certainly not dismiss offhand the opinion of many competent observers that the antitrust laws have proved on the whole an effective deterrent to collusive action "in restraint of trade."

A summary of the evidence insofar as it consists of statistics on the size of business enterprises, share of the volume of output or sales of particular products controlled by individual enterprises, studies of price leadership and common price action, and facts concerning collusive action, does not lead to a very clear picture of the extent of concentration of control and the importance of positions of monopoly power in American industry. That most industrial markets are only imperfectly competitive and that many have been at times and are now highly organized, at least on the side of the sellers, no one would deny. Whether competition is now more imperfect and monopoly more widespread than before the war or in the nineties is, however, a different question. Only to those who believe that fifty years ago American industry was highly competitive is the available evidence on concentration of control conclusive.

In addition to facts and figures on size of enterprises, share in the market, and agreements in restraint of trade, the behavior of prices has been advanced as indicative of the existence of monopolistic control. In the very interesting and illuminative pamphlet, *Industrial Prices and Their Relative Inflexibility*, Gardiner Means has called attention to marked differences in the number and amplitude of changes in the quoted prices of particular commodities during the depression. On the whole it is clear that the quoted prices of most industrial products were less "flexible" in this sense than the prices of agricultural products. These statistics bear an interesting resemblance to the statistics of "free" and "controlled" prices in the German economy.

It is true that Means attributed the relative inflexibility of industrial prices to the fact that they are "administered" and attempts definitely to disassociate this type of price behavior with the existence of monopoly power. But surely "administration" is simply a method of price quotation and has no necessary connection with price inflexibility. Vermont farmers "administer" the prices of the maple syrup they sell in the sense that a price is quoted at which the "buyers may purchase or not as they wish,"[8] but this does not prevent the price of maple syrup from adjusting itself fairly rapidly to changes in the market situation. In purely competitive market prices will change

___

[8] Gardiner C. Means, *Industrial Prices and Their Relative Inflexibility,* Senate Document No. 13, 74th Congress, 1st Session (Washington, 1935), p. 1.

with changes in demand or supply regardless of the method of price quotation.

Price stability in the presence of changing market conditions is, except for markets in which prices are conventionally or for institutional reasons stable, pretty good evidence of the existence of monopoly power. It is true that a monopolist aware of market changes and interested in maximizing his short-run profits would change his price with every change in the market. Nevertheless monopolists are not necessarily interested in maximizing their short-run advantage nor are they forced by the market to do so. There are many reasons why not only a monopolist but more particularly large sellers who do not enjoy a complete monopoly position should prefer price stability to price change. We do not need to consider those reasons here, the point being that in a purely competitive market prices could not remain stable with changes in the demand and cost conditions.[9]

Although price inflexibility in a serious depression is indicative of the presence of positions of monopoly power, there are many reasons why statistics of number and amplitude of changes in quoted prices do not throw much light on our question of the concentration of control in American industry. The prices of branded and trade-marked articles occupy an important place in the category of "inflexible prices" but, although a monopoly position is necessary for this type of price rigidity, it is by no means necessarily a monopoly dependent on large size or share of the market. Without some examination of the behavior of industrial prices in prewar depressions, it would be, of course, impossible in any case to use them as evidence of increasing price control. But apart from this, price statistics are so faulty as to injure seriously their utility for this purpose. The statistics take very little account of changes in quality of product or selling terms, which may be of importance in a number of industries. Then too, the prices quoted are in some cases not prices at which sales are made. There has been a good deal of criticism in Germany that the statistics of controlled prices concealed the very considerable price cutting and shading. There is very little reason to believe that American "inflexible" prices are exempt from this difficulty.[10]

[9] See John Kenneth Galbraith, "Monopoly Power and Price Rigidities," *Quarterly Journal of Economics,* May 1936, pp. 456–475.

[10] For Means' reply to this type of criticism see his articles, "Notes on Inflexible Prices," *American Economic Review,* Sup., March 1936, p. 23. In

Price statistics are no doubt adequate to show certain rough but very striking differences between the behavior of the prices of certain industrial products and agricultural commodities. But for the more subtle purpose of distinguishing the influence of monopoly power from the other influences, they are something less than adequate.

In conclusion it would be emphasized that the foregoing comments are not designed to suggest that American industry is effectively competitive or that nineteenth-century arguments concerning the coincidence of private and public interest, depending on the assumption of pure competition, have weight and merit. They have rather been concerned with the inadequacy and incompleteness of the popular thesis that in the postwar period American industry has exhibited so marked a tendency to concentration of control and the development of positions of monopoly power as to produce a quite different economic system than existed at a previous period. At least a part of the present emphasis on concentration arises, in all probability, from the illusion that at some not too remote period the economy was competitive.

---

this article he reports the results of an attempt to correct the index of price change for agricultural implements from 1929 to 1933. When his original figures showed a fall of 6 per cent, the corrected index gives a fall of 15 per cent in the prices of these products.

3

Price and Production Policies of
Large-Scale Enterprise[1]

I

The current emphasis on price policy, as against price, as a proper object of study represents recent economic reflection on the significance of expectations, uncertainties, market control, and the position of price as one among many selling terms. Policy implies some degree of control over the course of events and, at the same time, the use of judgment as to the probable consequences of alternative lines of action. In perfect markets, whether monopolistic or competitive, price is hardly a matter of judgment and where there is no judgment there is no policy. The area of price policy, then, embraces the deliberative action of buyers and sellers able to influence price; that is to say, it covers practically the whole field of industrial prices.

The preoccupation with policy questions certainly indicates a trend towards an inclusion in price analysis of an increasing number of institutional considerations. Pursued to its Hamiltonian end,[2] it implies not only an examination of the facts peculiar to each industrial market situation, but also a study of the conditions peculiar to each sale or purchase including what Messrs. Ford and Firestone dreamed in the night preceding the morning of their big tire deal. Particular circumstances may, indeed, justify so minute an investigation. It is submitted, however, that useful work in the field of industrial price policies requires a frame of reference of much greater generality. To the construction of such a frame of reference, which must take the form, I think, of a classification of market structures, recent theoretical work makes a useful contribution. It is, however, merely a starting point.

[1] Reprinted from *American Economic Review,* Supplement, Vol. 29, No. 1, March 1939.
[2] Cf. Walton Hamilton et al., *Price and Price Policies* (New York, 1938), Sections I and IX.

A firm may have a price policy by reason of the existence of rivals of whose action it must take account, of the desirability of considering the effect of present upon future price, of the possibility of its price in one market affecting its price in another, of the possibility of competing in other ways than by price, and for many other reasons. All these situations involve some degree of market control on the part of a seller or buyer. A position of market control, while a necessary, is not, however, a sufficient condition for price policy. In addition a seller or buyer must customarily conduct his operations by means of a quoted price. A dealer on an organized produce exchange may conduct transactions of sufficient magnitude to influence the market price. Yet if he buys and sells "at the market" it serves no useful purpose to attribute to him a price policy. I limit the meaning of this term, then, to buyers and sellers who enjoy some degree of market control and who carry on their purchases and sales through the medium of a quoted price.[3] Practically speaking this includes all selling transactions outside of agriculture and the organized produce and securities markets.

II

The size of a firm influences its competitive policies in a number of ways. In the first place the scale of its purchases and sales relative to the total volume of transactions in the firm's market is one indication of the extent of its market control. Taken in conjunction with other data it may throw a good deal of light on price and production policies. Certain authorities, on the other hand, brush aside figures on the relative size of firms as irrelevant and emphasize the decisive impor-

---

[3] R. F. Kahn, "The Problem of Duopoly," *Economic Journal*, March 1937, p. 4, distinguishes the following "extreme cases":

"(a) At one extreme we have the case where, in spite of a change in a competitor's price, firms' prices remain constant automatically until they are altered as a result of deliberation or experiment. . . .

"(b) At the other extreme is the case where it is the volume of sales that automatically remains constant until some other decision is arrived at."

The first case is practically significant and embraces the whole range of industrial market situations in which sellers act through price quotations. The second case, however, is unrealistic. If price varies from moment to moment with changes in market conditions it is more than probable that sales (for an individual seller) will vary also.

tance of the elasticity of the firm's demand curve.[4] It would no doubt be extremely convenient if economists knew the shape of individual demand and cost curves and could proceed forthwith, by comparisons of price and marginal cost, to conclusions regarding the existing degree of monopoly power. The extent to which the monopoly theorists, however, refrain from an empirical application of their formulae is rather striking.[5] The alternative, if more pedestrian, route follows the direction of ascertainable facts and makes use only of empirically applicable concepts.[6] One such set of facts embraces the data relevant to concentration.

Secondly, the absolute size of a firm, as measured by assets, employees, or volume of sales, is also relevant to price and production policies. The scale of operations may affect the number and character of the factors that are taken into account in the determination of policies; it may also affect the way the firm reacts to given market situations. Selling practices at the disposal of the large firm may be beyond the reach of its smaller competitors. Large oil firms characteristically brand their gasoline and differentiate it from the product of competitors by extensive advertising campaigns. Small firms may, by reason of their size, be forced to sell an unbranded product at a lower price. In a society in which size is popularly considered a menace, the large firm must consider carefully the probable reception of its price and production policies by public opinion and political agencies. There is some evidence that the United States Steel Corporation for a considerable period of time viewed with favor its dwindling share in the national market and, through its price policies, "held an umbrella" over the heads of its growing competitors. Recent aggressive price tactics on the part of this company may indicate that it no longer regards such policies as politically necessary. If the

[4] Cf. A. P. Lerner, "The Concept of Monopoly and the Measurement of Monopoly Power," *Review of Economic Studies*, June 1934.

[5] Some theorists, pursuing their analysis on a high plane, refer to their work as "tool making" rather than "tool using." A "toolmaker," however, who constructs tools which no "tool user" can use is making a contribution of limited significance. Some knowledge of the use of tools is probably indispensable to their effective fabrication.

[6] I should be far from denying, however, the value of theoretical speculation, even of a very abstract sort, in helping to ask the right questions of the data and in indicating the irrelevance of much factual material.

market be considered as embracing all the factors external to the firm which habitually influence its competitive policies, there can be no doubt that the size of the firm affects the scope and structure of the market.

The size of a firm likewise influences its reaction to given market situations. Economic analysis exhibits a disposition to treat the firm as a "profit maximizing" agency, the action of which in the market is independent of its internal organization. The growth of corporate bureaucracies (with the consequent institutionalization of management decisions), the separation of ownership from control, and the growing influence of labor organization on policy making are all factors "internal to the firm" which may and do affect its reaction to market situations. One of the questions raised by these considerations is the meaning and importance of administered prices. To this question I shall return in a subsequent section.

III

Current consideration of price policy is apt to take either one of two quite different directions. One approach, associated with the theory of oligopoly and monopolistic competition, starts with various elements of the market structure of the individual firm and derives therefrom conclusions regarding the price and production policy of this firm. The other begins with an examination of the behavior of prices and through correlation of various measures of price behavior with other measurable economic variables works back towards differences in the structure of markets in an attempt to explain the observed differences in price behavior.

The practical utility of the analytical method has been to focus attention on rivals' reactions as considerations in the determination of price and production policies and on the importance of non-price forms of competition. Whether the further elaboration of techniques of analysis yielding results of illusory exactness are useful is doubtful. The broad justification of this type of analysis must be that it provides a pattern of thought useful in separating data which are relevant from those which are irrelevant to the explanation of price and production policies. Certainly numbers of buyers and sellers in the market and the possibility of product differentiation are relevant. No one would deny, furthermore, that the position and shape of individual demand and cost curves would be relevant if ascertainable.[7] In the absence of such data, however, a realistic analysis of price and production policies may be unable to make much use of the constructions of recent monopoly theory.

A number of more specific strictures on the utility of this theory for price analysis may be offered. The static equilibrium assumptions implicit in this analysis rule out most of the considerations which are important for price policy. These considerations are in the main connected with industrial growth and decay and with the business cycle. The objection is not that monopoly theory is incompatible with an analysis that takes these considerations into account but that its constructions are irrelevant to the real problems. If we seek to build further on the existing foundation, the only part of that foundation which is likely to be found usable is composed of the ascertainable facts of numbers of sellers (and buyers) and product differentiation.[8]

Data on numbers, furthermore, tell us little regarding price and production policies unless there is further specification of market

[7] However true it may be that businessmen have a roughly accurate notion of the shape of the demand curve with which they are confronted, at least within a limited range, it seems extremely unlikely that economists will be able by independent investigations to ascertain this shape except by the roughest sort of deduction from other data. In certain favorable cases demand curves for a product may be drawn statistically; for other products we are able to surmise that the demand curve is elastic or inelastic. Cf. J. M. Cassels, *A Study of Fluid Milk Prices* (Cambridge, Mass., 1937), p. 41: "Certain fairly definite conclusions about the character of the consumer's demand for milk can be drawn from a general common sense analysis of the factors involved." By taking into consideration such factors as numbers of sellers, product standardization, and others one can, in some cases, proceed from a rough knowledge of the shape of the product demand curve to a rougher guess at the shape of the demand curve for an individual seller.

[8] Pigou would apparently deny that products for which substitution is not perfect can be in the same market. He defines the market at a "common nodal point" at which different units of an identical good are "available for purchase and sale" en route from the sellers' works to the buyers' home. Such a definition permits of a classification of markets only on the basis of numbers of buyers and sellers. (A. C. Pigou, *The Economics of Stationary States,* London, 1935, p. 78.) If different products are admitted to the market then the problem becomes one of (a) defining the group of products which are in the same market; (b) defining the geographical area within which buyers and sellers are in competition. It is on the basis of numbers and product differentiation that Machlup constructs his classification of markets, without, however, dealing with the question of how the geographical and product limits of the market are to be defined. Cf. Fritz Machlup, "Monopoly and Competition," *American Economic Review,* Sept. 1937.

structure. Elaborate speculation on the probable behavior of A based on the assumption that B will act in a certain way seems particularly fruitless. It recalls Morgenstern's discussion of the dilemma of Dr. Moriarty when confronted with the alternative courses open to Sherlock Holmes.[9] It should be a function of market analysis so to particularize as to reduce the area of necessary speculation to a minimum. The theory of oligopoly has been aptly described as a ticket of admission to institutional economics. It is to be regretted that more theorists have not availed themselves of this privilege. If they had, there would certainly be less of a disposition in the literature on the decline of competition to assume that in all markets dominated by a few sellers are to be found the same or similar patterns of price policy.

The statistical approach to price policy starts with an examination of price behavior and then proceeds to correlate various measures of price change with changes in other economic variables. Despite the recognized defects in price data, recent work along this line has made clear characteristic differences in the various groups of prices and has raised problems of admitted importance. Typically, however, this work exhibits certain weaknesses. First, it has been insufficiently recognized that, proceeding from the standard products of the raw material markets to the differentiated products of the highly fabricated goods markets, price as an index of the terms on which buyers acquire or sellers dispose of commodities tends to lose significance. The introduction of various forms of non-price competition and a proliferation of selling terms emphasize the necessity to take these considerations into account both in an analysis of sellers' price policy and in determining changes in the position of buying groups.[10] Second, the measures of price behavior customarily employed are fre-

[9] *Wirtschaftsprognose,* p. 98.

[10] In this connection it is necessary to distinguish between two quite different attacks on the validity of existing price data. It may be objected that the quoted price is inaccurate because it is not the price at which sales actually take place; e.g., the B.L.S. quotations on sulphuric acid were, during the depression, highly inaccurate since they represented unimportant sales to small purchasers while the bulk of the sales during this period were made at much lower prices to large industrial users. On the other hand it may be objected that the quoted price is inaccurate because it is merely one among many conditions of sale. In so far as the other conditions of sale cannot be legitimately reduced to price terms — and they usually cannot — this is not an objection to the validity of the price as such.

quently much too general to serve the purposes to which they are put. This is conspicuously true of commonly used measures of price sensitivity. An all-purpose measure of price sensitivity or flexibility is subject to as many and as serious objections as an all-purpose index number. Price is a function of many variables, and price sensitivity or flexibility acquires significance mainly as a relationship between price change and change in some one or more of these variables.[11] Prices may be sensitive to changes in inventories, demand, costs, and in other prices, or to changes in some of these variables and not in others. Third, the attempt to correlate measures of price behavior with other data such as industrial concentration and product durability on an economy-wide basis is apt to include irrelevant and exclude relevant determinants of price policy. It seems probable that empirical work will achieve better results by a more intensive examination of specific market situations. In selected industrial markets a study of the relation between changes in costs, inventories, sales, production improvements and other variables, and the magnitude and timing of price change may considerably increase our knowledge of price and production policies.

These strictures on current methods of interpreting price and production policies do not imply that analytical and statistical techniques are useless. On the contrary any classification of market structures designed to illuminate patterns of competitive policy must make use of them.

IV

It follows from what has been said that an adequate analysis of price and production policies requires consideration of (a) the influence of the organization of a firm on the character of the firm's reaction to given market situations; and (b) elements of market structure which include many more things than numbers and product differentiation. It goes without saying that a realistic treatment of

[11] Some of these relationships are, of course, much more important than others. I should be prepared to admit, with Lerner, Kalecki, and Dunlop that — at least for commodities for which price is the only significant selling term — the relationship between price and marginal cost is peculiarly significant both for analysis and policy. Cf. Lerner; M. Kalecki, "The Determinants of Distribution of National Income," *Econometrica*, April 1938; J. T. Dunlop, "Price Rigidity and Degree of Monopoly," a manuscript to be published shortly.

these questions necessitates the use of analytical tools which are amenable to empirical application. The problem, as I see it, is to reduce the voluminous data concerning industrial organization to some sort of order through a classification of market structures. Differences in market structure are ultimately explicable in terms of technological factors. The economic problem, however, is to explain, through an examination of the structure of markets and the organization of firms, differences in competitive practices including price, production, and investment policies.

A consideration of the relation of the organization of firms to price and production policies raises at the outset the question of administered prices. As currently used this is neither a clearcut nor a useful concept. In one sense it appears to relate to the methods by which a price is determined; in another sense to the way the price behaves. A price may be determined by administrative action; i.e., it may be quoted by a seller rather than determined by the higgling of buyers and sellers in an organized market. At the same time it may behave in much the same way as prices in organized markets. A manufacturer's price of cotton print cloth may be taken as an example. Furthermore, the attempt to contrast administered prices with market prices obscures the fact that all prices are market prices in the sense that market considerations influence their determination.

There is, nevertheless, an important kernel of truth concealed in this usage, to wit, the fact that firms are not, regardless of what economic theory may suppose, undifferentiated profit-maximizing agencies which react to given market situations in ways which are independent of their organization. The large corporation is a complex administrative unit in which control frequently bears a very attentuated relationship to owners' interests, in which management is increasingly professionalized, in which the character of labor organization may influence price and production decisions, and in which at best a considerable area of important price decision must be routinized and delegated to subordinates. Hence management, in the determination of price and production policies, is influenced not only by market pressures but also by considerations internal to the firm.

The United States Steel Corporation, considering all the quantity and quality variations involved in adapting forty or fifty basic products to the specifications of its customers, is faced with the problem of setting some fifty thousand prices. While market considerations may, at one time or another, influence the relationships between these prices, it is impossible to make independent decisions respecting prices with every change in the market situation even if such action were thought desirable. The result is that pricing on individual orders is delegated to price clerks armed with an elaborate book of extras and such specific directions as to its use as may be thought desirable. The International Harvester Company, in servicing its agricultural implements, manufactures and stocks some two hundred and fifty thousand separate parts. In pricing these parts considerations relevant to the organization and administration of the firm are probably at least as important as considerations relevant to the market situation.

The locus and character of control within the firm may likewise be relevant to basic price and production policies. The familiar contrast between a financial type of control primarily concerned with the conservation of assets and control by entrepreneurial types mainly concerned with expanding output and the firm's share in the market is doubtless too easy. Conservation of assets may necessitate an expansion of output and, after all, bankers called in to rehabilitate a declining firm have been known to advise price reduction as a remedy. Furthermore, in those cases in which the supposed influence of entrepreneurial and financial attitudes are sharply contrasted, e.g., automobiles and steel products, the differences can probably be more adequately explained by market conditions than by considerations relevant to the internal organization of firms. Nevertheless it is true to say that organizations make men, as well as the reverse, and in the making of men policies are also made. During the recent flurry of price cutting in the steel industry the president of the Steel Workers' Organization Committee announced that if price cutting continued organized labor might be forced to take action since "price cutting always leads to wage cutting." The character of control and the action of control in the determination of policy — including price and production policies — are influenced not only by the pressure of labor but by many pressures arising from group relationships within the firm. These relationships, furthermore, tend to influence the kind and caliber of men who are called to management positions in a concern.[12]

Economists have been singularly loath to investigate these semi-political relationships within large-scale enterprise which influence business policy. Where business policies are recognized as running counter to what would seem to be rational action in the market, the disposition has been to interpret them in terms of individual personalities. It was said that Firestone and Ford were sports, in the sense of deviations from the norm of entrepreneurial rationality. Or again, that what every industry dominated by a few firms needed was a Ford or Firestone, by which it was implied that economic rationality in such situations would lead to production restriction and price maintenance but that these policies were prevented, with advantage to the public, by the anomalous behavior of such entrepreneurs. No doubt Messrs. Ford and Firestone set the impress of their personalities on the policies of their respective industries, but the larger problem for economists to consider is the impress of large-scale business organizations on the character and functioning of the management groups that are called to control positions.[13]

[12] Cf. J. A. Schumpeter, "Der Unternehmer in der Volkswirtschaft von heute," *Struktur Wandlungen der Deutschen Volkswirtschaft*, 1: 303. In a "trustified" economy the performance of entrepreneurial functions is subject to a "mechanization and bureaucratization" of decision (*Willensbildung*). The type of business leader associated with large-scale enterprise tends to resemble the successful political figure, "a good minister, or bureau-chief." "The groups and interests who select the leader tend to agree on a compromise candidate — not always the man of highest ability. Even when the object is to find the 'best man' he may turn out to be not one who can run the concern but a man adept at manipulating public opinion and handling public relations."

[13] The effect of the development of what may be called a professional management point of view on corporate policies is a question too frequently neglected. As an expression of that point of view, cf. Owen D. Young quoted in J. C. Sears, *The New Place of the Stockholder* (New York and London, 1929):

"To whom do I owe my obligations?

"My conception of it is this: that there are three groups of people who have an interest in that institution [General Electric Company]. One is the group of fifty-odd thousand people who have put their capital in the company, namely its stockholders. Another is a group of well towards one hundred thousand people who are putting their labor and their lives into the business of the company. The third group is of customers and the general public. . . .

"One no longer feels the obligation to take from labor for the benefit of capital, nor to take from the public for the benefit of both, but rather to administer wisely and fairly in the interest of all."

V

When we proceed from a consideration of the effect of the organization of a firm on its reaction to market situations to a consideration of the elements of market structure and their relation to price and production policies, we are immediately confronted with the necessity of making clear the meaning of market and market structure. A preoccupation with logical elegance might lead us to define a market, with Pigou, as a nodal point at which a product, whose units are perfect substitutes for each other, are available for purchase and sale. Unfortunately, such a definition would effectively relegate all the important and interesting problems to the area of intermarket relationships. An alternative would be to conceive of a market as an area in geographic and product space bounded, in Joan Robinson's phrase, by a gap in the chain of substitutes. Within such an area, however, assuming that it could be defined, the position of individual sellers and buyers may be very different with respect to the influences affecting business policy. These and other considerations suggest that, at least in the industrial area, the market, and market structure, must be defined with reference to the position of a single seller or buyer. The structure of a seller's market, then, includes all those considerations which he takes into account in determining his business policies and practices. His market includes all buyers and sellers, of whatever product, whose action he considers to influence his volume of sales.

The classification of market structures on the seller's side consists, then, in grouping together those firms, in whatever industry, which operate under the same or similar objective conditions.[14] Among these conditions are the economic characteristics of the product: is it a producers or consumers good, is it durable or non-durable, is the product of an individual seller differentiated with respect to the products of other sellers in the same market or is it standardized? Another group of conditions relate to the cost and production characteristics of the firm's operation. The ratio of overhead to variable costs at given volumes of output and for given variations in volume of output, the flexibility of costs, locational factors, and the existence

---

[14] The author is at present engaged with his colleague, Professor D. H. Wallace, in working out a classification of industrial market situations.

of joint cost are all important. A third class of considerations has to do with the numbers and relative sizes of buyers and sellers of whose action our given seller has to take account and with the relative ease of entry for new firms. Among the demand conditions which are empirically determinable may be mentioned the trend of sales, seasonal and cyclical fluctuations in sales, and roughly, the knowledge possessed by buyers with respect to the quality and characteristics of the product. Differences in distribution channels provide another set of conditions of great importance for the policies and practices of a firm. The accurate specification and measurement of these and other market conditions with respect to an individual firm admittedly present great, but not insuperable, difficulties. Properly used, the available data should permit of an illuminating grouping of firms into classes exhibiting roughly the same type of market conditions. Under similar market conditions may not firms be expected to pursue similar policies and practices? A careful study of the empirically determinable differences in market structure may go far in explaining observable differences in policy and practice.

It may be objected that most of what are here called market conditions are already taken into account in traditional value and price analysis in much neater fashion. That is, at least in part, true in the sense that traditional analysis purports to focus the results of many policy determining considerations in the form of demand and cost curves which are, for different time periods and under certain qualifications, single valued functions of output. We can admit that if cost and demand curves for short, long, and intermediate periods were discoverable, rather than assumed, a large part of what is called business policy could be explained without resorting to so crude a device as a classification of market structures. It is, however, precisely because theoretical techniques of price analysis have been constructed without regard to their empirical applicability that such a classification is necessary as a first and primarily important step towards an understanding of business policies and practices.

Enough has been said to suggest that the size of firms is only one among many factors influencing price and production policies. It requires no more than a cursory examination to perceive that large firms confronted with different market situations pursue different policies and practices. In the automobile industry the existence of large firms and relatively small number of sellers was not incompatible with steadily falling prices which pushed the use of the product into lower and lower income classes until well into the 1920's. When large returns from price reductions seemed no longer possible, automobile manufacturers turned their attention to accelerating the replacement demand for new cars by yearly changes in the design and structure of their product. By and large it probably continues to be true that a strong tradition exists in the industry to the effect that a substantial price reduction or an improvement of the product should be made in each year's model. The shift in emphasis from price to product competition may well have been the result rather of a change in the economic age of the industry than a change in the size or number of sellers. Although the price and production policies of the automobile industry are frequently contrasted with policies in the steel industry, may we not expect the former to approximate the latter as demand for motor cars becomes almost entirely a replacement demand and as product improvement takes increasingly the form of mere design or gadget changes? The economic age of an industry exerts an important influence on the policies and practices of firms in the industry. There is a widespread conviction among businessmen that aggressive price competition is an effective policy only during the period of an expanding market and that with a relatively stable or declining demand some type of controlled competition is in the interests of all sellers in the market. Controlled price competition is not a policy limited to large firms or markets in which sellers are few, though of course numbers may be so large as to make effective control difficult.

In the steel industry, price and production policies differ markedly among products undergoing substantially the same fabricating process and sold by substantially the same firms. A striking example of a divergence in price policies over the cycle is suggested by the behavior of the prices of automobile body steel as compared with the prices of galvanized steel sheets in the period between 1929 and 1937. Both of these products are made in the same kind of mill and the technological process is very similar. One, however, is sold to a few large buyers and the other to many small buyers. Automobile sheet prices declined more sharply from the beginning of the depression and at the bottom were 38.5 per cent below the 1929 level while galvanized sheet prices were only 28.7 per cent below 1929. On the rise since 1933, the price of automobile body steel went up more slowly than that of galvanized steel sheets. During 1937, the price of the latter exceeded its 1929 level by 6.2 per cent while the price of the former was still 12.8 per cent under its 1929 level.

In the rubber tire market four large firms sell around 75 per cent of the total volume and there are in the whole industry no more than twenty-eight firms. Yet price and production policies would seem to be quite different than in other markets, e.g., cigarettes, in which firms are large and the number of sellers are few. Consideration of the structure of the tire market appears to indicate that the character of distribution channels exerts a decisive influence on price policies. In the market for tires as equipment on new cars the sellers are confronted with buyers each large enough to undertake tire production himself if dissatisfied with the price. In the replacement market a number of different distributive channels induces a discount structure which facilitates price cutting on the slightest provocation. While the personality of Firestone, plus the fact that his firm is admittedly a low-cost producer, has no doubt been an important factor, it seems probable that if Firestone, like God in another context, had not existed the structure of the tire market would have created him.

Another type of market in which the large firm has typically followed a policy of aggressive price competition is to be found in the field of distribution. Here the price we are concerned with is the spread between manufacturers' and retail prices. Forty or fifty years ago by all accounts the distribution patterns for most consumers goods sold at retail was highly standardized, with full-function wholesalers and retailers operating under a relatively inflexible mark-up system. The growth of chain stores and other types of mass distributors has probably contributed not only toward a lowering of the manufacturer-retail margin but toward making it more flexible over the cycle. This influence is likely to continue — unless checked by recent and prospective legislation — as long as mass distributors can acquire by aggressive price tactics an increased share of the available sales.

These examples seem to indicate that the price policies of large firms are apt to be influenced by the stage of economic development of the industry in which they operate, by the size of buying units, the character of distribution channels, and the possibility of obtaining an increased share of total sales of a group of products. There are, of course, many other elements of market structure which affect business policies and practices. In consequence it seems doubtful whether any useful generalizations can be made regarding the price and production policies of large-scale enterprise without further specification as to the market situations which confront such firms.

It may possibly be true that a rough inverse correlation might be demonstrated between concentration as measured by percentage of volume of output of a product produced by a given small number of firms and, for example, some measure of amplitude of wholesale price change over a business cycle. Would such a correlation, if demonstrated, reveal an important fact regarding short-run price policy of large-scale enterprise? I think not. In the first place such a correlation would be heavily biased by agricultural products all of which exhibit low concentration and high amplitude of price change. Everyone admits that the structure of agricultural products markets is at once atomistically competitive and incapable of realization in industry. The principal problem we are concerned with is whether within the range of fabricated products there is a marked relation between size of firms and the type of price policy which is followed. In the second place the available price data for fabricated products is inadequate for such a comparison for two reasons. For many products there is a marked discrepancy between B.L.S. prices and average net realization per unit of sale reported in other sources,[15] a discrepancy which varies considerably over the cycle. Furthermore, it is probably true to say that, in general, the more highly fabricated the product the less important is price as a comprehensive indicator of the terms of purchase and sale. That is to say, a study of price behavior would have to be supplemented by an examination of changes in product and selling terms.

As another example of the difficulty of establishing a relationship

[15] Bureau of Mines and Bureau of Census figures. In part, this discrepancy and the changes in discrepancy are the result of nonreported price cuts, in part, of changes in the complex structure of a commodity price that are not adequately represented in the reported price; e.g., the B.L.S. price for men's shirts is the relatively stable price of a high grade trade-marked product. The sale of this shirt fell off markedly during the depression in favor of lower priced and frequently unbranded shirts.

between size of firms and price policy through an examination of price behavior, consider the recent history of construction materials prices. Thirty-five B.L.S. prices of construction materials were higher in January 1938, than in 1929 or 1926; twenty-one prices, on the other hand, were lower at this date than the wholesale price index. An examination of these prices fails to indicate any well marked influence of size of firm. Among the high-priced products were structural steel, wire nails, cast iron pipe, and terne plate, all produced in industries in which a small number of firms produce a large percentage of output. On the other hand, the high-priced products included cypress lumber, shingles, yellow pine and maple flooring, and common building brick produced in industries in which the typical firm is small. Among the low-priced products were wallboard, glass, sewer pipe, and a number of porcelain products fabricated by large firms in industries with high concentration, and, on the other hand, a number of products typically produced by small concerns. It is difficult in this instance to discover any pattern of price behavior which would throw light on the relationship between size of firm and price policy.

The relative size of a selling unit, to recapitulate, is one element — doubtless a very important one — in the structure of a firm's market. As such it exerts an influence on the policies and practices of the firm. But firms of given size, relative to the extent of their markets, will follow very different price and production policies in different market situations. Differences in the character of price response to given changes in the cost or demand conditions facing a firm or group of firms is to be attributed both to differences in the internal organization of the firm and to differences in the structure of the market in which the firm, or group, is placed. An analysis of the relation between organizational and market differences and the character of price response is the central problem of price analysis. The relation of size to price policy is merely one part of the problem which, taken out of its setting, is not very amenable to fruitful discussion.

VI

In conclusion a few remarks may be offered on the relation of price analysis to public policy. A consideration of the consequences of different types of price response to changes in costs and demand for the functioning of the economy is the prerequisite to effective public action in the price area. These consequences can be usefully divided into two groups:

1. The effect of differences in price responses on the distribution of economic resources among different uses. This is the traditional monopoly problem. A monopoly position is supposed to lead to restriction of output and of investment in the monopolized area below that which is desirable and attainable with a greater degree of competition. A whole range of problems, therefore, centers around the effect of price policies and price relationships on the distribution of economic resources as between various uses.

2. The effect of differences in price response on continuity in the use of resources already invested or available in different uses. This is primarily a business cycle problem. It is frequently maintained that certain types of price response to changes in costs and demand conditions are more favorable to continuous employment than others. The second group of problems, therefore, turns around the effects of different types of price policy and behavior on the continuity of employment of economic resources.

The argument for both groups of problems runs from differences in market structure to differences in price response, and from differences in price response to the consequences of these differences for the functioning of the economy. Proposals for public action therefore must consider, first, what types of price behavior and price policy are most conducive to an effective use of resources, and, second, within what limits appropriate public action is likely to be able to influence price behavior.

Although a good deal has been written both on the effect of restrictive policies on the distribution of resources and on the effect of price policies on fluctuations in employment and output, very little has been done to formulate tests of undesirable price behavior applicable to public action. Specifically, what sorts of tests are indicative of the existence of a price sufficiently high to restrict output and investment below desirable levels? What types of price behavior in industrial markets would be likely over the cycle to promote a fuller use of economic resources?

Without attempting to answer these questions attention may be called to three issues of immediate importance in the price field facing economists interested in public policy.

First, is it desirable that during periods of business upturn and downturn prices respond readily (in ways that can be roughly specified) to changes in costs, sales, or other variables of determinable magnitudes? If not for all commodities, for what groups of commodities should prices be flexible?

Second, should certain types of price behavior, the use of price formulae, or particular price policies be accepted as prima facie evidence of violation of the antitrust acts?

Third, is price competition ever sufficiently ruinous to justify public action? What are the tests of ruinous competition and what type of public action is appropriate?

Insofar as the price and production policies of large-scale enterprise provide a proper field for public action, these are critical questions.

4

International Commodity Controls; Cartels and Commodity Agreements[1]

The word "cartel" is currently enjoying an extraordinary and somewhat curious vogue in the United States. Like many more or less technical words adapted for popular consumption, its meaning, while becoming more vague, has become more portentous. The overtones, moreover, are definitely sinister. If international finance is somehow more to be feared than that of the domestic variety, how much more is this true of international cartels! People are either for or against cartels, and very little of the recent literature is devoted to careful description or cool appraisal of cartel activities. Those opposed have relied on such words as "conspiracy," "monopoly," "Fascism," and "treason," while, on the other side, Lord McGowan of Imperial Chemical Industries describes cartels as a means of assuring orderly marketing, planned expansion of international trade, elimination of cutthroat practices, and all that is admirable and reasonable. It must be said that the anti-cartel people have been much more successful than the pro-cartel people in getting their favorite connotations accepted, at least in this country.

CARTELS

Cartels, in the narrow — and proper — sense, are agreements between firms in the same branch of trade limiting the freedom of these firms with respect to the production and marketing of their products. Typically, cartel agreements aim at the restriction of output or sales by the member firms, at an allocation of market territories between firms, and a fixing of the price of their products. Such restrictive agreements are, of course, illegal as between firms engaged in domestic trade in the United States, but American firms can form export associations which then, on occasion, have entered into inter-

[1] Reprinted from *Economic Reconstruction*, edited by S. E. Harris (New York, 1945).

national cartel arrangements with associations or firms in other countries. These American export associations are formed under the Webb-Pomerene law, which contains certain limitations now being tested in a series of antitrust cases. As stated by Wendell Berge, present Chief of the Antitrust Division of the Department of Justice, export associations are not permitted under the Webb law to enter into international agreements which

(a) restrain trade within the United States; or
(b) restrain the export trade of any domestic competitor or association; or
(c) enhance or depress prices within the United States, substantially lessen competition within the United States, or otherwise restrain trade therein.

Despite these limitations, American firms have in a number of cases entered into full-fledged international cartels fixing prices and allocating markets and, unless the Webb-Pomerene law is more strictly interpreted, may be expected to enter such cartels still more extensively in the postwar period.

Although cartel in the strict sense of the word means a marketing agreement between private firms, in current usage its meaning has been greatly broadened. It is used to include patent and process exchange agreements between firms in different countries such as those which have been consummated with foreign interests by Du Pont, Standard Oil, and International General Electric. Frequently, patent-exchange arrangements contain marketing agreements; indeed, the market agreements may be the real reason for exchange of patents and processing knowledge. This type of cartel arrangement is, perhaps, the one which primarily concerns American firms. Since, however, the market-control features depend in the main on the patent rights which are exchanged, the nature and extent of the restrictions on international trade involved and the means of avoiding or lessening these restrictions become technical patent questions which it is not our purpose here to discuss. International cartels are also interpreted to include joint ownership by potential competitors of foreign affiliates, such as the Latin-American Duperial companies jointly owned by Du Pont and Imperial Chemical Industries.

International cartels are sometimes formed under governmental auspices and with government participation; indeed, some of the best known — most notorious if you will — international cartels have been negotiated by governments. This was true of the prewar tin and rubber cartels. Government-owned enterprises may also — and frequently do — participate in what are, in other respects, private international cartels. As government participation increases — as it promises to do in the postwar period — the international cartel which in its pure form is an agreement between private firms, takes on the character of an international commodity agreement. The United States government has entered into commodity agreements respecting wheat and coffee, and agricultural interests are pressing for broader participation after the war. If other governments sponsor and participate in international cartels in industrial materials and manufactured products, not only will a considerable part of the international trade of the world be brought under a high degree of commodity control, but the distinction between cartels and commodity agreements will become progressively less meaningful. In any case, as the term "cartel" is now used, it suggests a much broader range of problems than those relating merely to international marketing agreements between private firms.

Before proceeding to a consideration of some of the problems which a policy with respect to cartels must take into account, two facts bearing on the formation of cartels should be emphasized:

1. Most of the important international cartels have arisen out of situations in which it could be plausibly argued that a serious lack of balance existed between productive capacity and current consumption of the products in question.

2. A functioning international cartel has usually required the effective prior "organization" of producers in the domestic market.

The formation of international cartels in rubber, tin, nitrates, steel, and many other important products was preceded by situations in the participating countries considered to be unsatisfactory by politically important producing interests. Productive capacity existed for outputs greater than could be absorbed on the world market at prices sufficient to maintain the owners of this capacity in the style to which they had become accustomed. In some cases, the number of workers employed was large and falling world-market prices had seriously influenced wage rates. In others, the exports in question were heavily relied on for government revenues and for foreign exchange. When producing groups are confronted with declining or inadequate markets, they turn naturally to methods of controlling output and price. If private action proves inadequate, appeal is made to the state and, if the groups in question are politically influential, the appeal is usually not made in vain.

Given excess capacity — either real or arguable — in politically important sectors of the economy, demands for relief will arise. Relief may be provided by limiting imports of the affected commodities, either directly or by protective tariff. Relief may be provided by export bounties, by production subsidies, and in many other ways. One of these other ways is the formation of an international cartel which will "adjust supply to demand" (i.e., restrict output); which will provide for "orderly distribution" (i.e., allocate market territories); and which will "stabilize prices" (i.e., raise prices). In the postwar period, partly as a result of war-expanded output, we may expect to be confronted by excess-capacity situations in many countries and on a large scale. The only successful remedies will be the maintenance of a high level of income in the principal countries of the world accompanied by a shift in resources out of war-expanded industries into other employment. Yet we may expect other remedies to be suggested which will take the form of restriction of imports, export subsidies, and international cartels with or without government participation. In many cases cartel agreements will appear to governments confronted by excess capacity or balance-of-payment difficulties to be preferable to other types of restrictive arrangements.

This will be particularly true in countries in which domestic industries are already well organized or, if one prefers a synonym, monopolized. The members of international cartels are ordinarily either very large firms controlling a predominant share of the export of the cartelized product from a given country or export associations including the principal exporters of such products. Restriction of output or exports, a typical cartel activity, frequently requires an allocation of shares in the restricted quantities as between the member firms. Such allocation, if it is to be effective, may require policing or control measures on the part of the export association. Unless export business is completely separated from domestic production, effective cartelization for exports is difficult without considerable control of the domestic market. English participation in the European steel cartel, for example, was impracticable as long as the tradition of competition between steel producers ruled the domestic market and, when English exporters were finally brought into the cartel, this action was accompanied by a substantial cartelization, at government insistence, of the domestic market.

Extensive American participation in cartels would likewise presumably require a considerable measure of cooperation between firms in the domestic market. Since, however, the United States is rather enthusiastically committed to an antitrust policy at home, such participation appears unlikely at least in those industries in which exporting firms are not only numerous but also engaged in production for the domestic market. Our antipathy to monopoly, however, is not shared by other countries. In many European countries international cartels will be favorably considered, along with import restrictions, export bounties, and other measures, as a means of coping with excess production in the postwar period. Industries are so organized domestically as to be able to take up with international cartels where they left off at the outbreak of war and to carry these arrangements to a bigger if not better future.

A discussion of the effects of international cartels may fairly center on the following three aspects of cartel practice:

1. Trade-Barrier Aspects. Cartels are said to involve privately imposed limitations on the free flow of commodities in international trade.

2. Security Aspects. The participation of American firms in international cartel arrangements is alleged to have involved restriction by these firms of the production and development of products and processes necessary to the war effort, and the use of American connections for enemy espionage purposes.

3. Political Aspects. International cartels are said to promote a relationship between private enterprise and the state which may involve (a) the use of the power of the state to further the purposes of private interests; and (b) the use by the state of business enterprises as instrumentalities of public policy.

There are also various cartel problems which might be treated under the general heading "economic warfare." International cartel connections have posed certain difficulties for blacklisting and other economic-warfare policies by reason of ambiguities of ownership and the mobility of assets involved in such connections. These problems are not, however, limited to cartels nor will they be of much significance in the postwar period.

CARTELS AS TRADE BARRIERS

There can be little doubt that international cartels on balance restrict the total volume of world trade, divert to a considerable extent the channels of world trade, and affect, through price and output controls, a considerable proportion of world trade. The primary purpose of cartels is to restrict the freedom of participating firms and associations to compete on the world markets, and cartels would not long continue to exist if prices and outputs under cartelization were not more satisfactory to participating members than they would be with competition unrestrained. Instances are numerous in which tariff reductions have not produced an expected increase in imports because market allocations by cartels have restrained foreign producers from selling outside of allocated territory. On occasion, it is true, cartel restrictions may have increased the total volume of world trade. High cartel prices have frequently brought into the market productive capacity and a volume of exports greater than would have existed had the cartels in question not been forced. If an international cartel, by threatening to cut prices in a particular country, prevents the installation of domestic capacity, imports into that country may be maintained and, along with them, world trade. This result has been achieved on more than one occasion in Latin-American countries. Such expansion of trade, however, is not likely to be adduced as a merit of cartelization.

The influence of cartels on the diversion of trade from normal competitive channels is undoubtedly greater than is their influence on the total volume of trade. International cartelization tends to divide the world into spheres of commercial influence by allocating to the nationals of particular countries exclusive selling rights — apart from outsiders — in allocated territory. American firms, through cartel arrangements, are normally assigned the United States market, sometimes the whole of North America, and on occasion parts of South America. British firms have special claims to Empire territory and, in the period before the war, the growing strength of German participation in a number of cartels led to the assignment of increasing areas of European territory to German cartel participants. In the period between the wars, mandated areas were frequently reserved by cartel agreement to the firms of the country holding the mandate and, as we shall see later, there is a clear tendency for cartel allocations to follow the lines of political influence.

Although, in general, international cartels tend to restrict the volume of world trade, it does not necessarily follow that restriction is in all cases undesirable nor that, under the competitive conditions facing American firms, American participation in such cartels would lessen our foreign trade.

Restriction of the exports of strategic materials to present aggressor nations may be one of the policies followed by an international security organization in the postwar period and, if so, fairly serious restraint of foreign trade will be involved. Unrestricted competition between the nationals of various countries may lead to the rapid exhaustion or the wasteful exploitation of irreplaceable resources; if so, the case for regulation and restriction is a strong one. In some branches of commerce, of a public-utility character, such as shipping, air transport, and international communications, competition between the nationals of the various countries concerned is not likely to produce desirable results and agreements limiting the freedom of the competing interests are probably necessary. The immediate postwar period will see a number of industries expanded beyond the needs of civilian consumption. Temporary control of international competition pending a conversion of facilities and a shift of man power into other employment is perhaps desirable.

All these areas of foreign trade in which a restriction of competition may serve broader interests than those of the producers immediately involved raise questions concerning the appropriateness of private cartels as the restricting and regulating agency. If an international agreement restricting trade is necessary to accomplish a purpose widely recognized to be within the public interest of several states, the agreement should presumably be consummated by public bodies rather than by private business enterprises. The word "presumably" is used advisedly, since the intervention of the state in foreign trade introduces a possibility of political conflict which may be more dangerous to the maintenance of peace than are conflicts between private cartel interests. The other side of the picture is that a tradition of governmental agreements on specific and relatively minor matters is probably necessary to broader international agreements on the vital questions of war and peace.

It does not follow that because international cartels restrict foreign trade, American participation in cartels will restrict American trade. With a goodly part of world trade already cartelized, it has been argued that American participation is necessary in order to maintain or increase our exports. It is said that by local price cutting, monopolization of distributing outlets, and other practices, fair and unfair, foreign cartels can effectively deny certain foreign markets to certain American products whereas, if American firms were members of the cartel, access to these markets would be secure. This argument is difficult to document and, on its face, not very plausible. High cartel prices abroad offer excellent competitive opportunities to American enterprise, and cartel practices have in all probability lost more business to American competition than they have ever gained from it.

A more serious danger to our exports rests in the influence which foreign cartels on occasion exert on the governments of their national participants. Through this influence tariff barriers may be raised against our products and our exports impeded by other forms of state action. Although American participation in international cartels might lessen these barriers, it would probably be at the expense of a smaller share of the foreign market than might be won by outright competition. Moreover, it is within the power of our government to deal with trade barriers raised against our products by the usual international bargaining processes. There is, however, truth in the contention that if the trade of the rest of the world is cartelized and our own exporters excluded from cartel participation, we shall purchase our imports at monopoly prices and sell our exports on world markets at competitive prices. The terms of trade, in technical language, may be turned against us by foreign cartel activities. Again, however, this is probably a matter to be handled through the bargaining powers of the American government rather than by permitting cartel participation to American export firms.

In general, it may be said that private cartel restrictions constitute a definite type of trade barrier, that the seriousness of this trade barrier is greatly increased by government support of cartel practices, and that neither world trade nor American trade is likely to increase through American participation in cartels, regardless of how widespread are cartel ramifications in other countries.

SECURITY ASPECTS OF CARTELS

The fierce light of Congressional investigation and antitrust prosecution has in recent years beaten on certain American firms which in the prewar years entered into patents and processing arrangements, mainly with German firms, involving, in a number of cases, market agreements extending considerably beyond legitimate patent rights. The committee hearings and the antitrust prosecutions have been surrounded by effective publicity on an absorbing subject, and the implications of the agreements have, in consequence, lost nothing in the telling. Out of the facts thereby revealed (of which the most complete compilation is in the Bone Committee reports) have grown various generalizations ranging from a description of the American participants as dupes and their firms as cogs in a "German master plan" to a characterization of international cartels as essentially Fascist institutions without differentiation between the Fascist potentialities of the various national participants. Whatever the generalization, there has been no doubt in the minds of the generalizers that American participation in international cartels is highly dangerous to American security.

Antitrust cases against American firms restrained by agreement with German firms in their freedom to develop or produce useful war materials were effective in the early stages of the war in eliminating these restraints and releasing, thereby, American production. The much publicized cases of magnesium, beryllium, military optical instruments, and synthetic rubber are too well known to require further comment. Whether the patents and processing agreements between American and German firms have, on balance, hampered American war production is, however, an open question. To answer that question we would need to know the value of the technical knowledge disclosed by both sides and the uses, considering the restrictions imposed in the contracts, to which this knowledge has been put. To date only one side of this story has been effectively told. There can be little doubt that the Nazi government exercised much more careful supervision of the disclosure by its nationals of technical knowledge having potential military usefulness than did the American government nor that, on occasion, the disclosure to American firms was accompanied by restrictions framed with an eye to the military ends of the Nazi state. It would be very difficult for the American government to exercise that degree of supervision without a pretty serious alteration of our political and economic traditions. No doubt the exchange of technical information by American firms holding important Army and Navy contracts will have to be scrutinized more carefully in the future, but it is more than doubtful whether the exclusion of these firms from an international exchange of patents and processing knowledge, even of the prewar type, would benefit this country either in war or in peace.

International cartel connections have been used by nationals of our present enemies for espionage purposes and, particularly in Latin America, for political propaganda and psychological warfare. It is hard to see, however, that these activities raise questions peculiar to cartels. Foreign affiliates and foreign agencies can and do serve much the same purpose. The intimate relations between nationals of different countries involved in the exchange of laboratory and processing information may be peculiarly suited to such purposes, but these arrangements do not necessarily involve participation in cartels.

There is, of course, a widely spread doctrine that the foreign economic interests of monopoly capitalists are a primary source of war and, since the interests of such capitalists are frequently served through international cartels, cartels are in some sense a menace to peace. "The internationalism of international cartels is the most dangerous type of internationalism." Insofar as cartel participants enlist the support of their respective governments, thus bringing the interests of the state into what would otherwise be the concern of private enterprise, there may be some truth in this thesis. The danger, however, lies primarily in substituting state conflict for the conflict of private interests, not in the attempt of business interests to lessen international competition by private agreements.

One of the most ominous attempts of organized business groups to secure state support for international restrictive arrangements, an attempt which, had it succeeded, would almost certainly have produced extreme international friction, was the Düsseldorf discussion undertaken shortly before the war by the leading British and German industrial associations. In a joint communiqué it was declared that:

Both organizations are fully aware that the advantages of agreements between the industries of two countries or of two regions could be frustrated by the uneconomic competition of the industry of another country refusing to join the agreement. In such cases it might become necessary for the organization to ask for the *support of its government*. Both organizations agree to ask for such support if the need arises.

POLITICAL ASPECTS OF INTERNATIONAL CARTELS

Although examples are not lacking of the use of international cartel connections to avoid legitimate obligations to government such as the payment of customs duties, compliance with domestic legislation, administrative rulings, and the like, the important political questions have to do with state action in the interests of cartel participants and the use by the state of the cartel as an instrument of public policy.

The American government, in keeping with our strong antitrust tradition, has pursued a policy of arm's-length dealing with business associations both in domestic and foreign trade that is unique among industrial nations. The British government went very far in the prewar years in permitting and encouraging business control of output and prices in the domestic market and the participation, through export associations, of British industries in international cartels. State assistance in the formation of cartels and the policing of cartel regulations was a common feature of continental industry, and the enlisting of governmental support in international cartel negotiations had become almost standard practice.

The granting of tariff protection to increase the bargaining position of their nationals in cartel quota allocations was a policy followed by many European governments. As Sir Alfred Mond, organizer of the British Imperial Chemical Industries, observed:

In negotiation, the man behind the tariff wall always has something with which to bargain, which the man in the Free Trade country has not. Any one who has had practical experience of bargaining with continental producers knows that the first thing they say is: "You cannot export to our country, because we have a tariff. How much of your market are you going to give us?"

Cartel participants have also solicited the help of their governments in enforcing domestic cartel regulations and in negotiating more effective international agreements. Private attempts to cartelize the production and export of tin and rubber were ineffectual, and it required the cooperation of the governments of the principal producing areas to make these attempts successful. Private cartel arrangements always run the risk of nonobservance by certain members of controls upon which the effectiveness of the cartel depends, and resort to government is frequently the only course of action which can assure satisfactory results.

For these reasons and because of increasing public awareness of the character of the trade barriers which cartel regulations impose, it is probable that, if the postwar period sees an expansion of international cartelization, it will be under the sponsorship and regulation of governments. Private interests would suffer thereby some infringement of their freedom of action, but cartel controls would be much more effectively enforced. Within this framework the term "regulation" should not be taken too seriously. The experience of European governments in the regulation of cartels is both extensive and unhappy. Government sponsorship of the participation by their nationals in international cartels would, no doubt, impose limitations on private action. Publicity might be required as well as the avoidance of the grosser forms of restrictive practice. But there is no reason to expect and, on the basis of experience, every reason not to expect, that effective regulation of cartel output and price policies in the interests of groups broader than those composed of cartel members would be accomplished. Governments will sponsor and regulate cartels with an eye mainly to the expansion of the exports of their nationals, and the more important foreign-trade interests are in the economy of a country, the more active will be government support and the less likely will be a consideration of anything other than export interests.

This view is further supported by the behavior of those government-owned firms which participated in essentially private international cartels in the period between the wars. Government-owned aluminum-, timber-, nitrogen-, potash-, and phosphate-producing or -exporting enterprises participated in all the restrictive practices pursued by the cartels of which they were members.

As governments penetrate into cartel activities, private controls are not only in part circumscribed, but cartel arrangements become available to the state as vehicles of foreign policy. In the mercantile period many foreign trading companies were semipolitical in character. The British government accomplished through the East India and the Levant companies tasks which, in the nineteenth century, were the sole prerogative of state officials. There is considerable evidence that semipublic cartels engaged in foreign trade may come to fulfill similar purposes: Mention has already been made of the use by the Nazis of German cartel connections to attain various military objectives. Cartels, moreover, have been one of the important instrumentalities in the integration, during the last four years, of European industry under German control.

If, in the postwar period, limited world supplies of strategic materials are to be produced and allocated by cartels with government participation, private interests are likely to be overshadowed by the security considerations of the government participants. Likewise spheres of political influence in Europe and elsewhere will have their effect upon the scope and function of cartel activities.

The interpenetration of government and business in foreign-trade activities creates problems which are likely to be of serious concern to this country. In the United States, more perhaps than in any other country, business has remained private, and public affairs have been carried on by public officials. Nor is our form of government well adapted to a flexible interrelationship of public and private interests in foreign affairs. It would be well for us to recognize that, abroad, the trend of events appears to be quite definitely in the direction of greater state participation in all forms of foreign economic activity.

COMMODITY AGREEMENTS

This interpenetration in other countries of government and business should be taken into account in the formulation of American policy toward intergovernmental commodity agreements. It is possible that the role of such agreements in postwar international trade will be large, and it is important that American interests with respect to such agreements be clearly perceived.

The traditional case for intergovernmental commodity controls rests upon certain characteristics of raw-material production; viz., a tendency toward the emergence of chronic surpluses, excessive price instability, and wasteful methods of exploitation. Chronic surplus production is particularly prevalent in agricultural industries, especially foodstuffs. The consumption of foodstuffs increases slowly and is not very responsive to a decline in price. The rate of growth of agricultural output per worker has, within recent years, been rapid. Under these circumstances the prices of agricultural products — apart from government subsidy — could be maintained only by a large transfer of workers out of agriculture. The worker-owner character of agricultural production, however, and the lack of jobs in industry have hampered such transfer with the result that, in the interwar period, the terms of trade between agriculture and industry tended to move markedly against agriculture. In this sense agricultural products tend to be produced in chronic surplus, and there are strong reasons for believing that this situation will persist in the postwar period.

The prices of both foodstuffs and industrial raw materials, moreover, are notoriously unstable. In the case of foodstuffs the unresponsiveness of demand to price changes together with large harvest variations and, in some cases, an inverse elasticity of supply with respect to price, makes for great price fluctuations. The consumption of industrial raw materials varies with industrial output and is complicated by large inventory accumulations and decumulations in anticipation of price changes. In the absence of output controls the prices of these materials tend to fluctuate wildly. It is argued, therefore, that intergovernmental commodity controls are advisable in the interest of maintaining raw-material price stability.

Finally, the unregulated overcropping of certain resources and the wasteful exploitation of irreplaceable deposits may be difficult to avoid without international commodity controls. Such controls have been applied with benefit to certain branches of the fishing industry and have an obvious potential utility in the field of metals and minerals.

This is the traditional case for intergovernmental commodity controls, and it is alleged that in the absence of such controls, countries, particularly the exporters of raw materials, will be inclined to take unilateral action which will hamper the flow of goods in international trade more seriously than would commodity agreements. In the postwar period, furthermore, the potential scope of commodity controls will probably be broadened to include intergovernmental action regarding strategic materials. Exports of strategic materials to potential aggressor nations may be subject to control. The competition of the great powers for control of existing sources of scarce materials may lead to some sort of intergovernmental agreement regulating the production and distribution of these materials.

Obviously, the area of possible intergovernmental commodity regulation is a large one. In formulating American policy in this area, however, it must be emphasized that (1) American interests run very strongly in the direction of a relatively unimpeded flow of commodities in foreign trade; (2) the United States is predominantly an importer and not an exporter of raw materials; and (3) it is impossible to undertake extensive international commodity controls without a pretty thoroughgoing control, either by government or by private monopoly, of the domestic market.

As an industrial country with a rapidly growing output potential, we are becoming a continually larger importer of raw materials and will be adversely affected by restrictive raw-material controls.[2] As a creditor country the United States has a primary interest in a large volume of international trade and in the convertibility of foreign currencies which is dependent on that trade. The maintenance of a high level of domestic employment is significantly dependent on our finding export markets for an increasing volume of industrial products. Finally, and most important, we have a strong political interest in preventing a development of world trade in the direction of economic blocs and spheres of influence.

If foreign-trade statistics are compared with national-income data, a close correlation is evident between changes in the national income and the size of our raw-material import balance. The larger the national income, the greater the excess of imports of raw materials and unprocessed foodstuffs over exports from the United States. It is probable, with a postwar national income of from $130 to $140 billion, that imports of raw materials and unprocessed foodstuffs will exceed exports by an amount of the general order of $750 million. Under these circumstances, it would seem extremely unwise for the

[2] The next two pages are largely taken from a contribution by the author to the Proceedings of the Norman Wait Harris Foundation meeting, September 1944, entitled, "The Future of Commodity Agreements."

United States to promote a system of international controls which is bound to increase the value of our imports more than the value of our exports.

Finally, international commodity controls, whether governmental or private, are ineffective without a prior organization of a system of domestic commodity controls. We have already gone a long way in developing such controls in the field of agriculture. How far do we want to go in this direction in the field of industrial products? Unless we wish to undertake an extensive reorientation of the relation of business to government in the United States, it would appear wise in formulating our policy toward intergovernmental commodity controls to draw a sharp distinction between owner-worker industries, typically agricultural, and others. And with respect to the former, it would be also wise to remember that our import interests in the products of such industries are more important than our export interests.

Within the framework of a commercial policy favorable to American interests, it must, however, be recognized that intergovernmental commodity agreements will have a place. Even after a transition period, in which disposal of war surpluses will call for international commodity action, intergovernmental controls will be necessary to meet a set of special situations. The export of strategic materials to potential aggressors may have to be limited; agreements regulating overcropping or wasteful methods of extracting irreplaceable national resources will inevitably increase in number and importance; unmanageable agricultural surpluses will exist in certain areas even on an optimistic forecast of world trade; in some commodity agreements, involving effective output controls, buffer-stock programs for evening out price fluctuations may be practicable.

However — and this is the central point — the use of intergovernmental commodity controls should be subordinated to the requirements of a commercial policy oriented in the direction of an expansion of world trade and a reduction of trade barriers. Such a policy will not bring about the elimination of all quantitative import restrictions, of all exchange rationing, or of all protective or preferential import duties. No more will it — nor should it — accomplish the elimination of commodity controls. What it should accomplish, however, is a recognition of commodity controls as an exceptional device whose use is strictly limited to exceptional situations.

POSTWAR PROSPECTS

The prospects for a liberal foreign-trade policy in the postwar period, including a policy of reducing private as well as public trade barriers, depend primarily on two conditions: the emergence of effective security cooperation among the great powers, and the development of domestic economic policies oriented in the direction of full employment. Effective cooperation among, at least, the great powers is a necessary but not a sufficient condition. In the absence of such cooperation the world might well tend to split into spheres of influence which will have serious economic as well as political connotations. A competition for available supplies of strategic materials would ensue which in itself would be sufficient to blast any chances of a liberal economic solution.

Domestic economic policies, furthermore, designed to promote reasonably full employment of resources are a *sine qua non* for such a solution. It was the depression of the thirties which produced that array of protective tariffs, exchange controls, quantitative limitations, currency depreciation, export subsidies, commodity agreements, and cartel restrictions which had by the end of the decade succeeded in putting international economic relations in a strait jacket. Prolonged depression in the postwar period would maintain all the old restrictions and, no doubt, add new ones.

Since governmental policy respecting commodity controls, public and private, is part and parcel of foreign economic policy broadly conceived, what can be accomplished in the field of cartels and commodity agreements is largely dependent on what can be accomplished in other areas. If the postwar world sees the development of an effective international security organization and sensible domestic policies, it may be possible by international agreement to get rid of the more restrictive types of international commodity controls along with other barriers to foreign trade. There are also other possibilities, in the imposed terms of a peace settlement, of important alterations in the European cartel structure which centered in Germany. It must be recognized, however, that such measures are not likely to be successful unless they conform to the long-run economic interests of the countries affected.

The interests of the United States, both political and economic, run so strongly, at this stage of affairs, in the direction of a liberal foreign policy that the appropriate attitude toward international commodity controls may be said to be predetermined. The fact that this attitude also conforms to a long-established antimonopoly tradition gives assurance that this aspect of a liberal foreign policy will probably have stronger domestic support than some others. It should be recognized, however, that if international events and domestic policies make the possibilities of a liberal international-trade world illusory, we may be confronted with the necessity of a rather drastic change in our attitude toward commodity controls both public and private.

5

Schumpeter on Monopoly and the Large Firm[1]

I

. . . the problem that is usually . . . visualized is how capitalism
administers existing structures, whereas the relevant problem is how it
creates and destroys them.[2]

Although Schumpeter's views on United States antitrust policy
represent a fairly familiar European reaction, in his case these views
were heightened by an annoyance with professional colleagues who
attempt to apply an economic analysis based on simple "models" to
the complicated world of reality; by the possession of a well-developed ideology concerning the evolution and functioning of capitalism that clashes rather violently with typical antitrust ideology; by
adherence to a distinctly aristocratic view of the distribution of talent
in the economy and in society; and, finally, by a rather low opinion
of the likelihood of developing, in a democracy, a public policy toward the large firm and monopoly that will be anything more than
an amalgam of the special interests of particular groups and the
rancor of disgruntled intellectuals. These elements combined to make
a rather explosive mixture, as can be seen by reading Chapters VII
and VIII of *Capitalism, Socialism, and Democracy,* which contain
Schumpeter's parting shot at antitrust policy along with certain other
distinguishing features of the current scene.

These chapters, which bring together and sharpen earlier views on
the role of the large firm in the competitive process, represent one of
the most effective as well as most drastic critiques extant concerning
traditional pattern of antitrust thought. The critique is drastic and
effective because it plausibly undermines the two main pillars of the
traditional ideology: first, that market power is the proper object of

---

[1] Reprinted from *The Review of Economics and Statistics,* Vol. 33, No. 2,
May 1951.
[2] Joseph A. Schumpeter, *Capitalism, Socialism, and Democracy* (New York,
1942), p. 83.

attack since power means the ability to exploit; and second, that the preservation of competition, meaning the exclusion of positions of market power, will assure the efficient use of resources. The essence of Schumpeter's position is that market power is necessary to innovation and that innovation is the core of effective competition.

The competition that counts is "the competition from the new commodity, the new technology, the new source of supply, the new type of organization (the largest-scale unit of control for instance) — competition which commands a decisive cost or quality advantage and which strikes not at the margins of the profits and their outputs of the existing firms but at their foundations and their very lives. This kind of competition is as much more effective than the other as a bombardment is in comparison with forcing a door, and so much more important that it becomes a matter of comparative indifference whether competition in the ordinary sense functions more or less promptly; the powerful lever that in the long run expands output and brings down prices is in any case made of other stuff." [3]

Schumpeter maintains that his argument is not a case against all antimonopoly policy but only a particular variety of policy. There may be "cases of restrictive or regulating strategy" that have "that injurious effect on the long-run development of output which is uncritically attributed to all of them." [4] He does not, however, give us much help in determining what business practices or strategies might be expected to produce expansive rather than restrictive results. What he has to say in criticism of existing policy constitutes a challenge that every serious student of the "monopoly problem" must take to heart. But whether his view of competition as the process of "creative destruction" could be made to yield principles applicable by government agencies and the courts in pursuit of a "rational" as opposed to a "vindictive" antimonopoly policy is a different matter.

II

American antitrust policy, as distinguished from the antimonopoly policy of most other countries, purports to be — and to some extent is — an attack upon positions of market power. Whereas legislation and administrative practice elsewhere has emphasized *abuse of* power, including the charging of unreasonable prices, as the proper object of

[3] *Capitalism, Socialism, and Democracy*, pp. 84, 85.
[4] *Capitalism, Socialism, and Democracy*, p. 91.

attack, and has recognized the possibility of "good" monopolies, American practice, within certain areas at least, has attacked market power as such. "The reasonable prices fixed today — may become the unreasonable prices of tomorrow" runs the language of a famous antitrust decision.[5] And with respect to certain kinds of agreements in restraint of trade, i.e., certain attempts to secure a position of market power, the judicial position has been that they are unreasonable and illegal *per se*.

Needless to say, however, U. S. antitrust policy has not been entirely consistent. Large firms enjoying a position of market power have remained immune, while associations with much less power have been broken up. Nevertheless, this inconsistency has been recognized, and within recent years the courts have proceeded some way toward its remedy. There is, moreover, a strong current of opinions both within and outside government that would go much further and faster than the Antitrust Division or Federal Trade Commission have been willing or able to go. Schumpeter was frequently inclined to confuse this current of opinion as to what antitrust policy *should* be, with the reality. Nevertheless, insofar as market power is really the subject of attack, Schumpeter's strictures apply to antitrust policy as enforced as well as to what may be called the core of antitrust ideology.

Market power, that is to say, some protection from a competitive forcing of prices toward short-run marginal costs, was, in his opinion, essential to successful innovation. This is recognized in the case of patent protection, but patents form only one example of a much larger class of restrictive devices without which the introduction of new processes, new products, or new forms of organization would frequently become impracticable. Innovation, by definition, is the introduction of new, that is to say, untried processes or products. What the new will involve in the way of costs or revenues is uncertain. If through business strategies, e.g., tacit agreement among leading firms not to enter each other's fields of specialization, or even by overt agreement to limit competition in certain areas, the risk attendant on large investment to introduce new products or processes is lessened, innovation may be encouraged.

That there is *some* truth in this contention can hardly be denied. A history of the growth of most large firms that have been important

[5] U. S. v. Trenton Potteries Co. et al. 273 U. S. 392.

innovators in their field would probably reveal, in addition to the patent protection they may have enjoyed, the use of various strategies and practices that in any proper antitrust interpretation would be called restrictive.[6] But how important these strategies and practices were to these firms as innovators, and whether on balance growth was encouraged or checked in the relevant industries and in the economy as a whole, would be difficult for even the most painstaking research to establish with assurance. The history of the firms and industries which Schumpeter cites in support of his thesis — the old Standard Oil Company, the Aluminum Company, rayon, and motor cars — is capable of yielding a rather different story.

Schumpeter is on surer — and also more important — ground in his evaluation of the results of innovation, that is to say, the relation of innovation to effective competition. Here he denies completely the significance for public policy purposes of any standard of evaluation derived from pure competition, marginal cost-price relationships, or other formulations of static economic analysis. His general position is best stated in a proposition quoted with approval by Pigou.

A system — any system, economic or other — that at every point of time fully utilizes its possibilities to the best advantage may yet in the long run be inferior to a system that does so at *no* given point of time, because the latter's failure to do so may be a condition for the level or speed of long-run performance.[7]

The condition of long-run effective performance is perpetual innovation — the "process of creative destruction" — and this condition is incompatible with those price-quantity relationships which, at any moment of time and assuming unchanging data, would be conducive to the most efficient use of resources. While applauding recent analysis in the field of monopoly and competition and of welfare economics which, among other things, has indicated how very restrictive are the conditions under which we are entitled to suppose that profit maximization is compatible with maximum output, Schumpeter was highly skeptical of any possibility of drawing from this analysis conclusions or principles useful in the field of public policy. "It is . . .

[6] Cf. P. B. Frankel, *Essentials of Petroleum* (London, 1946), for an interesting discussion of the rôle of restriction and innovation in the rise of the great oil companies.

[7] The quotation is from *Capitalism, Socialism, and Democracy*, p. 83. It is cited in A. C. Pigou, *Lapses from Full Employment* (London, 1945), p. 71.

always important to remember that the ability to see things in their correct perspective may be, and often is, divorced from the ability to reason correctly and vice versa. That is why a man may be a very good theorist and yet talk absolute nonsense whenever confronted with the task of diagnosing a concrete historical pattern as a whole." [8]

The role of the large firm in the competitive process and the significance of business strategies and practices in relation to the monopoly problem were, for Schumpeter, very much matters of diagnosing a concrete historical pattern as a whole. The historical pattern was that unfolded in the development of captalism and the essential fact about capitalism is the process of creative destruction. "It is what capitalism consists in and what every capitalist concern has got to live in. This fact bears upon our problem in two ways."

First, since we are dealing with a process that takes time, "we must judge its performance over time, as it unfolds through decades or centuries."

"Second, since we are dealing with an organic process, analysis of what happens in any particular part of it — say in an individual concern or industry — may indeed clarify details of mechanism but is inconclusive beyond that." [9]

This view of the proper approach to the problem of the large firm and monopoly takes the question pretty much out of the area of economic analysis and into one that Schumpeter was accustomed to call ideology. In fact, he once indicated to the author of this paper that he was anxious to clear existing work out of the way in order to undertake a study of the question whether anything could be said about the "monopoly problem" that was anything other than "sheer ideology."

Certainly Schumpeter had a well-developed "ideology" concerning capitalist development and the relation of the process of development to competition and monopoly. It was clearly opposed in his mind to what he thought of as antitrust ideology, which emphasized existing positions of market power and current business practices and strategies without considering the role these positions, practices, and strategies played in the process of economic development. But though his view of capitalist development might serve to cast doubts on the

---

[8] *Capitalism, Socialism, and Democracy,* p. 76, fn. 3. p. 83.
[9] *Capitalism, Socialism, and Democracy,* p. 83.

validity of particular antitrust actions, and though he might demonstrate that antitrust policy was, in general, "nothing but ideology," had he anything better to suggest? Were not all ideologies pretty much equal in the eyes of science?

This relation of "ideology" to science and logic was very much in the front of Schumpeter's thought in the late years of his life and formed the subject of his presidential address to the American Economic Association in 1948.[10] Here he argues that "ideology," giving this term a rather special meaning, viz., "the initial vision of the phenomenon we propose to subject to scientific treatment," [11] not only provides the impetus to new departures in scientific research but is not necessarily incompatible with objective research findings. The possession of an "ideology" is not necessarily incompatible with the drawing of objective conclusions from careful research but it may be, and it is clear that, in Schumpeter's view, the possession of a traditional antitrust ideology was apt to be. The antitrust vision, according to him, was of an economy of small enterprise capable, in the absence of growth of positions of monopoly power, of accomplishing an efficient allocation and use of economic resources.

> Theirs is the ideology of a capitalist economy that would fill its social functions admirably by virtue of the magic wand of pure competition, were it not for the monster of monopoly or oligopoly that casts a shadow on an otherwise bright scene. No argument avails about the performance of largest-scale business, about the inevitability of its emergence, about the social costs involved in destroying existing structures, about the futility of the hallowed ideal of pure competition — or in fact ever elicits any response other than most obviously sincere indignation.[12]

This is not the place to analyze Schumpeter's conception of the relation of ideology to science. It is clear — and not too surprising — that he regarded his own ideology of the nature of the captalism as being quite compatible with objective research. He obviously thought of the "process of creative destruction" as that "initial vision of the phenomenon" which had shaped and fructified his own scientfic work and might fructify the work of others. However, whether his own or the opposing antitrust view would prove to be the most useful

[10] "Science and Ideology," *American Economic Review,* March 1949, pp. 345–59.
[11] "Science and Ideology," p. 351.
[12] "Science and Ideology," p. 358.

ideological framework must depend, in his opinion, on the quality of the scientific work issuing therefrom. What is to be noted here is that Schumpeter recognized that his own views on the role of the large firm in the economy had a large ideological content, and that his opposition to antitrust policy represented in part a clash of ideologies that might or might not be resolved by subsequent research.

III

Two further strands in Schumpeter's thought must be briefly mentioned to round out his total conception of the monopoly problem and of antimonopoly policy. He had pronounced views on the scarcity of first-rate talent, including the ability to create and to organize new combinations of economic resources; he was also highly skeptical of the capacity of democratic government to devise and execute sensible policies concerning business organization and business practices.

Effective use of the limited supply of first-rate entrepreneurial ability requires opportunity to create and organize economic structures large enough to give full rein to exceptional talent. During the heyday of American capitalism, in fact — the late nineteenth and early twentieth centuries — a large percentage of the best brains in the United States were devoted to the formation of those huge combinations whose contribution to efficiency, he holds, is mainly responsible for the rapid growth in national output. Economic progress in the United States, according to Schumpeter, "is largely the result of work done within a number of concerns, at no time much greater than 300–400. . . ."[13]

As far as economic progress is the result of organized industrial research, current data indicate a much higher concentration than these figures would suggest. But innovation, as Schumpeter insisted, is something other than the discoveries of applied science. And whether in fact innovation in his sense has generally been the product of the largest firms, during the last few decades of American economic history, is seriously open to question.

During the nineteenth century innovation, according to Schum-

---

[13] *Business Cycles* (New York, 1939), II, 1044. Since the 300–400 largest firms in the United States control a high percentage of total business assets, this is not, perhaps, a very striking statement.

peter, was typically the product of new firms. "The new processes do not, and generally cannot, evolve out of the old firms, but place themselves side by side with them and attack them." [14] In the twentieth-century epoch of "trustified" capitalism, however, innovations issue from existing firms and, as indicated above, usually from large ones. Furthermore, although the creation of giant firms represents a high form of innovating ability that could not be expected to be brought to fruition except in a capitalism that gives full scope to exceptional talent, the process of concentration ends up by making innovation quasi-automatic.

It meets with much less friction, as failure in any particular case loses its dangers, and tends to be carried out as a matter of course on the advice of specialists. . . . Progress becomes "automatized," increasingly impersonal and decreasingly a matter of leadership and individual initiative.[15]

Thus although trustified capitalism could not be created without economic leadership of the highest quality, and although the large-scale organizations of a trustified capitalism function with the highest efficiency, the culmination of the process is a situation which makes exceptional entrepreneurial talent unnecessary. "Since capitalist enterprise, by its very achievements, tends to automatize progress, we conclude that it tends to make itself superfluous. . . ." [16]

This is a conclusion that can hardly be pleasing either to the defender of large-scale enterprise or to the exponent of aggressive antitrust policy. Nor is it a conclusion clearly substantiated by the facts. Schumpeter's analysis raises more questions than it answers. Did the huge concentrations put together during the first and second merger movements in fact promote efficiency and progress in efficiency? Is is true that during the last few decades innovation has come mainly from the very large firms? What is the evidence that, in an economy in which the large firm predominates, successful innovation becomes "quasi-automatic" and is no longer dependent on exceptional entrepreneurial ability?

[14] "The Instability of Capitalism," *Economic Journal,* September 1928, p. 384.
[15] "The Instability of Capitalism," p. 384. Cf. also "Der Unternehmer in der Volkswirtschaft von heute," in *Struktur wandlungen der deutschen Volkswirtschaft,* 1 (1928), 303, where these ideas are worked out in greater detail.
[16] *Capitalism, Socialism, and Democracy,* p. 134.

We have partial answers to some of these questions; further research can throw further light on others, particularly on the question whether innovation comes principally from large firms. In the main, however, the Schumpeterian view represents an historical interpretation of the process of capitalist development — a sort of *histoire raisonnée* of capitalism — that is hardly subject to proof or disproof.

IV

Particularly serious difficulties are presented when the attempt is made to apply Schumpeter's analysis in the field of public policy. Here the problems presented are what to do about a specific agreement in restraint of trade, a particular combination of hitherto independent firms, or a concrete set of business practices. If one took at face value his admonition that, since we are dealing with an organic process that takes time, a judgment on the consequences of any particular part of it — say a combination of hitherto independent firms — can only be an historical judgment, as these consequences "unfold over decades," and a partial judgment, since the repercussions reverberate throughout an economy which is in process of "organic development," informed public action would clearly be impossible. However, Schumpeter assures us that what he is opposed to is not every antimonopoly policy but only certain kinds of monopoly policy.[17]

What a "sensible" as opposed to a "vindictive" antimonopoly policy would presumably emphasize is mainly the possibility that various restrictive activities may be a necessary concomitant to innovation with its accompanying investment decisions, and that a firm producing new products and processes may be a more effective stimulant to efficient behavior on the part of others than a large number of routine competitors. What this appears to boil down to in terms of practicable application is a useful admonition that the existence of a large firm or a few large firms in a market is not necessarily incompatible with effective competition.

Schumpeter was highly doubtful, however, whether a sensible antimonopoly policy, even within this attenuated interpretation, was possible for American democratic government. It is impossible within the space available to do more than suggest the color of his argument.

[17] *Capitalism, Socialism, and Democracy,* p. 134.

Economic concentration, by diminishing the relative importance of individual business proprietors in society and thus weakening the position of the natural defenders of all business, contributes to an increasing political vulnerability of big business. Accompanying this decline in the strength of its natural defenders is an increase in the numbers and the organizational strength of those with an antibusiness bias and particularly those with a bias against big business. Even the executive of the large corporation requires an employee mentality. "Whether a stockholder or not, his will to fight and to hold on is not and cannot be what it was with the man who knew ownership and its responsibilities in the full-blooded sense of those words." [18]

The growing hostility of the environment, furthermore, is immeasurably increased by the current activity of that "scribbling set," the intellectuals, "who wield the power of the spoken and the written word" but who assume no "direct responsibility for practical affairs." [19] Among the intellectuals responsible for fomenting hostility to big business are those economists both in and out of government who propound an antimonopoly policy running in terms of standards derived from a static analysis of the conditions of pure competition.

Under these circumstances, "Even if the giant concerns were all managed so perfectly as to call forth applause from the angels in heaven, the political consequences of concentration would still be what they are." [20] One of the conclusions deriving from these political consequences is the improbability of shaping, through current democratic processes, a public policy toward the large firm in particular, and business practices in general, that will give due consideration to efficiency and to conditions conducive to progress in efficiency. Much more likely is a policy of vindictive harassment.

V

Schumpeter most certainly exaggerated the extent of the influence exerted on American business organization and business practices by antitrust policy. Furthermore, he painted a picture of antitrust objectives and of the ideological justification of these objectives that is in many respects distorted and out of focus. Nevertheless, his

[18] *Capitalism, Socialism, and Democracy*, p. 156.
[19] *Capitalism, Socialism, and Democracy*, p. 147.
[20] *Capitalism, Socialism, and Democracy*, p. 140.

powerful attack on the limitations of static economic analysis as an intellectual foundation for a public antimonopoly policy is highly salutary and profoundly correct. And his discussion of the political environment in which public policy toward business organization and business practices actually gets shaped is a useful corrective to the thinking of those colleagues who conceive that policy can be divorced from politics. Finally, although it is difficult to the point of impossibility to derive from Schumpeter's "process of creative destruction" an analytical framework on which applicable and effective antitrust standards might be built, his analysis suggests lines of research and invokes considerations that must play a role in formulating an acceptable public policy in this area.

PART II

WAGE-PRICE PROBLEMS

Introduction

The papers in Part II, with the exception of the disquisition on "labor monopoly" published as Chapter 10, are largely devoted to the behavior of prices and costs in the business cycle. Among the lesser products of the great depression in the United States was the discovery of the concept of price rigidity. The argument holds that the price system is composed of monopolistically determined prices that are inflexible to downward shifts in aggregate effective demand and competitive prices that respond flexibly to such shifts. It is remarkable what economists, both in and out of the government, and the representatives of various interest groups have been able to do with this concept. In the hands of the United States Department of Agriculture it practically became the cornerstone of a theory of depression and one of the main justifications for price support of agricultural products. If industrial prices were as flexible as agricultural prices, the argument ran, industrial output would be as well maintained as is agricultural output. But, if nothing can be done to make industrial prices more flexible, there is a strong case, on both ethical and economic grounds, for government support of agricultural prices.

Opposition both to the empirical foundation of the thesis of price rigidities and to the inferences drawn from the supposed facts did not lag far behind the statement of the thesis. The prices quoted by the Bureau of Labor Statistics tended to overemphasize, it was argued, the rigidity of certain groups of prices; industrial prices, in particular, are more flexible than the statistics indicate. Furthermore, there appeared to be little correlation between the competitiveness of markets and the cyclical flexibility of prices determined in these markets. The durability of the product, the stage of processing, and other factors appeared on examination to be more closely correlated with price behavior. Finally, if price flexibility were interpreted to mean responsiveness to cost changes, it was shown that differences in the flexibility of non-agricultural prices were not as great as supposed. Given information on wage rates and material prices, the behavior of finished goods prices could be "predicted" with some accuracy.

The supposed consequences of price rigidity for changes in aggregate output and employment were also questioned. Far from promoting depression, monopolistically inflexible prices were alleged to be a stabilizing influence via their effect on business expectations. From this preoccupation with the behavior of particular prices, attention shifted, under Keynesian influence, to the price level and to the relationship between the level of prices and the level of wage rates. Conceding that a fall in the price-wage level might, under appropriate monetary assumptions, stimulate employment via effects on interest rates and the real value of cash balances, both Keynes, and later Pigou, rejected price-wage deflation as a practical remedy for depression. But their argument assumed a competitive determination of both wages and prices and, consequently, a market-determined wage-costs-price relationship.

The possibility that differences in the degree of market control of wage rates versus prices might lead to changes in the relationship of the wage level to the price level raised a new set of hypotheses. Suppose trade-union control of wage rates permits a maintenance of the wage level while prices fall. Would this not shift income from potential savers who lack proper investment opportunities to spenders who face no difficulty in getting rid of their money? And would not this income shift be favorable to the maintenance of aggregate employment? The trade-union interest, almost to a man, voted "yes," and this intriguing possibility of employment promoted by an increase in real wages has since become something of a dogma in the American labor movement.

All these variations on the theme of price rigidity were essentially a product — though in part a belated product — of the great depression. The war and postwar inflation turned attention to another set of issues that has come to be known as the wage-price problem. Again, however, there appears to be a greater number of hypotheses than knowns in the system. A distinction is drawn between income inflation proceeding from events on the demand side and cost-price inflation proceeding from events on the supply side of the equation. But given a certain quantum of income inflation, it is by no means clear whether wage and prices influenced by the action of trade unions and firms having a large degree of market power do or do not increase more rapidly than these wages and prices would increase in competitive markets. Conceding that substantial areas of monopoly power exist in both labor markets and product markets, are the policies that issue from these areas of control stabilizing or unstabilizing with respect to the wage-price level? A lot seems to depend on the expectations created in the minds of business and labor leaders by governmental monetary and fiscal policies. If full employment is, in effect, guaranteed, moderation in union wage and business price policies may be difficult to maintain.

Despite considerable speculation on wage and price policies appropriate to an over-all stabilization program, particularly by the Council of Economic Advisers during Democratic administrations, no very sure light has been thrown on this problem. Generous use has been made of such words as "balance" and "harmony," but their meaning in relation to what wage-price relationships are conducive to an effective stabilization program at various stages of the cycle has proved elusive.

Chapter 6 on "Price Inflexibility" distinguishes various meanings of price flexibility and attempts to show that, in terms of frequency and amplitude of price change, Bureau of Labor Statistics price data show no evidence of increasing rigidity over time. As Schumpeter used to say, if one likes inflexible prices he calls them stable; if he doesn't like them he calls them rigid. Chapter 7 on "Price Policies and Full Employment" dates from the period shortly before the war when I was co-director of the Department of Labor Studies for the Temporary National Economic Committee. That this committee's investigation of various aspects of the monopoly problem in the United States was not perfunctory is indicated by the 39 monographs and 44 volumes of published hearings issuing therefrom. Among the aspects considered were the price policies of large firms, and the Committee was concerned with the consequences of these policies for full employment. The author's views on the feasibility and productivity of research on this problem were somewhat more sanguine in 1940 than later when he returned to this subject in a paper here published as Chapter 9, "Prices, Costs, and Profits."

Chapter 8, "Competition, Price Policy, and High-Level Stability," sketches — but no more than sketches — the thesis that the prime movers of increases in the price level on the upswing are prices determined in competitive markets and wage rates. Among the most important competitive markets are those for food stuffs and textiles, and prices in these markets rise rather easily with increases in aggregate expenditures. These items also bulk large in cost-of-living indices, and an upward movement consequently stimulates wage demands. The prices of most investment and durable consumers goods, on the other hand, rise rather sluggishly and tend to follow rather than lead increases in wage rates and raw material prices.

If there is a wage-price problem, it exists because of the ability of trade unions, large firms, and agricultural and other pressure groups to exert an influence on wages and prices that would not be felt in competitive markets. The only justification for including Chapter 10, on labor monopoly, in Part II is that it is concerned with the market power of one of the groups on whose action the existence of a wage-price problem depends. The emphasis of Chapter 10, however, is on broad public-policy issues rather than on union wage policies in the cycle, and the discussion is at least as relevant to the subjects considered in Part IV.

6

Price Inflexibility[1]

Recent work in the fields of price behavior, of monopoly problems, and of business-cycle research has been concerned with the phenomenon of price inflexibility. Much has been written about the causes of price inflexibility or rigidity, and the supposed consequences have been viewed with misgiving. It seems, furthermore, to be a widely held opinion that the price systems of industrially well developed countries, such as the United States, are becoming more inflexible. At the same time, no altogether satisfactory conception of what price rigidity means has been advanced, with the consequence that much of the statistical and theoretical work on this problem has tended to be either trivial or extremely vague. In truth, the study of price inflexibility has appeared at times to present the dilemma — too familiar in economics — of a choice between an institutional gathering of irrelevant data and a theoretical formulation of unanswerable questions.

The purposes of this paper are two: first to distinguish between various meanings of price flexibility and, second, to examine the frequency and amplitude of change in the monthly wholesale prices of the B.L.S. for the period 1890 to date.

I. MEANING AND MEASUREMENT OF PRICE FLEXIBILITY

It must be recognized at the outset that regardless of the meaning assigned to price rigidity it is probably impossible to determine whether the "price system" is now more rigid than it was, say fifty years ago. If attention is directed to the frequency of change of monthly price data, it has been shown that existing price series reveal no evidence of increasing inflexibility.[2] Additional material on this

[1] Reprinted from *The Review of Economic Statistics,* Vol. 20, No. 2, May 1938.

[2] F. C. Mills *Behavior of Prices,* National Bureau of Economic Research (New York, 1927), pp. 379–381; D. D. Humphrey, "The Nature and Meaning of Rigid Prices, 1890–1933" *Journal of Political Economy,* 45 (1937); Rufus S. Tucker, "The Reasons for Price Rigidity," *The American Economic Review,* 28 (1938).

point is presented in section II of this paper. If flexibility be defined as relative amplitude of price change, no evidence has been presented of increasing inflexibility. Relative amplitude, of course, may be measured in many ways. One measure, which is applied to wholesale price data in section II of this paper, reveals no increasing inflexibility.

Nevertheless, in some important sense, the price system may very well be more rigid than it once was. We know that a group of products whose prices are flexible by any test, i.e., agricultural commodities, have been decreasing in importance in terms of proportion of their value to the value of total output. We know that public-utility services, the prices of which are rigid by any test, have been increasing in importance. For large numbers of prices, statistical data relevant to the problem are unavailable. Finally, the price series for many commodities which have undergone a marked change in quality — automobiles may serve as an example — are quite useless for a study of price inflexibility. The price system may then be more rigid than it was a half century ago, although it is impossible to demonstrate that this is so.

A judgment on the question of changing flexibility, furthermore, depends not only on the meaning assigned to price flexibility but on the purpose in view. Price series are not equally important for all purposes nor can their importance be estimated by calculating the value (or value added) of the commodities they represent, assuming this to be possible. For example, in business-cycle analysis certain price relationships are presumably much more important than others, and an increasing inflexibility in these relationships has much more serious consequences for economic stability. The flexibility of variable cost elements of which wage rates are the most important components would seem to be of great importance. The relationship between the prices of existing capital goods and the prices of new capital goods is of decisive significance. If, on the other hand, an attempt is made, by a study of price behavior, to estimate the extent of monopoly control that exists in the economy, a different relative importance may have to be assigned to the various price series.

The study of price inflexibility for various purposes is one in which theoretical analysis and statistical research might well join hands. It is nowhere declared in the Constitution that all prices are created equal. It behooves the student of "rigidities," therefore, to draw lines and make distinctions. This can hardly be done without some theoretical preconceptions of how the economic system functions. The first purpose of this paper, however, is not to consider what prices and price relationships are important for various purposes but to examine what meanings have been and may be assigned to the term price inflexibility.

STATISTICAL MEASURES OF PRICE FLEXIBILITY

Price flexibility may be and has been considered to be a phenomenon of price behavior, of relationship between price change and change in price determining variables, and of relationship between actual and desirable price behavior. We might, without impropriety, call the first the statistical, the second the theoretical, and the third the normative meaning of price flexibility. A purely statistical treatment of price flexibility, undertaken without preconceptions or policy judgment, is limited to the observed data of price behavior. Such a treatment may measure flexibility by frequency of price change, amplitude, rate of change between high and low points or vice versa, time lag between turning points of price trends, and in other ways. There are, moreover, different ways of measuring amplitudes, rates, and time lags.

Means interprets flexibility principally in terms of frequency of price change, although for the period 1929 to 1932, he correlates frequency of change in wholesale price data with amplitudes;[3] Galbraith thinks that amplitude of price change may be a more significant measure of flexibility than the frequency;[4] Mills, in his *Prices in Recession and Recovery,* treats flexibility in terms of "time differentials in price adjustment to changing conditions." [5] Differences in these "time differentials" lead to "price disparities," the concept with which he principally works.[6] As long as flexibility and disparity are

---

[3] Gardiner C. Means, *Industrial Prices and Their Relative Inflexibility,* 74th Congress, 1st Session, Senate Document No. 13 (Washington, 1935).

[4] J. K. Galbraith, "Monopoly Power and Price Rigidities," *Quarterly Journal of Economics,* May 1936.

[5] Published by National Bureau of Economic Research (New York, 1936), p. 33.

[6] "We define as a price disparity the condition prevailing after a shift in price relations to which there has not been complete adaptation among elements of the economic system at large. We take the term adaptation, in the above definition, to mean such adjustment in respect of the volume or

measured by price changes and price relationships, the meaning of these terms is to be sought in the field of price behavior. When, however, they are used to state a relationship between price changes and actual or possible changes in other economic variables within the system, they acquire a theoretical or normative meaning in the sense in which these words are used above.[7]

The statistical measures of price flexibility call for three comments. In the first place, they are the only measures of price flexibility which permit any extensive quantitative treatment of the available data. All of the factual studies of price inflexibility have used some simple satistical concept of flexibility. It may well be that a more significant meaning of flexibility is of a relationship between price changes and changes in other economic variables, e.g., a relationship between price and marginal variable cost, but the difficulties of using such a concept are so great that no study of price flexibility has been made along these lines.

Secondly, studies of flexibility in this pure price behavior sense, may well suggest relationships and conclusions which are useful to an understanding of the economic system. For example, numerous statistical studies of frequencies of price change for masses of wholesale price data all show, except for periods of great price disturbance such as the war years, a characteristically and markedly U-shaped distribution with heavy concentration of items in the low and high frequencies of change. As Means[8] has concluded and Humphrey[9] has

character of production, allocation of man-power, investment of capital, distribution of income, or disposition of other elements of economic life as may be necessary to a working balance of economic elements, with effective utilization of available productive resources." Mills, p. 34.

[7] Although Professor Mills in his operations used flexibility in its purely statistical, price-behavioristic sense, in his Chapter I on "General Aspects of Recent Price Movements" he seems also to use the terms flexibility and disparity as stating relationships (a) between actual and (in some sense) equilibrium prices, and (b) between actual prices and those prices which would permit a healthy functioning of the economic system. These are meanings which we have called, above, theoretical and normative. Cf. the definition of flexibility as "a time differential in price *adjustment* . . ." (Italics mine). Also, page 34, "The definition [of price disparity] goes back to a rather vague conception of a state of balance, or equilibrium, or mutual adjustment among the working parts of an abstract entity called the economic system."

[8] *Industrial Prices.*

[9] "The Nature and Meaning of Rigid Prices."

emphasized, this probably means that the prices included tend to be determined in at least two quite different sets of buyer-seller relationships. The structure of wholesale markets is likely to be such as to produce *either* very frequent price changes *or* relatively infrequent price changes.

Thirdly, no very important or meaningful interpretation of the data of price behavior can be made without assumptions or findings regarding the behavior of other variables in the economic system. The conclusion mentioned above that different frequencies of price changes probably indicate different buyer-seller relationships, or structures of wholesale markets, rests on the assumption that for all products whose prices are quoted there are continual changes in amounts offered and demanded, stocks on hand, and other "price determining" variables, such that if all the markets were as competitive as those for agricultural products, all the prices would change frequently. This assumption is probably valid, and no doubt there are other probable or easily verifiable assumptions regarding the behavior of related economic variables which would permit interesting and important interpretations of statistical price flexibilities. Unfortunately, however, it seems to be thought in some quarters that statistical observations of price inflexibility lead directly to important conclusions concerning the structure and functioning of the economic system. It is asserted that inflexibility in this sense signifies a situation of "acute distress in the price system." It is concluded, because the prices of agricultural products fell during the depression without much decline in output while the output of industrial products fell without much decline in price, that, if the prices of the latter had declined, output would have been maintained. It is frequently inferred, because many prices are now rigid, that the degree of monopoly control must now be greater in the economy than it was at some time in the past. All of these deductions seem to be highly dubious to say the least.

If statistical studies of price flexibility are to throw light on the functioning of the economic system, a distinction must be made between price series which really indicate price changes and those that do not. For a product which changes markedly in quality from year to year, a price series is meaningless for the purpose of measuring flexibility. In the second place, such studies should be accompanied by studies of changes in demand, costs, and other data if significant conclusions are to be drawn from price behavior. In the third place, the studies should be adapted to particular purposes.

THE ANALYTICAL MEANING OF PRICE FLEXIBILITY

The meaning of price flexibility, which we have called the theoretical, attempts to focus attention on the relation between price change and changes in price determining variables. It is obvious to everyone that if there is no change in supply and demand conditions the fact that the price does not change is no very significant evidence of inflexibility. If, on the other hand, the price does not change in response to changes in these conditions there may be inflexibility in some sense that is important for economic analysis. The problem is to examine differences in the reaction of prices to changes in the price determining variables.

Price flexibility may then be thought of in terms of the rate or degree of movement or adjustment of a price from one position determined by given conditions to another indicated by a change in these conditions. Obviously, if the conditions include all the price determining variables, the position of a price at any point in time is completely determined, and there is no object in speaking of flexibility as a rate or degree of adjustment since the price is always perfectly adjusted. Problems of relative price flexibility arise because with a change in *certain* of the conditions one price will react more quickly or in a different way than another.[10]

Prices, in this sense, are flexible or inflexible relative to changes

---

[10] Suppose, for example, that commodity A is sold in a purely competitive market while for commodity B there is only one seller. The demand curves for both commodities shift to the left and become less elastic. The price of commodity A will decline, but the price of commodity B may well remain constant assuming that the sellers in both markets attempt to maximize short run profits. If the structure of the market is included among the price determining factors, there is no reason for holding that the price of B is less flexible than the price of A since the adjustment to the changed conditions is as perfect and as rapidly consummated in the one case as in the other. If, on the other hand, the structure of the market is not considered, the price of A, *with respect to the change in the demand conditions,* is more flexible than that of B.

in given variables. H. L. Moore has used the term flexibility in this way.[11] His coefficient of simple flexibility states the relation between a relative change in quantity and the relative change in price. Given the demand curve, this coefficient is the reciprocal of the Marshallian elasticity of demand. His coefficients of partial flexibility indicate the relation between a relative change in one or more variables of which price is a function and the relative change in price. This, of course, is simply a mathematical formulation of relationships assumed to exist between economic variables with no attempt at practical application. The application of these formulae certainly presents grave difficulties. But, if flexibility is defined as a relationship between price change and change in price determining variables, the quantitative analysis of relative price flexibility must lie in this direction.

Meanwhile various relationships between price and other variables which are important for particular problems may be studied. For many commodities the relation between inventory changes and price changes are significant. A price which is flexible with respect to inventory changes will ordinarily fall with an increase and rise with a decrease of stocks on hand. Inflexible prices will tend to remain constant regardless of inventory changes and adjustments made entirely by varying the output. The prices of new automobiles seem to be inflexible in this sense. For certain problems, it may be useful to compare the flexibility of a group of prices with respect to their responsiveness to inventory changes, or to compare the flexibility of a particular price for different periods of time.

The relation of wage rates to changes in the volume of employment or unemployment may yield a meaning of flexibility of use in another type of problem. The relative flexibility of wage rates would seem to be better indicated by some measure of the responsiveness of wage rates to changes in employment than by statistics merely of the frequency or amplitude of changes in wage rates. For some purposes it is possible that the relation between price and the degree of utilization of existing productive capacity might yield a useful measure of price flexibility.

[11] "Elasticity of Demand and Flexibility of Prices," *Journal of the American Statistical Association*, 18 (1922); and "Partial Elasticity of Demand," *Quarterly Journal of Economics*, 40 (1926). Cf. F. C. Mills, *Behavior of Prices*, pp. 140–151.

The point of the foregoing remarks is, first, that for purposes of economic analysis price flexibility is best understood as a relationship between price change and change in other economic variables; and, second, that in this sense there is no one measure of price flexibility. There are many measures, though some are more important than others and may be used for different purposes. It follows that it is impossible to arrange prices in order of their flexibility or to compare the flexibility of prices now and at some time in the past without specifying the context in which the term is used.

Myrdal, in his "Equilibrium Concept as an Instrument of Monetary Analysis," seems to have a different notion of price flexibility.[12] "We could," he says, "group all prices statistically according to the speed with which they change under the influence of a changing impulse. The *speed of reaction* of prices of different goods, and for the same goods in various markets, depends upon the different institutional circumstances — based on law, convention, consumption habits, methods of production, etc. — which determine the conditions of reaction for the different markets; conditions relating not only to demand and supply, but also to demand- and supply-prices."

If we knew what was meant by a "changing impulse" and where this impulse impinges on the system of prices, it might indeed be possible to group prices according to their speed of reaction, or to their flexibility. But the impulse may lead to a quite different set of price reactions depending on whether it consists in a shift in demand conditions, a change in costs, a change in stocks on hand, or — if it takes the initial form of a change in monetary expenditure — whether this change affects first one group of markets or another.

It is not the purpose of this paper to consider in detail the possible measures of what we here call theoretical price flexibility or to attempt to arrange them in order of their importance for the study of, for example, the business-cycle problem. Again, it may be stated as the writer's conviction that this is a field in which only the joint application of theoretical and statistical techniques is likely to prove fruitful. There remains to be examined the normative meaning of price inflexibility.

---

[12] Gunnar Myrdal, "Der Gleichgewichtsbegriff als Instrument der geldtheoretischen Analyse" in *Beiträge zur Geldtheorie,* edited by F. A. von Hayek (Vienna, 1933).

PRICE INFLEXIBILITY AND ECONOMIC POLICY

Price flexibility in the normative sense may be considered a relationship between actual and desirable price behavior. This use of the term attaches the meaning of flexibility to economic policy. Prices in this connection may be inadequately flexible, adequately flexible, or too flexible to promote satisfactorily a given policy objective.

In an unregulated, competitive milk market the price may fluctuate sharply from day to day with changes in the quantity of milk brought in to market. The introduction of sellers' control or some form of regulation may considerably reduce the price fluctuations. Is the price of milk in this market still a flexible price? If we assume that the purpose of the control is to adapt the average yearly changes in the supply of milk to the growth of population in the area or to a change in some other quantity, the price may be adequately or inadequately flexible. In the absence of regulation, the price may be too flexible for this purpose if it has the consequence of causing farmers, in disgust, to turn to some other pursuit.

Implicit in much of the discussion of price rigidity is a normative conception of flexibility. Prices are often considered rigid not because they change infrequently, or fail to respond to changes in some economic quantity, but because they do not behave as they should behave if economic stability, or some other desirable objective, is to be attained. Frequently, the supposed behavior of prices in a purely competitive market is accepted as the standard from which to measure the inflexibility of actual price behavior. The sort of price behavior assumed to obtain in a purely competitive market would, it is maintained, tend to minimize the adjustments in "real" variables necessary to the maintenance or reestablishment of full employment and the effective utilization of economic resources. A disparity between the actual and the competitive price is then accepted as evidence of inflexibility.

An application of the normative concept of price flexibility requires a judgment of the probable consequences for relevant economic quantities of types of price behavior different from the one actually under observation. This judgment may be sound or unsound depending, among other things, on the experience and diagnostic competence of the one who judges. In any case, opinions are continually being offered of the relative inflexibility — in this sense — of particular prices, and it is safe to say that a great deal of the writing on rigidity, at least in business-cycle literature, is concerned with this meaning of the term.

Let us assume, to illustrate the point, that the demand curve for sheet steel — of certain specifications — is, during a depression, shifting continually to the left. Steel makers, following a price leader, make a slight cut early in the depression which has the effect (or at least it is so interpreted by the sellers) of causing the buyers to hold off, waiting for further cuts. As a result, the price of sheets is not cut again until near the end of the depression when it is sharply slashed. Has the price been flexible or inflexible during this period? Statistical observation yields one set of answers depending on what measure — frequency, amplitude, or some other — is applied. A study of the relation of price to other variables — costs, inventories, unfilled orders, and so on — yields another set of answers. A third type of answer, which is important for economic policy, may be derived by comparing the effect on various relevant economic quantities of the actual price policy with the probable economic effects of some one of a series of other possible price policies.

The problem can be made more specific if we assume as the desideratum an attainment of the maximum hours of employment of labor in steel during the depression consistent with a price policy that the industry will accept or can be made to accept. One of the important considerations is the probable effect of the size and timing of price cuts on the size and distribution of demand during the period. Burns, following Clark[13] and having in mind recent price policies in the steel industry, ventures the opinion that "a halfway policy of grudging reductions when there is a general shrinkage in business activity and reduction of the prices of other products is the one most calculated to induce a general expectation of more severe cuts, and a postponement of purchases."[14] Whether or not this is true, a judgment that some other possible price behavior would result under these circumstances in a fuller employment of steel labor

[13] J. M. Clark, *Economics of Overhead Costs* (Chicago, 1931, fourth edition), p. 406.

[14] A. R. Burns, *Decline of Competition* (New York, 1936), p. 246.

leads to the conclusion that the actual price behavior was inadequately flexible *with respect to the given policy objective.*

The normative view of price flexibility, needless to say, yields different conclusions as to the relative flexibility of prices depending not only on the choice of objectives but also on the setting — particularly with respect to the time period involved — of the problem. Automobile prices, changing once or twice a year, may be inadequately flexible to eliminate or diminish an undesirable seasonality in the demand but sufficiently flexible to produce as stable a demand over the cycle as any price behavior, within the range of possibilities, could be expected to produce. Building labor wage rates may be inadequately flexible over the cycle with respect to a possible and desirable regularization of building and employment but sufficiently flexible over a longer run to induce a satisfactory number of laborers to enter or leave this range of occupations.

It is perhaps unnecessary to say that the application of this conception of price flexibility is surrounded with great difficulties. The writer is not prepared to say, however, that it is altogether useless. In any case it approximates what most people, including many economists, seem to mean when they talk about price rigidity and its consequences.

II. FREQUENCY AND AMPLITUDE OF CHANGE IN WHOLESALE PRICES

It must be emphasized, by way of preface to the statistical treatment to follow, that the data do not "prove" or "demonstrate" that the price system in the United States is as flexible now as it was a half century ago. What the data seem to indicate is that, with respect to the monthly quotations of wholesale prices collected by the Bureau of Labor Statistics, 1890 to date, (1) there is no evidence of decreasing frequency of price change; (2) for one type of amplitude measurement there is no evidence of decreasing average amplitude of price change for various groups of commodities relative to the average amplitude of price change for agricultural commodities or for all commodities; (3) there seems to be a fairly well marked correlation between frequencies and amplitudes of price change in the two periods, 1890–1897 and 1929–1936, for which these data were correlated.

The price system or price structure includes, of course, "all quotations on commodities, services, equities and other disposable values which are expressed in pecuniary terms." [15] Certainly for most of these quotations there are no available series running over a considerable period of time. It is possible that a careful selection from all the available price series might produce a group more or less representative of the price system as a whole. But a consideration of the number of significant ways in which price flexibility may be defined and measured together with the additional data which would be required to make some of the more significant of these measurements possible compels a skeptical attitude toward the possibility of returning a sensible answer to the question whether the price system is now more or less flexible than it once was.

The B.L.S. wholesale price series, which constitute the most extensive body of price data easily available, are themselves, it has been frequently observed, subject to serious limitations for purpose of price flexibility studies. The most serious difficulty is probably change in the quality of the product of which prices are quoted. So serious is this difficulty in certain cases that a more careful study would probably exclude a number of series. Additional difficulties are created by divergence between quoted and actual prices, which seems to be most frequent and important in the rigid price group, the exclusion of changes in selling terms, and others.[16] In all probability, however, this latter type of limitation is not so serious for an historical study of changes in price flexibility as it is for a comparison of the relative flexibility of prices in a given period. It seems likely that the commodities exhibiting differences between actual and quoted prices in earlier years are frequently the same commodities which show these differences now.

FREQUENCY OF PRICE CHANGE

It has already been pretty conclusively shown that, as regards frequency of price change, there is no evidence that wholesale prices are any less flexible now than they were in earlier periods. The material here presented merely tends to corroborate these findings. The

[15] F. C. Mills, "On the Changing Structure of Economic Life," in *Economic Essays in Honor of Wesley Clair Mitchell* (New York, 1935), p. 371.
[16] See for a discussion of these difficulties G. C. Means, "Notes on Inflexible Prices," *American Economic Review*, Supplement, March 1936.

arrangement by F. C. Mills, in his *Behavior of Prices*, of 206 series
of wholesale prices, 1890–1925, in order of frequency of price change,
indicated quite clearly that the frequencies in the earlier periods
showed much the same type of distribution as in the later.[17] Humphrey, analyzing the data presented by Mills, together with Means'
data for the period 1925–1933, has shown that the bulk of the rigid
prices — by this test — are now, and have been during the whole
period, prices of finished goods, while the bulk of the flexibility prices
have been prices of raw or semi-finished materials. He concludes
that, "the U shape [of the frequency distribution in all periods]

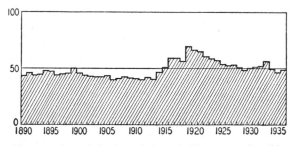

Chart 1. Annual Ratios of Actual Changes to Possible
Changes in Wholesale Prices Quoted in U. S. B.L.S.
Index, 1890–1936 (unit: one per cent).

results from the fact that two or more families of prices have been
included in the single frequency distribution."[18] Tucker, analyzing
wholesale price data for earlier periods[19] has found that infrequency
of price change was characteristic of a large proportion of these
prices a century ago.[20]

    Chart 1 presents in graphic form the annual ratios of the actual
number of changes to the possible number of changes of all prices
quoted in the B.L.S. index from 1890 to 1936 inclusive.[21]

    Except for the war — and immediate postwar — years, the ratios

[17] Mills, pp. 379–381. This was true except for the war period when the
percentage of inflexible prices decreased.

[18] "The Nature and Meaning of Rigid Prices," pp. 651–661, 657.

[19] Drawn from A. Bezanson, R. D. Gray, and M. Hussey, *Wholesale Prices
in Philadelphia, 1784–1861* (Philadelphia, 1937), and wholesale price data in
the Aldrich report.

[20] "The Reasons for Price Rigidity."

[21] This measure is suggested by Mills. See *Behavior of Prices,* p. 57.

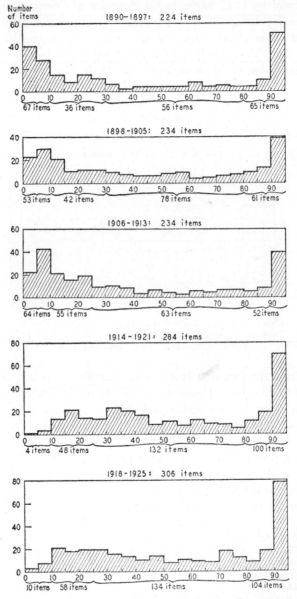

[*Chart 2 is continued on facing page.*]

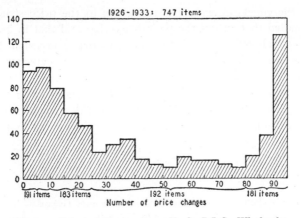

Chart 2. Selected Items from U. S. B.L.S. Wholesale Commodity Price Index Distributed According to Frequency of Price Change.

indicate no great change, and certainly no significant trend in either direction is visible. During the entire period, the number of price series included increased from some 224 to approximately 750, but an attempt has been made by the Bureau of Labor Statistics in the earlier as in the later period to secure a representative coverage of wholesale price data.

Chart 2 presents a frequency distribution, by order of frequency of price change for eight-year periods, of all prices represented in the B.L.S. index.[22] The segment of the chart representing the period 1926–1933 is taken from Means' *Industrial Prices and their Relative Inflexibility*.

The eight-year period was chosen in order to make the data comparable with those presented by Means in his original chart, from a consideration of which so much of the discussion of frequency of price change has sprung. There is no peculiar significance to a period of that length. Any length will do that is short enough to permit a comparison of price behavior at the beginning and end and at various intervals throughout the whole period and long enough to

[22] Only those price series were included which had a continuous existence throughout a period. With respect to the selection and elimination of other series, the author followed, after correspondence, Dr. Means' practice.

include the effects of serious disturbances to the price structure. It will be noted that two of the periods overlap and that in both these periods, which reflect the disturbances to prices occasioned by the war, the percentage of prices which belong in the category of rigid, is small.

Apart from these two periods, the percentages of items which fall in the "rigid" and "flexible" price categories remain remarkably stable. In Table 1, these percentages are given for the first and last periods.

Table 1

Percentage of Price Items in Frequency Groups,
1890–1897 and 1926–1933

Group[a]	Percentage of 224 items, 1890–1897	Percentage of 747 items, 1926–1933
1	29.91	25.59
2	16.07 ⎫	24.50 ⎫
3	25.00 ⎬ 41.07	25.60 ⎬ 50.10
4	29.02 ⎭ 54.02	24.23 ⎭ 49.83

[a]Group	Frequency of price change (number of changes in 94 opportunities for change)
1	0–9
2	10–24
3	25–79
4	80–94

These data on frequency of price change are chiefly significant in relation to the thesis that there has been a pronounced shift within recent decades from prices which changed from day to day, in response to daily changes in supply and demand conditions, to prices which remain, for a considerable period of time, fixed. The history of wholesale prices since 1890 does not seem to substantiate this thesis. What the evidence appears to indicate is that certain groups of prices, notably those of agricultural products and certain other raw materials, have remained flexible — in this sense — throughout the whole period, while the prices of manufactured and processed goods, which were largely inflexible in the later periods, were also inflexible in the earlier.[23]

It may be, of course, that at some more remote period, a larger segment of the price system than at present responded to the impact of day to day changes in supply and demand conditions. Is it not probable, however, that this type of price behavior has for a very long time been largely confined to more or less "organized" markets such as the grain market, the stock market, the market for textile fabrics, and that horse trader's market, so beloved of classical economic theory, in which a relatively large number of buyers and sellers are assembled in one place — or in close contact — for trading purposes? There is not much evidence that retail prices, the prices of the services of factors of production, and a large percentage of wholesale prices, have ever exhibited this type of behavior.

AMPLITUDE OF PRICE CHANGE

A study of relative amplitude of change in wholesale prices, although the technique may be more open to question, appears to lead to much the same result. There is little evidence of increasing inflexibility in wholesale prices — in this sense — over the period 1890 to date. The amplitude of change in the price of any commodity for a given period is here defined as the percentage ratio of the difference between the highest and lowest monthly quotation for a period and the arithmetical average of the monthly prices for that commodity. For example, if the highest monthly price quotation for No. 2 hard wheat in the period 1890–1897 is $1.50, the lowest $.50, and the average $1.00, the amplitude of price change is 100. The arrangement of the wholesale price series for any period in order of amplitude reveals, as one would expect, a wide variation in this type of price behavior (Chart 3).

We are not, however, so much interested in the amplitude differences between commodity prices in any period as in the question whether these differences show a marked tendency to change over

[23] A study of the 141 prices which have had a continuous representation in the B.L.S. index since 1890 leads to the same conclusions. The frequency distributions by eight year periods have, except for the war period, shown pretty much the same shape throughout. The charts were not presented here because they seemed redundant.

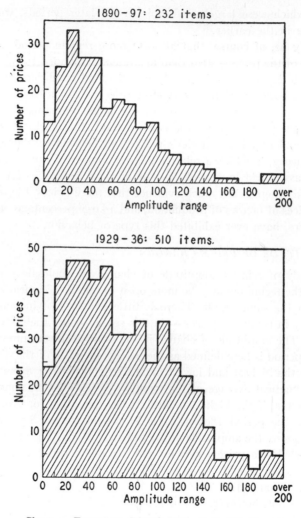

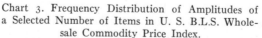

Chart 3. Frequency Distribution of Amplitudes of
a Selected Number of Items in U. S. B.L.S. Wholesale Commodity Price Index.

time. Specifically, do certain prices or groups of prices tend to become more inflexible (in terms of amplitude of price change) in
relation to an average of all prices or of some other group of prices
— such as farm product prices — which there is reason to believe

are flexible in every sense of the term flexibility? The reason, of course, for comparing relative amplitude differences rather than absolute amplitude differences for commodity groups between different periods is the fact that all prices (the price system) have been sub-

Table 2

Average Amplitude of Price Change for Ten Groups of Commodities, by Eight-Year Periods, 1890–1936[a]

Group	1890–1897	1898–1905	1906–1913	1914–1921	1922–1929	1929–1936
Farm products	113.44	89.67	92.65	138.49	74.96	118.06
Foods	80.62	62.21	55.47	138.07	63.06	94.19
Hides and leather products	34.50	22.58	28.33	164.25	57.02	69.53
Fuel and lighting materials	61.70	83.79	30.22	103.08	62.73	65.25
Metals and metal products	51.31	58.18	40.09	159.36	49.31	34.32
Building materials	39.43	61.84	43.20	137.61	46.10	63.03
Chemicals and drugs	63.71	39.31	41.99	105.53	36.92	45.77
Housefurnishing goods	22.12	26.00	42.27	50.05	26.16	23.21
Textile products	36.95	38.87	28.02	178.32	51.34	73.30
Miscellaneous	39.36	43.33	37.98	103.87	39.98	56.39
Average	54.31	52.57	44.01	127.86	50.75	64.30

[a] For the first three periods, the figures are the unweighted averages of amplitudes of the prices in each group. For the last three periods (for which weights were available), the averages were calculated in accordance with the formula

$$\frac{\text{(sum of items} \times \text{weights)}}{\text{(weights)}}$$

The weights used may be found in appendix B of the following B.L.S. Bulletins: for 1914–1921, #320; for 1922–1929, #473; for 1929–1936, #573. The unweighted average of amplitudes could, of course, have been used for all periods. But, on the assumption that the B.L.S. in the earlier period weighted by number of items alone, while in later periods the procedure was items times weights, the method here followed seemed preferable. It is unlikely that the results would have been very different had weights been eschewed throughout.

Strict care was taken that the average amplitude of any series should not be based on less than the full eight year span. Since the commodity list changed greatly over the entire period covered, a considerable proportion of the series for any period was found to be incomplete and so not available for use in computing the average. But since the weights — for the last three periods — were based upon the full list, a correction for these omissions had to be made. This was done by taking the ratio of the total weights of each classification for each period to the weights of the commodities available, and multiplying the weighted sum of these commodities by this percentage before dividing by the sum of the weights to obtain the average.

ject to general disturbances of very different magnitude in different periods. The fact that metal prices showed an average amplitude of change for the period 1906–13 less than the average amplitude of change for the period 1890–1897 is irrelevant, for practically all groups of commodities in the later period exhibited smaller price changes than in the earlier. A marked change in average amplitudes relative to the average of all commodity prices or particular groups of prices *may*, however, be significant.

Table 2 indicates that the average amplitude of price change of farm products exceeded the average amplitude of price change for all other groups in every period except 1914–1921. For various reasons, discussed above, the war period is not typical and should be neglected in a study of trends in price flexibility. The commodity groups are those which the B.L.S. has used since 1931 in its classification of wholesale prices.

Table 3 gives the ratios of the average amplitude of price changes in the various groups for each period to the average amplitude of price change for farm products. It is difficult to detect here a marked trend in the relative flexibility of any group of prices. If the prewar periods be compared with the postwar periods, hides and leather and textile prices seem to be relatively more flexible in the latter period than in the former. On the other hand, metal and chemical and drug prices — particularly if attention is focused on the last period — seem to exhibit relatively less flexibility. It may be, of course, that

Table 3

Ratios of Average Amplitude of Each Group to the Average Amplitude of Price Change of Farm Products, by Eight-Year Periods, 1890–1936
(*Unit: one per cent*)

Group	1890–1897	1898–1905	1906–1913	1914–1921	1922–1929	1929–1936
Foods	71.07	69.30	59.87	99.69	84.12	79.78
Hides and leather products	30.41	25.18	30.57	118.60	76.06	58.89
Fuel and lighting materials	54.38	93.44	32.61	74.43	83.60	55.26
Metals and metal products	45.23	64.88	43.27	115.06	65.78	29.06
Building materials	34.75	68.90	46.62	99.36	61.49	53.38
Chemicals and drugs	56.16	43.83	45.32	76.20	49.25	38.76
Housefurnishing goods	19.49	28.99	45.62	36.13	34.89	19.65
Textile products	32.57	43.34	30.24	128.76	68.48	62.08
Miscellaneous	34.69	48.32	40.99	75.00	53.33	47.76

an increasing relative inflexibility of a group of prices is hidden by this classification. Changes in the weight of individual prices within a group either by a change in the number of prices in the group or a change in the weights themselves may also possibly distort the result.

An alternative method is to select those prices which are most inflexible (in terms of amplitude) in each period and to examine changes in their relative inflexibility. Table 4 indicates the average amplitude of price change of ten per cent of the most inflexible prices in each period and the ratios of these averages to the average of all prices. There is no apparent tendency for the inflexibility of the most inflexible prices to increase relative to the average amplitude of price change for all commodities.

Table 4

Part A: Average Amplitude of Price Change of Ten Per Cent of
Commodities Lowest in Amplitude in Each Period[a]
Part B: Ratio of Above Averages to the Average Amplitude of
Price Change of All Commodities

	1890–1897	1898–1905	1905–1913	1914–1921	1922–1929	1929–1936
A	10.17	13.25	4.71	70.73	12.65	15.13
B	18.72	25.20	10.70	55.31	24.02	23.53

[a] For the first three periods, the figures represent an arithmetic average of the ten per cent lowest amplitudes. A different method, however, was necessary for computing the averages of the last three periods since those averages in Table 1 had been computed in accordance with the formula

$$\frac{(\text{sum of items} \times \text{weights})}{(\text{weights})}.$$

Thus in order to make the ratios commensurable above and below the line, the ten per cent lowest amplitudes in the last three periods were obtained by taking ten per cent of the sum of the weights of all commodities and adding the lowest amplitudes until their weights equaled ten per cent of the total weights. All those commodities were excluded from consideration which in no period (for which B.L.S. weights are available) had a weight of more than .02. Thus, presumably, unimportant commodities have not been allowed to influence these ratios.

As was true of the statistics on frequency of price change, the data on amplitudes support perhaps a negative thesis. They serve principally to awaken doubt as to the validity of the widely held opinion that prices, in terms of frequency and amplitude of price change, are

becoming less flexible. For the wholesale price data of the Bureau of
Labor Statistics, this seems definitely not to be true. At least it is
now encumbent on those who maintain the thesis of increasing inflexibility to state clearly what they mean by price inflexibility and
to present their evidence.

RELATION OF FREQUENCY AND AMPLITUDE OF PRICE CHANGE

Means' study of frequencies and amplitudes of price change in the
period 1929–1933 showed a rather striking correlation.[24] The scatter
diagrams presented in Chart 4 tend to corroborate the existence of
such a correlation, though amplitude is here defined somewhat differently.

A rough but unmistakable correlation between frequencies and
amplitudes of price change appears to exist for the periods 1890–
1897 and 1929–1936. On the whole, prices which change frequently
also show wide variations from their average for the period, and vice
versa. In the diagram for the later period where price of foods and
of farm products are represented by crosses, it can be seen how large
a percentage of the flexible price group these constitute. How is this
correlation to be interpreted?

As stated above, it is probably fair to assume that for all products
there are day to day changes in amounts offered and demanded,
inventories, and other "price determining" variables, such that, if
the buyer-seller relationships were the same for other products as for
agricultural products, all prices would be flexible in a *frequency*
sense. There is not the same warrant, however, for assuming that the
quantitative changes in these variables is such that, if buyer-seller
relationships for other products were the same as for agricultural
products, the *amplitudes* of price changes would be similar. Although
many explanations of why prices which change infrequently also tend
to exhibit low amplitude of price change are possible, it nevertheless
seems probable to this observer that two factors are of paramount
importance, inflexibility of variable costs and opportunities for price
control, particularly by sellers.

The inflexible prices are predominantly those of finished and semi-
finished goods. For the producers of these goods, wage rates and

[24] *Industrial Prices*, p. 3. Amplitude is there defined as the ratio of 1932 to
1929 price.

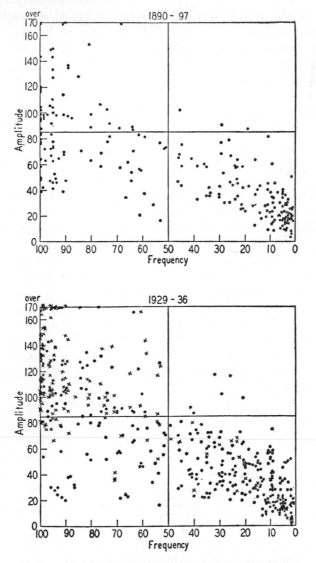

Chart 4. Correlation of Frequency of Price Changes to
Amplitude of Price Changes in U. S. B.L.S. Wholesale
Commodity Price Index,

other variable cost items are frequently subject to contractual arrangement and change slowly.[25] It is, furthermore, in this range of products that monopoly positions of various sorts are, within this section of the economy, chiefly to be found. Adjustment to changing conditions takes the form of output changes and changes in quality of product more frequently than in the case of foods and farm products. There is, however, no evidence, in the data we have considered, that this type of non-price adjustment is more important in the later than in the earlier periods.

REMARKS

In conclusion it may be said that there are many legitimate meanings and measures of price inflexibility. These may be conveniently grouped into (1) those which consider inflexibility as a type of price behavior; (2) those which consider it as a relationship between price and change in other economic variables; (3) those which treat inflexibility as a relationship between actual and desirable price behavior. A study of the behavior of prices leads to little understanding of the functioning of the economic system unless this behavior is related to changes in other economic quantities. Thus, for analytical purposes, the important meanings of price flexibility are to found in the second group. Even within this group, however, there is no one meaning of price inflexibility. What measure of inflexibility is used depends largely on the purpose of the analysis.

Although a study of frequency and amplitude of change in monthly quotations of wholesale prices lends no support to the thesis that the "price system" is becoming more inflexible in a price behavior sense, it may well be that with respect to those price responses to change in economic quantities which relate to business fluctuations, the "system" *is* becoming more inflexible. Furthermore, even though prices are now no less flexible, in this sense, than they once were, it is possible that price inflexibility is a more serious obstacle to the

---

[25] Over a large part of agricultural output, it is difficult to see that variable cost considerations have any significant relation to price. In more or less specialized farms, where the employment of labor is also small, practically all costs seem to be constant with respect to such variations in expected output as come within the farmer's calculation. A determined number of acres is subjected to a routine of cultivation which apparently varies little with considerable change in price expectations.

maintenance of economic stability now than it was a half century ago. A rapid rate of population growth and the existence of unexploited natural resources in an earlier period may have made price adjustment then less necessary than it is at present to recovery from depression and to the reëmployment of idle resources.

7

Price Policies and Full Employment[1]

PROBLEMS FACING THE TEMPORARY NATIONAL ECONOMIC COMMITTEE

The circumstances leading to the creation of the Temporary National Economic Committee (the so-called Monopoly Investigation) heavily emphasized the relation of business price policies to the functioning of the economic system. The Congressional resolution creating the Committee was formulated in the midst of the business recession which became evident in the fall of 1937. Political exigencies created by the attempt of anti-administration forces to exploit this situation to their advantage, by variations on the theme of a "Roosevelt Recession," led to a counterattack on the policies of "big business." In the phraseology then current, "big business" had "priced itself out of recovery."

The opportunity to direct attention to the economic consequences of business price policies was welcomed by a number of government agencies concerned with this problem. The Antitrust Division of the Department of Justice, under the leadership of Robert Jackson, had for some time laid emphasis — reiterated in the report of the Department for 1937 — on the importance of considering the *consequences* of business policies rather than the *intentions* behind these policies in the enforcement of the antitrust acts. Certain circles at the Federal Reserve Board were inclined to attribute to the rapid rise in the prices of a number of industrial products an important role in cutting short the recovery of 1934 to 1937. In the Department of Agriculture the relative inflexibility of industrial prices during the downturn from prosperity to depression had become the cornerstone of what amounted to a theory of the business cycle.

During the winter of 1937–38 a "business price-policy" theory of the recession was proclaimed by a number of administration spokes-

---

[1] Reprinted from *Public Policy,* edited by C. J. Friedrich and Edward S. Mason (Cambridge, Mass., 1940), Vol. I.

men, notably Messrs. Ickes and Jackson. In February 1938 a Committee on Price Policy appointed by the President called attention to the fact that "the prices of some items are still at the highest levels reached in 1937; some are even higher than in 1929."

The Committee further observed,

When high prices sharply curtail sales there is a real danger. This is shown by our recent experience with housing. A year ago there was a serious shortage. We had unused productive resources ample to overcome the shortage. Yet all the major elements in housing costs advanced so sharply by the spring of 1937 as to kill a promising expansion of activity in an industry whose restoration is vital to continued recovery.

These views regarding the relation of price policy and price behavior to the functioning of the economy were underlined in the President's "Message on Monopolies" of April 29, 1938.[2] As a formulation of monopoly problems the President's message was novel in at least two respects: (1) in its emphasis on a "concentration of economic control" which influences in many ways the activities of business firms; and (2) in its emphasis on the relation of price policies and price behavior to fluctuations in employment and volumes of output.

With respect to the latter, the message summarizes a number of observations on this relationship in the statement,

One of the primary causes of our present difficulties lies in the disappearance of price competition in many industrial fields, particularly in basic manufacture where concentrated economic power is most evident — and where rigid prices and fluctuating payrolls are general.

Reflecting this emphasis on business price policies, the Congressional resolution creating the Temporary National Economic Committee enjoined the Committee with the duty of investigating "the matters referred to in the President's Message," including "the effect of the existing price system and the price policies of industry upon the general level of trade, upon employment, upon long-term profits, and upon consumption."[3]

It must be recognized that, in technical economic literature, prob-

[2] Senate Document No. 173, 75th Congress, 3rd Session. Message from the President of the United States transmitting recommendations relative to the strengthening and enforcement of the antitrust laws. April 20 (calendar day, April 29), 1938.

[3] Public Resolution No. 113, 75th Congress, June 16, 1938.

lems concerning the relation of price behavior to the full and efficient use of economic resources are in a somewhat anomalous position. During the nineteenth century — and in fact until fairly recently — it was widely accepted, in accordance with Says's law, that both the long-run allocation and organization of economic resources and the short-run adjustments necessary to reestablish a full employment, temporarily disturbed, are — and should be — accomplished by the type of price changes which are "automatic" in freely competitive markets. An increased awareness of the extent of business price controls, together with a more intensive examination of price behavior, has made it clear that price adjustments are not as "automatic" as had been supposed. At the same time postwar business cycle theory, with its emphasis on fluctuations in the volume of investment, has directed attention away from price adjustment as the central aspect of the problem of maintaining or restoring full employment.

While it is recognized that the way prices behave on the downturn and upturn may have "something to do" with the extent of depression or the character of the recovery, many proposals for public action designed to promote economic stability and reëmployment are apt to assume price behavior as given. In part this minimizing of price problems is probably the result of the very great difficulty of distinguishing between price behavior which promotes and that which retards recovery and full employment; in part, no doubt, to a reasonable suspicion that even though this distinction were made not much could be done about it.

This paper is not primarily concerned with the relative importance of a public policy with respect to prices as against other forms which public action might take to promote full employment. Nor is it concerned with the various possible techniques of public action considered elsewhere in this volume by Mr. A. H. Feller. Section I attempts to make clear why business price policies are of public concern. Section II attempts to formulate some of the public policy issues in the field of prices which are relevant to the work of the Temporary National Economic Committee.

I

PUBLIC CONCERN WITH BUSINESS PRICE POLICIES

The price system — or cost-price structure — composed of all the prices of individual commodities and services offered for sale, may be regarded as an elaborate indicator of the economic alternatives open to producers and consumers. To the consumer the structure of prices indicates the terms on which he can acquire the goods for which he spends his money income. To the producer the structure of prices indicates the terms on which he may dispose of his goods and services or acquire the goods and services of others. Any change in this price structure involves a change in the alternatives open to some or all producers and consumers. Since the price system defines, in important respects, the conditions on which producers and consumers engage in economic activity, in influences, on the one hand, the efficiency with which economic resources are used to satisfy human wants and, on the other, the size of the income streams which flow to those who, as owners or workers, participate in the process of production.

In an economic system in which no single buyer or seller was able to influence the price of the goods and services bought or sold, the structure of prices would more effectively determine the economic action of producers and consumers than, in fact, it does today. Such a situation substantially exists, for sellers, in the markets for the principal agricultural crops and, for buyers, in the principal consumers' goods markets. The individual farmer, not being able to influence the price of the produce he sells, determines what crops he will produce and what acreage he will sow in view of the *existing or expected price situation.* As a result of the action of hundreds of thousands of independent farmers (together with other influences which lie outside their control) the price structure of agricultural prices changes in ways which may influence the kinds of quantities of farm products produced in the next crop period. The structure of prices thus influences the action of individual farmers, but the action of individual farmers does not in any significant degree influence the structure of prices.

Likewise, the individual housewife governs her purchases with reference to the existing structure of prices in the consumers' goods markets. If the price of beef is high, she may switch to pork; if citrus fruits are cheap, she may introduce grapefruit to the breakfast table. As a result of the action of millions of housewives the structure of consumers' goods prices changes, and in consequence of these changes individual housewives alter their buying practices. Again the structure of prices influences the actions of the individual purchaser, but the action of the individual purchaser does not influence the structure of prices.

If all markets were organized, on both the buying and selling side, in such a fashion that no individual buyers or sellers could influence the price, then all producers and consumers would be constrained to seek their economic advantages under the conditions laid down by the existing or expected price structure rather than by attempting to change or to maintain prices. No firm or group could have a price policy any more than a farmer or housewife can have a price policy.

The principal problems faced by the Committee in the price area arise because in fact, particularly in the industrial sector of the economy, buyers and sellers can and do influence price. The buyers in the raw tobacco market are so large and so few in number that the purchases of any one of the principal companies necessarily influence the price producers secure for their crop. In the market for many heavy steel products the position of the United States Steel Corporation is so dominant that its action cannot fail to be important in the determination of prices. For many consumers' goods, firms can, through heavy selling expenditures, influence consumers' choices and consequently the prices that are charged for the product.

The control of buyers or sellers over prices can be and is accentuated by collusive action, by trade association practices, and by pricing techniques. The important fact, however, is that, given the ability to influence price, buyers and sellers can have a policy with respect to price — they can raise or lower prices or keep them stable even though external conditions change somewhat. The price policy followed will influence the behavior and structure of prices, and the structure of prices will have consequences for the functioning of the economy. The situation in most industrial markets is not one in which firms are limited, in pursuit of their economic advantage, to the production and distribution of goods under conditions determined for them by an existing cost-price structure. The possibility is also open to them to influence, to their advantage, the terms on which they buy and sell.

This does not mean that a buyer or seller can completely determine the price at which he buys or sells. No firm, no matter how strong its market position, can determine the price of its products without any regard for whatever competitive situation exists. The Aluminum Company of America, which produces 100 per cent of the virgin ingot aluminum made in this country, is forced to take account in its price policy of the competition of scrap aluminum, imports of virgin ingot, iron and steel, and nonferrous metal substitutes. Any business man, as a matter of fact, is so acutely aware of the competitive elements in his market that he is prone to ignore, or even deny, the existence of any control over price. We are presented, in consequence, with the spectacle of the representatives of industries in which concentration is very marked, asserting — and believing — that the prices of their products are determined by the impersonal forces of supply and demand.

Although all firms operate in markets in which they meet the competition of rival producers and rival products, there is for most firms an area of control within which the formulation of a price policy is possible. Certain competitive and collusive tactics, furthermore, have the effect of widening this area. The wider (or more expansible) the area, the greater may be the incentive to pursue profits by other means than by increased production and distribution of goods.

The types of price policy which may be used to widen or exploit market control positions are as numerous as the types of market situations which firms confront. Faced during a business recession with a demand temporarily inelastic, a firm may decide on a policy of price maintenance. To increase sales might require a sharp reduction in price, to the disadvantage of the firm in question. To be able to influence price by increasing or decreasing sales indicates a control position for the firm. The decision to maintain price is a policy decision designed to take advantage of this control position. Other sorts of price-policy decisions are evident in the classification of customers for the purpose of charging different prices to different groups, selling only at delivered prices, following the price leadership of a particular firm. All are dependent on the existence of some degree of price control.

It does not follow that, just because the market position of buyers or sellers permits the determination of price policy, this policy necessarily runs counter to the public interest. Still less does it follow that public action should be taken to eliminate the possibility of price control on the part of buyers or sellers. Such action would probably involve a breaking-up of concerns (an atomizing of competition) on a scale undreamed of by even the most enthusiastic of trust-busters. On the other hand, it *does* follow that in those areas in which firms are able definitely to influence price, price policy becomes a matter of public concern. The structure and behavior of prices impose a set of conditions which seriously influences the functioning of the economic system. The structure and behavior of prices, at least in the industrial sector, is largely the result of price-policy decisions.

THE LACK OF STANDARDS OF UNDESIRABLE PRICE BEHAVIOR

The case for public concern with price policies and price behavior can be outlined in the following propositions:

(1) The behavior of prices has an important influence on the functioning of the economy.

(2) Certain types of price behavior are more conducive than others to full employment and the efficient use of economic resources.

(3) It is possible, at least in part, to discover which types of price behavior encourage and which handicap the fuller attainment of these objectives.

(4) It is possible, at least in part, to facilitate by public action price behavior which encourages, and to prevent price behavior which handicaps, the attainment of these objectives.

With respect to this case, it may be observed that propositions (1) and (2) would receive general, even universal, acceptance. However, when the argument proceeds from a general indictment of "undesirable" price behavior to a specification of what types of price policy and price behavior are undesirable — and why — agreement is by no means general. The truth of this statement is easily demonstrated. The basing-point system of price quoting as practiced in steel, cement, and other industries has been the subject of active investigation and discussion by government and private experts for at least fifteen years. Whether this system produces results much less desirable than the results of any probable or attainable alternative method of price determination is still a matter of acute controversy.

The relative inflexibility of industrial prices during a downturn of business activity, to take another example, has been demonstrated beyond the possibility of doubt. Moreover, there would probably be general agreement to the proposition that a greater responsiveness of some prices to a decline in costs and volume of sales would contribute to the stability of employment and output. But when it comes to a specification of what prices should decline, in what manner, by how much, and within what limits appropriate government action can be expected to accomplish this result, the record is relatively blank.

Until recently public policy in this country has not been concerned with non-predatory price policies of independent firms outside the public utility field. The antitrust acts have been enforced against agreements destroying the independence of firms in the field of price and other policies. They have also been enforced against price policies — particularly price discrimination — designed to drive rivals from the field or to prevent the entry of potential competitors. With respect, however, to price policies independently determined within the framework of the existing structure, of industrial markets the administration of the antitrust acts has been conspicuously silent.

Recent legislation has set off certain areas within which price policies and price behavior have been recognized as the concern of public policy. The NRA offered a striking, though temporary, example. Of more permanent significance has been government action with respect to agricultural commodities, coal, oil, and sugar. It is interesting to note that public policy in these areas has induced price increases either by means of or accompanied by restriction of output. Presumably the problem primarily presented in other economic areas is not one to be met by facilitating restriction of output and price increases but rather the reverse. Consequently, recent legislation does not throw much light on the question of devising tests of desirable and undesirable price behavior encountered in the industrial sector.

The President's message on monopolies offers the suggestion that certain techniques of price-making or types of price behavior might be accepted as prima facie evidence of violation of the antitrust acts. The implementing of this suggestion either by means of additional legislation or reinterpretation of the antitrust acts would definitely represent a change of public action in the field of business price policies. The extent of this change, however, would vary markedly, depending on which one of two quite different meanings is implied. Certain pricing techniques or types of price behavior might be accepted as prima facie evidence of collusion or lack of independence on the part of buyers or sellers. The existence of identical bids, rotating bids, basing-point practices, and others may serve as examples. If these and other pricing techniques are to be accepted as prima facie evidence of an absence of free competition or of independent competitive action, the scope of the antitrust acts is, to be sure, extended. But the extension is along traditional lines as respects both the nature of the evil to be corrected and the remedies to be applied. The evil is still conceived to be an interference with the independence of rivals in what would otherwise be a more freely competitive market. The remedies would still consist in eliminating the interfering practice, thus restoring the independence of rival firms.

Another interpretation, however, is possible. Among the examples of undesirable price behavior cited in the President's message is price inflexibility or rigidity. While price stabilization and other questionable policies *may* be the result of practices which fall within the existing — or an expanded — meaning of the antitrust acts, this is by no means necessarily so. In markets in which firms enjoy some degree of price control — and this embraces practically all markets outside of the agricultural sector — price stabilization and other questionable policies may represent merely the attempt of independent firms to pursue their advantage within the existing framework of the market. In such a situation price becomes a matter of policy. Instead of pursuing economic advantage within the limits of an existing price system firms are typically in a position to influence directly — or indirectly through various forms of non-price competition — the price of the product they buy and sell.

If, now, price behavior is to become the concern of public policy directly, rather than merely as evidence of the existence of practices violative of the antitrust acts, as traditionally interpreted, either tests of desirable (or undesirable) types of price behavior or price policy of a somewhat novel sort will have to be devised. Neither the evils to be remedied nor the remedies to be applied fall completely within that conception of the monopoly problem embraced by the antitrust acts.

Section II of this paper presents an attempt to analyze public policy issues in the field of prices. It should be emphasized at this point that a useful examination of the desirability or undesirability of particular types of price behavior or policies cannot proceed by means of a study of prices alone. A consideration merely of differences in the behavior of a large number of price series over a period of time reveals little data of use either for the diagnosis of economic ills or for public policy prescription. In the first place, price, as a sum of money changing hands in connection with a purchase or sale, is only one of many items indicative of the terms on which the buyer acquires or the seller releases the commodity in question. Competition in the markets for fabricated products exhibits a continually increasing emphasis on non-price forms. Discounts, free deals, product changes, selling outlays not only change the inducements to purchase and sell but affect, in many cases drastically, the terms on which commodities change hands. An analysis of price behavior which took no account of changes in non-price terms of purchase and sale would, in the case of many products, be of questionable utility.

Secondly, even if all non-price terms could be reduced to price terms — which for many products is impossible — a study of price behavior alone would be unlikely to yield results of value for policy formation. The determination of price takes place within the limits of forces which lie outside the price-maker's control. An increase in wage rates or the price of materials imposes certain conditions on a seller which must be taken into account in the pricing of his product. A judgment on his price policy, therefore, cannot be formulated without an understanding of the limitations, and changes in the limitations, within which he operates. A price, for example, which is insensitive by any of the current measures of prices change, may be sensitive with respect to changes in the conditions which a business man must take into account. In other words, the formulation of an opinion on the relative desirability of a specific example of price behavior requires an intensive examination of costs, demand, and other conditions in the market.

A consideration of the forces lying outside a price-maker's control impels a final cautionary observation. This paper deals primarily with business price policies as reflected mainly in the movements of prices at wholesale. These data, needless to say, form only a part of the total cost-price structure. Another important part of that structure is made up of the prices of services, particularly wage rates. It is not a function of this paper to deal with the consequences of the behavior of wage rates for the functioning of the economy. It is perhaps unnecessary to emphasize that these consequences may be important. A change in wage rates involves a change in the cost conditions under which firms operate which almost necessarily produces a change in the prices of products. In 1937–38, to take an example, the prices of a number of agricultural implements increased to a level considerably above the prices for these articles in 1929. A judgment, however, as to the desirability or undesirability of these price changes is impossible without a consideration of the fact that hourly wage rates in this industry increased to from 25 to 50 per cent above their 1929 level.

To an examination of the possible consequences of price policies and price behavior for the functioning of the economy we now turn.

II

ISSUES IN THE FIELD OF PRICE POLICIES

The price policies of business firms influence in important ways the structure and behavior of prices. The structure and behavior of prices in turn have serious consequences for the functioning of the economy. The purpose of this section is twofold: on the one hand, to indicate the broad issues in the area of the relation of price behavior to the functioning of the economy, and, on the other, to focus attention on certain problems in this area which appear amenable to investigation.

The joint resolution creating the Temporary National Economic Committee defines in a general way the scope of the problem. The Committee is to investigate "the effect of the existing price system and the price policies of industry upon the general level of trade, upon employment, upon long term profits, and upon consumption." These agenda may be conveniently grouped, for purpose of discussion, into the effects of the existing price system and price policies upon (1) efficiency in the use of economic resources and (2) the distribution of the national income among the various participants in the process of production. A consideration of price policies in relation to the "general level of trade" and "employment" emphasizes the existence of recurring or continuing unemployment of labor and capital which is an important manifestation of inefficiency in the use of resources. The effects of the price system and price policies on profits is a part of the consequences of this system and these policies for the distribution of income. Their effects upon consumption are in part to be discovered by way of an examination of the distribution of the national income, in part through a consideration of other aspects of the problem of efficiency. This section is limited to a consideration of some aspects of the relation of price policies to economic efficiency.

PRICES AND EFFICIENCY

The term "efficiency" in general implies a skillful use of given means to achieve given ends. In the economic area the means are the available supplies of human abilities, the material, and the natural resources seeking employment. The end is the greatest possible satisfaction of human wants for the products and services which can be produced by these resources within the general limitations imposed by existing social and economic institutions. An approximation to this objective requires a fairly continuous, full employment of the available resources in ways which yield high productivity. Granted that the productivity of resources already employed is not adversely affected thereby, any policy which puts to work unemployed resources increases the efficiency of the economic system as a whole. Granted further that total employment is not adversely affected, any policy which facilitates a transfer of resources from less to more productive uses increases efficiency. This distinction between the productivity associated with a given rate of employment and fluctuations in this rate suggests that the problems revolving around the relation of price policies and price behavior to efficiency may well be divided into two groups. One group of problems is concerned with distribution of resources as between different uses, different types and sizes of business organization, different geographical locations, and different techniques of production and marketing. The existing structure of prices influences this distribution of resources; changes in price relationships, affecting volumes of output and the disposal of new investment, slowly change the distribution of resources. Certain price policies and types of price behavior are more conducive to an efficient distribution and use of a given volume of employment of human and material resources than others. However, in the main, these policies can work out their effects only through a long-run adjustment of capital investment and a relocation of labor and material resources.

The second group of problems is concerned with changes in the rate of employment. A somewhat regular fluctuation in the rate of employment is an important characteristic of the business cycle. There is some reason for believing that certain price policies and types of price behavior are less conducive to a rapid and serious decline in the rate of employment of men and materials than others. On the other hand, it is fairly clear that the behavior of prices on the upturn has a good deal to do with whether or not a recovery will be sustained. The relation of price behavior to the rate of use of resources, however, is by no means entirely a problem of the business cycle. Events of the last decade have emphasized the possibility that serious unemployment of resources may be continuous. One of the important issues to be investigated, therefore, is the possibility of stimulating the reemployment of idle resources through a change in price policies. In fact, in the contemporary setting, this may be said to be the crucial issue.

This distinction between the effect of price policies and price behavior on the long-term distribution and organization of resources and the effect on changes in the rate of employment of existing resources is not a mutually exclusive distinction. Public action designed to influence the distribution and organization of resources would have repercussions on the rate of use. On the other hand, an attempt to increase the rate of use of resources by almost any feasible policy would have repercussions on their distribution and organization. Nevertheless, this distinction is necessary and useful in order to bring into focus the primary issues in the field of price policy.

The basing-point system of price quoting, for example, which has existed, in various forms, for a long time in the steel industry has influenced the location of basic production as well as fabricating and finishing plants. It is alleged that the present locations are not the most economical and that, furthermore, the continued existence of the basing-point system encourages a wasteful cross-hauling of products. A public policy designed to correct these alleged evils by changing the methods of pricing could only accomplish its objective through a slow adaptation of the location and organization of resources to the changed pricing system. There would undoubtedly be repercussions on the rate of utilization of equipment and man power in the steel industry. While these probabilities would have to be taken into account in the formulation of a public policy regarding the basing-point system, the main considerations have to do with long-term efficiency in organization and location.

One of the questions, to take another example, which excited controversy following the business downturn in 1937 was whether the prices of certain products, particularly construction materials, had not increased so rapidly in 1936 and 1937 as to handicap a sustained recovery. Assuming that these price increases were recognized at the time as undesirable and justifying public action, the considerations mainly involved would have to do with the possibility of stimulating by such action a continued increase in the rate of use of resources. Very possibly the appropriate policy would have long-term repercussions on the distribution of investment and the organization of resources in certain areas. These repercussions would be secondary, however, to the main considerations in question.

This distinction between the consequences of price policies and price behavior for the allocation, as against the rate of use, of resources is advisable not only because the economic issues in the two types of questions are somewhat different, but also because it is probable that the public action appropriate to dealing with these questions would be different.

Economic research has emphasized chiefly two aspects of the relation of price policies to long-term efficiency. The first has been concerned with the effects of price policy and price behavior on the allocation of economic resources, i.e., the problem of over- and under-investment; the second with the supposed waste of resources in various forms of non-price competition.

The first problem is the monopoly problem as traditionally conceived. The possession of a considerable degree of market control has been understood to permit a seller to charge a price higher than would be charged by the sellers of the same product were the market more competitive. The high price restricts the volume of sales and output, and consequently the employment of resources necessary to the production of the required volume. The unutilized resources are forced to seek employment elsewhere, with the result that overinvestment develops in the more competitive sectors of the economy. It is argued that a transfer of resources from the areas of overinvestment to the areas of underinvestment would permit a substantial increase in the national income.

The validity of this argument does not depend on the assumption that economic resources are fully employed. A transfer from less productive to more productive uses would increase the national income produced at any given level of employment. Nevertheless, if there are large amounts of unemployed resources any transfer difficulties which may be involved are probably accentuated in importance. To restrict output in the bituminous coal industry, for example, in the face of a considerable volume of unemployment elsewhere is probably a more serious step than it would be if employment were relatively full.

There can be little doubt, though the evidence is scattered and difficult to interpret, that existing over- and underinvestment have serious consequences for long-run efficiency in the use of resources. For example, if a given level of employment could be maintained, there is every reason to believe that a transfer of resources from some branches of agriculture, the bituminous coal industry, and some branches of the cotton textile industry to certain industrial sectors of the economy would increase the national income. In order to maintain this level of employment, however, the long-run price policies in these industrial sectors would have to be modified to permit an increase in sales and volumes of output. Just what these industrial sectors are and what modification of price policies would be necessary are precisely the problems, related to long-run efficiency, which have to be solved.

A comprehensive solution to the first problem would obviously require some measure of desirable investment by means of which to test the extent of over- or underinvestment in different economic uses. While the formal requirements of a desirable amount of investment can be approximately stated, no tests which are entirely satisfactory and applicable to particular situations, given the available data, have been devised. In the absence of such tests public policy is apt to resort to evidence which is fragmentary and unsatisfactory.

In the economic sectors alleged to be characterized by overinvestment the evidence usually adduced is of low prices, rapid turnover of firms, low profits and wages, the existence of unutilized capacity, and "market demoralization." In the economic sectors in which underinvestment is considered to exist, the evidence presented is of high prices, prices which fail to fall with technological improvements, high profits and returns to labor, and comparatively full utilization of capacity. Outside the public utility field direct price or output regulation has been applied in this country only to the overinvestment areas. The Bituminous Coal Act and the Agricultural Marketing Agreements Act provide for minimum prices for coal and milk. The Sugar Act and the Agricultural Adjustment Act attempt control of output.

It is obvious that public intervention in these areas is likely to be politically much more feasible than in the underinvestment, restricted output areas. Producers will accept — and frequently demand — public action designed to restrict output and raise prices, whereas action designed to expand output and investment and to reduce prices may be bitterly opposed by the interests affected. Although a good case can be made out for the restriction of output in these and other areas and the transfer of resources elsewhere, this case depends on (1) a definite limitation of the economic sector to which these remedies are applied, and (2) the adoption of policies designed to promote expansion and reëmployment elsewhere in the economic system. The standards of proper prices and output written into recent legislation certainly do not provide tests the application of which would be likely to limit restrictive policies to a small sector of the economy. Both the "parity price" of the Agricultural Adjustment and Agricultural Marketing Agreements Acts and the "average cost of production" of the Bituminous Coal Act, if applied throughout the economic system, would imply a wide expansion of restrictionist policies. One of the serious issues confronting public policy in the price field would seem to be the formulation of tests of "excessive" or "ruinous" or "cutthroat" competition sufficient to indicate the desirability of restricting output and diverting resources into other channels. The existence of prices lower than "parity prices" or than prices covering "average cost of production" provides no such test.

In the second place, restrictionist policies have not hitherto been accompanied by price and output policies designed to encourage expansion in the underinvestment sectors of the economy. Yet this is the crucial aspect, for public policy, of the relation of price policies and price behavior to long-term efficiency. To deal with this problem effectively would require tests indicative of the existence of price policies and price behavior unduly restrictive of output and investment. The tests currently applied are fragmentary and almost wholly inadequate. The Federal Trade Commission, for example, cites as partial evidence of unduly restrictive price policies the fact that the prices of certain agricultural implements did not fall as much as (or rise more than) the prices of "implements somewhat comparable to farm implements in materials and labor" in the period 1929 to 1937. The articles with which agricultural implements are compared are four-door sedan automobiles, one and a half ton trucks, gas ranges, electrical refrigerators, ice refrigerators, warm-air furnaces, and hot-water boilers. While such a comparison may suggest the necessity of further investigation into the reason for the differences in the price behavior of these articles, it can hardly be accepted of itself — nor would the Commission so claim — as evidence of undesirable price behavior.

The existence of high profits over a long period of time in an industry which is not growing rapidly may be indicative of underinvestment. On the other hand, in a rapidly expanding industry such as rayon the persistence of high profits may simply reflect a necessary and unavoidable lag of productive facilities behind an even more rapidly expanding demand. A study of profit records can provide necessary but not sufficient evidence of the existence of output and investment restriction. An examination of the degree of utilization of installed capacity may produce further relevant data. If public action in this area is contemplated, however, more comprehensive data is required. It is also clear that the formulation of satisfactory tests of restrictive price policies would necessitate a more thorough-going comparison of cost-price relationships in different industrial markets than any hitherto undertaken.

While the relation of price policies and price behavior to the over- and underinvestment of economic resources presents a serious problem, it appears unlikely that further price research will lead to immediately practical results. This does not mean that such research is useless. On the contrary, a careful investigation of the relationships of costs, prices, output, and investment in different types of industrial markets can probably contribute substantially to an understanding of the consequences of business policies for the long-term distribution of resources. But this is definitely long-term research. It is possible that effort expanded elsewhere will yield results of more immediate utility.

Before turning to these problems it is necessary to call attention to the fact that the relation of price policies to long-term efficiency embraces other questions than the under- and overinvestment of resources. Price policies reflect, and in turn influence, the organization of resources within, as well as their distribution among, different uses. Price discrimination, for example, may affect the size of buying as well as selling firms, the location of fabricating plants, and the expansion of particular kinds of distributive channels. These consequences all involve questions of long-run efficiency. Certain of these questions, such as the economic consequences of basing-point systems and of price discrimination in favor of mass distribution are in the forefront of public discussion. Here again, however, the formulation of applicable tests of what are optimum sizes of business firms, optimum locations for productive capacity, and optimum distributive channels has lagged behind the recognition of the importance of these problems.

Of more immediate importance would appear to be an examination of the possibility of further expansion of output and employment in particular industries. Such an examination is concerned with price policy only in the broadest sense. Expansion of output may require a redesigning of products, the use of different distributive channels, coöperation among producers in different industries, or a change in any of the other terms on which buyers are offered commodities or services.

In a period of full employment the expansion of a particular industry or group of industries would presumably involve a transfer of resources employed elsewhere. Whether or not such a transfer would be desirable would depend on considerations of over- and underinvestment and other aspects of long-term efficiency discussed above. In a period, however, of widespread and continuous unemployment an expansion of particular industries *may* make possible a net increase in employment with or without a considerable transfer of resources already employed. A consideration, therefore, of these possibilities would appear to offer one of the most immediately practicable opportunities to make a contribution to public policy in the field of price research.

At the present time it is generally recognized that an important factor contributing to continued unemployment is the extremely low volume of new investment. To some, the remedy appears to be government borrowing and spending to absorb the funds which, under other circumstances, have flowed through the channels of private investment. Others look for new industries to open up these channels. There is, however, no particular virtue in the newness of an industry. A continued expansion of already existing industries may serve the purpose of inducing investment and increasing employment. To encourage expansion, however, may require a change in price policies. To establish the character of the required change is, therefore, the problem.

There are certain fields in which investigation appears to promise better results than in others. One of these fields embraces a group of consumers' durable-goods industries which have provided large and, until recently, increasing opportunities for investment and employment. These industries, in their process of development, exhibit striking similarities. A period of rapid expansion of output accompanied by product improvement and price reduction has been followed by a flattening of the growth curve. For many of these industries the demand has become almost entirely a replacement demand and, since replacement may be postponed, an exceedingly fluctuating one. While, for certain of the products involved, families in the upper income levels are almost completely equipped, this becomes progressively less true in the lower income groups. Obviously, if these industries are to enjoy an additional period of expansion, ways must be found to carry sales into the lower income groups.

For some of these products, notably electrical equipment, the relevant price is the price per unit of service, which is affected not only by the price at installation but by the durability of the product, the cost of servicing, and the price of electric current. For others the relevant price is the difference between the price of a new article and the turn-in value of a used one, and conditions in the secondhand market clearly have repercussions on the volume of sales of new products. For others a continued expansion in sales may involve a redesigning of the product to meet new needs, the provision of adequate consumer financing, or the exploration of new channels of distribution. A thoroughgoing examination of the possibilities of continued expansion for this group of industries may make an important contribution to employment.

A second fruitful field of investigation seems to be indicated by recent experience in the field of electric power consumption. Some evidence, particularly in the Tennessee Valley area, suggests that electrical companies habitually underestimate the elasticity of the demand for their product in domestic consumption. In those cases in which a substantial rate reduction would lead to so large an increase in sales as to increase — or at least not substantially reduce — net revenue, such a reduction is clearly desirable. An expansion of output and, subsequently, of investment in this important industry may make possible a substantial increase in employment. The whole field of public utility industries is peculiarly adapted to studies of demand elasticity both by reason of the fact that the product sold is a relatively standard unit of service and because the areas of sale for individual producers are isolated. The existence of public regulation in this field, furthermore, makes it easier than elsewhere to put the results of such investigations into practice.

A third field of investigation is presented by the construction industries. The demand for construction represents a joint demand for a wide variety of materials and labor and contracting services. A substantial reduction in the prices of particular materials or labor services involves a relatively small reduction, at best, in the cost of construction. It is therefore not within the power of suppliers of particular materials or services to stimulate the demand for construction even by drastic price reductions. By reason of the complementary character of materials and services, these suppliers are faced with demands which are highly inelastic. The inelasticity, however, is in large part the result of the way economic resources are organized in this branch of industry. A substantial change in the organization might produce substantially different results. The extent to which certain fabricators of construction materials are experimenting in the field of construction indicates some of the possibilities. A study of the probable effects of simultaneous changes in materials prices and wage rates on the cost of construction is clearly a fruitful field of price research. It may serve to indicate those areas in which price reductions are likely to prove of greatest assistance in stimulating expansion in the construction industries.

The examples just cited are representative of a type of problem to which it is believed price research, broadly understood, can make a practical contribution. A change in price policies in these or other industries leading to an expansion of sales and output could, under certain circumstances, induce a substantial net increase in employment. An increase in output of a particular product, not accompanied by an increase in investment, and leading merely to a diversion of consumer spending from other products to the one in question, would not, of course, be likely to produce such a result. The volume of consumer spending involved in questions of this sort cannot be accepted, however, as fixed. A change in the terms on which a product is offered may lead to an increase in consumer spending, and, if the increase in output produces an increase in net investment, it will lead to an increase in consumer incomes.

A concentration of attention on the possibilities of output expansion through a change in pricing or market policies does not mean that other aspects of the relation of price policy and price behavior to long-run efficiency should be neglected. It has always been recognized, considering the structure of prices as a whole, including the prices of labor and other factors of production, that appropriate price adjustment may increase employment and promote a more efficient utilization of economic resources. Price research has not been particularly successful to date in suggesting standards of appropriate price adjustment. There are, furthermore, political and economic obstacles to some types of price adjustment which may make the application of such standards impracticable. Nevertheless there clearly remains an important area within which price research may make an effective contribution to a public policy.

NON-PRICE COMPETITION

A second broad aspect of the relation of price policies and price behavior to long-term efficiency on which attention has traditionally centered has to do with the increasingly important phenomena of non-price competition. Business firms not only pursue their advantage by adjusting prices to the existing market situation; they also attempt to increase their sales and improve their position in the market by changing their products, their location, by advertising and selling expenditures, and in other ways. The whole group of business policies designed to increase the sales of a firm within a given price range may be roughly designated non-price competition. It is clear not only that the character and importance of non-price competition affects the significance of price as an expression of the conditions on which sellers dispose of and buyers acquire products but also that the price policies of a firm are only a part, and are closely influenced by other aspects, of the firm's sales policy.

Certain types of non-price competition are presumably desirable; others are, prima facie, wasteful. To the extent that waste may be involved, it is not usually the result of restrictionist policies designed to exploit an existing market control position. On the contrary, the fields in which the prima facie case for the existence of wasteful non-price competition is strongest are frequently industries and markets in which the competing firms are small and the rivalry between them intense. This rivalry, however, may involve large expenditures in ways that make no commensurate contribution to the satisfaction of consumers' wants. Large expenditures, for example, on the advertisement of various cosmetic and drug preparations may represent a very considerable waste of resources.

Non-price competition offers means by which a seller can augment his price control and lessen the rigor of direct price competition. He accomplishes this objective by differentiating his product from that of his immediate rivals. In a market for a graded product, such as No. 2 northern wheat, where the units offered for sale by one seller are perfectly substitutable for those of another, such competition for business as exists must take the form of direct price competition. If it were possible for a seller to offer a superior quality of wheat, or to convince buyers that his product was superior, he would be in position to command a price differential and to influence the size of that differential by varying the quantity of his product offered for sale. This is substantially what happens in markets for other than graded products.

With respect to the *seller's* interest, it makes no difference whether price control is secured by means of a given expenditure on product improvement or by a similar expenditure devoted to persuading buyers that a nonexistent difference is real. Clearly, however, the bearing of these two types of expenditure on the *public* interest is different.

Whether sellers will resort to efficient or wasteful types of non-price competition will depend largely on the knowledge of the product possessed or obtainable by buyers. Business buyers are, in general, well informed and frequently buy only upon specification and testing. Consumers, on the other hand, in a wide variety of products are unable to form an accurate impression of relative merits and demerits. Consequently an important and observable difference exists between the methods of non-price competition in the producers' goods and in the consumers' goods areas. In the former area competition, in general, is on the basis of quality, accuracy of specification fulfillment, servicing, speed and assurance of delivery, and, of course, price. Advertising expenditures are usually relatively small, and selling activity is frequently associated with technical advice and servicing. In the latter field advertising expenditures are frequently considerable. Packaging and style factors are important, and brand names loom large. This does not mean, of course, that these types of non-price competition are necessarily wasteful.

The economic opportunities offered by various types of non-price competition may lead to the entry into different markets of large numbers of small high-cost firms, each owing its existence to its ability to attract a group of customers who prefer its product to the closely similar product of rival sellers. Small retail grocery stores scattered over an urban area may offer a trading convenience to the immediately surrounding public which permits them a higher price than that charged by their larger low-cost downtown competitors. The proliferation of gasoline stations seems to have been induced by consumers' preference for particular brands. While one station at a given street intersection might be operated more efficiently than the two or three or four among whom the business is actually divided, the competition between brand names encourages this division.

Although the possibilities of product differentiation may, in these and other cases, encourage the establishment of small high-cost firms, in other situations non-price competition may make the entry of new firms extremely difficult. For many products consumers are highly brand-conscious. A branded and nationally advertised product usually sells at a higher price than unbranded products of similar grade and quality. It is safe to say that in the cigarette and gasoline markets, for example, it is extremely difficult for a new firm to achieve consumer acceptance no matter what the quality of its product.

It is clear that if consumers were able accurately to judge the merits and serviceability of competing products, and utilized this knowledge in economically rational choices, price differences would more closely reflect quality differences than in fact they do. However, with the enormous increase in the number, variety, and importance of synthetic and highly fabricated products, for which the ingenuity of American enterprise has been responsible, an acquisition of the required degree of knowledge is difficult, if not impossible. Consumers' ignorance has opened up a wide field of economic opportunity for methods of non-price competition of dubious merit.

An attempt has been made to grapple with the problem of wasteful versus useful non-price competition by making a distinction between "rational" and "irrational" consumers' preference.

Irrationality . . . is to be detected by imagining that each consumer is forcibly removed from the firm with which he is accustomed to deal to some other firm which meets the same want at a cost which, according to the general consensus of the market, is the same as that incurred hitherto. [The market organization] . . . is irrational to the extent that the consumer suffers no loss of satisfaction as a consequence of such diversion.

[The market organization] . . . is purely rational if it takes its basis in preferences which correspond to real satisfactions. Insofar as the forcible transfer of a consumer from one firm to another has no effect on his scale of preferences for the products of the different firms, the imperfection of the market may be said to be rational.[4]

[4] R. F. Kahn, "Some Notes on Ideal Output," *Economic Journal*, March 1935, p. 26.

While such a distinction may serve to clarify thought regarding the issue involved, it seems clear that it neither offers tests which can be applied directly nor suggests factual investigation likely to lead to the formulation of such tests. Investigation relevant to public policy in this area must take account of two aspects of the problem: (1) the relation of non-price competition to the behavior of prices, and (2) the effect of non-price competition on the costs of production of, and the quality changes in, the commodities in question. The first type of study is concerned with the effect of non-price competition (or some aspects of it) on the price terms on which buyers acquire goods. The second is concerned with the probable effects of the elimination of some kinds of non-price competition on the costs of producing these commodities.

A study of some aspects of the first question seems to show that for many consumers' products buyers are highly brand-conscious, and that the prices of a number of branded products respond less readily to cost reductions than the prices of similar, though un-branded, products. It is probably fair to conclude from this and other evidence that branding and advertising a product permits the seller to escape from some of the rigor of price competition. This type of study could be fruitfully pushed much further. An examination of the consequences of various types of non-price competition on the behavior of prices not only may illuminate the varying significance of price in different markets, as one of the conditions of sale, but it is also one essential avenue of approach to the problem of wasteful versus useful methods of competition.

The second type of study is more difficult but also more important for the question at issue. On the condition that certain types of non-price competition were eliminated or regulated, what would be the probable effect on the cost of producing the commodity in question? How much, for example, would the elimination of contiguous gasoline stations and the consolidation of business in the hands of fewer units be likely to reduce the cost of distributing gasoline? The grading of gasoline would presumably reduce the importance of brands in determining consumers' preference and consequently the incentives of refiners and distributors to advertise and to place new service stations close to already existing stations. An estimate of the probable savings is relevant to public policy on the grading of this and other products. Equally relevant is the question whether such savings would be apt to be passed on in the form of lower prices to consumers.

What effects, to take another example, would a limitation on advertising expenditures in particular fields be likely to have on the volume of sales of the goods in question, the distribution of these sales between existing firms, and the costs to the sellers of producing and distributing the commodities? Such questions are extraordinarily difficult to answer, but they lie at the bottom of the question of the waste of economic resources in non-price competition.

PRICE BEHAVIOR IN RELATION TO EMPLOYMENT AND OUTPUT

Business price policies not only influence the direction of investment of fixed capital, the location of labor resources, and other aspects of the long-term pattern of industrial organization; price policies also presumably influence the rate of employment of labor and capital. Large and fairly regular fluctuations in the rate of employment are characteristic of the business cycle and an important aspect of the problem of economic efficiency.

Recent studies of cyclical price behavior have directed attention to price-stabilization policies as evidenced particularly by the relative inflexibility of industrial prices on the downturn. It is alleged that the failure of industrial prices to adjust to changes in material and labor costs and to changes in demand intensifies and prolongs depression and retards recovery. The role of price policies in the upswing is at least as important an aspect of the relation of price behavior to cyclical fluctuations in employment, although it has been relatively neglected. It should be noted in this connection that prices which are inflexible on the downturn may be flexible on the upturn. The prices of a number of building materials, iron and steel products, and agricultural implements, to mention no others, moved downward very little between 1929 and 1932 but moved upward fairly freely in the period 1934–1937.

The price data primarily utilized in studies of price inflexibility are commodity prices at wholesale. These prices form only one sector of a system of prices which includes wage rates, building and land rents, retail prices, public utility and railway rates, interest charges, and other prices. Obviously the effects on the rate of employment of greater or less flexibility of commodity prices will be different from the effects of greater or less flexibility in the price system as a whole.

In considering questions involving the influence of a continuing pattern of price relationships on the allocation and use of economic resources the repercussions of price changes on total money income and spending have been, and can be, neglected. These repercussions, however, become the center of the problem as soon as attention is directed to the relationship of price behavior to changes in employment and output in the economy as a whole. Most discussions of price policies in recession and recovery have neglected this fact. It has been too easily assumed that total money income is independent of a change in prices and wage rates, and that consequently any reduction in prices or wage rates will necessarily increase total employment, since it reduces the costs of some of the commodities or services for which this given money income is spent.

A recognition of the interdependence of prices, costs, and money incomes focuses attention on the necessity of examining the effect of given price changes on total money incomes and spending. A price reduction may increase total employment if it leads (1) to the spending of a larger share of existing money incomes; (2) to a transfer of income from income hoarders to income spenders; or (3) to an increase in money incomes through an increase in investment. If it leads merely to a transfer of a given volume of spending from certain commodities to others, it may produce no change in total employment, although a shift in spending from commodities produced at a low ratio of labor to total costs to commodities produced at a high ratio may increase the employment of labor at the expense of other factors.

If attention is focused on industrial price policies — i.e., on the behavior of the prices of manufactured products at wholesale — it must be recognized that the relative inflexibility of prices other than wholesale commodity prices constitutes, on the one hand, a limitation on the possibility of change in wholesale prices and, on the other, a limitation of the probable effect of increased price flexibility on the rate of employment and volume of output. Within these limitations the questions at issue are (1) what types of price policy and price behavior are likely to lessen the decline in rate of employment on the downturn from prosperity to depression, and (2) what types of price policy and price behavior are conducive to sustained recovery.

Contemporary discussion has defined the issue in this area as the consequences for output and employment of the relative inflexibility of industrial prices. The measures of price inflexibility which have been used are measures of frequency, amplitude, and timing of price change, and not of the responsiveness of price to changes in cost and demand conditions. Yet it must be admitted that it is the lack of responsiveness of price to changes in these conditions rather than "inflexibility" as such which has significance for the functioning of the economic system.

Mere measures of price change may nevertheless yield a roughly accurate indication of relative price responsiveness in a downturn from prosperity to depression, since in such a period nearly all commodities are subject to the same sort of change in cost and demand conditions. The wage rates and material costs relevant to the production of one commodity will fall by a smaller percentage than those relevant to the production of another, but they will fall for both. The demand for one product will decline further than another, but they will both decline. Under these circumstances a price which changes infrequently or by a small percentage or which turns down later is, prima facie, a price which is insensitive in the proper sense of the word. If it is inflexible by all these tests the case is strengthened. To proceed beyond this to a measurement of the relative responsiveness of prices would require an examination of the behavior of the material prices and wage rates relevant to the production of different commodities.

It would probably be wise, in such an examination, to distinguish between commodities with respect to which price inflexibility is accompanied by large expenditures on non-price competition and those for which this is not true. The prices of many consumers' goods items — for example, wearing apparel sold at definite price lines — are inflexible, but producers compete avidly for business by product changes, changes in packaging, free deals, and in many other ways. The real problem of price inflexibility lies mainly in the field of producers' materials where fewness of sellers makes possible price stabilization policies unaccompanied by extensive non-price competition. In these fields a closer examination of the relation of material prices and wage rates to the price of the products will throw much needed light on the relative insensitivity of industrial prices.

Given the needed information on the relation of costs to prices, there remains a question that is central to public policy in this area: How sensitive should prices be to a cyclical decline in costs if price behavior is to facilitate the economic adjustments necessary to recovery? This problem is usually envisaged in terms of the price and output relations of individual products. The question is put: How much would the sales of a given product increase if the price were reduced by a given amount? The problem of price insensitivity on the downturn is, however, much broader than this. A price reduction is likely to affect the money incomes of the selling and buying groups, and consequently is likely to have repercussions on other prices and quantities. Furthermore, an isolated price reduction, other prices remaining insensitive, will have a different effect on the sales of the product concerned than if many prices are reduced.

Studies of the relation of price inflexibility to output changes on the downturn from 1929 to 1932 have led to the conclusion that, in general, outputs of those commodities fell least whose prices fell most, although there are many exceptions to this generalization. It is clear, however, that a distinction should be made between commodities for which demand is postponable and those for which it is not. With a marked decline in spending, the sales of the first type of product will probably decline regardless of price; the sales of the second are likely to be well maintained regardless of price.

Commodities for which demands are postponable are luxury goods, products where purchase requires a large initial expenditure, products whose life in use is subject to considerable extension. In general these commodities belong in the class of durable goods. If a distinction is made between durable and non-durable goods, the relationship between price changes and quantity changes is likely to be much more illuminating than if all products are lumped together for the purpose of such an analysis.

The sales of durable goods fall markedly on the downturn, principally for two reasons. In the first place, the rate of use of these goods can frequently be continued for some time without replacement. The rate of use of automobiles as measured by gasoline consumption or car registration fell very little from 1929 to 1932, though new car sales fell violently. The rate of use of houses as measured by occupancy remained practically stable, while new construction sank nearly to zero. Secondly, and as a result principally of the extensibility of use, replacement may be delayed in expectation of price declines. It is this speculative aspect of the demand for durable goods which has led some observers to question the efficacy of price reductions as a stimulus to further sales during the downturn. Certainly it behooves both business and government to consider the effect of the way price is cut on the volume of sales. It is quite possible that, while a crumbling price will lead buyers to withhold purchases, sharp and sizeable price reductions, effectively timed, would have the opposite effect.

More important than the manner of price decline is an investigation of the probable consequences on volumes of output and employment of simultaneous price reductions for a number of products. A reduction of the prices of electrical appliances, electrical rates, and installation costs would probably have a very different effect on sales of electrical equipment even during a downturn than a reduction in equipment prices alone. A common reduction in building material prices, contracting charges, and building-labor wage rates would probably produce very different results in the housing field than a reduction in the price of one or a few materials.

If an objective of public policy is the facilitating on the downturn of those price adjustments necessary to early recovery, it will probably be found that certain prices and price relationships are much more important with respect to this objective than others. Interest rates belong in this category, and it may plausibly be argued that a reduction in the prices of captial goods may have the same effect of increasing the prospective yield on new capital investment as a reduction in the rate of interest. At the present time, however, it must be said that this problem has not been investigated with sufficient thoroughness to permit conclusions. It stands as one of the important questions requiring further examination.

Finally, a public policy designed to promote greater price flexibility on the downturn will have repercussions on the flow of income and expenditure. These repercussions in turn affect the volume of output and employment. A consideration, therefore, of the probable influence of price changes on hoarding and spending is a part of the problem of price inflexibility.

In conclusion it may be said that, while readjustments in the price system form one of the conditions necessary to recovery, this is by no means the only condition. Studies of price inflexibility have thrown some light on types of price behavior which presumably handicap the attainment of this condition. Nevertheless, these studies must be pushed much further, and more attention must be paid to the relative responsiveness of the prices of particular commodities and services to changes in costs.

The question of what price policies and types of price behavior are conducive to a sustained recovery, and particularly what types are not, was undoubtedly one of the most important price policy issues broached in the discussions preliminary to the creation of the Temporary National Economic Committee. The view was widely held in Washington and elsewhere that the rapid rise in a number of industrial prices had an important effect in terminating recovery. It was the opinion of the President's Committee on Prices

that a sharp rise in prices encouraged speculative inventory buying which, combined with the decline in housing construction, laid much of the ground for the present recession. We must do everything we can to prevent this from happening again.[5]

The question what price policies are conducive to sustained recovery is not limited exclusively to a period of cyclical upswing, nor does it relate exclusively to reëmployment induced by business spending. The effect on employment and output of any net increase in spending, public or private, will probably be affected by the way prices respond to this increase. Here again, as on the downswing, the question of the relation of price changes to the rate of employment is different if all prices are considered than if attention is limited to the field of commodity prices at wholesale.

If attention is so limited, it must be recognized that business firms are confronted with a price system in which many prices relevant to their costs and to the character of the demand for their product are largely outside their own control. In such circumstances a judgment on the effect of business price policies on recovery must take account of the area within which changes in price policies are both possible and likely to influence spending. For many consumers' goods — notably cotton textiles — the relative rigidity of retail prices means that considerable variation can take place in wholesale prices with no

[5] Press Release, February 18, 1938.

effect on volume of consumer sales. The rapid increase in hourly wages from November 1936 to June 1937 — though earnings are by no means identical with labor costs — is obviously relevant to a judgment on the increase in prices of manufactured products during the same period.

Although the question of price policies proper to sustained recovery

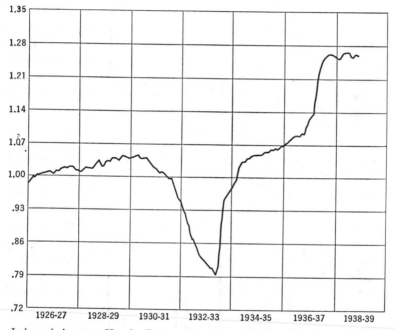

Index of Average Hourly Factory Earnings, All Wage Earners, in 25 Industries, 1926–1938 (1926 = 100). Source: National Industrial Conference Board.

has occupied a prominent place in public discussion, it must be recognized that the issues have not been very satisfactorily formulated, nor have standards of proper price policies been forthcoming. Some price increases are presumably necessary to overcome resistances to increased volumes of output. Increases in wage rates and material prices must be largely passed on in increased prices of the product if business firms are to have an incentive to produce. Over and above increases in hourly wage rates and material prices, some increase in costs may be involved in more intensive utilization of fixed plant and equipment, though at rates of utilization common in recent years in most American industries this is probably small. Large and sustained price increases over and above those necessary to overcome such resistances are impossible without some considerable degree of market control. It is probable that a study of changes in the relationship of material prices and wage rates to prices of products may reveal at least the more obvious cases in which price increases are the result of market control positions.

Although the case is by no means conclusive, there is a strong presumption that prices which increase faster than is necessitated by the increase in wages and material costs handicap a sustained recovery. Such increases may well lead to a larger speculative inventory accumulation of materials and finished products than would accompany a slower price increase. On the other hand, the release of a potential demand for particular durable goods created by depreciation, during depression years, of plant, equipment, and housing may be indefinitely postponed by too rapid an increase in the prices of these goods. Furthermore, the exploitation of a temporarily favorable market situation by price increases may lead to the building-up of cash reserves which remain uninvested in the absence of expectations which only a sustained recovery would justify.

There is some evidence that business firms in 1936 and 1937 took an excessively short-run view of recovery and pursued price policies designated to produce maximum temporary profits. In many cases, undoubtedly, such policies were the result of a financial position weakened by years of persistent losses. In any case, it seems probable that price policies pursued in expectation of short-run recovery had something to do with making the recovery, in fact, short-run.

SUMMARY

The price system, or cost-price structure, is one indicator of the conditions on which producers and consumers engage in economic activity. In an economy in which no buyer or seller was able to influence prices, producers and consumers could scarcely be said to have a policy respecting price. Outside the markets for agricultural products and — on the buyers' side — the markets for consumers' goods, however, some ability to influence price is an almost universal characteristic of selling, if not buying, activity. Although the area within which prices may be influenced by individual buyers and sellers differs widely from market to market, the existence in all markets of this area of discretion creates the possibility of a policy with respect to price.

The attempts of sellers and buyers to seek their advantage by adjusting and controlling prices influences the behavior of prices in ways that are of consequence for the functioning of the economy. Not only is the distribution of resources between various uses, and of income streams as between the different groups of income recipients, influenced, but also the rate at which resources are utilized. In consequence, business price policies become a matter of public concern. It does not, of course, follow that all price policies should become the object of governmental action; still less does it follow that government should take action designed to make the formulation of price policy impossible.

Outside of the field of public utilities, price behavior has not been considered, until recently, of direct public concern. Implicit in the legislation and interpretation of the antitrust acts has been the conception that the price adjustments of individual firms independently determined under conditions of free and fair competition require no public scrutiny. The acceptance of various types of pricing techniques as prima facie evidence of violation of the antitrust acts, while involving a broadened interpretation, is perfectly compatible with this conception. On the other hand, if the behavior of prices is to be examined with respect to its consequences for the functioning of the economy rather than as evidence of the existence or nonexistence of a state of free competition in the market, other standards of judgment are involved.

Very little progress has been made as yet in the formulation of such standards. At the present junction what seems to be needed is a clearer formulation of the issues and a direction of attention to those problems which appear amenable to investigation. It is to these questions that the foregoing discussion has been directed.

8

Competition, Price Policy, and High-Level Stability[1]

It seems necessary, at the outset, to devote a certain amount of attention to the meaning of high-level stability in the American economy. I take it for granted that stability does not mean absence of change. The economy is stable in terms of output and employment if output and employment in the expanding industries and areas are about sufficient to absorb resources released by the contracting industries and areas. In this sense of the term the American economy, over the last year or so, has presented a remarkable example of high-level stability. Employment has declined in certain industries geared to war production and, more recently, in a limited number of nondurable goods industries, but the workers there released have been absorbed into employment elsewhere in the economy in remarkably effective fashion. The economy while highly dynamic has succeeded in maintaining a very high level of output and employment. The much advertised recession, which was just around the corner, has either come and gone or is still around the corner.

During this same period, however, we have witnessed a drastic increase in prices and the end is not yet in sight. Since January 1946 the level of wholesale prices has risen by more than 40 per cent, and the cost of living by more than 20 per cent. This represents a serious degree of inflation by comparison with any period of similar length in the past history of the United States. Organized labor and those dependent on profits can more or less protect themselves against this situation by successive rounds of wage and price increases. Nor is this process likely to degenerate into a galloping sort of inflation largely because there exists in the economy a very sizeable group of people who are dependent on relatively fixed income whose response will be to tighten their belts and reduce their consumption. It can be

[1] Reprinted from *Pricing Problems and the Stabilization of Prosperity*, Second 1947 Economic Institute, Chamber of Commerce of the United States, Washington, 1947.

argued, furthermore, that there are certain advantages to be found in this increase in prices; it reduces the burden of the national debt and the incomes going to an unproductive rentier class in society. On the other hand a continuation of this process is likely to be accompanied by a breakdown of some pretty fundamental institutions and services in this country. Municipal services in particular but also federal and state services are already in a bad state from the loss of effective personnel and the situation is going to get worse. The educational system of the country is already far gone in the process of disintegration and it is going to take a long time to build it up again.

All in all I do not believe, despite the fact that employment and output have been high, that we can describe conditions of the past year or so as high-level stability. Stability is not compatible to my mind with a 25–30 per cent per annum increase in wholesale prices.

Employment and output have been high despite a very substantial shift in demand among the products of various industries because the American economy as a whole has been confronted with a very large volume of effective demand for its products. It may be taken for granted that a high level of employment and output can be maintained if effective demand is maintained. Furthermore we have been told by the past generation of writers of fiscal policy just how we need to go about it to maintain effective demand. Unfortunately these same writers have not told us how, while maintaining that demand necessary to the full employment of resources, we can also maintain some stability of wage rates and prices.

They have, it is true, recognized the existence of a problem but they have usually shrugged it off with more or less serious admonitions to business and to labor to exercise discretion and good judgment. It is by now clear, as it should have been clear earlier, that price and wage levels are not going to be stabilized by the self-restraint of business or of organized labor. As long as the economy is confronted by the volume of effective demand that is deemed necessary for the maintenance of full employment we can be nearly certain that, in the absence of price and wage controls, we shall have inflation. On the other hand if effective demand is not maintained we can be equally certain that high-level stability of employment and output will not be maintained. This is about where the problem stands now. Without an adequate counter-cyclical fiscal program high-level stability of output and employment is unlikely. With an adequate fiscal program a free market economy seems inevitably to generate strong inflationary pressures.

DIFFERENT PRICES SHOW DIFFERENT TYPES OF BEHAVIOR

Turning now to the second term in the subject assigned to me, i.e., price policy, I should like to consider the behavior of different prices in the price system as the economy approaches high levels of employment and output. The thesis I want to defend, at the risk of considerable oversimplification, is that wage rates and competitively determined prices are the dynamic price elements which drag along in their wake, but sluggishly and slowly, the prices of products produced in highly concentrated industrial markets. Needless to say, the relative stability of industrial prices is not to any large extent to be attributed to the superior moral character or even the superior wisdom of those who determine these prices. The explanation of differences in price behavior and in price policies is to be found mainly in the differences of structure of different product and service markets. As far as motives are concerned I assume that when business firms see an opportunity for profit they take it and that when labor union leaders see another dollar in the till their thoughts turn to wage rate increases. When these motives are converted into action the effect on prices and wages will depend mainly on the market structure within which this action takes place.

It should require no extended argument to demonstrate, nor statistical material to illustrate, the fact that the prices of industrial products are relatively stable. This is, of course, as true of the downswing of the cycle as it is of the upswing. Here we are concerned with the behavior of prices in the present period of more than full employment. It is not the prices of iron and steel, petroleum products, heavy chemicals, aluminum, glass or other items produced in the highly concentrated industrial sectors of the economy that have led the way in the present upswing of prices but rather grains, poultry and dairy products, textile fabrics, lumber and other items produced in what we are accustomed to call competitive markets. It is not the prices of motor cars as sold by the "big three" that have soared out of sight but rather the prices of so-called used cars sold on more competitive markets. And when the output of the concentrated industries has risen in price the cause of the rise in price is, as likely as not, to be found in substantial wage rate increases.

This phenomenon was, of course, familiar during the war period as well as after. It was the large scale enterprises of the country that gave least difficulty to price control authorities and the highly competitive industries that gave most difficulty. Whatever the nature of the monopoly problem at other times and places, at this particular junction of incipient inflation public authorities should thank heaven for a substantial degree of concentration in the American economy.

THE DYNAMIC ROLE OF "SMALL-ENTERPRISE" PRICES AND WAGE RATES

Now why is it that the prices of goods in the heavily concentrated industrial sector of the economy are relatively stable or inflexible both in the upswing and the downswing of the cycle? It would be impossible to answer this question in satisfactory fashion without examining the structure of particular industrial markets but there are certain characteristics common to all or most of the industries here under consideration that go far toward explaining this phenomenon. Among these characteristics I should consider the following to have special importance: the tendency of variable costs per unit of output to be stable with respect to changes in the volume of output; the existence of possibilities of expanding sales through advertising or product changes without resort to price inducements; price policies which of necessity take account of the probable price reaction of rival firms; a traditional concern with antitrust policy which forms part of the peculiar sensitiveness of large firms to adverse public reaction.

If you will permit this oversimplification, what we may think of as a typical industrial market situation is one in which three or four large firms account for a high percentage of the total sales of the industry, in which these firms enjoy some substantial opportunity to use non-price competitive techniques, a situation in which they typically regard their variable costs as constant with respect to output and finally a situation in which the firms are sensitive to the possibility of adverse public and legal action. In markets of this sort there is a strong tendency toward stability of prices over the cycle.

By way of contrast, in agriculture, in many branches of the textile industry, lumber and elsewhere the course of events during a cyclical upswing seems to be about as follows: an increase in demand leads to an increase in price which is almost immediate unless stocks are unusually large. The increase in prices is followed by an increase in output but at costs which soon begin to rise. Costs rise both because of a resort to higher cost sources of supply and because higher prices have to be paid to attract resources including labor into the industries in question. The sequence of events seems to run from demand to prices to costs. This sequence is well illustrated by the relationship between these variables in competitive fields of enterprise during the war.

In the area of large-scale enterprise, however, the sequence of cost-price relationships appears to run in the other direction. An increase in demand will be followed by an increase of output accompanied by no, or a very small, price increase. This situation may persist for an increase that carries output nearly to capacity operations depending largely on what happens to material prices or to wage rates. In the absence of substantial changes in material prices or wage rates, variable costs per unit of output remain constant or rise very slowly, and since overhead is spread over an increased volume average costs decrease and profits increase markedly. Under these circumstances the impetus to a price increase seems mainly to come from the costs side, i.e., from an increase in material prices or wage rates. The increase in material prices, in turn, is likely to be significant depending on whether these materials are produced under competitive conditions or in the large enterprise sector of the economy.

If this view is approximately correct — and I believe that it is — the dynamic elements in the price system are mainly wage rates, particularly the rates of organized labor, and the prices of goods produced in the small enterprise sector of the economy. Furthermore the dynamic elements act and react fairly strongly upon each other. Costs of living depend quite substantially on the prices of goods produced in the competitive sector of the economy. An increase in the cost of living certainly provides, at the least, a strong talking point for wage rate increases. On the other hand, an increase in money wages cannot help but increase the demand for the output of this sector of the economy, and, as we have seen, the relationship between an increase in demand and in prices is close and immediate in the area of competitive production.

We could hardly have a better illustration of the interconnection between the dynamic elements of the price system than confronts us at present. The prices of agricultural products are definitely on their way up with obvious consequences for the cost of living. The cost of living can hardly continue to rise without another round of wage rate increases. The prices of industrial products are caught in the middle and regardless of the reluctance of large scale enterprise to undertake another round of price increases, the prices of their products are likely to be drawn upward by the behavior of the more volatile elements in the price system.

MARKET STRUCTURE AND PRICE STABILITY

This digression concerning differences in price behavior in various parts of the economy has drawn us away from the explanation of why prices in highly concentrated industrial markets are relatively stable. There is more to that question than is contained in a discussion of the relation of changes in the rate of output and costs. In the markets now under discussion there is one or a small number of firms each so large, relative to the total market, that a variation in its volume of sales will have price effects that must be taken into account. How they are taken into account constitutes the core of what is customarily called price policy.

To have a price policy implies that the price at which a firm sells is not determined exclusively by market forces outside its own control. The possible courses of action open to the firm confronted by this situation are numerous. Recognizing that, under existing conditions, increased volume can not be obtained except by price reductions, the firm may try to change these conditions by increasing advertising expenditures. The firm may also attempt to increase sales without reducing prices by one or more of a large category of possible courses of action that are usually described as non-price competition. The term price policy, as I am using it here, embraces the whole range of devices by means of which the firm attempts to influence its volume of sales within the limits of the basic demand and cost conditions which lie outside its control.

Even if it is impossible to influence sales without resort to price changes it by no means follows that price changes will be made. In markets dominated by a small number of sellers, any given firm, before changing its price, will have to take account of how its competitors are likely to react to this price change. If a price cut is met by rivals the firm may gain little volume and actually lose revenue by the price cut. If a price increase is not followed the firm may lose largely both in sales and revenue. Under these circumstances the firm may be well advised to leave its price unchanged.

This situation seems, in fact, to be typical of many industrial markets during most of the business cycle. In the absence of substantial change in material prices or wage rates the volume of sales can and does increase without any marked change in prices. A price increase is not necessary to induce increased volume since variable costs seem to be fairly constant with increasing volume pretty much to the limit of designed capacity. As output increases toward this limit no firm increases its price for fear its rivals will not follow. Likewise, as output falls, variable costs per unit are relatively unaffected. And no firm reduces its prices because a price cut is likely to be followed by all firms. Meanwhile a very active competition of a non-price variety may well be in process. Admittedly this is an oversimplification of the situation but it seems to hold true in many industrial markets.

The type of market structure that produces a high degree of price stability over the cycle is neither predominantly monopolistic nor predominantly competitive. It exhibits a blend of monopoly and competitive elements and it is the particular nature of this blend that results in the tendency toward price stability. If these markets were either more competitive *or* more monopolistic, it seems likely that prices would respond more sensitively to changes in demand conditions than in fact they do. If they were more competitive, the individual seller would not be concerned with the question whether his rivals would meet a price increase or decrease. If these markets were more monopolistic, the firm would either have no rivals to take into account, or if there were rivals, responses to changed market conditions would be governed by understandings or agreements among the firms. As it is, there is sufficient monopoly influence in these markets to prevent price cutting when demand recedes. There is also enough competition both to resist price increases in response to increases in demand and to lead to an active cultivation of non-price forms of rivalry.

PUBLIC OPINION AND "BIG BUSINESS" PRICING

Up to this point we have discussed industrial price stability with reference to monopoly and competitive elements in the market. It would be unwise, however, to take leave of this subject without recognizing the substantial influence that public attitudes and public policy have on industrial prices. The large-scale firm in the American economy is in a highly vulnerable political position. The antitrust mentality is deeply ingrained in the American people and the antitrust laws are merely a legislative embodiment of a profound suspicion of business size. The public reaction, therefore, to a rapid increase in industrial prices is apt to be very different than to a comparable rise in agricultural prices or in the prices of other products of small enterprise. The management of large firms, the leaders in particular industrial fields, are as well aware of this as anyone else, and the probable effect on public relations of a sizeable price increase is certainly taken into account. It would be difficult to explain the behavior of certain industrial prices at the present juncture without resorting to this kind of consideration. Certainly petroleum prices and the prices of a number of other products could be raised by the leading firms without any loss of business to rivals. That such prices are not raised is to be explained by semi-political considerations rather than by the economic elements of market structures. If anyone doubts the importance of this influence in the United States let him consider the behavior of industrial prices in a Latin American country, say Argentina or Brazil, in the face of the inflationary pressures that now impinge on this country.

WHY WAGE RATES TEND TO "LEAD THE WAY" FOR RISING INDUSTRIAL PRICES

Returning now to the dynamic elements in the price system, which there is reason to believe are mainly competitively determined market prices and the wage rates of organized labor, why is it that, in the typical industrial markets now under discussion, wage rates tend to push up prices as the economy approaches full employment rather than following prices as they tend to do in more competitive markets? The answer again has mainly to do, I believe, with the structure of the markets in which wage rates and prices are determined.

Although a comparison of the monopoly power of a labor union in the labor market with the monopoly position of a firm in its product market presents serious difficulties, there are certain respects in which the power of particular labor monopolies seems much stronger than does the monopoly power of most large-scale enterprises. Furthermore it seems certain that labor leaders are less inhibited by public relations considerations in the use of what monopoly power they have than are large-scale enterprises. An industry-wide labor union may control the supply of labor for the whole industry.

If so, it is in the same position with respect to this labor supply as a single firm would be with respect to output if it were the sole producer in the industry. That particular blend of monopoly and competitive elements which helps to explain price stabilization policies in the product market is absent in such a labor market. Add to this the fact that labor is not inhibited by an antitrust policy or, at least not to the same degree, by the public animus against business giantism, and one has at least part of the explanation of why it is that increases in wage rates are a primary factor in pushing up sluggish industrial prices.

If we may conclude then that industrial prices tend to adjust themselves slowly to price changes elsewhere in the system, what is the effect of this price inflexibility on high-level stability in the economy as a whole? At the present juncture, facing as we are heavy inflationary pressures, the relatively sluggish adjustment of industrial prices can only be judged to be a stabilizing factor. The more sluggish the adjustment the better. When one turns, however, to the effect of inflexible prices on employment and output over the cycle one raises a question about which economic thought to date is, to say the least, confused and confusing. Personally, I should support the view that the inflexibility of industrial prices tends to even out cyclical fluctuations in employment and output. At the same time I should have to say that on this matter economic thought is badly divided.

On the whole question of the proper relation of costs, prices and profits at any particular stage of the cycle no one, so far as I know, has had anything very convincing to say. In a highly productive, wealthy economy such as ours, it is probably true that on the average and over the long run a low profit-high wage relationship is conducive to the maintenance of high-level employment. Unless consumption can be sustained at a high rate — and this means high wages — the capacity for saving in the American economy at any level approaching full employment is such as to create a most difficult investment problem. As far as cost-price relations are concerned, this would seem to argue for a much higher break-even point than is customary in American industry — though how this is to be achieved I not know.

THE "HIGHER-WAGES-FOR-STABILIZATION" THEORY

A recognition of these factors, however, throws little or no light on the question which cost-price-profit relation is conducive to the attainment or maintenance of high-level employment over any particular short-run period. At the beginning of this year a report by Robert Nathan and, in more restrained language, the President's first "Economic Report" under the Employment Act of 1946 advanced the view that prices and profits were too high and wages too low to sustain high-level employment. Since Nathan saw no prospect of adequate price reduction, it would require in his view large wage increases to sustain an effective demand sufficient to take off the market the flow of goods foreseen for 1947 at full employment. The President's report contented itself with a recommendation of selective price reductions and wage rate increases.

Now the fact of the matter is that economists at the present time do not know anywhere near enough to be able to predict, on the basis of current wage, price, profits, and employment data, what the effective demand and, consequently, the level of employment and output are likely to be over the ensuing short period. As things have turned out wage rate increases have done little but push up prices, and it is hard to see under the circumstances how they could have been expected to have any other effect.

Apparently we are in for another round of wage increases shortly. Is it too much to hope, however, that we shall be spared further talk of the necessity of increasing wages to maintain purchasing power to maintain output and employment? Admitting that over the long-run and in the absence of extensive government intervention, a high wage-low profit relationship is probably necessary to the maintenance of high-level stability, it does not follow either that it can be brought about by wage rate increases or that this or any other particular relationship is the desirable one at a given stage of the business cycle.

WOULD MORE HIGHLY COMPETITIVE MARKETS HELP?

Finally let us return to the first term of our subject, namely, competition. We have seen that one of the important consequences of that blend of competitive and monopolistic influences characteristic of industrial markets is a relative stability or inflexibility of prices. It would be quite impossible, most people agree, by antitrust or any other sort of policy, to bring about a really competitive adjustment of industrial prices to the upswings and downswings of the business cycle. Furthermore, in my opinion, it would be dubiously desirable even if it could be done. Prices would fall very low in periods of depression and rise to extremely high levels in boom years. The profits of business enterprise could be measured only in negative figures in depression and would soar to astronomical heights in prosperous years. What this would do to speculation, to business planning and to labor relations is perhaps not too difficult to foresee. In fact, I doubt whether we want a sensitive competitive adjustment of industrial prices to the swings of the cycle.

What we do want from competition is a process by means of which over the long run — and not too long a run at that — consumers get the results of a vigorous and independent probing of the possibilities of cost and price reduction in the American economy by independent buyers and sellers. In recent years various people concerned with public policy in the area of industrial organization have been looking for a practicable standard of competition more consonant with the fact of American industrial life than the standards customarily advanced by economic theorists or antitrust lawyers. They reject, on the one hand, pure competition or any variant of it, as a norm of desirable business behavior; on the other hand, they insist that the tests of monopoly ordinarily suggested in antitrust actions are frequently either insignificant or misleading and, in any case, have meanings that vary greatly with the industrial context. The term usually applied to describe such a standard is "workable competition."

Now it must be admitted that to date very little progress has been made in giving precision to this notion. About the only *general* specification of workably competitive market structures that can be advanced is the following: workable competition implies the availability to both buyer and seller of an adequate number of alternative courses of action. Obviously the word adequate puts a heavy premium on judgment of the significance of facts in particular industry situations. It is clearly not enough that buyers have a number of sellers from whom to choose or that sellers have a number of customers to whom they can sell. There must be on the part of buyers and sellers an independent probing of the possibilities in the situation. Beyond this point it is impossible to go in any general discussion of workable competition. Further meaning can be added only by breaking down the problem into the context of particular market situations.

There is, however, one aspect of this problem to which, in closing, I wish to direct attention and that is the relevance of numbers of buyers and sellers in a given market to the monopoly problem. It may be said, I think, that large numbers are a sufficient though not a necessary condition of workable competition. If these numbers are large enough to prevent any serious consideration of interdependence among firms they are probably also large enough, in the absence of government support, to make collusion impracticable or ineffective. The industry may be unprogressive and existing methods may involve serious wastes but there is nothing in the situation to prevent individual firms from exploring demand elasticities and possibilities of cost reduction. If measures need to be taken to improve efficiency they will definitely not be measures leading in the direction of more competition.

THE PRACTICAL VIEW OF "WORKABLE COMPETITION"

The fact that large numbers of buyers and sellers *will* insure workable competition does not mean, however, that such numbers are necessary. Whether or not competition is in fact workable in a market dominated by three or four large sellers depends on a number of considerations such as the rate of technical change or innovation, conditions of entry, trade association practices, volume of imports and others. Furthermore, the way these considerations blend in any particular market context is sufficiently complex to render a final judgment possible only in terms of the net effect on courses of action open to suppliers or customers of the industry in question.

In particular one should be cautious in attributing monopolistic significance to size of firm or percentage of sales in a market subject to active product or process innovation. This is presumably the basis for the common-sense view that the automobile industry is a highly competitive industry despite the fact that, at least before the war, 90 per cent of the sales of popularly priced cars were made by three firms, two of which persistently earned high rates of profits. I suggest that the common-sense view is probably right.

9

Prices, Costs, and Profits[1]

The wild free days of the "Keynesian revolution," when devotees
of the "New Economics" attempted, on the basis of a simplified
"Keynesian model," to forecast unemployment twelve months hence
and then soberly proposed the public expenditure of X billion dollars
to "offset" the projected "deficiency" in aggregate expenditures, are
long since past. Williams was one of the first and one of the most
effective of the critics, insisting that beneath and behind those
Keynesian aggregates lurked "more things than were dreamed of" in
the new philosophy. Among these things were variabilities in the
behavior of prices, costs, and profits.[2]

One of the assumptions of the simplified Keynesian analysis was
that wages, prices, and profits were determined in purely competitive
markets. It followed from this assumption that increases in wages or
prices accompanying an expansion of aggregate expenditures were, up
to the limit of full employment, "necessary" to the absorption into
employment of unemployed resources and that it was only after full
employment was achieved that inflation emerged as a serious problem.
Of course bottlenecks of various sorts might produce undesirable price
or wage increases if the expansion in expenditures was very rapid.
These were, however, merely technical difficulties likely to be quickly
overcome. And, although it was recognized by Keynes — who was
usually more cautious than his immediate followers — that the
policies of employers and trade unions might have "considerable

[1] Reprinted from *Money, Trade, and Economic Growth, In Honor of John
Henry Williams* (New York, 1951).

[2] John H. Williams, Statement before the Joint Committee of the Economic
Report, July 2, 1947, *Hearings before the Joint Committee on the Economic
Report* (Washington, 1947), p. 204.

"The great challenge of the postwar period is whether in the conditions of
a free society, without the regimentation of a war economy, we can continue
to enjoy a large, growing, and reasonably stable volume of production and
employment. . . .

"The heart of the problem lies in the relations of prices, costs, and profits."

practical significance" in producing price and wage increases, these "positions of semi-inflation" offer a very imperfect analogy "to the absolute inflation which ensues on an increase in effective demand in circumstances of full employment." [3]

In fact, the influence on wages and prices of large firms and trade unions is a matter of primary importance both for the analysis of and prescription for economic instability. But whether realistic assumptions concerning the behavior of wages and prices can be worked into a useful model of the trade cycle and, in particular, whether public wage and price policy can contribute to a stabilization program without killing the prospect for future growth is a different question.

A generation of writers on the subject of price flexibility has contributed little that is conclusive to our understanding of the relationship on the downswing between price and wage behavior and employment and output in the economy as a whole. There may be some arrangement of leads and lags that facilitates the maintenance of output and employment but, if so, we do not yet know at all definitely what this arrangement is. In the Keynesian analysis prices fall with marginal prime costs, and since in the system as a whole prime costs are essentially wages which are spent, the decline in aggregate costs is equivalent to the decline in aggregate expenditures. The strength of organized labor may hold up money wages but by so doing it holds up prices and, consequently, real wages, both as cost and as income, are unaffected. It follows, abstracting from the effect of price changes on expectations and possible dishoarding induced by low prices, as, indeed, the Keynesian model does, that it makes no essential difference to a stabilization program, except for remote and uncertain effects via the rate of interest, whether wages and prices fall or do not fall.

When the effects of price changes on price expectations are introduced into the problem, one can arrive at any solution that is desired merely by choosing among assumptions concerning the elasticity of price expectations. If it is assumed that a fall in prices creates expectations of a further fall, then it may well be that an increase in the flexibility of prices on the downswing will augment instability.

[3] J. M. Keynes, *The General Theory of Employment, Interest and Money* (New York, 1936), pp. 301–302.

It may be true that a fall in particular prices induces such expectations, but by no means necessarily. There are certainly cases in which it is the failure of a price to fall that sets up expectations of a decline rather than the reverse, and for the price system as a whole no one to date has been able to show how an increase in the number of centers of resistance to price decline will affect aggregate expenditures and, via expeditures, the volume of output and employment in the economy as a whole.[4]

It is possible, on the other hand, to arrive at conclusions on this matter if one assumes that prices are inflexible to changes in wage rates and, indeed, a number of people have.[5] A fall in wage rates, prices being unaffected, would decrease real wage rates. The orthodox economists, and on this point Keynes would have to be classified as orthodox, would argue that a reduction in real wages would tend to increase employment and output. But the effect would be slow, depending on expansion of investment, changes in production methods in response to changes in the relative prices of factors, etc. It is possible, on the other hand, to imagine that, in the short run, aggregate real income would not be very much affected and that the reduction in money wages would merely shift real income from wage to non-wage receivers. If one makes further appropriate assumptions concerning the savings habits of wage and non-wage receivers, the conclusion can be reached that a wage decrease will reduce employment and a wage increase will increase employment.

This view of the matter has in fact become official dogma in the American labor movement or rather what has become official is the

---

[4] Cf. T. de Scitovsky, "Capital Accumulation, Employment, and Price Rigidity," *Review of Economic Studies,* Feb. 1941, pp. 69–88. Scitovsky maintains this thesis but, in the writer's opinion, unsuccessfully. He holds that (p. 77), "Consumers will regard the movement of a few isolated prices as a normal phenomenon, due to causes inherent in those commodities. Only when price-changes become very general or very drastic will they begin to suspect 'trouble on the side of money' and wake up to the realisation of a shift in its value. This threshold of consciousness, we submit, is the boundary line between a stable and an unstable economy." But people may well become conscious of "trouble on the side of money" for other reasons than price decline; e.g., because output and employment decline. Assuming that a decline in business activity is expected, the failure of particular prices to fall may increase rather than diminish the expectation that they will fall further.

[5] E.g., M. Kalecki, *Essays in Theory of Economic Fluctuations* (New York, 1939), particularly Chapter 3.

view that wage increases could always increase employment were it not for the nasty business habit of increasing prices to cover the increased wage. In this connection it should be remembered that while the prices of industrial products are sticky, they do not seem to be particularly sticky to wage-rate changes. They tend to the sticky with respect to changes in demand, but the variants of full-cost pricing to be found in American industry usually provide for a change in prices with any marked change in labor or material costs. What the theory then becomes is a belief that an increase in wage rates *would* increase employment *if* prices could be restrained from rising.

One obvious restraint would be the imposition of price controls and many labor economists have come to the conclusion that the use of wage policy to maintain or increase employment requires the use of price controls.[6] Others have concluded that although it is not possible at every stage of the cycle to increase wages without increasing prices, it *is* possible at certain stages. Robert Nathan appears to be the leading custodian of this view and the appropriate stage of the cycle appears to him to be the initial stages of the downturn when the prospect of declining demand may effectively restrain business from increasing prices. Since we are here concerned with examining the relation of wage-price behavior in the downswing to a stabilization program, this view merits attention.

It would have to be said that this policy confronts certain difficulties connected with short-run forecasting that have already plagued Mr. Nathan and his confreres. One has to know when a downturn really is a downturn. It has to be remembered that in 1945 the expected deflation, which according to these views could only be held off by raising real wages, failed to materialize. It must also be recalled that, in the spring of 1947, when Nathan and his group again foresaw a downturn and called for a simultaneous increase in money wages and reduction in prices, the economy refused to behave as expected.[7]

[6] E.g., Eugene Forsey, "Trade Union Policy under Full Employment" in Lester and Shister, *Insights into Labor Issues* (New York, 1948). Forsey takes it for granted that labor will demand not only a rate of increase of real wages that keeps pace with productivity but a redistribution of income in its favor. He considers this to be necessary to the maintenance of full employment and concludes, rightly enough, that such a full-employment policy could only be brought about by "planning" including price controls.

[7] Robert R. Nathan and Oscar Gass, *A National Wage Policy for 1947* (Washington, 1946).

In the spring of 1949, however, there was unmistakable evidence that a downturn of some sort was in progress. In two documents prepared for the C.I.O.,[8] Nathan and his associates called for an increase in real wages to be brought about either by an increase in money wages or a reduction in prices, or both.

The thesis of these documents is that the time to raise wages is when profits and investment have started to decline.

> Profits are still high but declining. If business falls much further, profits will decline precipitously. A major depression will see profits replaced by losses. If the business community acts now to help stop the recession, profits will continue to be earned. . . .
>
> If business can afford to cut prices, it can afford to raise wages and other types of labor income. One or the other has been necessary all during the last nine months.[9]

Again, in a later publication, Nathan summarizes his views succinctly:[10]

> It is our contention that wage rate increases in profitable industries during the summer of 1949 would result in increased total spending in the economy. Business would find it difficult to pass along these wage increases in the form of higher prices. . . . Wage increases based on ability to pay would not significantly depress business expenditures at a time when investment outlays are declining largely because of inadequate consumer expenditures to support the peak rate of investment expenditures. Increased purchases on the part of those who receive wage increases would enlarge consumer demand, place props under declining investment, and make more universal the ability to pay higher wages.[11]

This contention raises two questions. Will a wage-rate increase, under the circumstances of the summer of 1949, lead to an increase in prices? If it is not followed by an increase in prices, will the increase in money wages in a few industries, including steel, produce an in-

---

[8] *A National Economic Policy for 1949* (Washington, 1949), and *Economic Position of the Steel Industry, 1949* (Washington, 1949).

[9] *A National Economic Policy for 1949*, p. 37.

[10] "Comments of Sumner H. Slichter" on the Steel Report, *The Review of Economics and Statistics,* Nov. 1949, pp. 288–289.

[11] It should be pointed out that this quotation implies an assumption that investment outlets depend directly upon consumption and that increased consumption means a necessary increase or maintenance of investment. Neither assumption is universally correct. See, for example, J. R. Hicks' reference to "autonomous investment" in his *Contribution to the Theory of the Trade Cycle* (London, 1950), Chapter V.

crease in aggregate real expenditures favorable to output and employment in the economy as a whole? An answer requires us to choose among so many possible values for the relevant variables that no definite reply can be given to either question.

An examination of what in fact happened to price does not help us very much with the first question. The steel wage settlement in September 1949, which increased labor costs, on the average, about 10 cents an hour was followed by a substantial increase in prices. But it is always possible for the advocates of the Nathan policy to reply that this increase would have taken place with or without a wage increase. And it is in fact true that prices in many areas stiffened with the upturn which became evident towards the end of the summer of 1949. On the other hand, if prices had not risen, it would have been possible for opponents of the Nathan position to say that, in the absence of the increase in wage costs, steel prices would have fallen. *Ex post* statistics are by no means conclusive for either side.

Approaching the problem *ex ante,* Nathan appears to rely on competitive pressures augmented by unfavorable business expectations to prevent a wage increase from generating a price increase. If competition were "pure," prices being equal to marginal costs, an increase in wage rates that increased short-run marginal costs could not fail to lead to a price increase. But however competition in the steel industry may be described, it is certainly not "pure." It would be easy to set up a "market model" capable of translating a substantial wage-rate increase into a zero-price increase. Presumably the "kinked" demand curve hypothesis would play a part in such a model. On the other hand, with the market demand for steel products being quite clearly, under the circumstances assumed here, price inelastic in the short run, it does not require a stretching of the imagination to conceive of a relation among firms such that prices could move upward fairly easily with cost increases even in the initial stages of a business downturn. It would seem incumbent on those who argue that a wage-rate increase in a particular industry will not produce a commensurate price increase to indicate what combination of competitive and monopoly elements is relied on to produce this conclusion. The postwar experience has indicated that governmental and quasi-governmental exhortation is not a particularly important element in the process of price determination.

If, however, for the sake of argument we assume that prices do not rise with an increase in wage rates, what is likely to be the effect of the wage increase, in the early stages of a downturn, on the economy as a whole? The Nathan thesis maintains that the result of such a wage increase is to transfer income from profits, which, considering the current business outlook, are not likely to be invested, to wages which are sure to be spent. Consequently, aggregate real expenditures are increased, the demand for consumers' goods is sustained and, indirectly, the outlook for investment is improved.[12]

It is certainly possible that, under given circumstances, this chain of events might follow a wage-rate increase. Whether it did or not would depend on the immediate effect of the wage increase on employment in steel via the shape of existing cost functions and, over a somewhat longer period, via a substitution of other factors for labor; on the marginal propensity to consume of steelworkers; on dividend policies of steel companies, their investment program; on the state of confidence of investment plans of industry generally, and other matters. It would depend, in other words, on a number of magnitudes which, in the present state of our knowledge, we have no means of estimating or foreseeing. The fact of the matter is that we cannot prescribe a *universally* valid wage-price policy designed to check a cyclical downswing, and the forces shaping a particular situation are usually not shown until too late — if then.

"If business can afford to cut prices," says Nathan, writing in the summer of 1949, "it can afford to raise wages and other types of labor income. One or the other has been necessary all during the last nine months." [13] One can perhaps agree that for business as a whole the effect on income of a price cut versus a wage increase is a matter of indifference.[14] But, of course, business never acts as a whole. It makes a great deal of difference to the competitive position of a firm or an industry whether prices are cut or wages increased. But again this is no argument for cutting prices as a means of sus-

[12] But as already pointed out, in footnote 11 above, a mere rise in aggregate expenditure will not necessarily either increase or maintain aggregate investment.

[13] R. R. Nathan, footnote 9 above; the sentence quoted ignores the role of profit expectations upon autonomous investment.

[14] But longer-run effects of a wage increase upon the substitution of capital for labor need not be the same as for a price reduction, and could be adverse to labor.

taining output and employment in the economy as a whole. Just as for wages we do not know what prices to cut, and when, in order to attain this objective.

There is an argument of some validity to the effect that, periodically, small recessions have a beneficial effect in curtailing inefficient operations and tightening up business practices. "In the optimistic climate of a mild expansion, ventures are undertaken that might not be risked in a perfectly stable world. And mild contractions make for efficiency by bringing about shakedowns of business practices." [15] One can accept this argument, however, without supporting either a policy of price reduction or of wage-rate increase as a means of bringing about increased efficiency. The fall in profits which motivates the inquiry into production methods can come about through small variations in output without any marked assistance from wage or price changes.

The argument stated in the last few pages is not, however, a plea for greater stability or rigidity of prices or wages on the downswing. It is a confession of ignorance with respect to the question what type of wage and price behavior is best suited to check the downswing of a particular business cycle. Only one thing is fairly clear; in the present state of short-run economic forecasting a public policy which attempts to sustain aggregate expenditures by wage-rate increases which, because of adverse business expectations, will not, it is believed, induce price increases, rests on very shaky foundations. It did not work in 1945, it did not work in 1947, and it did not work in 1949. Under the circumstances such a policy is likely merely to feed the fires of inflation.

This danger, however, is, for obvious reasons, much more serious on the upswing. If a downswing is really underway, the fall in profits and, even more, in profit expectations, will be sufficiently drastic, whatever happens to prices, to establish a strong resistance to wage-rate increases. This deterrent is absent from periods of expanding business activity.

[15] Research and Policy Committee of the Committee for Economic Development, *Monetary and Fiscal Policy for Greater Economic Stability* (New York, 1948), p. 10.

Large increases in money wage rates, of course, can take place over time, and have taken place, without producing a marked upward movement in the level of prices. Over the last century the fourfold increase in average real hourly earnings has been realized by increases in money wages rather than by a fall in prices. From mid-nineteenth to mid-twentieth century the upward secular trend in the level of wholesale prices probably becomes a slight downward trend when adequate account is taken of product improvement. During the same period the trend of money wage rates was sharply upward. The increase in money wage rates takes place, or course, principally during periods of expanding business, but how the increase in real wages tends to be distributed over the cycle is still fairly obscure.

If large increases in money wages have occurred over time without leading to comparable upward movements in price trends, why cannot that pattern be continued? Perhaps it can; it may be that the rate of productivity increase will continue sufficiently high to permit, on the average, a two or three per cent per annum increase in real wages without inducing an upward trend of prices. And if the upward trend of money wages tends to exceed this rate, the ensuing pressure for labor-saving innovations may produce an unexpectedly high rate of increase in labor productivity. On the other hand, some new features have been added to the functioning of the economy which cast doubt on such optimistic prospects.

The most important of these features are first, the adoption by government, including the Government of the United States, and apparently on a permanent basis, of fiscal policies oriented toward full employment; and second, the growth of organized economic interests capable of influencing in the market the money compensation of their membership. Both the change in public policy and the growth in market control are connected with the emergence of strong, well-organized economic groups. How these groups affect the level of prices, moreover, is as much a matter of politics as it is of economics.

So far as the United States is concerned, the period of critical growth in the strength of organized interests was in the 1930's. The great depression may not have heralded the onset of economic stagnation in any technical sense, but it produced a change in the process of wage- and price-determination that may have consequences just as drastic for the functioning of an enterprise economy. The change with respect to a large segment of the wage structure and to the price of important farm products is conspicuous and obvious; it is to be seen in the great expansion of collective bargaining and the adoption, on what seems to be a permanent basis, of price supports for farm products. The change in the process of determining industrial prices is more subtle and represents the continuation of a trend, already marked, in the direction of business practices designed to shelter profits against the effects of cost increases and price declines.

If we may conjecture — and it must be admitted that propositions in this area are largely conjectural — wage-price relationships were significantly different from current relationships fifty years ago, when labor was relatively unorganized and competition more characteristic of product markets than it is today. We may suppose that cyclical upswings, pushing demand functions to the right, permitted an increase in prices which in turn pulled up wage rates and other factor prices. On the downswing, prices again moved ahead of wages. The prices of farm products, representing a large fraction of the cost of living, were traditionally among the most volatile of prices whose fluctuations tended to augment that relative decline in real wages on the upswing and relative increase on the downswing which Marshall and his contemporaries thought characteristic of the cycle.

A policy of supporting farm prices at high parity levels tends to eliminate the influence of the market except in periods of crop failure or of unusually high economic activity. Furthermore, the levels tend to move up with the level of nonfarm prices. The prices of industrial products tend to become unresponsive to demand changes either on the upswing or the downswing but quite definitely responsive to changes in factor prices among which wage rates are of overwhelming importance. Under these circumstances, the stage is set for persistent upward pressure on the price level with an aggressive labor movement the active element and with business and agriculture organized for effective defense of profits and of farm incomes.

It is generally agreed that money wages can increase without upward pressure on the price level if the rate of increase does not exceed the average rate of increase in productivity. The rate of increase in money wages could conceivably be substantially higher than this without producing an increase in the price level if farm prices and profits could be prevented from rising.[16] Product per man is a figure secured by dividing the value of total product by the number of gainfully employed. It may be argued that if the increase in the value of the product can be monopolized by a particular group among the gainfully employed, the rate of increase in the real income of the members of that group can be substantially greater than the rate of increase in average per capita productivity for the gainfully employed as a whole.

As we have seen, however, both the farm and the business groups are sufficiently well organized to prevent this from happening. If organized labor presses for a rate of increase in per capita money wages substantially higher than the rate of increase in per capita productivity, one of the results may be price inflation. It may be, but not necessarily; depending in part on whether labor pressure for higher wages is limited to wage bargaining or whether it also includes political pressure for the maintenance of full employment. Unless monetary and fiscal policy are oriented toward the maintenance of full employment, union pressure for higher wages is likely either to meet with effective resistance from employers who foresee difficulties in raising prices or, if such resistance is ineffective, with unemployment.[17] Inflationary pressure on the price level *might* come either from an excessive demand for goods supported by monetary-fiscal policy or from a wage-price spiral generated by the wage and price pressures of organized labor and business groups. It is unlikely, however, that either influence would be sufficient without the other.

The most effective deterrent to union pressure for increased wage rates appears to be fear of strike losses rather than fear of unemployment. In a dynamic economy where the volume of employment in a particular industry or area is the resultant of many influences, the effect on employment of a given increase in wages is uncertain and, in any case, slow in appearing. It is unlikely, therefore, to be con-

[16] As indicated below in the text, however, we must not neglect the effects such a policy could have upon employment via possible adverse repercussion upon *net* new investment due to the unfavorable price-cost expectations such a policy might create.

[17] In this connection it should not be assumed that mere government deficits would necessarily suffice to maintain full employment from *private* industry. If the inflation is regarded as temporary, long-run net investment expectations, especially autonomous ones, may become adverse, and full employment be rendered maintainable only by direct government investment.

sidered by union leaders to be a weighty factor. Furthermore, even if some unemployment is foreseen as the result of a wage increase, it may be among nonmembers or among members whom the union leadership does not have to take into account.

Strike losses, on the other hand, are real, are foreseeable, and affect that core of union membership to which union leaders are accountable. Although the considerations leading to union action are by no means purely monetary — and indeed in certain cases may be very little influenced by monetary factors — the length of the strike that may be involved in enforcing a wage-rate increase, and the costs attendant thereto, are ordinarily of primary importance. Whether the fear of large losses enters into union calculations depends mainly on the resistance to union demands offered by employers. Such resistance in turn depends in part on whether the wage increase can be passed on in the form of a price increase and in part on how such an increase, if it takes place, is likely to affect the employers' competitive position.

If a single employer in a competitive industry is faced with a wage-rate increase, his competitive position is obviously endangered. His resistance to the wage-rate increase, on the other hand, will be tempered by the fact that a strike will divert business to his competitors. If wage rates are determined for a whole industry or area, the influence of a wage increase on the competitive position of a single employer may be much less. Consequently, the incentive of employers to resist the wage increase may be less. On the other hand, their power to resist, if they are united into an employers association, will be much greater than that of a single employer. Whether they use this power will depend in part on how a wage-rate increase is deemed to affect the competitive position of the industry or area.

There is a widespread tendency in all industrialized countries for union influence on wage rates to be generalized over a continuously broader area. This may occur through a broadening in the coverage of formal wage negotiation; it may also occur through a process of wage leadership such that the wage settlement in a few key industries becomes the pattern for wage settlements in many others. As this occurs the resistance of employers stemming from fear of losing competitive position becomes less. There remains, however, the question whether wage-rate increases can be passed on as price increases.

Since this depends largely on the level of effective demand, we are forced back to a consideration of monetary-fiscal policy as the key to the behavior of employers confronted with demands for increased wages.

If monetary-fiscal policy is strongly oriented towards the maintenance of full employment and both unions and employers can count on the stability of this policy, the opposition to wage-rate increases is apt to be slight. If wage increases are fairly uniform, percentage-wise among industries and areas, the competitive position of particular industries and areas will not be adversely affected; if monetary-fiscal policy assures the maintenance of effective demand, prices can be adjusted upward fairly readily to wage increases.[18]

Suppose, for example, that governments accept the basic principle underlying the recommendations of the United Nations Group of Experts on *National and International Measures for Full Employment:*

> The basic principle underlying these recommendations is that compensatory measures aimed at producing an expansion of effective demand should be brought into operation automatically whenever the actual level of unemployment (as a percentage of wage-earners) exceeded a pre-announced level by a stated percentage, for three consecutive months.[19]

The announcement of such a policy will necessarily and strongly influence the expectations of unions and employers. It goes far to ensure that wage increases can be passed on as price increases. Such opposition as employers would be likely to offer to wage increases would be limited to situations in which the wage increase would adversely affect competitive positions. But as wage increases are generalized this source of opposition also tends to disappear.

The Group of Experts recognizes that, "The general responsibilities assumed by the government for the maintenance of full employment also enhance the government's general responsibilities for maintaining the stability of the price level." [20] And they go on to say:

---

[18] But see footnote 17 above.

[19] Report by a Group of Experts appointed by the Secretary-General (Lake Success, New York, United Nations, Department of Economic Affairs, Dec. 1949), p. 40.

[20] Report by a Group of Experts, p. 84.

If there is evidence of a continuous general upward pressure of money wages exceeding substantially the rate of increase of productivity and leading to offsetting price increases, the situation requires such action by the government, jointly with organized labour and employers' associations, as would ensure that any wage increases that may be granted will not result in a general price inflation.[21]

What line of action this portends is not very clear. But earlier in their report the experts allege that "The measures recommended in the present report to sustain effective demand do not involve any basic change in the economic institutions of private enterprise countries." [22]

If this statement has any relevance at all to the United States, it must mean that so-called direct controls, including price and wage controls, are not regarded as necessary to the maintenance simultaneously of full employment and stability of the general price level. This could only be true, in the writer's opinion, if labor and business groups capable of influencing the incomes of their participants were very considerably atomized.

Space is lacking either to develop this proposition fully or to indicate in any detail what kind of stabilization program might be compatible with "the economic institutions of private enterprise countries." But in general it may be said that such a program involves, first, a governmental policy toward business and labor organizations designed to ensure that wage and price decisions are made with regard to the effects of these decisions on the competitive position of individual firms and, second, that fiscal and monetary policy fall substantially short of guaranteeing the employment of all but a fixed percentage of wage earners.

CONCLUSION

It remains true, to paraphrase Professor Williams, that, given an appropriate monetary-fiscal policy, the answer to the question whether "we can continue to enjoy a large, growing, and reasonably stable volume of production and employment . . . lies in the relations of prices, costs, and profits." It would have to be said, however, that with respect to relative prices, costs, and profits we can make almost no universally valid statements about their relation to

---

[21] Report by a Group of Experts, p. 85.
[22] Report by a Group of Experts, p. 7.

economic stability. Particular downswings or upswings, under particular circumstances, *may* be halted by special relationships of costs and prices but not only is our theory incomplete, but also the relevant data on which to base a conclusive policy statement is virtually never available in time.

With respect to wage and price levels and the incomes of various groups of participants in the production process, certain things may be said which have at least negative utility to a public stabilization program. Business and farm groups in the United States have substantial power to protect farm incomes and profits against increases in the prices of products and services consumed by these groups; organized labor has substantial power to force increases in money wage rates. It seems, therefore, futile to expect that, without direct controls, wage-rate increases at a rate greater than the increase in average productivity will not be followed by price increases.

Under these circumstances, a persistent upward pressure on the price level can only be avoided if there is adequate opposition to excessive wage increase. The real opposition lies in the possibility of large strike losses inflicted by employers who fear either an injury to their competitive position or an inability to pass on wage increases in the shape of price increases. The fear of loss of competitive advantage is lessened as "patterns" of wage settlements are generalized over the economy. The fear of inability to raise prices would be lessened by expectations generated by a governmental full-employment program.

It probably follows that if "the conditions of a free society" desired by Williams are to be maintained, employment policy must fall short of a full-employment guarantee and that government must interpose limits to the development of economic pressure groups.

10

Labor Monopoly and All That[1]

Whether labor unions are monopolies is a question hardly worth asking and, if asked, hardly worth discussion. Whatever else a union is, it is certainly an agreement among workers not to compete for jobs. If unions are not monopolies, working men have been deliberately sold a "bill of goods" for many long years by slick operators who have repeatedly promised to "take labor out of competition." The interesting questions would appear to be: of what are unions monopolists; how much market power do they have and how do they use it; are there degrees of power and types of use that call for public intervention; and, if so, are "unreasonable" manifestations of labor monopoly appropriately handled by policies primarily designed to deal with monopoly problems in product markets or is another type of policy required? It is obviously impossible adequately to discuss so broad a range of questions in the time available to us. What I propose to do is to consider some of the determinants of the degree of market power and its use by "labor monopolies" and to do a little prospecting around and about the concept of "unreasonable" power.

UNIONS IN THE MARKET

Monopoly power is obviously a question of degree. In commodity markets a pure seller's monopoly, if it means anything at all, can only mean that buyers confronting this seller have no alternative except to purchase from him. But since, in some sense, all commodities and services compete with each other for consumer dollars, it follows that to be "pure" the monopolist would have to control the sales of all goods and services. Even then he might encounter competition from the do-it-yourself contingent. Certainly if his control falls short of all goods and services offered for sale, his market power will be

[1] Reprinted from Industrial Relations Research Association, *Proceedings*, Eighth Annual Meeting, Dec. 1955.

limited by the alternative open to buyers to spend more or less on the products of other sellers. Similarly a pure labor monopoly can only mean the total control of the supply of labor by a single seller or, if you prefer, a single negotiator for the sale of labor services. Anything short of that would confront the seller, or negotiator, with competitive limitations to his market power.

Unions are, of course, organized for purposes other than bargaining advantage. Consequently it is possible — though barely possible — to imagine a union with no market power. Unless, however, its members think there are advantages to be obtained from the employer in the area of wages, hours, and working conditions greater than could be obtained by individual negotiation, the union is not apt to be long-lived. If we accept the degree of market power essential to the continued existence of a union as the lower limit, and a monopoly of all labor as the upper limit, the market power of currently functioning unions will fall somewhere between. They are all monopolists to a degree, and the degree will be largely determined by their success in controlling the alternatives open to relevant groups of employers.

Each employer with whom a union negotiates must be denied access to alternative sources of labor supply. The number of employers sought to be controlled will depend on competitive relations in product markets. If product transport costs are high, it may be sufficient to organize employers in a regional market only. If there exists a national market for the product, the market power of the union will depend either on organizing employees on a nation-wide basis or on devising means of excluding competing products from organized local markets. Nor may it be enough to deny all employers in a relevant product market access to alternative sources of labor supply. Under certain circumstances the market power of the union can be increased by denying the employer access to alternative labor saving techniques. Market power is dependent not only on control of the supply of labor but also on control of the supply of jobs. Finally, assuming adequate control of the supply and demand for labor among some relevant group of employers, the market power of the union may be increased if advantage can be taken of elasticities of the demand for the employer's product. This may, on the one hand, involve control of the entry of new firms and, on the other, control of the price of the product sold.[2]

The market power of a union may be roughly measured by its ability to raise the price of labor above the level attainable in the absence of the union. What for reasons of simplicity is here called price is better considered as a utility index of acceptable combinations of wage rates, hours worked, and other "working conditions." What is here called labor is some group of working men in whose interest the union negotiates. For the present we are concerned with the determinants of market power, leaving for later consideration the characteristics of the unit that exploits market power. Even if a union has complete control of the supply of labor, wields substantial influence over the number of job opportunities, and is in a position to determine the conditions of entry of new firms and the way existing firms take advantage of the elasticity of demand for the products they market, the power of the union is still limited. There may be close substitutes for the product in question produced by firms whose employees are outside the control of the union under consideration. Furthermore, there may be a wide discrepancy between the union's judgment of its market power and the fact. This happens all the time in product markets, and there is no reason to believe that unions are immune from such mistakes. A union, for example, that hopes to strengthen its market position by denying employers access to superior technology may wake up to find that demand has shifted away from the products in which it has interest to others. No union is likely to have sufficient market power to be able to ignore competitive influences from areas outside its control.

It is obvious that in the process of acquiring and using market power union activities may impinge either on the labor market or the product market. But it is not at all clear where the labor market leaves off and the product market begins. Nor, assuming we know where the product market begins, is it at all easy to determine what types of labor intervention lessen competition in the product market and what do not. If union rules deny the use of spray guns to paint-

[2] The demand for labor is, of course, a derived demand and, for particular types of labor services which are complementary to others, the derived demand may be highly inelastic. Hence an organization — say a craft union — capable of taking advantage of this inelasticity may, at least in the short-run, command a high degree of market power.

ing contractors, is competition among these contractors thereby lessened? Presumably if there is a large number of contractors in the market and they continue to act independently of each other, competition, as the term is explained in the textbooks, remains intact.

If the labor market embraces that group of economic activities which a union may seek to influence in its attempt to increase its power to improve wages, hours, and working conditions, there is really no tenable distinction between labor markets and product markets. There is literally no entrepreneurial activity in the production and sale of goods that cannot conceivably be influenced by union activities to the advantage of union members. Certainly the attempt of the antitrust division, preceding the decision in the Hutcheson case, to draw a distinction between "legitimate" union concern for improving wages, hours, and working conditions and "illegitimate" activities that interfered with business competition was ludicrously ineffective.[3] Any attempt to set out the limits of the market power of unions will have to consider union activities on both

[3] It is interesting in this connection to compare the Antitrust Division's statement (Thurman Arnold) of "illegitimate" union practices with the A. F. of L. replies (T.N.E.C. Hearings, Part 31A, pp. 18, 175–79).

1. "The strike of one union against another union certified by the N.L.R.B. to be the only legitimate collective bargaining agency with whom the employer can deal."
Reply: "A union certified by the N.L.R.B. may certainly be guilty of negotiating an unfavorable wage contract or imposing arbitrary dues or arbitrary leadership."

2. "A strike to erect a tariff wall around a locality."
Reply: "His illustrations prove that he considers it to be unlawful for unions to seek as much work as possible for their members. Surely it cannot be denied that efforts on the part of a labor union to increase the amount of work for its own members have a direct connection with wages."

3. "The exclusion of efficient methods or prefabricated materials from building construction."
Reply: "Surely unions may, in the language of Mr. Justice Brandeis 'join in refusing to expend their labor upon articles whose very production constitutes an attack upon the standard of living.'"

4. "The refusal of unions to allow small independent firms to remain in business."
Reply: "The so-called independent contractors or vendors are in truth employees, and certainly the competitors of employees."

5. "The activities of unions in imposing and maintaining artificially fixed prices to consumers."
Reply: "The crux of the problem is, when are prices artificially fixed? Would it, for example, be an unreasonable restraint of trade for unions to enforce a

sides of the market; its success in controlling not only the supply of labor but the demand for labor. And any exploration of union activities on the demand side of the labor market will inevitably penetrate deeply into the functioning of product markets.

WHAT KIND OF MONOPOLY?

Having set out some of the factors that influence the degree of monopoly or market power that a union may possess, let us turn now to a consideration of the nature of the organization that presumably exploits this market power. An examination of business monopoly problems makes it clear that a given degree of market power, however measured, can be variously used depending, in part, on relationships among those who hold this power. Market power may be held by a single seller, a small group of sellers each of whom acts with regard to the reaction of others, a cartel, a trade association, and, no doubt, by other combinations. The market conditions external to the group may be similar but differences in relationships within the group can produce a wide variety of responses to these external conditions. Insofar as the theory of the firm has attempted explanations of business behavior in situations in which power is held by a group the members of which act independently or in some sort of collusion, it has done so by asking how firms attempting to maximize profits would act subject to various restraints imposed either by the probable reactions of other firms or by the regulations of a collusive agreement. But it has proved very difficult to specify restraints that have any claim to generality and the meaning of profit maximization under such circumstances itself becomes ambiguous. Consequently, examination of business behavior tends at this point to abandon theoretical models and to retreat into the institutional atmosphere of industry studies. The rock on which the more general analysis founders is the complexity of relations among a group possessing market power.

If we attempt to relate this experience to the study of labor monopoly, the first thing we need to recognize is that whatever else it may be, a trade union is not a seller of labor services. If a union con-

---

price so as to maintain a living wage by cutting out sweatshop competition?"
6. "The make work system."
Reply: "Employers will always claim that a few extra hours of work by a smaller number of employees renders useless and unnecessary a greater number of employees."

trolling the supply of labor in a defined market were to act as a
monopolistic seller of labor services, it would presumably, on the
analogy of a monopolistic seller in a product market, attempt to take
advantage of any differences in demand elasticities in different segments of the market via a policy of wage discrimination and, in
other ways, so act as to maximize total receipts for services rendered.[4]
How to distribute these receipts among union members would ration-
ally be determined on the basis of some calculation of incentives required to bring forth the necessary services. Obviously unions not only
do not but cannot act as rational monopolistic sellers of labor services.

In the first place, even though the union is the sole negotiator in
a given market there is considerable ambiguity in determining the
numbers for whom it negotiates. Not all may be union members and
within the union certain blocs of members may have preferred positions that, at the least, may influence acceptable gradations among
wage rates. In other words the union view of the quantity axis in the
familiar diagram that depicts the results of quantity-times-price calculations is not quite the same as the perspective, say, of a seller of
cement.

In the second place, there is a still greater ambiguity about the
nature of the unit of sale, i.e., of labor services. The union presumably negotiates with respect to a bundle of benefit called wages,
hours, and working conditions. But "working conditions" in particular have a way of appearing on both sides of the bargain. The
terms affecting "working conditions" offered by the buyer of labor
services as a part of the "price" for these services may affect the size
of the unit of services he in turn receives. In other words, the supply
and demand functions for labor services may not be completely independent of each other.

In the third place, the union is clearly not in the same position to
package, ship, and otherwise dispose of its product as, say, a seller

[4] Although it is probably correct to say that, in general, unions do not act
like systematic discriminators, my colleague Martin Segal has called my attention to a number of interesting examples of discriminatory action: the
rubber workers not only discriminate among tire-making firms but also negotiate different rates (for the same job) within one firm depending on the nature
of the product and the elasticity of demand for the product. The teamsters,
at least in certain geographical markets, appear to consider the elasticity of the
demand for the service in setting rates for virtually identical trucking jobs.

of cotton grey goods. In fact if the union does not handle its material very carefully, it is not likely to have any product at all. The necessity to persuade, discipline, cajole, and take the other steps required to maintain morale and cohesiveness in the organization clearly sets important limits to what the union can and cannot do in negotiating for the sale of labor services. For all these and other reasons the union is not a seller of labor services but a negotiator for the sale of a not very clearly defined product, representing a not very easily determinable number of men, and operating in an environment that pretty seriously limits the application of any maximizing principle.

To say, however, that a union is not a monopolistic seller of labor services is not to say that it is not a monopoly organization. If we are permitted again to draw analogies from the commodity market, the form of business monopoly that most closely resembles the union is a price cartel with sufficient control over entry and output to make its price policy effective but lacking the device of profit pooling and the powers required to make profit pooling effective. Such a cartel can obviously not pursue the price and output policies that would be followed by a single seller operating in the same market. The prices that would maximize the profit of the various firms constituting the cartel will normally be different and consequently the cartel price has to be some sort of compromise. Since profits are not pooled, each firm has an interest in its continued existence as a firm and consequently the cartel cannot do what a single seller would supposedly do, shut down inefficient facilities and attempt to minimize costs for the total output. The union is normally faced with somewhat the same problem of reconciling divergent interests and taking care of employees in high cost locations even though it might be better for the union as a whole if jobs could be concentrated in high profit concerns.

Although a cartel is not a single-firm monopoly, no one has any hesitation in describing it as a monopolistic organization. Nor should there be any hesitation in so characterizing a trade-union. The exploitation of its market power by a cartel — or similar loose business arrangements — has been characterized by Fellner as "limited joint profit maximization." [5] Any attempt so to characterize a union's ex-

---

[5] William Fellner, *Competition Among the Few; Oligopoly and Similar Market Structures* (New York, 1949). Cf. in particular Chapter VII.

ploitation of its market position would probably have to stress the "joint" and the "limited" and play down the element of "maximization."

STRUCTURAL AND PERFORMANCE TESTS
OF MARKET POWER

We have now said something about the character of the market confronted by unions and the varying degrees of "occupancy" of the market — if I may be permitted this term — that a union may possibly achieve. We have also considered briefly some of the relations between the union and its membership that might be expected to influence the way in which a market position is exploited. Given the market position and the internal organization of a union, would it be possible to say anything useful about the wages, hours, and working conditions that collective bargaining is likely to produce in that market? Or conversely, given the performance of a union as revealed in the terms and administration of its collective agreements, would it be possible to say anything about the market power possessed by the union?

There has been a good deal of examination in recent years of at least one aspect of union "performance" — the effect of labor organization on hourly wage rates — with fairly inconclusive results. Paul Douglas, writing in 1930, found that while in the 1890's and early years of this century "unionists were able to secure for themselves appreciably higher wages and shorter hours than the mass of the workers," since 1914 "the wages in the non-union manufacturing industries have risen at least as rapidly as have those in non-manufacturing trades." [6] Arthur Ross, on the other hand, after a study of B.L.S. wage data 1933–45 concludes that "Real hourly earnings have advanced more sharply in highly organized industries than in less unionized industries, in periods of stable or declining membership as well as periods of reorganization." [7] Studies by Dunlop[8] and

---

[6] Paul Douglas, *Real Wages in the United States* (1930).

[7] Arthur M. Ross, "The Influence of Unionism Upon Earnings," *Quarterly Journal of Economics*, Feb. 1948, p. 284.

[8] John T. Dunlop, "Productivity and the Wage Structure," in Lloyd A. Metzler et al., *Income, Employment and Public Policy, Essays in Honor of Alvin H. Hansen* (New York, 1948).

Garbarino[9] cast doubt on any very strong influence of unionization on inter-industry wage structures. Clark Kerr, summing up the results of these and other investigations, concludes: "One consequence of contemporary institutional controls in the labor market is evident. They conduce to the single rate within the craft or industrial field which they cover. The best, although not thoroughly convincing, evidence now indicates they have surprisingly little effect, however, on inter-industry differentials, confirming the conclusions of Paul Douglas of a quarter of a century age."[10]

If we turn to the writings of those who have most strongly emphasized the dangers of labor monopoly, we find many ominous statements about distortions of the wage structure, and sabotage of the price system but almost no factual information to support such statements.[11] Are we to conclude that because the factual investigators of union performance have found no striking evidence of significant effect on wage differentials and the theorists of labor monopoly have failed to demonstrate their case empirically, the degree of market power possessed by unions is small? Some writers appear to think so but the conclusion seems to me premature.

Similar difficulties confront judgments, based on evidence regarding business performances, of market power in product markets. Repeatedly, in the administration of the antitrust laws, the courts have wisely refused to answer the question whether the prices — or some other aspects of performance — of a combination are "unreasonable," by some test of what would be reasonable under competitive conditions, and have found violation in the mere existence of the combination. And, insofar as the courts have tended to move away from "abuse of power" and toward the existence of "power itself"

---

[9] J. W. Garbarino, *A Theory of Inter-Industry Wage Structure Variations,* (Institute of Industrial Relations, University of California, 1950).

[10] "Labor Markets: Their Character and Consequences," I.R.R.A. *Proceedings,* 1949, p. 78.

[11] E.g., various writings of Charles E. Lindblom, Fritz Machlup, and Henry Simons. Cf. Lindblom, *Unions and Capitalism,* p. 5: "Unionism will destroy the price system by what it wins rather than by the struggle to win it. It sabotages the competitive order, not because the economy cannot weather the disturbance of work stoppages but because it cannot produce high output and employment at union wage rates. Nor can the economy survive the union's systematic disorganization of markets and its persistent undercutting of managerial authority."

as evidence of monopolizing or attempting to monopolize in cases involving large firms, the tests of market power have tended to emphasize structural rather than performance considerations. If the degree of monopoly possessed by a firm is to be estimated by comparing the prices, output, investment, and profits of this firm with what these prices, output, and investment of profits would be if the firm were subject to competitive restraints, two major difficulties arise. First, there is the question of standards; are the restraints to be those associated with pure competition or with some sort of "workable" competition, and, if the latter, what sort? Second, there is the problem of isolating the effect of market power on the prices, output, investment, and profits under observation from other influences. The study of business performance has its uses in estimates of market power in conjuction with structural evidence but only in rather special situations can performance tests alone yield unambiguous findings.

So far as I can see, the same difficulties plague attempts to estimate the market power of unions by means of observations of union performance. Again there is the question of standards. Are we comparing the behavior of union wage rates with the assumed behavior of wage rates in a purely competitive labor market, which is apparently what Machlup has in mind? [12] Or is the standard of comparison the assumed behavior of wage rates in the absence of unionization, which is apparently what Reynolds and various other people consider to be appropriate? [13] Secondly, assuming we have chosen our standard, will we find it possible to isolate statistically the influence on wage rates, or other dimensions of performance, of union power from all the other influences at work in a changing economy? A failure to establish empirically a clear connection between unioniza-

[12] Fritz Machlup, "Monopolistic Wage Determination as a part of the General Problem of Monopoly," in *Wage Determination and the Economics of Liberalism,* U. S. Chamber of Commerce, 1947, pp. 69, 70.

[13] Lloyd Reynolds, *Structure of Labor Markets; Wages and Labor Mobility in Theory and Practice* (New York, 1951), p. 259. Kerr, "Labor Markets: Their Character and Consequences," distinguishes between "perfect" labor markets in which "physical movement of workers and the wage setting process" are intermingled with the emergence of "one wage for labor" and "natural markets." He reports of the latter that all the evidence indicates a wide range of wage rates for equal qualifications — due to limited knowledge on the part of the worker and a "restricted conception of himself."

tion and the terms of the wage bargain does not, to my mind, dispose of the question of labor monopoly.

In product markets, it is much easier to assemble information relevant to the market power of a firm by considering the limitations imposed by the firm's position in the market than by observing the firm's performance, and I suspect this is true of the market power of unions. Needless to say, it is not at all easy in either case to evaluate this information. If we are to consider the area of freedom open to the union in wage negotiations as well as the limitations imposed by the external market environment, we must presumably start with the product market which defines the employers with whom, and the number of jobs with respect to which, the union will desire to negotiate. Unless all the employers in a well-defined product market are included, the union's area of freedom is bound to be severely circumscribed by the product substitution of non-union for union output. Given complete control of the jobs in a well defined product market, the union may be able to increase its market power by setting limits to the introduction of labor-saving technological changes or by increasing the number of jobs by "featherbedding" operations. There may also be opportunities of taking advantage of demand elasticities in the sale of the product by controlling or influencing output and price. The union might be said to occupy its market fully when all opportunities of improving wages, hours, and working conditions, within the unavoidable limits imposed by the elasticity of product demands and unalterable production functions lie within its control.

The union in the course of acquiring its market position may find it necessary to engage in organizing strikes and secondary boycotts; to press for closed shops; to absorb "independent businessmen-workers" into the union or drive them out of business; to insist on the employment of non-working standby crews, and do many other things designed ultimately to improve wages, hours, and working conditions. All or most of these are "well established practices" of trade unions, and Lester admonishes us, "Merely to condemn as 'monopoly' almost every well-established practice of trade-unions serves, therefore, to confuse rather than to shed light on, the significant issues." [14] I agree that to *condemn* these practices as monopolistic is wrong since

---

[14] Richard A. Lester, "Reflections on the Labor Monopoly Issue," *Journal of Political Economy,* Dec. 1947, p. 526.

condemnation implies a judgment based on some public interest standard. But to *analyze* these practices in relation to the market power or degree of monopoly achieved or achievable by unions seems to me not only desirable but necessary. Needless to say, the conclusions of such analysis have no necessary relevance to a public interest finding of "unreasonable" power or "abuse of power."

I take it for granted that all these and other union practices contribute — or are thought to contribute — to improvement of wages, hours, and working conditions. Consequently I agree with Lester that there is no reason for selecting out certain of these practices, such as the closed shop or industry-wide bargaining, as monopolistic to the exclusion of others. Certainly these particular practices may in various circumstances increase the degree of union power but so does any kind of labor organizing. The union is a monopolistic arrangement by definition and it may be reasonably assumed that a union will take such steps as it can to increase the degree of its monopoly control in order the better to perform the functions for which it was organized.

At the same time it has been emphasized that the union is a very special kind of monopoly organization, negotiating on behalf of its members rather than selling their services, and constrained by various internal and external political considerations in its conduct of negotiations. There is no reason to expect then that the market power possessed by a union will be translated into a certain predictable pattern of economic performance via some sort of wage-maximizing motivations and procedures. If we turn to commodity markets, the closest resemblance is a particular kind of cartel which, though it does not behave as a single monopoly seller would behave, is a monopoly organization for all that. And so is a labor union.

UNREASONABLE UNION POWER

It needs to be recognized at the outset of any discussion of "appropriate" limits to union power or use of power that this is a political question. There is no possibility, by means of an application of the principles of economics, the philosophy of the common law, or any other technique of analysis or body of doctrine, of arriving at an "optimum" solution to this problem. The determination of wages and working conditions through the process of collective bargaining is

highly valued by important elements of the community not only because of "bargaining" considerations but because it permits the participation of labor in a process of industrial self-government. Under
the Wagner Act collective bargaining was the preferred method of
wage determination and even under Taft-Hartley it is an approved
method. But collective bargaining inevitably requires the existence
of unions with a substantial degree of market power. In general,
the more power unions have the more rapidly unorganized sectors
of the economy can be brought within the framework of collective
bargaining and the more deeply union representatives can penetrate
into the process of joint labor-management decision-making. Those
who set a high value on this process are apt to take the position that
since collective bargaining is a "good thing" public policy should
favor whatever measures are necessary to expand it.[15]

It is equally clear, on the other hand, that a substantial degree of
union power can adversely affect the functioning of competition in
both labor and product markets. I say *can* rather than *will* both
because the evidence is unclear and because there is a difference between the possession and the exercise of market power. There is a
substantial body of opinion favoring the maintenance of competition
and, *ipso facto,* whatever measures are necessary to attain these
ends. Furthermore, some attach value to continued opportunities for
self-employment even in areas where so-called "businessmen-workers" are in competition with union members.[16] And others point out
that individual workers can be "oppressed" by union as well as busi-

[15] Cf. for example the statement of Nathan Feinsinger in *Hearings on the
Taft-Hartley Law before the Senate Committee on Labor and Public Welfare,*
81st Congress, 1st Session, Pts. 4-6, p. 2569: "If our national policy is to be
effectuated through collective bargaining, we cannot simultaneously encourage
a competing system of individual bargaining. If collective bargaining is to be
free **and** voluntary, we cannot have governmental intervention, except to
insure the conditions under which free bargaining can take place."

[16] Cf. the opinion of Frankfurter, J., in the case of International Brother-
hood of Teamsters, Local 309, v. Hanke, 339 U. S. 470 (1950) at p. 475:
"Here we have a glaring instance of the interplay of competing social-economic
interests and viewpoints. Unions obviously are concerned not to have union
standards undermined by non-union shops. This interest penetrates into self-
employer shops. On the other hand, some of our profoundest thinkers from
Jefferson to Brandeis have stressed the importance to a democratic society of
encouraging self-employer economic units as a counter-movement to what are
deemed to be the dangers inherent in excessive concentration of economic
power."

ness power. Thus there appears to be a set of respectable values held by a considerable number of people that is unlikely to be realized without some check to union power, and I suppose it would have to be said that for those who esteem hightly the benefits — supposed or real — of a competitive price system, the check would need to be sharp and severe.

A conflict of *some* magnitude between the values of collective bargaining and the values of competition seems to me inescapable.[17] Under these circumstances how much of the one, as against how much of the other, a democratic society will permit itself to have will, in the last analysis, be determined at the polls. All that an "independent" and "objective" student can hope to contribute is a somewhat clearer understanding of the question how much of the one of necessity has to be sacrificed in order to secure some part of the other. This seems to me a fruitful field of inquiry for those interested in public policy in this area. Even if we set a high value on collective bargaining we can recognize that there are some types of union practice that seriously damage the competitive process without adding very much to the union's ability to attain its ends. And, no doubt, similar conclusions could be reached by asking the question whether the competitive process would really be damaged very much by certain union practices that are essential to effective collective bargaining. But this type of inquiry is detailed and difficult, and I propose here to avoid it in favor of the much easier task of commenting on certain proposed solutions to this question of the appropriate limits to union power and its use.

Let us consider first the implications of the so-called self-interest doctrine; that so long as a union acts in its own self-interest and

---

[17] This conflict is stated in somewhat exaggerated form by Neil Chamberlain, commenting on a statement of Joseph Spengler's on unions' monopolistic control of the wage rate: "Here is a problem couched in terms which are familiar to generations of economists bred on liberal economic traditions. But its very statement in these terms robs it of its real significanre — that the development in industrial relations represent not just a threat to the workability of the price system but a challenge to its philosophical and ethical foundations. . . . Satisfaction in the process of production, enjoyment of the job and the worker society which it represents, are important parts of living." Joseph J. Spengler, "Power Blocs and the Formation and Content of Economic Decisions," I.R.R.A. *Proceedings,* 1949, p. 174. Chamberlain's statement is at p. 200).

eschews violence and coercion no limits should be placed by government on the acquisition and use of union power. So far as federal legislation is concerned this doctrine was, of course, in effect between 1941 and 1947, after the Hutcheson decision[18] and before the enactment of Taft-Hartley.

I should like to state with respect to this doctrine three not very startling or novel propositions. There is really not much basis in either logic or experience for believing that an unimpeded economic struggle among large-interests groups will lead to sociably acceptable results. Government can, in fact, go rather far in limiting the acts of unions in pursuit of their interest without substantially damaging the collective bargaining process. The view that a free enterprise economy implies no constraint of the self-interest pursuits of economic units has as little validity for labor as it has for business.

There are some, of course, to whom the struggle of large groups means competition. "I have seen the suggestion made," said Justice Holmes sixty years ago, "that the conflict between employers and employed is not competition. But I venture to assume that none of my brethren would rely on that suggestion. . . . it is plain from the slightest consideration of practical affairs, or the most superficial reading of industrial history, that free competition means combination, and that the organization of the world, now going on so fast, means an ever increasing might and scope of combination. . . . Whether beneficial on the whole, as I think it, or detrimental, it is inevitable. . . ."[19]

Justice Holmes was a very great man, but his ideas on the nature of competition, I confess, have always struck me as being rather peculiar. The stricture that unions should act only in their own interest is really not very much of a stricture, as experience since the Hutcheson case has shown, and, despite the writings of my col-

[18] U. S. v. Hutcheson, 312 U. S. 219 (1941). In Justice Frankfurter's famous phrase, "So long as a union acts in its self-interest and does not combine with non-labor groups, the licit and the illicit under Section 20 are not to be distinguished by any judgment regarding the wisdom or unwisdom, the rightness or wrongness, the selfishness or unselfishness of the end of which the particular union activities are the means."

[19] O. W. Holmes, J., in Vegelahn v. Gunter, 167 Mass. 92 (1896). My colleague Archibald Cox calls it to my attention, however, that a review of Holmes' labor decision reveals his position as falling substantially short of full acceptance of the self-interest doctrine.

league Galbraith, I do not really believe that there is an historic law to the effect that the appearance and use of power will be inevitably checked by the appearance of a countervailing power.[20] The historic forces may have to be nudged and assisted by action of the state designed to moderate the action in their own interests of economic groups. This has been found desirable, in this country at least, with respect to business enterprises and there is no reason to believe that the self-interest of labor groups is any more closely identified with the public interest than that of General Motors.[21]

Nor do I think that government intervention to limit unions in the pursuit of their interest means the end of collective bargaining. One does not have to be a supporter of Taft-Hartley to hold that after eight years' experience under that law American workers are not yet slaves. After all, as McCabe has pointed out, "The Wagner Act took unions out of the category of private clubs in which the Supreme Court found them in Adair v. United States and Coppage v. Kansas." [22] And they have never returned to that category. There is a view, vigorously expressed by various labor leaders in the hearings on Taft-Hartley,[23] that any public interference with the self-interest pursuits of a union is incompatible with the operation of a

[20] Cf. J. K. Galbraith, *American Capitalism: The Concept of Countervailing Power* (Boston, 1952).

[21] On the relation of the labor interest to the public interest see an interesting paper by E. H. Chamberlin, "The Monopoly Power of Labor," in *Impact of the Union; Eight Economic Theorists Evaluate the Labor Union Movement,* edited by David McCord Wright (New York, 1951).

[22] Testimony of D. A. McCabe, *Hearings,* Senate Committee on Labor and Public Welfare, 81st Congress, 1st Session, Parts 1–3, p. 1564.

[23] Cf. for example, the testimony of John L. Lewis, *Hearings,* Senate Committee on Labor and Public Welfare, 80th Congress, 1st Session (1947), p. 1984. The statement of William Green (*Hearings,* pp. 992–994) is equally illuminating regarding labor attitudes toward any limitation of self-interest pursuit by unions. When Senator Ives pointed out that there was probably going to be legislation regulating secondary boycotts and jurisdictional strikes and that it was important that this legislation be as sensible as possible, Mr. Green replied in effect: (1) The present proposals are impossible; (2) it is all a very difficult question and a commission ought to be set up to study it; (3) what can Congress do about it anyway; are you going to put people in jail for refusing to work?; (4) the whole question should be left to the "House of Labor" to determine.

Philip Murray's contribution was that if there are any abuses in the labor movement, the Committee should persuade "Willie" Green to sit down with "Phil" Murray to see how they can be ironed out (p. 1089).

free enterprise economy. But, in the words of Justice Holmes, "I venture to assume that none of my brethren would rely on that suggestion."

We must, of course, recognize that in the United Kingdom and the Scandinavian countries public policy in effect sets little or no limit to the self-interested action of trade unions. It we had time, and the competence, it might be useful to speculate on the lessons of this experience for the United States. Certainly on one definition of "good labor relations" it might be said that in these countries labor relations are better than they have been over the last two decades in the United States. But this definition appears to exclude from the meaning of "good labor relations" certain adverse effects on consumer interests and, in England at least, some considerable part of the good relationship between labor and management seems to have been purchased by effective collusion against the consumer.[24] In certain of the Scandinavian countries, notably Norway, the management of labor relations appears to have required a large step toward the application of a public wage-price policy as an essential element in the administration of a planned economy. I am very far from contending that even this cost of attaining good labor relations is necessarily excessive. But, if these are the costs, they should be recognized and, in the political process through which public policy gets determined, they should be compared with the supposed advantages that might accompany an unimpeded pursuit of self-interest by organized labor.

There is, furthermore, the question whether institutions and policies that work in a certain way in another country would function in the same fashion in the United States. In this connection I am impressed by the words of Judge Amidon in Great Northern Railway v. Brosseau.[25] After pointing out that Section 20 of the Clayton Act

[24] See, e.g., the comment of W. Arthur Lewis on the decision in Crofter Handwoven Harris Tweed Co., Ltd. v. Veitch and Another, 1 All.E.R.142 (1942) in *Overhead Costs* (London, 1949), Ch. VI: "Businessmen seeking to advance their private trade interest may not only combine with each other, but also bring their workers into the scheme, and promise them part of the swag; even this was hardly in doubt after the decision in Reynolds v. Shipping Federation, Ltd. (1923, Ch. 28). Now we know that they may use not only their own workers, but workers in any other industry who happen to belong to the same union."

[25] 286 F. 414 (1923): "In Great Britain strikers and the new employees are a part of the common life of the community. They mingle freely with one another. The opportunities for peaceful persuasion are a part of the daily

was pretty much copied from Section 2 of the British Trades Dispute Act of 1906, he emphasizes the enormous differences in the application of these two sections in the two countries and concludes, "The contrast between the situations in England and the United States presents an impressive example of how differently the same statute works in countries whose habits of life are different."

The facts cited here refer, of course, to the early 1920's when labor relations in this country were vastly different from now. But the observations of Judge Amidon are still relevant to the question whether in this country an unlimited pursuit by trade unions of their own self-interest would tend to produce the same kind of labor-management relations as in England, with or without the presence of a Sherman Law.[26]

I do not know what the answer to this question is. Here I wish merely to emphasize that the self-interest doctrine will inevitably lead to action that impinges on various values that may, somewhat loosely, be said to be bound up with the maintenance of competition. The self-interest doctrine then can be pushed to an extreme only by those who are willing to assign zero magnitudes to these values. If it is not to be pushed that far, what kinds of limits have been or may be suggested?

THE DOCTRINE OF EQUAL BARGAINING POWER

One of the oldest defenses of union organization depends on the supposed desirability of equalizing bargaining power between employees and employers. This argument appears in every textbook in economics and as a statement of policy is written into paragraph 2 of the Wagner Act.[27] One clear implication of this defense is that there are appropriate limits to the power of unions. If equality in the

intercourse. There the private armed detective is unknown. . . . The writ of injunction in strike cases has been unknown in England during the period when it has attained such universal use with us."

[26] It should be noted, furthermore, that trade unions in the United Kingdom are substantially limited in their pursuit of self-interest by extensive foreign competition, and the balance of payments considerations involved in a heavy dependence on foreign trade, and by their association with a political party that has been and at any time may be asked to assume the responsibilities of government.

[27] National Labor Relations Act of 1935, par. 2: "The inequality of bargaining power between employees who do not possess full freedom of association or actual liberty of contract, and employers who are organized in the

bargaining relation is desirable a growth of union power beyond the extent necessary to secure equality would appear to be undesirable. Do we have here a useful suggestion concerning the proper distinction between reasonable and unreasonable union power?

I think not. Although there is some minimum of market power without which a union cannot bargain effectively or even exist as continuing organization, to attempt by public action to equalize power on different sides of the labor market is neither possible nor desirable. In the first place, the standard suggested by the doctrine of equal bargaining power is clearly non-operational. Does the U.A.W. have greater or less bargaining power than General Motors? I don't know. Not only do I not know but neither I nor anybody else has a very good idea what information, if diligently collected, would permit an answer to that question. It is difficult enough — some would say impossible — to form an objective judgment on whether the market power of a business firm exceeds or falls short of some permissible standard. But to estimate whether a labor union and a business firm confronting each other in wage negotiations have or do not have approximately equal bargaining power seems to me, by at least another order of magnitude, more difficult.

In the second place, equality of bargaining power, if attained, has a very different significance in different market contexts. If the negotiating parties are surrounded, on either side of the market, by effective competitors the results are likely to be quite different than if both are entitled to be called monopolists. The theory of bilateral monopoly tells us that stalemate is a distinct possibility and the more equal the negotiators the more likely is this possibility.

In the third place, the doctrine implicitly assumes that the attainment of equality is compatible with the efficient operation of organizations on both sides of the market. Why should this be necessarily so? If workers are unorganized, we would not recommend, I presume, that firms be reduced to that size necessary to the attainment of equality of bargaining power with individual workers. Nor should we, I think, suppose that there is any virtue in the proposition that

corporate or other forms of ownership association substantially burdens and affects the flow of commerce, and tends to aggravate recurrent business depressions, by depressing wage rates and the purchasing power of wage earners in industry and by preventing the stabilization of competitive wage rates and working conditions within and between industries."

the size of the union, or of a union bargaining unit, be adapted to the scale considerations that influence the size of firms. Both firms and unions have scale problems of their own and there is no reason for believing that what is optimum on one side of the market will produce an equality of bargaining power with the optimum size on the other side of the bargaining table.

For all these reasons I suggest that the doctrine of equal bargaining power, having done its duty in the early history of trade-unionism, be decently interred and quietly forgotten.

UNION INTERFERENCE WITH BUSINESS COMPETITION

Finally, let us consider briefly the suggestion that at least one guide line to the proper limitation of union powers may be provided by considering the effect of union action on business competition. Since the Hutcheson decision there has been much discussion of this possibility, and many bills designed to accomplish this objective have been presented to Congress. Unfortunately the line separating trade-union action limiting competition in labor markets from trade-union action limiting business competition in product markets is not self-evident. As we have seen, union efforts to improve wages, hours, and working conditions can spread rather indiscriminately among labor and product markets, and business competition may be adversely affected at a number of points. Let us consider briefly some of the possibilities.

First, there is the question of the effect of union action on the number of firms in the market. Should unions be permitted to drive independent business-workers out of the market? It is clear that their continuing competition may adversely affect union wage scales. On the other hand, to eliminate them may adversely affect competition in the product market. Should unions control the entrance of new firms through what is essentially a licensing process as allegedly has been done in the Pacific Northwest under conditions locally and familiarly known as "Dave Beck's N.R.A."? Should unions exclude from a local market the competition of firms located outside the market by refusing to work on their products? This appears to have been a fairly common practice in recent years, and by no means all boycotts of this sort have been attempts to organize the unorganized employees of outside competitors.

Second, there is the question of union action interfering with the independence of price and output decisions by firms within the market. Should there be allowed to be accomplished by unions what would be condemned as a *per se* violation of the antitrust laws if undertaken by business firms? My colleague Professor Cox, in what is by far the most penetrating discussion of labor and the antitrust laws that I have seen, favors an amendment of these laws condemning "agreements with employers, fixing prices, limiting production or cutting off access to a market." [28] It is not altogether clear, however, how far this condemnation is meant to go. Cox admits that union action limiting output presents a difficult problem. Were John L. Lewis' famous memorial days merely an attempt to spread the available work among union members or did they represent an attempt to maintain the price of coal by limiting output? He apparently also does not want to include in this condemnation union action designed to exclude the introduction of labor saving techniques and equipment and to "make work" by requiring the employment of non-workers, though this type of action would almost certainly be struck down by the antitrust laws if attempted by a combination of employers.

Third, there is the bothersome question of who is a worker and who is a businessman. However far one goes in supporting the self-interest activity of unions it is assumed that certain limitations to union power are provided by the arms'-length and independent bargaining of businessmen on the other side of the market. But what if the wages of labor are essentially a share of the proceeds and dependent on the quantity and price of the workers' output as in the case of various east and west coast fishermen's associations? In this situation the only limitation to be found is the elasticity of the demand for the product. And what may become of arms'-length bargaining if managerial employees up to and including the president of the company are brought within the ranks of union membership? The United Mine Workers, at least before Taft-Hartley, frequently proclaimed their aims to include organizing everyone up to and including the mine superintendent. The Wagner Act defined employee as "any employee" and, as Justice Douglas pointed out in his dissenting opinion in the Packard case, if foremen are employees so are "vice presidents, managers, assistant managers, superintendents, as-

[28] Archibald Cox, "Labor and the Anti-Trust Laws; A Preliminary Analysis," *University of Pennsylvania Law Review,* Nov. 1955.

sistant superintendents — indeed all who are on the payroll of the company, including the president." [29] He goes on to say that if the majority view of the Court prevails, "The struggle for control or power between management and labor becomes secondary to a growing unity in their common demands on ownership" or, one might add, on the consumer.

Finally, there is the most bothersome question of all, the question of so-called "management prerogatives." We expect from our system of enforced competition, I take it, not only a limitation to business power but the maintenance of an environment in which business rivalry will produce a continuous flow of new and better products and new and better ways of producing existing products. One important presumption underlying this policy is that business has a substantial area of freedom to innovate and to explore ways of achieving cost reduction and product improvement. Union action *could* diminish this area of freedom rather drastically and this diminution *could* at all points be closely related to a legitimate union concern with wages, hours and working conditions. E. Wight Bakke, in a perceptive paper on collective bargaining, points out that a business enterprise is a risk taking organization in which management wants to preserve as much freedom of action as possible. The union, on the other hand, is a security seeking organization one of whose objectives is a reduction in the area of employer discretion.[30] At the Labor-Management Conference in 1945, management representatives wanted an assurance that collective bargaining would not be allowed to encroach on a specific set of "management prerogatives." The labor representatives, while recognizing that "the responsibilities of management must be preserved," took the position that collective bargaining is an "expanding process" which must necessarily encompass new subjects.[31] One can agree with Richard Lester that unions do not normally desire to "take over" the functions of management but at the same time be impressed by the potential limitations to the effectiveness of business competition that inhere in a gradual cur-

[29] Packard Motor Co. v. N.L.R.B., 330 U. S. 483.

[30] E. Wight Bakke, "Organizational Problems in Collective Bargaining," in *Wage Determination and the Economics of Liberalism,* Economic Institute of the U. S. Chamber of Commerce, 1947.

[31] Cf. George W. Taylor, *Government Regulation of Industrial Relations* (New York, 1948), pp. 237–238.

tailment of management's area of freedom through the process of collective bargaining.[32]

These seem to me the principal ways in which union power may impinge upon business competition. There may be others.[33] I do not propose to attempt here an evaluation of the effects on competition of various lines of union action but wish merely to emphasize that those who consider that the appropriate limits to union power should be established at the point where union action adverses affects the process of business competition may be embracing a lot of territory.

In conclusion let me reemphasize the view that the determination of the "proper" limits to union power is not completely amenable to logic and experience. We are concerned here with values that are to some degree conflicting and how these values are to be reconciled is a part of the political process. At the same time I feel that the gulf between those on the one hand who believe that there is no problem of labor monopoly worth mentioning and those on the other hand who believe that it is the problem of our generation is unnecessarily wide. Is it not possible for those who set great store by collective bargaining to recognize that there are areas in which union action may encroach rather seriously on other values and where limitations may be imposed without significant injury to the process of collective bargaining itself. And is it not also possible for those who set great store by the maintenance of a competitive society to recognize that the spread of unionism does not necessarily mean that all is lost.

[32] Richard A. Lester, *Labor and Industrial Relations; A General Analysis* (New York, 1951), p. 209.

[33] I have not discussed at all the so-called wage-price problem though this is probably the area in which there is the greatest latent concern for the effects of trade-union action on the functioning of the economy. Insofar as there is a wage-price problem it certainly involves the relationships of large groups, unions and firms, but it is not very amenable to analysis in terms of particular markets. Industry-wide wage increases, whether or not negotiated by industry-wide bargaining, provide an excellent rationalization for simultaneous price increases and probably facilitates price leadership. Furthermore business will be less reluctant to increase prices if "key" wage bargains bring about similar wage increases in economically adjacent industries. And such reluctances as union leaders have to pressing for a continuous succession of wage-rate increase or that business may have in granting such increases will be considerably mitigated if both groups can count on a fiscal policy that in effect guarantees full employment regardless of what happens to the price level.

PART III

RAW MATERIALS, SECURITY, AND ECONOMIC GROWTH

Introduction

The papers in Part III are somewhat tangential to the main theme of this volume. They represent interests acquired during the war in the Office of Strategic Services and on the staff of the Joint Intelligence Committee and, later, as a member of the President's Materials Policy Commission.

The first three chapters of Part III are principally concerned with two major issues. To what extent is the security of the United States likely to be endangered by the elimination of important foreign sources of raw-material supply? Must the United States encounter over the next few decades increasing real costs of raw materials and if so, what would this do to our prospect of economic growth? The first question belongs, in a sense, to the pre-atomic age, but it much exercised military planners and business advisers to the military in the periods before, during, and just after World War II. Furthermore, vestiges of the thought then current appear to remain in our stockpile and other policies, despite the fact that the development of military technology seems to have made somewhat irrelevant attempts to assure in advance a four- or five-year supply of industrial materials for an economy whose productive capacity is assumed to remain intact.

It was and is the author's view that those responsible for raw-material supplies in wartime tend enormously to underestimate the possibilities of civilian rationing and technological substitution. Powerful support for this view is available in the experience of Germany in World War II. The Germans mounted and sustained for five years a tremendous military effort with — by our standards — incredibly small supplies of strategic raw materials. They did it largely by rationing and substitution. This process, of course, if extempore and unrehearsed, may involve substantial costs and some loss of quality. But there is no reason why it should be extempore, and it is relatively easy for a country with the natural resources of the United States to assure itself of raw-material supplies for wars of World War II magnitude. The only hitch is that we seem to have passed out of the era of such wars.

The second question is more enduring. The last century has witnessed a continuous decline in the real cost of producing foodstuffs and industrial raw materials, and this decline has contributed substantially to the economic growth of the western world. During most of this period the United States has been a large net exporter of these products, but towards the end of the 1930's we began to be a net importer. In 1952, the date of the publication of the report of the President's Materials Policy Commission, we were importing some 9 to 10 per cent of our total consumption. This shift in the position of the United States from net exporter to net importer has been accompanied in the rest of the world by a significant upsurge in the rate of population growth with a commensurate increase in requirements for foodstuffs and raw materials. Are we and other countries now confronting a long-term trend of increasing real costs for meeting these requirements?

The P.M.P.C. thought not, at least over the next quarter-century, providing that conditions of international trade permit raw materials and foodstuffs to be produced in low-cost areas, and providing that technological developments now visible over the horizon are realized. Known mineral reserves and potential soil fertility are adequate to the supply, within this time period, of twice or more the current annual requirements without substantial increases in real cost. But what if governmental policies do not permit the expansion of foodstuffs and raw materials in low-cost areas? The P.M.P.C. envisaged a situation by 1975 in which the United States would import roughly 20 per cent of its consumption of these products, assuming that trade barriers were no higher than at present. If, however, foreign sources of supply become inaccessible, what would this do to the real costs of meeting our raw material requirements and what repercussions would an increase in real costs have on the American rate of economic growth? It is the author's view that the American economy is relatively invulnerable to this contingency, at least for the next few decades, and this view is argued at some length in Chapters 12 and 13. Furthermore, since the value of industrial materials is less than 10 per cent of the aggregate value of finished output, a small increase in the real cost of raw-material supply is not likely to offer a substantial check to economic growth.

Chapter 14 on world "Energy Requirements and Economic

Growth" was prepared for the United States delegation to the International Conference on the Peaceful Uses of Atomic Energy, Geneva, 1955, in collaboration with the staff of the National Planning Association Project on the Economic Aspects of the Productive Uses of Nuclear Energy. It is an attempt to project the rate of growth of world energy requirements, to establish certain relationships between economic growth and energy requirements, and to consider the effect of a reduction in energy costs on economic development.

II

American Security and Access to Raw Materials[1]

The foreign policy of the United States appears to have two primary political objectives: the maintenance of peace, if possible; and, if this becomes impossible, the maximization of military effort against its enemies. This duality of purpose raises a number of perplexing questions. If we could assume with Clausewitz that the making or avoidance of war simply involves a choice between means — the end being given — then these questions would disappear. As it is, we have to recognize that in fact the pursuit of peace may well involve actions which tend to diminish United States military potential and that attempts to maximize military potential may well increase the possibility of war. Under these circumstances only a compromise solution seems sensible. We must consider best how peace may be maintained, but be ready to reject those methods which would leave the United States defenseless in the event that war cannot be avoided.

Economic considerations bulk large in connection with both these objectives.[2] The development of a maximum military potential involves economic calculations at every turn. So also does the choice among economic alternatives affect in many ways the prospect for peace. For the purposes of this discussion, however, the analysis will be limited to certain economic elements involved in the maximization of war potential.

It is useful to distinguish between the strategic and economic considerations affecting national defense. The strategic considerations may be regarded primarily as matters of space and geographical position. The economic factors would have to do with supply of matériel. It is obvious, however, that the two factors are interdependent.

---

[1] Reprinted from *World Politics,* Vol. i, No. 2, Jan. 1949.

[2] Pursuit of the political objectives of preparedness and peace may interfere with the maximum attainment of prosperity. For present purposes, the absolute priority of these two political objectives over any economic objectives of foreign policy is taken for granted. With Adam Smith, it is assumed that defense is more important than opulence.

The choice of strategic objectives depends substantially on the quantity of military resources available; strategic considerations, in turn, will heavily influence the volume and character of the requirements imposed on the economic system. The strategist recognizes this interdependence when he speaks of "trading space for time." The economist refines the conception when he says that what is substituted are the military resources which it would take time to organize and produce.

It is out of this interdependence that there arise some of the most complex questions involved in maximizing war potential. And it is the necessity for reconciling strategic and economic considerations which makes it both difficult and important to answer the particular question: "What bearing has control of the sources of raw-material supply on the military potential of the United States?"

THE ECONOMIC RAW-MATERIAL BASE
IN PEACE AND WAR

For ordinary peacetime production the United States depends on raw-material supplies from every part of the globe: tungsten from China, mica and burlap from India, copper from Chile and West Africa, graphite from Madagascar, and so on. If raw-material interest be defined in terms of the effect of the availability of a particular source of supply on national output, then it is obvious that we have raw-material interests — which are a part of economic interests more broadly defined — everywhere. And in order to estimate the extent of our interest in a particular source of supply we should have to take into account the possibilities of substitution in the event that this source were cut off. Now the possibilities of substitution are usually very numerous. The same raw material may be drawn from other geographic sources; scrap yields in the United States may be increased; other materials may be substituted in various uses; finished items may be redesigned to eliminate entirely the need for this material, and so forth. If the possibilities of substitution are fully exploited it will usually be found that any deficiency can be made good. But — and this is the point to be stressed — making good the deficiency involves a cost.

The cost should properly be measured as the amount by which national output would be reduced — all possibilities of substitution having been exhausted — if a particular source of raw-material supply were cut off. Since the factor which ultimately limits national output is the supply of available labor, the extent of our interest in a particular source of raw-material supply can be roughly measured by the increased labor requirements necessitated by the elimination of this source. If this measure is applied, it will no doubt be found that the economic interest of the United States in certain raw materials and in various geographical sources of supply is sufficient to justify careful planning in peace to assure their availability in time of war. Planning is equally important in avoiding or minimizing the loss of time that may be involved in any process of substitution.

A number of ways of assuring wartime supplies of scarce materials are at hand: the material may be stockpiled; domestic sources may be reserved for military use; domestic sources for all uses may be conserved by limiting peacetime exports or encouraging peacetime imports; technical problems involved in substitution may be overcome by peacetime research in preparation for the eventualities of war. How far any or all of these measures should be carried is a question that can be answered only by examining particular raw-material situations. It goes without saying that a study of these problems is important and that the steps necessary to assure the availability of scarce raw materials should be taken.

All this is too obvious to require extended discussion. But let us take a further step and ask whether there are raw-material interests so vital to the defense of the United States as to require, in time of war, a diversion of military resources for their protection. The answer depends upon the area that the United States will be called upon to defend. It is generally accepted that such an area would for strategic reasons include as a minimum, North America, the Caribbean, and the northern half of South America. If we control this space, it can be said with some confidence that the United States has no outside raw-material interest to which substantial military resources need be diverted.[3] It must be remembered that we are talking here in terms of a minimum. The larger the strategic area required by the armed forces, the easier it becomes to substantiate the case.

[3] In the following discussion, the sources and requirements of raw material for atomic warfare are neglected. The author, through lack of knowledge, is not prepared to assess the significance of this omission.

In order to demonstrate the truth of this proposition conclusively, it would be necessary to show either or both of the following: (1) that the loss of any or all of raw-material supplies from outside this area would, after full allowance is made for substitution, involve a relatively small loss in the output of war material; (2) that the defense of any or all sources of raw-material supply outside the strategic area would involve the diversion of military forces from important strategic objectives. It is probably impossible, for lack of relevant facts and figures, to prove this case by direct evidence. However, the indirect evidence appears to be sufficiently strong to carry conviction.

Before discussing this evidence, it is pertinent to emphasize one thing: it is almost inevitable that the military will, on this sort of question, receive poor advice from civilian specialists. This is so for two reasons. The civilian expert, by the nature of his job, is bound to have an inflated estimate of the importance of the materials with which he is concerned. During war he is faced on all sides by shortages; he is assailed by clamors from processors all of whom insist that their requirements are vital. Even though infinite possibilities of substitution exist, no one wants to substitute, and all insist that without the material in question their plants will have to shut down. Consequently the raw-material specialist comes to the conclusion that if we don't get that next shipload of graphite from Madagascar, if we don't hold on to the New Caledonian supply of nickel, if the North African sources of the supply of red squill fall into enemy hands, the war production of the United States will be doomed. The possession of these areas consequently becomes to him a vital economic interest.

In the second place, the raw-material specialist has no proper estimate — nor can he be expected to have — of what the cost to our war effort would be of diverting military resources from strategic to economic objectives. Surely it may be taken for granted that the over-all military objective is the destruction of the armed strength of the enemy and that this requires a substantial concentration of our own striking force. If the military listened seriously to the clamor of raw-material experts, they would probably so disperse our military resources in the defense of this, that, and the other "vital" economic interest that no effective striking force could be assembled.

The proper objective of economic planning and economic policy is thus the elimination of "vital" economic interests. If the planning is ably done, the whole of the armed strength of the United States should be available for the attainment of military objectives. Any serious dispersal of strength for the defense of economic objectives should be considered to be a failure of economic policy.

Returning now to the main argument, what is the evidence that the loss of any or all of the sources of raw-material supply lying outside the strategic defense area of the United States would not seriously handicap our war production? The evidence, as has been indicated, is chiefly indirect, and the principal witness for the defense is Germany. It is unnecessary to undertake quantitative estimates of German war production. It will, perhaps, be admitted that Germany waged quite a sizeable war for a period of almost six years. It will certainly be admitted that Germany waged this war with quantities of raw materials that were incredibly small in comparison with the quantities available within the strategic area of the United States. Germany's supplies of iron and steel, coal, aluminum, magnesium, lead and zinc, although not large by our standards, were adequate for both military and civilian requirements. Her supplies of petroleum products and rubber, though heavily dependent on synthetic production, were also adequate for military and essential civilian needs, at least until the final year of the war. Supplies of copper, tin and all the ferro-alloys were ludicrously small by our standards. Yet Germany managed, by exploiting the possibilities of substitution to the full, to meet her own war requirements and the essential civilian requirements in Germany and Europe for the whole period of the war. It is worthwhile to look at Germany's consumption of these metals, from 1938 through 1944.

During this period when German consumption of these "essential" materials remained almost constant, German production of finished military items increased three to fourfold. The production of aircraft increased from 8000 in 1939 to 40,000 in 1944; tanks from 750 in 1939 to 3900 in 1944; and the output of weapons and ammunition tripled.

Although annual consumption of copper in the United States during the war years was approximately ten times the German con-

German Consumption of Metals, 1938–1944[a]
(in thousands of metric tons, metal content)

	1938	1939	1940	1941	1942	1943	1944
Copper	448.3	324	292	392	238	221	219
Tin	20.4	6.8	8.5	10.9	8.3	9.5	7.7
Ferro-alloys							
Nickel	12.4	10.1	11.6	9.2	8.0	9.4	9.5
Molybdenum	....	3.4	2.2	2.2	1.8	0.8	0.7
Chrome	27.4	48.1	35.3	43.3	38.4	38.7	42.4
Manganese (ore)	135.9	....	130.2	152.1	124.1	178.5	....
Wolfram	4.3	4.2	3.7	3.4	3.0	2.2	1.5
Vanadium	0.7	....	0.8	1.4	1.8	3.0	....
Titanium	4.9	....	5.9	7.1	8.5	9.2	....

[a] The data comprising this table were assembled by the *United States Strategic Bombing Survey* from the following German sources: *Statistische Schnellberichte zur Kriegsproduktion, Hauptabteilung Planstatistik, Planungsamt* (Speer Ministry); *Monatliche Rohstoffübersichten, Statistisches Reichsamt, Abtg. VIII;* and *Statistische Zusammenstellung, Metallgeschaft, A.G.*

sumption, and American consumption of tin nearly twenty times the German, it is interesting to note that German stocks of these metals increased throughout the war and were more than twice as great at the end of 1944 as at the end of 1938. American consumption of all the ferro-alloys was a multiple of German consumption, ranging from about 10 in the case of manganese ore to 40 or 50 in the case of nickel.

It is quite clear from all this that Germany managed to fight a first-class war on very small quantities of "essential" raw materials. How was it done? The answer embraces a wide range of devices: substitution of plentiful for scarce metals, redesign of equipment eliminating or curtailing scarce metal requirements, extensive collection of scrap, paring of civilian requirements. The over-all economic effect of the shortages that required these methods was no doubt an increase in labor requirements per unit of finished output. The point is, however, that this increase was not enormous; it was rather easily held to manageable proportions. In a few cases — but the number is very few — there is some evidence that the quality of the finished product deteriorated. This deterioration, however, does not seem to have impressed those who had to face German equipment on the battlefield. The moral, for our purpose, seems to be that the potentialities for substitution and replacement of raw materials in a modern economy are enormous.

British and American technical intelligence services have by now collected a large body of information concerned with Germany's management of the problem presented by raw-material shortages. A careful examination of this information will obviously help to understand the problem with which we are here concerned. Dipping briefly into these sources, one comes up with these findings:

At the beginning of 1942 German locomotives required 2.3 metric tons of copper. By the middle of 1943 these requirements had been reduced to 237 kilograms, a reduction of approximately nine-tenths.

The quantity of copper used in U-boats was reduced during the war from 56 to 26 tons on the average.

Iron radiators were substituted for copper radiators in all German motor vehicles.

The use of alloy steel was virtually eliminated in railway car construction. The very difficult problem presented by shortages of ferro-alloys was reduced to manageable proportions largely by the substitution of the relatively plentiful alloys — vanadium and silicon — for the less plentiful. Vanadium, for example, was substituted for molybdenum in gun tubes under 21 cm. Nickel was replaced by vanadium in gun tubes 10.5 cm. and under.

New processes were devised to make possible the working of lower grade ore supplies, as in the case of chromium ores from the Balkans. Perhaps most important of all, the very large quantities of scrap, which exist in any highly industrialized economy, were systematically collected and utilized.

It is not pretended that the German management of raw-material shortages was accomplished without cost. Obviously labor requirements were substantially increased, and in a few cases some sacrifice in quality of finished product was involved. The loss of time involved in substitution must also be taken into account. The point, however, is that the additional labor requirement imposed by raw-material shortages made up a small percentage of the total labor requirements of a war economy.

A consideration of economic interests raises problems that are essentially quantitative. The real question, however, is, how important is a particular interest? The criteria lie first, in the loss of output involved in a sacrifice of this interest, all possibilities of substitution having been exploited; and secondly, in the size of the military force that, in time of war, would need to be diverted from other uses in order to protect this interest. Applying these tests to sources of raw-material supply lying outside the strategic area of the United States, it is difficult to find anything entitled to be called a vital economic interest. If all these sources were eliminated — a very drastic assumption — the increase of manpower requirements involved in the substitution of other sources and other materials, would probably be small in comparison with total wartime manpower requirements. On the other hand, the diversion of military resources required to defend even a limited number of these external sources of raw-material supply might well be large.

THE CASE OF OIL

A possible exception to this generalization may be offered in the case of Middle Eastern oil. It will, perhaps, be worthwhile examining this case in some detail. The experts tell us that, at current rates of consumption, the proved oil reserves of the United States will last no more than fourteen years. Since, however, the extent of proved reserves continues to be increased by exploration, we should have to add an unknown number of years to this estimate. Moreover, the strategic area of the United States includes the Caribbean with its sizeable oil reserves. It is impossible to say how long the oil resources of the Western Hemisphere, proved and unproved, would last at expected rates of consumption but even a very cautious estimate would put it at not less than twenty-five years.

Although rates of consumption will certainly increase it must also be noted that current consumption includes substantial though diminishing exports of oil from the Western Hemisphere to other areas. We are exploiting our oil reserves at a rate much greater than is desirable or necessary. It is obviously to our national interest that the reserves of other areas, and particularly of the Middle East, which has by far the largest, should be developed and that the rest of the world should be supplied from these sources rather than from the

Western Hemisphere. It is even possible to supply a part of our own requirements from imports rather than from oil produced in this hemisphere. By these methods the life expectancy of Western Hemisphere reserves could be very greatly strengthened.

Finally, there is the question of substitutes, immediately of synthetic petroleum, and ultimately, perhaps, of other forms of energy. Apparently, in the years immediately before the war, the cost of synthetic petroleum was approximately three times the cost of the natural product as produced in the United States. Technical development has already narrowed the gap between the cost of the synthetic and natural products and promises to do so further. It is quite probable, therefore, that synthetic petroleum will come forward as an effective substitute before our reserves of natural petroleum are exhausted. It is to be regarded as altogether probable that if, twenty-five years from now, we had to depend substantially on synthetic supplies to meet military requirements, and if adequate preparations had been made for this eventuality, the addition to labor requirements involved would be found to be remarkably small.

What the argument adds up to is this: It is extremely important for the United States to have an oil policy, but it does not follow that Middle Eastern oil is a vital economic interest in the sense that military resources should be allocated to this area for its defense. Indeed, the principal objectives of a national oil policy should be, first, the conservation of Western Hemisphere resources, partly by the acceleration of oil development elsewhere, and secondly, the alleviation of friction among the great powers in the exploration and development of oil resources. An effective pursuit of this policy would probably dispose of Middle Eastern oil as a vital economic interest of the United States.

Of course the possibility of finding that Middle Eastern oil lies within the strategic area of the United States should not be excluded. If a Western Alliance were to be composed of Great Britain and the countries of western and southern Europe, it is conceivable that for strategic rather than for economic reasons we would have to protect the area. That would be up to the military. But given adequate preparation, and given such a Western Alliance, it is equally conceivable that we could exclude the Middle East from our catalogue of vital interests and still supply our allies as we did during the last war.

DEFENSE OF THE STRATEGIC BASE

Up to this point a sharp distinction has been drawn between economic interests outside and inside the strategic defense area of the United States. Attention has been limited to raw-material interests, and the discussion has turned upon our ability to reduce military commitments outside the strategic defense area to a minimum. But it is obvious that the separation of a strategic defense area from other space had more significance in the time of Mahan than it has today. With the development of air and underwater methods of attack, military frontiers both on land and water tend to lose clarity of definition. Consequently it becomes necessary to examine economic interests within as well as outside of our strategic defense area. As soon as economic interests within this area come into question, it becomes clear that there are interests that are vital in the sense that their defense may well justify the diversion of military resources. This is so for two reasons: (1) there are sources of supply, but particularly plant installations, whose destruction would be a more severe shock to the economy than would be the cutting off of any given external source of supply; (2) the military resources required for the special protection of these sources or installations may be assumed to be relatively small as compared with the resources necessary to defend most positions outside our strategic area.

The protection of the bauxite routes from the Guianas to American ports, or ore passage through the Great Lakes, and of a large number of plant installations throughout the United States no doubt merits the diversion of certain quantities of military resources. Nevertheless, it must be stressed that military objectives have priority and, unless the claims to protection of various economic interests are scrutinized with the greatest care, it will be easy to fritter away the possibilities of offensive action.

During the war a great deal of attention was given to economic objectives in the selection of air targets. This analysis though mainly directed toward objectives in enemy territory has of course equal applicability to the selection of those installations in our own territory which it is most important to defend from enemy air attack. Although substantial progress was made during the war in refining the analysis, much can still be done. The techniques are mainly available and only need to be carefully applied. The problem is essentially one of estimating the interdependence among various kinds of quantities in an economic system. What one would like to know is what effect the destruction of a particular installation or source of supply would have on the output of various types of finished products and within what period, taking account of the possibilities of substitution. This is a problem for which careful economic analysis can yield results much more accurate than anything accomplished in the field of target selection during the war.

In fact, this seems to be one of those cases in which the expenditure of a few hundred thousands of dollars in peacetime on scientific research, taking care that the findings are always kept up to date, could save billions in time of war by avoiding a faulty allocation of military resources in the defense of economic objectives at home or in the attack on economic objectives in enemy territory. Such a project may be justified by quoting language already used: the purpose of economic analysis and economic policy geared to national defense is to eliminate or minimize those economic interests that need to be defended. The purpose of economic analysis and policy vis-à-vis the enemy is to avoid an expenditure of military resources on economic objectives of little or no significance.

ECONOMIC WARFARE

Since the economic factor looms so large in military calculations, and since the determination of a strategic area may well result in part from economic requirements, it is worth examining the over-all effectiveness of the economic weapon in war. One gets the impression that during World War I the accomplishments of economic warfare were much greater than in World War II, despite the enormously increased use of air power in the attack on economic objectives in enemy territory. This was so for two principal reasons. In the first place, in the earlier conflict the enemy was really confined to a narrow space. An elaborate series of measures ultimately depending on sea power caused him to be effectively limited to the resources of this area. In the second place, and much more important, techniques, both mechanical and administrative, adapted to the economizing of resources were relatively undeveloped. Processes of substitution were carried nowhere near so far as in World War II. Furthermore, ration-

ing of scarce commodities and the effective use of a priorities system
were measures that had scarcely begun to be developed. Consequently,
the German military effort was reduced by shortages of various sorts,
and lack of food contributed significantly to demoralization back of
the line. The Germans learned much from this experience. Improvement in German administration of economic resources before and
during World War II was at least as impressive as German developments in military technology, and probably had as important an
influence on keeping Germany in the war. If the proper wartime objective of economic policy is the minimizing of economic limitations
to military action, it can be said that in most respects German economic policy was admirably conceived.

As a result of its admitted achievements in World War I, the
Allies, but particularly Britain, entered World War II with absurdly
exaggerated notions of the importance of economic warfare. Even
after Germany had conquered the resources of the European continent, it was widely believed that if she could be denied the importation of such necessities as rubber, oil, ferro-alloys, and copper,
shortages of these materials would seriously diminish the size of her
military effort. A comparison of German resources with the requirements of the British and American armed forces was, of course, in
large part responsible for the illusion. A civilian expert, acquainted
with American military requirements for, say, oil, copper and nickel,
can scarcely be blamed if on studying the quantities of these materials known to be available to Germany he concluded that the
Germans were indeed in a bad way. The conclusion, however, was
wrong and, as we have seen, it was wrong because it seriously underestimated the economies possible through substitution and the application of effective raw-material controls. If these possibilities have
a bearing on the proper estimation of our own raw-material interest,
so likewise do they have a bearing on intelligence estimates of enemy
strength.

Despite what has been said, it is still a matter of some importance
to deny the enemy access to raw materials. But its importance must
be measured in terms of the relatively small increase in labor requirements he will thereby have to face. The larger the economic space
possessed by the enemy and the more highly developed his technology
and his methods of raw-material controls, the less effective will be

the traditional methods of economic warfare. To these traditional methods, however, there is now added the ever increasing effectiveness of air bombardment.

This is not the place to assess the relative importance of economic objectives (mainly air targets) as compared to military objectives in World War II. It will, perhaps, be admitted that the economic system of all countries subject to air bombardment stood up surprisingly well and continued to meet military requirements even when subjected to heavy air attack. Whether decisive results could have been achieved through bombardment of industrial installations if the weight of the attack had been increased, or whether these resources might better have been diverted to attack on the armed forces of the enemy, will probably prove to be a subject of lively debate for some time to come.

Concerning the prospective importance of economic objectives, two divergent trends appear to be in operation. On the one hand, developments in military technology continue to enhance the importance of economic objectives. Not only are the possibilities of striking far behind the enemy's military frontier continually being widened through the development of air power, but the weapons of attack seem progressively to favor industrial installations rather than armed forces. On the other hand, the economic space available to belligerents may be increasing, and the technology and economic controls necessary to the flexible use of economic resources within that space are certainly improving. What the result of these two divergent trends may be with respect to the future importance of economic objectives, we are not yet in a position to say.

It is possible, however, that economic warfare which yielded large results in World War I and disappointing results in World War II may, in consequence of these developments, return to a position of first-rate importance.

12

Raw Materials, Rearmament, and Economic Development[1]

I. CURRENT MATERIALS SHORTAGES IN RELATION TO THE REARMAMENT PROGRAM

Shortages of industrial raw materials have been much to the fore during the past year and are likely to be with us until the peak of the rearmament effort is past. Steel, copper, and aluminum are under tight control, and the use of a host of other materials is subject to some degree of limitation. The insatiable raw-material requirements of the American economy oriented towards military production and operating at full employment have had serious repercussions on the availability of material supplies for other countries, and an International Materials Conference has been established to attempt to bring about an equitable sharing of these supplies.

The material shortages that currently confront us, however, are primarily the product of an armament *build-up* and may be expected to disappear once the rate of armament production reaches a stable level. While an economy geared to armament production shows a marked increase in requirements for certain kinds of materials, its over-all material requirements are not much larger than are the civilian material requirements of the same economy operating at a similar level of output. At work currently, however, is the principle of acceleration. For a period of time, the movement towards a given level of armament production involves a disproportionate increase in materials requirements for production facilities and the filling of pipe-lines. If we could count on the maintenance of a given level of armament production, once that level is reached, material shortages of the type we now face would disappear rather rapidly. It may well be, however, that the next few decades will witness an alternation of armament scares and periods of relative relaxation. If this is so, we

[1] Reprinted from *The Quarterly Journal of Economics,* Vol. 66, August 1952.

might well experience a series of material shortages as the economy swings from a build-up of military output to an expansion of civilian production and back again. While these grim possibilities of recurrent shortages are worth examination, I wish to turn in this paper from the short-run problem to a consideration of the long-range materials prospect facing the United States and the free world.

II. THE LONG-RUN OUTLOOK

Over the longer run, a "shortage" of raw materials means essentially an increase in material prices relative to the price of services and of fabricated products. The principal question with which this paper is concerned is whether economic growth in the United States and the Free World is likely to be handicapped over the next few decades by rising real costs of industrial materials. Security considerations impinge on this argument mainly as they affect the costs of meeting materials requirements in a state of quasi-peace.

If we accept the current Bureau of the Census median estimate for population growth in the United States, and if we assume that the per capita productivity of the labor force increases at the slightly less than 2 per cent per annum rate that has been maintained over the last few decades, the Gross National Product of this country would approximately double over the next twenty-five years. Since the current activity of the durable-goods industries, which are heavy consumers of materials, is abnormally high and since there may be a long-term trend toward tertiary production which is less heavily material-consuming, the material requirements of the American economy may somewhat less than double over the same period. The rates of growth in the other principal industrial areas of the Free World, mainly western Europe and Japan, will probably be somewhat less than this. On the other hand, materials consumption in other areas that are ripe for industrialization, notably Latin America and Southern Asia, may increase at a much more rapid rate. However, it should be noted that since the United States consumes about one-half the raw materials of the Free World and, with western Europe and Japan, accounts for well over 80 per cent, even very high rates of industrialization in the rest of the Free World would not change the total rate of increase by very much. Perhaps, for the purpose of assigning some reasonable order of magnitude to the raw-material problem, we might assume that by some time in the decade of the 1970's, free world requirements are, in the absence of war, likely to double.

This presents us with a formidable problem. In real terms the U. S. consumption of minerals, including oil, increased by five times between 1900 and 1950. We are now projecting for 1975 a rate of consumption roughly ten times the rate for 1900. Can these requirements be satisfied and, if so, without a substantial increase in real costs?

If we turn our attention to the United States and concentrate on so-called exhaustible materials, the picture, though undeniably obscure, presents certain potentially disturbing features. What we should like to know, of course, for every one of the important minerals used by industry, is the total amount of the material in the United States recoverable at various levels of cost. What is available in fact is information concerning the proved reserves of commercial grade plus geological estimates of the percentage of the earth's crust constituted by the mineral in question. In between these estimated magnitudes there exists a vast gulf of uncertainty. For certain minerals it is clear that the so-called proved reserves are not much more than the mining industry's working inventory which can be expanded whenever the industry sees fit to do so. For others there may be reason to suspect that the present estimate of proved reserves represents about all of the mineral that is likely to be obtainable in the United States at current costs and with presently available techniques of discovery.

Despite this uncertainty, however, there are various facts that help to indicate the probable trend in the relationship between U. S. output of and requirements for exhaustible materials. For certain important materials the country was, before the war, either self-sufficient or on a net export basis. It is now a net importer of these materials which include oil, copper, lead, zinc, iron ore, and other less important items. The available evidence concerning oil and various other minerals, moreover, indicates pretty clearly a rising real cost of discovery. In addition we know that with respect to copper, lead, and zinc, the trend has for decades been toward the extraction of lower and lower grade ores. Finally is should be mentioned that there has not been a really important new discovery of some of our most important metals for at least three decades. When these facts are added to scattered evidence concerning the potential availability of minerals of lower grades in the United States, it appears highly probable that in the absence of increasing imports or improved techniques of discovery, the relative price of many mineral products in this country is apt to increase sharply.

What has been said about the United States has, of course, been true of western Europe for a long period of time. Not only will an increasing percentage of western Europe's materials requirements have to be imported but for certain important items, with respect to which the area has been relatively self-sufficient, the prospect is for increasing dependence on foreign sources. In the field of energy resources, despite the maximum development of hydroelectric power, it seems probable that western Europe will become a net importer of coal on a sizeable scale and, barring war, it is plausible that the area's requirements for petroleum will triple during the next quarter century.

If, then, we consider how the rapidly growing materials requirements of the industrial areas of the world are to be met, it is clear that without a large expansion of output for export in the so-called underdeveloped areas of the world or large technological improvements in the discovery, extraction, or processing of materials, or both, the material requirements of the industrial areas will be met either not at all or only at sharply rising real costs. Before proceeding to a consideration of the conditions of expansion of raw-material output in underdeveloped areas, it is necessary to consider briefly the potential impact on the raw-material problem of technological development. The existing level of technological knowledge of synthetics and of other possibilities of materials substitution is sufficient to set very real limits to the dependence of this country on imports of raw materials and to the rise in real costs that a lack of availability of imports would otherwise entail. There are, furthermore, technological developments just over the horizon that will still further reduce these limits. It is important that the current and potential impact of the state of technology on the raw-material problem be recognized not only in this country but throughout the underdeveloped areas of the world.

It was mentioned above that the cost of finding oil in this country is probably — and rather sharply — on the increase. In the absence of substitutes this would mean an increase in the price of crude oil mitigated by an increasing flow of imports. However, with presently available technical knowledge, it is estimated by the National Petroleum Council [2] that petroleum products can be produced from shale at no more than 25 to 30 per cent above the present price of these products; the Bureau of Mines says that shale oil is currently competitive. There are 125 billion barrels of oil in high-grade shales in this country and other hundreds of billions in lower grades. Furthermore, the hydrogenation and synthesis of coal, although at present more expensive than the production of oil from shale, give promise of further substantial technological development. Consequently the extent to which the cost and price of natural crude oil will rise in this country seems strictly limited.

Or, to take another example, consider the iron-ore situation in the United States. The approaching exhaustion of the high-grade Mesabi ores has already driven American companies to search for, and to find, large and rich deposits in Venezuela, Labrador, Liberia and elsewhere. At existing price levels we may expect to see over the next few decades a large expansion in the share of our domestic requirements met from imports. If, however, the conditions affecting the exploitation of foreign reserves should worsen in such fashion as substantially to raise the cost of imported ores, our practically unlimited Taconite ores would come into production on a large scale.

The existence of these reserves, which developing technology will make available at prices not much higher than current iron-ore prices, sets a very real limit to the future increase in the price of ores from other sources.

So it is with synthetic wool and other textiles, synthetic rubber, and a number of other synthetic materials the production of which is indefinitely expansible in the United States. The current and potential availability of these materials at prices somewhat higher than the current world market prices for the natural materials will continue to set ceilings beyond which the prices of these natural materials cannot rise for long without curtailing imports into the United States.

The effect of developing technology upon materials availability

[2] Report of the National Petroleum Council's Committee on Synthetic Liquid Fuels Production Costs, October 31, 1951.

is by no means limited to the exploitation of lower-grade ores and the production of synthetic substitutes. As the history of the last fifty years will show, the "mix" of the materials flow into American fabricating facilities is highly flexible. Over the next few decades we may expect to see a rapid substitution of aluminum, magnesium, titanium, and other expanding materials for materials whose output can increase only at rising costs. We shall continue that process of "engineering out of" tin and other scarce or vulnerable materials in which we have been engaged for some time past.

The principal relevance of current and potential technological development to the materials problem under discussion here is that it holds real possibilities for sharply restraining the increase in real costs of materials input to which the American economy would be subject if we should not be able to look toward an expansion of foreign sources of supply. At something like pre-Korean price relationships, however, we should, in fact, expect to see expanding American materials requirements increasingly satisfied from foreign sources. This has been the trend of the last few decades and there is no reason, except a sharp increase in the relative cost from foreign sources, why this trend should not continue. In other industrial areas of the world where the possibilities of substitution from domestic materials sources are not as real as in this country, an expansion of imports from foreign sources is likely to persist despite a substantial increase in relative prices. It appears, therefore, that the cost conditions under which expansion of materials production may occur in the underdeveloped areas of the world have an important bearing on the prospects for continued economic growth in western Europe, Japan and, to a smaller extent, in the United States.

III. FOREIGN SOURCES OF SUPPLY

The areas of the world to which we must principally look for expansion of minerals output for export are the Near East, south and southeast Asia, Africa, and Latin America. As potential producers and exporters of mineral products, excluding oil, Africa comes first and Latin America second. The Near East is, of course, the prospective supplier of nearly the whole of western Europe's oil requirements and may well become an important exporter to the United States. If we fasten our attention on minerals and look in particular at the high tonnage materials, including oil, iron ore, copper, lead, zinc, manganese, and bauxite, it can be said with fair confidence that the known and inferred reserves of these minerals in the underdeveloped areas of the world are large enough and of sufficiently high grade to meet the Free World requirements for at least the next twenty-five years at little or no increase in real costs. In fact we can extend this range of materials very considerably and still say that if resources were relatively free to flow to lowest-cost sources it is unlikely that economic growth in the Free World would be handicapped over the next few decades by rising real costs of mineral materials. In fact, however, there may be serious governmentally imposed impediments and the result may well be a substantial worsening of the terms of trade for manufactured products. The current and potential technological possibilities of substitution could moderate this shift but could hardly prevent it. What happens therefore to the conditions under which materials will continue to be produced for export in the underdeveloped areas of the world is an important aspect of the problem.

The major part of the production for export of mineral products in these areas has been carried on by western European and American capital under the ownership and control of a relatively small number of large companies. Oil company investment abroad has accounted for three-quarters of the total American private investment abroad since the war and, if prospective free world requirements for oil are going to be met through the same channels in the future as they have been in the past, the private foreign investment for petroleum expansion in the Near East, Venezuela, and elsewhere will continue to be very large. Although private U. S. capital invested in foreign mining enterprises increased by not much more than $100 million between 1930 and 1950, current expansion of iron-ore properties and the increase in other mining facilities that would have to be undertaken if Free World requirements for minerals are to be met largely by private production in underdeveloped areas, presages a much higher rate of increase over the next quarter-century. Are we going to witness such an expansion and, if so, is it going to take place through the medium of foreign private investment?

If the areas in question were all colonial possessions of western powers, there is little doubt that both questions would be answered in the affirmative. Furthermore, it would be argued, at least in the West, via the doctrines of geographical specialization and comparative cost, that the well-being of the underdeveloped areas would advance more rapidly through expansion of raw-material output than by large-scale diversion of resources into industrial production. And, within limits, it is by no means clear that this is not so.

We may take it for granted, however, that, with the possible exception of the African colonies of European powers, things are not going to work out in this fashion. In south and southeast Asia many of the important raw materials countries have recently thrown off colonial status and have taken their economic development in their own hands. In the Near East a fanatical nationalism has cast its shadow over any future expansion of foreign investment. In Latin America independent and sensitive governments increasingly resent the stigma of economic colonialism that frequently is attached to economies oriented heavily towards raw-materials exports. The political and economic differences among the areas in question and among the countries making up each area are great but, by and large, all these countries share the ambition to develop economically, and almost invariably economic development is interpreted to mean industrialization.

Industrialization may not be the road to economic salvation indicated by the signpost of comparative costs but it is widely suspected in the underdeveloped areas that this signpost is heavily warped in a westerly direction. For one thing the doctrine takes no account of what happens during cyclical depression to an economy which is strongly oriented toward the production for export of one, or a few, price-sensitive raw materials; for another, comparative cost is a static doctrine that does not reckon with a technological dynamism associated with industrialization that may affect conditions of production throughout the economy. The proper allocation of resources of today may, under the impact of industrialization, become the improper allocation of tomorrow. While there is merit in both of these contentions it is easy to exaggerate their importance and to appraise falsely their significance for raw-materials development.

The experience of the 1930's indicated what *could* happen to the foreign exchange earnings, government revenues, and the whole prosperity of an economy producing a few raw materials for the world market. Furthermore the 1930's followed upon a decade which, for agricultural raw materials, was also one of surplus. It is now fairly clear, however, that the change in the terms of trade unfavorable to raw materials during the interwar period marked the culmination of a trend that, by the end of the period, was already beginning to be reversed. And although the 1930's indicated what *could* happen to industrial demands for raw materials there are sound reasons for believing that it is not going to happen again. Countries producing raw materials seem excessively preoccupied — at least in international conferences — with the experience of the 1930's and unwilling to turn their attention to long-term historical and prospective growth rates in raw-material requirements. Certainly recessions of the 1949 variety and worse can and will happen; certainly, also, the percentage decline in the exports of raw materials will be a multiple of the decline in national income of the industrial countries importing raw materials. This constitutes a serious problem and merits attention to policies both national and international for mitigating the effects of the instability of the foreign exchange earnings of materials exporting countries. But the problem to be attacked appears to be one, henceforth, of evening out relatively small variations from a pronounced upward trend of materials requirements.

The more important *caveat* to the implications for economic development of the doctrine of comparative costs has to do with what Marshall would have called the external economies connected with expansion of output of industrial products and services. These "economies," so-called, are not only external to the firm but also to the industry. In an economy on the verge of industrialization one thing very much leads to another. In fact it is misleading to give the name "economies" to the creation of what are really new productive functions facilitated, it is true, by the expansion of output of particular products, but in no proper sense "induced" by this expansion. At a certain stage of industrialization, as the example of Japan shows, the whole economic environment may be changed with effects that permeate through every form of economic activity.

While recognizing these possibilities there are, however, certain limits to the rate at which this process can proceed even under the most favorable circumstances and it does not follow that the attainment of a satisfactory or an optimum rate means industrialization *à outrance*. Clearly the possibilities of capital formation either from domestic savings or foreign investment set some sort of limit. Equally clearly, if industrialization means diversion of labor away from agriculture, the possibilities of releasing labor for industrial employment may require a substantial increase in agriculture productivity. In considering the advantages of industrialization in backward areas what is frequently encountered is a comparison of the very low productivity of labor in primitive agriculture with the very high productivity of the same or similar labor in industry working with western techniques and machines. In all the industrial countries of the world, and particularly in the United States, statistical increases in per capita productivity are in part the result of a mere shift in employment from low productivity agriculture to high productivity industry. But a comparison of these relative productivities in underdeveloped areas stacks the cards much too heavily in favor of industrialization. Productivity in agriculture in most of these areas is as susceptible to improvement by the use of western methods as is productivity in industry.

The application of western methods requires capital not only for industry but for agriculture and, if economic development is to mean growth in national income and national wealth, and not merely industrialization, some sort of balance has to be struck between the expansion of agricultural and the expansion of industrial output. One of the considerations affecting this balance is the availability of foreign capital for certain uses but not for others. Another consideration has to do with quantities of domestic resources that are likely to be diverted from other uses and into the employments favored by foreign capital. If foreign capital can make a large contribution to the area's well-being with a relatively small diversion of local resources, it would appear desirable to encourage investment whether for raw-material or industrial expansion. If, however, foreign investment heavily influences the allocation of local resources it may fasten on the area a specialization which though satisfying the current comparative cost conditions is not conducive to economic growth.

It is the contention of this paper that the expansion of mineral production is, in general, not only compatible with the economic growth of underdeveloped areas but may greatly facilitate industrialization in these areas. Mineral development has been to date largely undertaken by foreign capital and, given proper encouragement, additional capital is available in quantity for expansion of output. Such development can rarely take place without the expansion of auxiliary facilities — railroads, roads, port development, electric power, and the like — which have a contribution to make to general economic development. Mineral production requires the development of technical skills on the part of the local employees of foreign mining and petroleum companies that are readily usable in other types of industrial development. The yield to the source countries in government revenue and foreign exchange earnings tends to be a high percentage of the value of mineral output and can provide the financial basis for a domestic development program. Finally, the diversion of domestic resources away from other objectives tends to be relatively small.

Venezuela is, of course, a particularly striking example of a favorable juxtaposition of mineral and general economic development, but the argument has wider validity. Petroleum royalties account for 97 per cent of Venezuela's exchange earnings and 60 per cent of government revenue. The oil industry, on the other hand, employs less than 5 per cent of the labor force. The government has in its hands the means to finance a large program of general economic development and has, in fact, undertaken important steps in this direction. Since the oil industry can look forward confidently to a very large expansion and since to oil has been added the prospects of large royalties from iron ore development, together with a great auxiliary expansion of transportation and other public utility facilities, the potentialities of general economic development in Venezuela seem most promising.

The same complementarity between minerals production for export and the possibilities of general economic development exists elsewhere. One may lament the fact that the Bolivian balance of trade is too heavily dominated by tin exports and the Chilean balance by copper exports. But the most effective answer to this is a better use of the governmental revenues and foreign exchange receipts of an expanding minerals export for general economic development.

IV. OBSTACLES TO THE EXPANSION OF FOREIGN
SOURCES OF SUPPLY

It has been the argument of the preceding paragraphs that, granted a relative freedom to develop low-cost resources, the minerals requirements of the Free World could be met for at least the next twenty to thirty years with little or no increase in real costs, and that the general economic development of source countries could be greatly stimulated by this expansion of mineral production for export. The argument is not here extended to agricultural materials and foodstuffs produced for export for two reasons. First, with currently used techniques, expansion of agricultural output may well encounter rising real costs. Second, the labor requirements for an expanded agricultural output could certainly conflict with an economically justifiable degree of industrialization. How these considerations would be affected by the spread of superior agricultural techniques is difficult to estimate. It is possible that improved methods in agriculture might release labor for industrialization at a rapid rate while still permitting the satisfaction of Free World requirements for foodstuffs and agricultural raw materials at existing terms of trade. An examination of these possibilities, however, lies outside the limits of this paper.

Granted that mineral production could be expanded with no substantial change in the relative prices of materials and fabricated products and that the general development of underdeveloped areas could be greatly facilitated by this expansion, does it follow that events will take this course? To answer this question easily in the affirmative would be to ignore the evidence of increasing difficulties confronting foreign investment in resource development and of an increasing reluctance on the part of private capital to risk these difficulties.

The difficulties do not lie primarily in the obvious conflict of interest between foreign investors and the governments of source countries over the division of profits of minerals development. No doubt these governments are showing themselves to be increasingly hard bargainers and no doubt occasionally the terms offered are such as to discourage investment. But the principal difficulties are concerned with doubts whether bargains once made will be kept and with limitations that source countries seek to impose on the control and management of foreign enterprises within their borders. Oil companies can live with a fifty-fifty division of earnings; it is questionable whether they can live — or at least expand — under the threat of overt or "creeping" expropriation.

Space is lacking for an adequate discussion of the principal obstacles to private foreign investment. There should be mentioned, however, the legal uncertainties concerning the status of foreign ownership such as those that have deterred investment in Brazil since the end of the war; the requirements in many areas for extensive local participation in management; limitations on the scope and direction of operations; excessive requirements concerning numbers to be employed and continuity of operations; the administration of import and export controls; limitations on conversion of profits into dollars; and others. Perhaps more important than any of these is the growing uncertainty whether the conditions of operation which are bad today may not become much worse tomorrow.

It is not the purpose of this paper to examine into the question of what steps the United States might take to lessen or to avoid the effects of these obstacles on the cost of our materials supplies. One route obviously lies in the direction of attempting to improve through negotiation with foreign governments, tax concessions, and other measures, the conditions under which U. S. producers can operate abroad. Another opens up the possibility of the assumption by government of some of the increasing risks of foreign operations through insurance, long-term contracts, price guarantees, financing, etc. We may be sure that the greater the extent to which this route becomes available the less will investors and producers be willing to proceed without help. A third line of attack would be the provision of capital and technical assistance to foreign governments to develop their own resources. It is obvious that if this path is followed very far, other sources of capital will dry up fast. Finally we could increasingly direct resources into technical research for synthetics and other substitute materials to lessen our dependence of foreign sources of supply.

It would be interesting to speculate on what combination of policies would permit us to satisfy our materials requirements at least cost. To do so, however, would divert attention away from our main argument. Reasons have been advanced for believing that although mineral resources exist in the underdeveloped areas of the world in such quantities and grades as to permit a meeting of Free World requirements over the next quarter-century at no increase in real costs, governmental policies in these areas may well prevent this from happening. If so, it seems likely that economic growth both in the industrialized and the underdeveloped areas of the Free World may be hampered.

A substantial rise in the real price of imported minerals would not be a very serious problem for the United States. It would be a much more serious matter for industrial areas more dependent on foreign sources. And if, to rising costs of minerals, are added worsening terms of exchange of manufactured products for agricultural materials and foodstuffs, there emerges for western Europe and Japan a balance-of-payments problem of great difficulty. It becomes, then, important to distinguish those segments of the problem that might economically be solved to the advantage of all concerned from those that involve a real divergence of interest.

V. MATERIALS SECURITY

It has been emphasized that the United States, confronted with rapidly growing materials requirements, can avoid resort to higher cost domestic sources only through technological development or through increased reliance on foreign sources of supply. Governmentally imposed obstacles to the expansion of output could substantially increase the cost of materials procurement abroad. And increasing dependence on foreign sources of supply raises a security problem, the solution of which inevitably increases the cost of meeting our long-run materials requirements.

Wartime materials consumption, although not much larger in the aggregate than peacetime consumption at equivalent levels of employment and production, demands very much larger quantities of particular materials. Furthermore, the advent of war would deprive us of certain customary overseas sources of supply and the greater the dependence of the economy on imports the larger the impact would be. For both of these reasons provision must be made in advance of war for meeting wartime materials requirements. This responsibility is the inevitable by-product of the current international situation, it has been recognized by government, and the cost of materials security must be admitted to be an essential element in the total cost of meeting our long-run materials requirements.

There are several ways of providing increased materials security. All are costly, and the central question of economic policy involved is how to secure adequate materials availability at minimum cost. Stockpiling is the best known device and for storable materials of high value and small bulk it is usually the most practicable and the cheapest. Some materials, however, such as oil and, to a limited degree, rubber, are not storable; others, such as iron ore or pig iron, are consumed in such volume as to make stockpiling in adequate quantities impracticable. For still others, of which bauxite may be an example, stockpiling may most cheaply and adequately take the form of in-the-ground storage of proved high-grade domestic deposits.

If stockpiling, either in warehouses or in the ground, is not the answer, attention must be given to expanding output in safe areas, even though this may be high-cost output, or in constructing stand-by facilities. Safe area does not necessarily mean within the borders of the United States though it should properly mean the area which we are militarily committed to defend. The diversion of military forces to the defense of material sources of supply will only rarely be found to be the most economical way of providing materials security.[3]

During the last war we were forced into a large-scale diversion of labor and of scarce materials to the construction of synthetic rubber plants. These were maintained as stand-by capacity after the war and are now put to effective use. Large stand-by facilities should be provided to assure the adequate availability of petroleum products, and additional transporation facilities are needed to safeguard our supplies of other materials. Finally, materials security may be increased by advance "engineering out of" various materials which are likely to be excessively short in wartime. Much too little attention has been given to this possibility in the United States.

The point that needs to be stressed is that all these methods are costly. When everything possible has been done to minimize costs, it will still be found that the necessity of providing materials security will inevitably increase substantially the cost of meeting our over-all materials requirements. Consequently, it is necessary that we do not

[3] Cf. E. S. Mason, "American Security and Access to Raw Materials," *World Politics,* Jan. 1949. Reprinted as Chapter 11 above.

allow security interests, which are real and important, to be used to lead us into wasteful methods of assuring materials availability when less costly methods are at hand. The protectionists have in the security argument a potent instrument with a limited field of valid application. Its use should be confined to these limits.

VI. CONCLUSION

If consideration is limited to the mineral requirements of the United States, there is reason to believe that security interests will increase the cost of meeting these requirements and that obstacles to the expansion of output in underdeveloped areas may also do so. Although no attention has been given to the question here, it may be stated as the author's opinion that U. S. requirements for agricultural materials are likely to be satisfied over the next two or three decades at little or no increase in real costs. Taking materials as a whole the American economy may, then, face a slight increase in the unit cost of meeting its requirements. Increases in the real costs of particular materials will, in most cases, be strictly limited by substitution possibilities. When account is taken of the fact that the value of raw-material production — excluding foodstuffs — is not over ten per cent of the total value of U. S. output, it must be concluded that the increases in real costs of materials production here contemplated are not likely to handicap economic growth over the next few decades. Although it has been impossible, for lack of space, to consider the situation faced by other industrial areas of the Free World, a warning must be given that, particularly when foodstuffs are included, the raw-materials prospect for these areas looks rather different.

13

An American View of Raw-Material Problems[1]

The Report of the President's Materials Policy Commission[2]

The report of the President's Materials Policy Commission published in June of this year is, to say the least, a comprehensive document. It purports to cover all materials except foodstuffs and to survey the materials problems not only of the United States but of the western world. Since the author of this paper was a member of the Commission he does not pretend to speak with critical objectivity of the Report; nor does he pretend to represent the views of his fellow Commissioners. The following remarks are rather the reflections of one individual on some of the issues that impend in the raw materials area.

The appointment of the Commission a few months after the outbreak of the Korean War indicated a serious and growing concern in the United States for the continued adequacy of raw-materials supplies. Rates of consumption during World War II were, of course, huge, and the extraordinarily high production of durable goods during the postwar period created abnormally large requirements, particularly for mineral raw materials. Added to this were the increased and speculatively accelerated material demands of the Korean War and rearmament. During the period from 1940 to 1952 shortages of important raw materials in the United States have been sufficiently serious to justify direct government controls in nine of the twelve

[1] Reprinted from *The Journal of Industrial Economics,* Vol. I, No. 1, Nov. 1952.

[2] Volume I, *Resources for Freedom,* presents the general analysis and the Commission's recommendations. Volume II, *The Outlook for Key Commodities,* in addition to discussing particular materials, includes the projections of material requirements, data on mineral reserves and the production and consumption measures used by the Commission. Volume III, *The Outlook for Energy Sources,* discusses coal, electric power, natural gas and oil. Volume IV, *The Promise of Technology,* contains the major technological papers prepared for the Commission by various research departments and laboratories. Volume V, *Basic Reports to the Commission,* includes staff papers.

years. And, during the same period of time, there may have occurred a reversal of long-term downward trend in the real cost of producing raw materials.

Although the establishment of the Commission coincided with, and was probably induced by, the reappearance of serious shortages of materials, its concern has not been with the short-run problem but rather with what may be expected over a longer period of time, a period somewhat arbitrarily defined to embrace the next quarter-century. Short-run variations in supplies and requirements, the well known volatility of raw material prices, which may well be accentuated if the postwar pattern of alternate reduction and increase in armament expenditure is continued, are considered only in relation to the long-run availability of supplies. The major problems considered by the Commission arise, on the one hand, from the effects of exponential rates of economic growth on requirements for raw materials and, on the other, from the possibility that, at any time, an outbreak of war may simultaneously and radically change materials requirements and remove customary sources of supply. These are the real materials problems that, over time, confront the Free World.[3]

THE TERMS OF TRADE

The projections of materials requirements used by the Commission assume for the United States a 28 per cent increase in population during the next quarter century and a 2½ per cent per annum increase in the per capita productivity of the labor force. These assumptions yield a doubling of gross national product by the mid-1970's. If this growth rate is realized it is projected that over-all materials requirements will be some 60 per cent higher in 1957 than in 1950, with minerals requirements rising some 90 per cent and the requirements for agricultural products by 40 to 50 per cent.

The conclusion that a doubling of gross national product could be accomplished with a consumption of raw materials only 60 per cent higher than in 1950 may seem surprising. During the postwar years, however, including 1950, United States production of durable goods, which are heavy materials users, has employed a higher percentage of

[3] Nothing is said in this paper concerning raw materials in relation to military security. This subject is treated in the Report, Vol. I, Section VI, *Foundations for Security*, and is referred to in various sections of the other volumes.

the labor force than can be expected to continue. Then, too, there is a fairly clearly marked trend towards a higher degree of fabrication of materials, which yields over time a lower material input per unit of national output.[4] Finally, although it is not visible in the statistics of employment during the last two decades, there probably exists an underlying trend towards tertiary employments, which are not heavily materials-consuming.[5]

Growth rates in the United States may well exceed those in most other industrialized areas of the free world. On the other hand, given a rapid industrialization of underdeveloped countries, their materials requirements could increase at a much higher rate than is projected for the United States. Even very high rates, however, would not greatly affect the total figures, since the percentage of raw-materials consumption accounted for by those countries is very small It is, perhaps, not unreasonable to assume for the free world as a whole, over the next quarter-century, something less than a doubling of gross income accompanied by a 60–70 per cent increase in consumption of raw materials including foodstuffs.

One of the central questions, having particular urgency for industrial countries heavily dependent on imports of raw materials and foodstuffs, is what, under these circumstances, is likely to happen to the terms of trade of manufactures for primary products.[6] If the

[4] E.g., in dollars of constant value, each dollar of raw materials cost in 1900 yielded $4.20 in finished products and services; in 1950 the figure was $7.80.

[5] The projections of materials requirements are discussed in detail in a paper by Arnold C. Harberger, published in Vol. II.

[6] If resources are fairly free to move among countries, a worsening of the terms of trade for manufactures will mean real costs for primary production rising in relation to real costs of manufactures the world over. In any particular country — in varying degrees depending on how effectively economies are sheltered by transport costs and on the shape of domestic cost functions — resources tend to be reallocated in line with the changing terms of trade. Thus in both industrial and raw-materials-producing countries a movement of the terms of trade against manufactures leads to higher imputs into primary production. Barriers to trade and to the movement of resources and, in particular, domestic policies favourable to industry or vice versa, can cut this connection. Thus a primary producing country can find its own terms of trade of primary versus manufactured output turning against primary production even though, in international trade, the movement is in the reverse direction. Needless to say, it is the trend of real costs of both primary and secondary production (rather than the terms of trade) that is relevant to growth of national income.

terms of trade are not to worsen for producers of manufactures, 50–60 per cent expansion of primary production must be accomplished at real costs that decline approximately as rapidly as may be expected for manufactured products. It may be anticipated with some confidence that the real cost of fabrication *will* decline as improved technology reduces the factor inputs required to convert a bale of cotton into yards of fabric, tons of iron ore of given grade into tons of ingot steel, and cubic yards of clay into brick. Can and will improved technology and organization accomplish a similar reduction in the real costs of wringing primary products from a limited physical environment?

It is fairly clear that, during the period 1875–1940 the real costs of primary production have not only declined as rapidly as the real costs of fabrication but more rapidly and that the economic growth of western Europe and the United States has been heavily dependent on the rate of improvement of primary production. During the twenty-five years preceding 1900 the terms of trade moved strongly in favor of manufactured products. The fact that this movement was temporarily checked during the period 1900–1914 may have had something to do with the apparent slowing down of per capita productivity both in Britain and the United States during these years. The very great improvement in their terms of trade during the inter-war period certainly sheltered Britain from the full economic consequences of the great depression.

The Report of the President's Commission does not attempt to arrive at conclusions concerning the probable movement of the terms of trade. On the basis of date assembled by the Commission, however, certain tentative propositions seem warranted. Granted a relative freedom for resources to move to lowest cost sources of supply and for materials to move to highest priced markets, there is little evidence to support the contention that terms of trade must necessarily turn sharply against manufactures. This appears to be true even if a large increase in population is assumed. If, in fact, the terms of trade do worsen substantially for manufacturers, it will be mainly because currencies are not convertible for purchase in lowest priced markets, because certain countries embark on irrational programs of industrialization, because increased obstacles are placed in the way of the flow of foreign capital particularly into minerals development, and because, in general, policies of self-sufficiency reign supreme.

A substantial worsening of the terms of trade for manufactures brought about by diversion of resources towards industrialization in the primary producing countries would obviously affect adversely the interests of the industrial countries of western Europe, Britain and Japan. The concomitant improvement in the terms of trade for primary production, on the other hand, would not necessarily promote the interests of the raw material producing countries if it is purchased at the expense of a drift from low-cost imported manufactures to high-cost domestic production. For reasons that will be developed presently, the extent to which a development of the sort here indicated could affect growth rates in the United States is substantially less than in most other countries. On a broader view, however, the interests of the United States could not help but be seriously threatened by a series of measures that may not only check the rate of economic growth in the free world as a whole but impose on certain countries problems of adjustment to which their economic and political structures are not well adapted.

This problem of bringing about a balance between industrial development and raw-material expansion that will facilitate economic growth not only in industrial but in primary materials producing countries is obviously one of the critical problems of international organization. The President's Commission quite naturally looks at the question mainly from the point of view of the United States which is likely to become an increasingly important net importer of mineral products though it may continue to be a net exporter of agricultural materials and foodstuffs. Currently the import of minerals is overwhelmingly from American-owned production abroad, and consequently a central concern of the Commission is how obstacles to the expansion of minerals output under American ownership and control may be overcome. When agricultural production is included and the interests and ideologies of other countries fully taken into account, it seems possible that a broader view of feasible international arrangements and a more venturesome consideration of alternative economic instruments than the Commission was willing to attempt may have to be undertaken. However that may be, it is necessary at this point to consider further the proposition that a substantial change in the terms of trade adverse to manufactured products is more likely to be the result of national policies of self-sufficiency than of the inevitable pressure of increasing requirements on limited natural resources. The relevant evidence may most conveniently be discussed under the headings agricultural resources, minerals, and energy resources, though the latter two categories obviously overlap.

AGRICULTURAL RESOURCES

The Commission's Report deals at length only with the situation in the United States, though a careful consideration of the American data makes it possible to venture an opinion on agricultural prospects elsewhere.

The leading conclusion that emerges from a study of the American material is that U. S. requirements for domestically produced foodstuffs and agricultural raw materials can easily be satisfied over the next quarter-century with a continually declining employment in agriculture. Currently — and for the last ten years — the United States has been a net exporter of agricultural materials on a small scale and could produce a large surplus for export with little increase in the agricultural labor force. It probably would become a large net exporter if foreign currencies were freely convertible into dollars. As it is, an important problem confronting the United States is how to bring about an expansion of industrial output sufficient to absorb into the working force the workers released by improvements in agricultural technology.

The projected increase in American requirements for agricultural products for 1975 as compared with consumption in 1950 is 40 per cent (42 per cent for foods and 25 per cent for non-food products). To satisfy these requirements from U. S. sources, agricultural output would have to increase 1 per cent per annum cumulatively. The average annual increase achieved during the decade 1939–49 was 2.75 per cent with a 10 per cent decline in the agricultural labor force.

The 40 per cent increase in U. S. agricultural output assumed to be required by 1975 ought to be rather easily accomplished with a smaller labor force than now (roughly 10 million). Indeed the agricultural labor force will have to decline if farm incomes and the income of farm workers are to increase commensurately with incomes projected for the rest of the population. Nor will much new land have to be brought into cultivation. The projected increase of output is what is conservatively possible on existing land if techniques now known are more widely used and if appropriate changes are made in current patterns of land use.

There is not much doubt that at existing price relationships, American agricultural output could increase over the next quarter-century by much more than the projected 40 per cent. If foreign demand were available, it is probable that an expansion of exports rather than a reduction of the farm labor force would be the alternative chosen.

This evaluation of agricultural possibilities can be applied without much modification to the Canadian situation. The possibilities of large expansion of agricultural output also exist for those other traditionally great exporters of primary products, Australia and Argentina. If these possibilities are not realized, it will be largely because of national policies unfavorable to primary production. One does not have to accept completely Colin Clark's characterization of the Australian "paranoiac national preconceptions towards urbanization and industrialization" [7] to agree that Australia's contribution to her own impoverishment and that of the rest of the world is an important one. A study of what has happened to national income per capita in Australia since 1900 when it was nearly as high as that prevailing in the United States should be enough to induce sobering thoughts in the minds of most enthusiasts of industrialization. As for Argentina the recent conclusions of a British journalist that "Peron's gamble on industrialization has brought Argentina agriculture close to bankruptcy without achieving any lasting economic benefits," appears to be not only succinct but accurate. [8]

The rapid rates of increase of agricultural output per capita that have been realized over the last decade in the United States and Canada and that would be possible, with different domestic policies, in Australia and Argentina, are by no means limited to these coun-

[7] Colin Clark, "Halfway to 1960," *Lloyd's Bank Review*, April 1952, p. 3.
[8] Jack Winocour, "Argentina's Economic Crisis," *Fortune Magazine*, May 1952, p. 95.

tries. Britain and the Scandinavian countries show increases nearly as large as the United States and there have been smaller per capita increases elsewhere in western Europe.

All things considered, it seems probable that countries that export manufactured products for foodstuffs and raw materials could obtain their imports without any markedly adverse change in price relationships if it were possbile for them to buy in the cheapest markets and if resources were free to flow into the most productive opportunities. For some materials-importing countries, however, lack of currency convertibility will prevent purchase in the cheapest market. And for some materials-exporting countries discrimination against primary production will substantially reduce supplies. The net effect of these impediments *could* be a substantial worsening of the terms of trade of manufactured products for agricultural raw materials.

When one examines the list of agricultural raw materials and unprocessed foodstuffs that bulk most largely in international trade (cotton, wool, rubber, jute, wheat, coffee, tea, cocoa, rice, etc.), there appears to be no economic reason why, with continued technological improvement, an expansion of the magnitude necessary to satisfy requirements over the next quarter-century cannot be accomplished at declining real costs. A possible important exception is meat and an inevitable exception is timber. On the North American continent, timber until recently has been produced and sold at prices very little higher than sufficient to cover cutting and handling costs. Even in western Europe it is doubtful whether timber prices have been adequate to cover the full costs of replacement. As replacement costs come to determine timber prices, this situation will change; indeed the real price of timber in the United States has risen sharply over the last decade. This, however, is an exception.

MINERALS

An appraisal of the outlook for mineral raw materials must start from the fact of the overwhelming importance of coal, petroleum, and steel (such minerals as sand, gravel, and common clays are here excluded from consideration because they are almost everywhere available in unlimited quantities). For any industrial country a 10 per cent increase in the real price of coal, steel, and petroleum would be much more serious than a 50 per cent increase in the real price of all other minerals taken together.

The consumption of steel in the United States — and in most other industrial countries — is more than twice as great tonnage-wise as the consumption of the total of all other metals. The next most important metal both in weight and in value is copper, soon to be displaced from this position by aluminum.[9] In recent years the U. S. consumption of copper has averaged around a million and a half tons and the current price is about 25 cents a pound. By comparison the average consumption of ingot steel has been about 100 million tons and the current selling price is 5 to 6 cents a pound.

The President's Commission finds some evidence that during the decade 1940–1950, the long-preceding trend of rather sharply declining real costs of production of minerals in the United States was reversed. This evidence, however, is by no means conclusive. What is much clearer is the fact that over this same period the United States has ceased to be a net exporter of mineral products and has become a large net importer. Furthermore there is no doubt that, given opportunities for expansion of output in the principal minerals-producing countries no worse than exist currently, U. S. mineral imports will greatly increase over the next quarter-century.

The questions of interest are what are the technical conditions confronting output expansion in the principal minerals-producing countries of the world; are the technical possibilities likely to be realized in the face of increasing obstacles to foreign investment; how seriously would rising real costs of imported minerals affect the prospects of economic growth in the United States and elsewhere?

While reliable data on ore bodies are hard to obtain, there is enough information available on measured and indicated reserves[10] to justify

---

[9] Gold is excluded from this discussion of industrial metals.

[10] According to U. S. practice, measured ore is ore for which tonnages are computed from the results of detailed sampling. In no case are the stated limits "judged to differ from the computed tonnage or grade by more than 20 per cent." "Indicated ore is ore for which tonnages and grade are computed partly from specific measurements — and partly from projection for a reasonable distance on geologic evidence." "Inferred ore is ore for which quantitative estimates are based largely on broad knowledge of the geologic character of the deposit and for which there are few, if any, samples or measurements." Report to the Commission from the United States Geological Survey and Bureau of Mines, Vol. II.

the statement that, were resources free to move to lowest cost sources of supply, projected requirements for the principal metals could, without much doubt, be satisfied over the next quarter-century at declining real costs.[11] This means real costs at present points of principal consumption, and the statement is made with full recognition of the difficulties of access to some of the richer ore bodies. There are one or two apparent exceptions among important metals of which lead may be the most significant. Even in these cases, however, it is difficult to judge whether reported known reserves are anything more than working inventories that can and will be extended as occasion warrants. When, furthermore, one takes account of the fact that most of the mineralized areas of the world have been nowhere near as intensively explored as the mineralized areas of western Europe and the United States and of the further fact that the detection of ore bodies by surface outcroppings is even now giving way to new techniques that give promise of locating deposits without benefit of outcroppings, this optimistic view is reinforced. At some stage an inescapable shortage of minerals may threaten but there is no evidence that this impends during the period in question. The difficulties and obstacles that may, over the next quarter-century, substantially raise the real costs of meeting mineral requirements are not to be attributed to the "niggardliness of nature."

These obstacles are rather the result of attitudes and policies in resource countries, the uncertainties arising out of the cold war and the general state of military insecurity, and the lack to date of constructive suggestions, on the national and international plane, as to how these difficulties may best be overcome. Most of the production of minerals for export is in the hands of a few large petroleum and mining companies. The resource countries are either independent states many of whom discriminate heavily against foreign capital, particularly with respect to the development of natural resources, or the colonies of European powers many of whom tend to discriminate against all except the nationals of the metropolitan country.

The Commission conducted an interesting and illuminating survey of the opinions of the principal U. S. companies engaged in foreign

[11] The information on reserves is summarized by countries in a set of tables in Ch. 11 of Vol. I. It is considered in more detail in Vol. II, which deals with specific materials.

mining and petroleum operations, some of which are made available in the Report. It is clear that the main obstacles encountered by American companies are not so much connected with the division of earnings between company and source country as with the imposition of conditions adversely affecting efficient operations, with limitations on the repatriation of earnings, and, above all, with uncertainty as to whether conditions under which operations are conducted, though not very good today, may not become very much worse tomorrow.

It is the opinion of the Commission, fully shared by the writer, that the development of mineral resources by western European and American capital and enterprise and with growing local participation is usually the most efficient way of expanding output. Furthermore, as the author has argued elsewhere,[12] such an expansion is not only compatible with general economic development but can be of very great assistance to such development, as the Venezuelan experience indicates. Not only is foreign capital, on appropriate terms, available for mineral expansion but it brings with it extensive auxiliary sources such as port facilities, roads and power plants, and, in distinction to many types of agricultural expansion, does not involve a diversion of large quantities of local resources.

The Commission's proposals for government action to overcome obstacles to foreign investment in resource development run along somewhat conventional lines: extension of investment treaties, negotiation in special cases of executive agreements applicable to minerals productions, tax concessions by the American government on foreign investment income, bilateral tax treaties, insurance against expropriation and inconvertibility of earnings, reduction of tariffs and other barriers to imports of materials into the United States. Frequently action by investors themselves can be of greater assistance in securing a welcome from source countries than anything government can do for them. A number of instances are cited of encouragement by American companies of local investment and management participation, the initiation of extensive training programs, and arrangements looking towards a transfer of ownership to the nationals or the government of the source country after a period of time.

[12] E. S. Mason, "Raw Materials, Rearmament, and Economic Development," *Quarterly Journal of Economics,* Aug. 1952. Reprinted as Chapter 12 above.

It seems quite possible, however, that the application of the full range of proposals here envisaged, both for investors and for government, including, in the case of strategic and critical materials, long-term government purchase contracts and financial assistance to American mining companies operating abroad, may not be sufficient to bring about an expansion of minerals production sufficient to meet projected requirements. In a number of areas effective mineral development waits on general developmental measures such as the provision of railway and road systems, electric power facilities, housing, port development, etc. The International Bank and, to a smaller extent, the Export-Import Bank are available in this area as lending institutions. And, despite the smallness of their contribution to date in the minerals field, the technical assistance programs have large potentialities. Since the President's Commission was exclusively concerned with materials problems, international public lending and technical assistance in support of general development are given somewhat peripheral treatment in their Report. It seems possible, however, that a satisfactory solution to the problem of raw-material expansion in the underdeveloped areas of the world may not be found outside the context of a satisfactory program of general economic development.

Concerning the over-all minerals situation, it is the writer's opinion, based primarily on the data made available in this Report, (1) that there are no insuperable technical obstacles to meeting free world requirements over the next quarter-century at declining real costs, and (2) that if, on the contrary, real costs increase sharply it will be primarily the consequence of mistaken national policies and of a failure to devise institutional and international arrangements adapted to the contemporary situation.

Assuming a pessimistic outlook, what would be the effect on the growth rates of industrial economies of increasing real costs of mineral raw materials? If iron and steel (or iron ore), coal and petroleum are excluded, the effect even of a substantial rise in real costs could not be very serious. The value of the consumption by industrial countries of all other minerals is a small percentage of national income. The inclusion of steel, coal, and petroleum makes a substantial difference. And, of course, if industrial countries confronted rising real costs of agricultural products, including foodstuffs as well as of mineral raw materials, per capita growth rates could well be negative.

With attention here focused on minerals, it is evident that differences in the vulnerability of various industrial economies to increases in real costs of materials from current sources are very great. These differences depend on the relative availability of substitute resources, of technologies capable of exploiting these resources and on institutional flexibilities within the various economies. The United States quite clearly is in a relatively good position to protect itself against the adverse effects of rising real costs of minerals from current sources. There exist within the borders of the United States very large deposits of lower grade iron ore that could be used with a relatively small increase in the cost of producing pig iron; extensive deposits of oil shale that will come into use if and when the real price of natural petroleum increases by 20–25 per cent: very large quantities of coal and more than adequate supplies of the different materials required for the expansion of various increasingly important types of synthetic products. Improved technology, moreover, offers large possibilities of materials saving in the redesign of end products, the more extensive reuse and recovery of scrap, and the development of alternative sources of supply and of substitutes.

This relative invulnerability of the United States to rising real prices of materials from existing sources could have rather diverse consequences. A sharp and sustained rise in these prices could take the United States out of competition with other industrial countries for the available supplies of materials, thus perhaps alleviating Mr. Bevan's fears that this country, having exhausted its own natural resources, is about to exhaust the natural resources of the rest of the world. On the other hand, such a shift would not only intensify the "dollar shortage" but would lessen that economic interdependence among countries of the Free World on which the hope of effective intergovernmental cooperation so largely depends.

ENERGY RESOURCES

The Free World situation with respect to energy resources is very much the same as it is for mineral raw materials. When full account is taken of the substitutabilities of coal, petroleum, natural gas, and hydroelectric power, and the flexibility of conversion of one energy source into another, there are no overwhelming technical obstacles to the satisfaction of projected energy requirements at real costs that — if not declining — at least need not rise very much. Here again if various countries encounter sharply rising energy costs, it will, in the main, be the result of a combination of barriers to trade, obstacles to the flow of investment funds, military insecurity and the failure to devise international arrangements adequate to meet these difficulties. Furthermore, the economics of different countries exhibit a wide range of vulnerability to rising energy costs.

As compared with other industrial countries an extraordinarily high percentage of American energy requirements are met from petroleum and natural gas. Over the next quarter-century this percentage is expected to increase. During the period since the war about 40 per cent of U. S. energy and heating requirements has been met by coal, roughly 35 per cent petroleum, nearly 20 per cent by natural gas and not over 5 per cent by hydroelectric power. This contrasts with the situation in 1900 when roughly 90 per cent of the energy and heating requirements of the United States war supplied by coal.

American energy requirements are projected to double by 1975. Although coal production is expected during this period to increase from something over 500 million tons to about 900 million, the share of the energy burden assumed by coal is projected to decline to less than 40 per cent. The position of petroleum is expected to remain about the same, natural gas will carry an increased burden, and hydroelectric power will, perhaps, decrease slightly.

If these expectations are realized, it is probable that the real price of natural gas will rise somewhat but not enough to check the expansion of demand of this extraordinarily convenient fuel. The real price of petroleum may also be expected to increase somewhat but any increase will be limited by the availability of petroleum imports and of petroleum from shale and, later, coal. On the other hand, there is no technical reason for expecting an increase in the real price of coal and since, for industrial purposes, coal and fuel oil are closely interchangeable, it seems likely that American industry will be able to count on fairly constant energy prices for the indefinite future.

The principle uncertainty in the U. S. energy situation concerns the future of natural petroleum production. For the last quarter-century, despite a three-fold increase in petroleum consumption, U. S. measured reserves have increased sufficiently to guarantee a 12–14 years' supply at current rates of consumption. The accelerated rate of discovery, however, has not prevented the United States from becoming a net importer to the extent of 300 million barrels per annum, and it seems highly probable that not only the volume but the percentage of domestic consumption imported will increase. U. S. dependence on imports of petroleum could increase very greatly. Whether or not this happens depends not only on domestic production of crude oil but on what happens to the price of both imports and domestic production. At a price not much higher than the current price of crude oil, the production of oil from shale will become possible. It is estimated that the upper limit of shale-oil production in the United States is not less than 2½ billion barrels per year which is somewhat greater than total current consumption. Beyond that there are the very large coal resources of the United States available for synthetic petroleum production.

There is, then, nothing in the present outlook that argues for a large increase in the real price of petroleum in the United States. The chief question concerns the share of U. S. petroleum requirements to be met by domestic natural production, imports, shale oil, or synthetic oil from coal. The main energy problems confronting the United States are concerned with ways and means of meeting the suddenly imposed conditions of total war. The steadily increasing requirements associated with economic growth can probably be satisfied at little or no increase in real costs.

The energy outlook for Britain and for western Europe, on the other hand, is clouded by the almost complete dependence of the area on imported liquid fuels, the lack of indigenous supplies of natural gas, and the probability that large increases in coal production, if forthcoming at all, will be at increasing costs. Certain countries, notably Norway, Sweden, and Switzerland, are adequately protected by the availability of hydroelectric power. Others, including Denmark and Austria, as noted in the Economic Survey for Europe in 1951, are currently pinched by the high price of imported coal.[13]

[13] *The European Coal Problem,* Economic Commission for Europe (Geneva, 1952), Ch. 6.

The small but important amounts of coal now imported from eastern Europe are likely to be absorbed in the near future by internal development. If western Europe becomes increasingly dependent on imports of coal from the United States the landed price may well be reduced from current high levels but it can hardly fall below the highest cost European production.[14] Increasing dependence on American output is bound not only to increase the total cost of meeting European coal requirements but to confront those countries particularly dependent on this source with a difficult payment problem.

A worsening of the western European energy situation can only be avoided if the area can count on Near Eastern production of petroleum and, possibly, of natural gas. The President's Commission projects a tripling of the petroleum requirements of western Europe and Britain by 1975. There are no technical reasons why an increase even more rapid than this could not be attained without encountering rising real costs. The real problems have to do with difficulties confronting capital expansion in the area and with payments questions. It is furthermore technically possible to pipe large quantities of natural gas, now unutilized, to western Europe at costs substantially less than the current price of manufactured gas.[15] In a situation, however, where an expensive installation could be rendered useless by any one of the countries in which it is located or easily overrun in case of war, it is unlikely that the required capital investment will be forthcoming.

TECHNOLOGY AND RAW MATERIALS

Surveying the raw-material outlook as a whole, including agricultural materials and foodstuffs, mineral materials, and energy sources, the data assembled by the President's Commission suggest strongly to this observer that the materials requirements associated with a doubling of the real incomes of free-world countries could technically be met over the next quarter-century at declining real costs. Nor does this conclusion depend on impossible assumptions concerning the mobility of resources, freedom of trade and exchange

[14] *The European Coal Problem*, p. 153. The E.C.E. suggests that, "if the trade were organized on a permanent basis," the cost of American coal landed in Europe might be reduced to $15 from present prices which, "on rush order," sometimes reach $25 a ton.

[15] Cf. Report, Vol. I, Ch. 21.

convertibilities. It *does* require a moderation of national policies now oriented towards self-sufficiency, a greater willingness on the part of primary producing countries to provide a hospitable reception to foreign capital, and the working out of international arrangements looking towards the provision of adequate lending and technical assistance.

The establishment of conditions conducive to economic growth in both industrial and primary producing areas involves issues that extend beyond the sphere of raw-material production. Even within this narrow sphere the Report under consideration is not unduly venturesome, particularly in its treatment of international possibilities. But it is important to distinguish those factors bearing on the real costs and terms of trade for primary products that come under the Ricardian heading of "the natural and irreplaceable qualities of the soil" from those that are amenable to change by national policy and international arrangement.

If adequate policies and arrangements are not forthcoming, the relative vulnerabilities of industrial countries to rising raw-materials costs will depend largely on technological potentialities in relation to alternative materials sources at the country's disposal and on the flexibility of institutions to shifts in material sources and uses. The possibilities of materials substitution in the United States are very large, and the President's Commission devoted substantial attention to the relation of technological developments to the raw-materials problem.[16]

Improved technology holds possibilities for commercial extraction of low-grade ores, the "recycling" of materials currently going to waste, the production of substitutes and synthetics, the redesign of equipment away from the use of scarce materials. Of perhaps equal importance is the devising of ways and means to bring economically substandard operations up to the level of the best. A consideration of both problems — how to overcome institutional obstacles to efficient operations, and how to secure a desired rate of technical improvement in the extraction and use of materials — raises im-

[16] One of the sections of Vol. I is specifically concerned with technology; the treatment of particular materials in Vol. II and Vol. III pays particular attention to technological possibilities; the whole of Vol. IV is devoted to the reports of various research departments and foundations on the technology of materials.

portant questions concerning the role of the price system and the sharing of responsibility between government and business.

The "proper" answer to these questions will vary markedly among countries. The President's Commission prescribing for American conditions see changes in relative prices as the principal allocator not only of labor and capital in raw-materials production but as indicator of the areas in which research expenditures are needed. "But," it is asserted, "to believe in a minimum of [Government] interference is not to believe that this minimum must be set at zero." In fact the American government already takes a large hand in raw-materials production, and public policy will have an important part to play in any satisfactory meeting of U. S. materials requirements over the next quarter century.

Research conducted under government auspices has made a major contribution to the phenomenal increase in American agricultural productivity over the last decade. Moreover, the Department of Agriculture has developed in its Extension Service a highly effective means of transferring the results of research to the farm. Despite these achievements the divergence between what is produced and what could be produced on the same land and with the same man power with better farm plans for the use of land, optimal application of fertilizer and equipment, is very large. In recent years governmental assistance in the preparation of production plans for individual farms has substantially increased agricultural output; a more extensive use of fertilizer and equipment may require not only instruction but improved credit facilities. In any case the removals of obstacles to the use of known techniques can make an important contribution to meeting U. S. requirements for foodstuffs and agricultural raw materials. Of necessity government bears the main responsibility for this accomplishment.

The management of forest properties provides another example in which the incentive to private enterprise provided by changes in relative prices can be usefully supplemented by government action. The first requirement, certainly for sustained-yield management of woodlands, is a real price for forest products sufficient to cover the full cost of reproducing these products. But the required price increase, per unit, can be more or less depending on how effective a use is made of the whole product of lumbering operations. Here the work of forest-products laboratories, government financed and sponsored, in devising new uses for timber and waste products has been and will continue to be important. Furthermore, since two-thirds of the woodlands of the United States are in holdings too small for efficient operations, economies of scale are likely to be realized only through institutional changes that facilitate the grouping of properties or their co-operative management. Even with these changes, government assistance in the development of effective cutting and seeding practices is necessary for efficient management. It is as true of forest as of agricultural land that the meeting of expected requirements depends as much on the spread of known technology as it does on new methods. In both, government has an important role to play.

Government action in the field of minerals production has taken the form of geological surveying and mapping, direct exploration for a limited number of "strategic" materials, the provision of a special set of laws relating to the exploration and development of mineral properties on public lands, the granting of special tax incentives, research into new sources and uses of materials, and, on a limited scale, the provision of financial assistance to small mining operations. In the minerals area, as in others, chief reliance is placed on private enterprise guided by the operations of the price system. But again, business functions within the context of important governmental limitations and direct participation. And the extensive use of tax concessions for oil and mining operations certainly involves a substantial modification of the price system.

Public action designed to spread the use of existing technology and the development of new methods in the minerals field can be illustrated by two examples. The first relates to the present laws governing the exploration for minerals on public lands which have survived practically intact from the days of the "gold rush" in 1849. Not even well adapted to pick and shovel operations dependent on the discovery of outcroppings these laws are totally unsuited to new techniques that search for minerals underground. The leasing system that permits exploration concessions over large tracts, now used in the United States in the development of petroleum, sulphur, and potash, can be and should be extended to other minerals. If and when it is, there is some reason to believe that the success attending the search for oil may be approached for some other minerals.

The second example has to do with recent work by the Bureau of Mines on the use of substitute materials. Practically all of the American investigation to date of the production of oil from shales has been conducted by the government. When and if the United States is confronted by a declining rate of discovery of natural petroleum, this work will be well advanced. The Bureau of Mines has developed a method of extracting manganese from slag that gives promise of providing a partial substitute for imports upon which the United States is currently almost entirely dependent. The work of the Bureau on the concentration of commercial grade iron ores from low-content taconites and on other materials problems had also been effective.

These examples of public action directed towards the removal of obstacles to the use of existing technology and to the development of new methods in agriculture, forestry and mining must not be allowed to obscure the central dependence in the United States — in the writer's view, a proper dependence — on the function of private enterprise under a relatively free price system. They may serve, however, as a caution to British readers to accept with a grain of salt the common export view of the American economy as a free enterprise system operating in a political void, a view that the Report here under consideration does not, perhaps, altogether successfully escape.

THE INSTABILITY OF RAW-MATERIAL MARKETS

It is impossible to conclude a discussion of raw-material problems — even one as brief as this — without some mention of the relative instability of raw-material prices and the supposed consequences. Many competent observers consider instability to be *the* materials problem. Those who espouse this view will complain — and from their point of view rightly — of the scanty attention paid this question in this Report.[17]

There is, of course, no doubt concerning the fact of relative price instability, a fact redocumented by a recent United Nations report.[18] Nor is there doubt concerning the hardships inflicted by a sharp fall

[17] Cf. Vol. I. Ch. 15, "Reducing Market Instability," and a technical paper in Vol. V, "Stockpiling Materials for Security."

[18] Economic and Social Council, "Relation of Fluctuations in the Prices of Primary Commodities to the Ability of Underdeveloped Countries to Obtain Foreign Exchange," New York, 1951.

in prices on raw-materials producers or the severity of payment difficulties encountered by both importing and exporting countries as a result of the gyrations of these prices. The behavior of raw-material prices and the consequences thereof since the beginning of the war in Korea are too freshly in mind to be ignored. Despite these facts, about all the President's Commission has to suggest is a more responsible management of stockpile procurement, avoidance of restrictive commodity agreements in favor of multilateral contracts of the type of the International Wheat Agreement, and a tentative espousal of international buffer stocks on an experimental basis.[19]

There are, of course, strong equity considerations favoring government action to relieve the distress of producers, particularly of agricultural raw materials, occasioned by declining demands to which no effective supply adjustment can be made. Many countries have taken such action, frequently, as in the United States, by price supports. The Commission, however, was not primarily concerned with the broad range of questions here at issue. Price instability was considered relevant to the Commission's assignment only to the extent that the long-run adjustment of raw-material supplies to requirements was thereby adversely affected.

It can certainly be argued that expectations of a relatively stable price trend will bring forth investment at lower costs per unit of investment than will expectations of wide price fluctuations around this trend. It is furthermore reasonable to expect, if relative price stability is the product of a lessening of fluctuations in quantities taken off the market by the operations, say, of an international buffer-stock program, that ouput per unit of investment would be increased. Both changes would work in the direction of lower real costs, over time, of primary production. The main questions are, would buffer-stock operations produce these price expectations, and if so, at what level?

Much more important than these hypothetical reactions of investors to a stabilization of raw-materials prices are the demonstrated reactions of governments to an absence of stability. The real argu-

[19] The Commission, of course, favors international raw-materials allocation during a period of shortages such as we have witnessed since the beginning of the Korean War.

ment for stabilization is that without it, trade and production restrictions, almost invariably outlasting the crisis that evokes them, are likely to be imposed by governments.

It is, however, open to question how much of the instability of raw-material markets is amenable to purely commodity solutions. Certainly the largest contribution that can be made to evening out the demand for primary products will come from the domestic income and employment stabilization programs of the principal materials-importing countries. These programs and policies will not eliminate recessions of the 1949 variety nor will they prevent rearmament booms of the type in 1950 to 1952. There is reason to believe, however, that they not only can but will prevent a recurrence of the experience of the 1930's. If so, commodity solutions to the problem of instability become less important but more practicable.

The President's Commission sees substantial merit both in multilateral contracts of the wheat agreement variety and in international buffer stocks.[20] Both types of arrangements leave price-making forces relatively free and seek merely to confine price fluctuations within a limited range. If a buffer-stock management enjoys substantial freedom of action and if all that needs to be considered is the probable reaction of individual buyers and sellers to price changes, the elimination of extreme price fluctuations through a proper adjustment of floor and ceiling prices should not be too difficult. Nor would the operations of buffer stocks in the face of fluctuations of the magnitude of 1949, or even of 1938, require the maintenance of very large stocks. It is of the essence of the problem, however, that the clients of the buffer-stock management are governments, and moreover governments frequently besieged by organized and highly vocal economic pressure groups. Whether in boom times producing countries would willingly see their export prices limited to a fixed ceiling via the competitive selling of the Buffer-Stock Authority and

---

[20] The Commission warns, however, with respect to the Wheat Agreement, that "Since the world price has been the maximum agreement price for the entire life of the agreement, the exporting countries have borne the full costs of stabilization. Since the major exporters (the United States and Canada) enjoy a strong balance of payments situation, this has not given rise to serious problems. The real test would come when importing countries many of whom are in weak international financial positions, were faced with the obligation to purchase at agreement prices above the world price."

whether consuming countries would witness with pleasure the competitive bidding up of the price of their imports by the same Authority, are statements open, at the least, to serious question.

Despite these difficulties it is the author's view that buffer stocks hold substantial promise of achieving a measure of stability and that the President's Commission might well have taken a somewhat more positive position. On the other hand it is difficult to accept the optimistic view, frequently advanced concerning what can be accomplished by buffer-stock operations.[21] International experience with this institution has been negligible and the difficulties attendant on the negotiations and administration of other types of international commodity arrangements do not suggest an easy path for this one. There is, furthermore, a special consideration that necessarily impresses an American Commission recommending action in this field. The significance of the United States as a raw-material importer and exporter, coupled with the probability that it would have the privilege of contributing most of the financing required to maintain inventories, would saddle this country with an unavoidable responsibility for decisions to accumulate or dispose of stocks. Such decisions are bound to be displeasing either to producing or consuming countries. This is not an adequate reason for avoiding international responsibilities but it suggests an experimental approach pending a further assessment of the character and magnitude of those responsibilities.

[21] E.g., W. Arthur Lewis in his excellent *Economic Survey 1919–1939* (p. 174) goes so far as to say: "The creation of international buffer stocks would be the greatest single contribution that could be made to international stability. If the machinery for operating such stocks had existed in 1929 there would have been no major slump, much higher standards of living all around, and no second world war."

14

Energy Requirements and Economic Growth[1]

It is becoming evident that in atomic energy a great new source of power has been made available to do the work of the world. How important this new source of usable energy is likely to be in conventional energy applications over the next few decades will depend primarily on its cost in relation to the cost of energy from conventional fuels. This in turn will in part depend on how rapidly the requirements of energy from all sources increase in relation to the available supplies. The significance of "conventional energy applications" and "the next few decades" needs to be emphasized.

Any imaginative discussion of the prospective uses of atomic energy exposes a multitude of possibilities. If we explore other planets in atomic-powered space ships or descend into the ocean's depths with a future Captain Nemo in his atomic-powered submarine, there is no telling what we may not discover that is relevant to our inquiry. We shall in fact be deliberately unimaginative. Our primary concern here is with the effects of nuclear energy on the availability and costs of power from central stations.

The period under consideration is also a matter of importance. Enough is known about the reserves of conventional sources of fuel to be able to surmise that over the next few decades the world's energy requirements, at any practicable rate of growth, can be satisfied from conventional sources at costs that, indeed, may increase, but need not increase very much. Over much longer periods of time, however, the situation could be very different. In the long run it is conceivable that nuclear power could become the *sine qua non* for continued economic well-being.

[1] This paper was prepared with the collaboration of the staff of the National Planning Association Project on the Economic Aspects of the Productive Users of Nuclear Energy, and was presented as one of the contributions of the United States Delegation to the United Nations Conference on Peacetime Uses of Atomic Energy, Geneva, 1955. Gratitude is also due Harold J. Barnett and Joseph Lerner of Resources for the Future, Inc., for their assistance in the preparation of the paper.

We are, then, concerned here with the question of how much difference the availability of central station atomic power will make over the next quarter- or half-century to the economic prosperity of various parts of the world. If we may assume that the availability of nuclear energy will lower the cost of power in those areas in which power costs are now high and will moderate a tendency for costs to rise in those areas in which they are now low, what will be the consequences for rates of economic growth, the location of economic activity, and the flow of resources and products in international trade? Answers to these questions must obviously be speculative. Some light, nevertheless, may be thrown upon them by examining the data relevant to past relationships between economic growth and energy consumption, to geographical differences in power costs, and to the relative importance of power as a cost of production.

The first section of this paper considers briefly the problem of estimating energy requirements. The second section discusses the complex relationship of economic growth and the use of energy. The third introduces the element of cost and considers how differences among areas and over time in the availability and costs of energy have affected the character and rate of economic growth. The fourth section of the paper examines some of the broad implications of prospective changes in energy requirements and energy availability.

I. ESTIMATING ENERGY REQUIREMENTS

It is obvious that energy consumption is closely tied to economic growth, and some of the major aspects of this relationship are examined in the next section. The proper starting point for estimates of future energy requirements is, then, a consideration of the prospects for economic growth. Any projection of energy requirements based on past trends involves an implied assumption that economic growth will continue at something like historic rates. In any attempt to predict economic growth rates for the world we enter a realm of high — but not sheer — speculation. Barring war or other catastrophe, for certain areas it is possible to say that the patterns and rates of energy consumption are sufficiently stable to project future trends with some confidence; for other areas it is possible to indicate the principle sources of uncertainty.

A number of countries have established growth rates of sufficiently long standing and exhibit sufficient stability in the relative importance of the energy-intensive sectors of their economies — manufacture, transport, and mining — to permit an estimate of probable energy requirements. The United States and most western European economies belong in this category and there are some others. These countries will be termed mature industrial economies, and account at present for over 60 per cent of the total energy consumption of the world.

Careful projections of energy requirements have been undertaken for the United States and western Europe, and they typically indicate a rate of increase of Gross National Product not very different from historic rates, and for reasons to be explained later, rates of energy consumption about the same or somewhat less than the trend of G.N.P. The President's Materials Policy Commission projected approximately a 3 per cent per annum rate of increase for energy consumption in the United States from 1950 to 1975. On the basis of less substantial evidence the P.M.P.C. also projected a 3 per cent rate for the non-Soviet world as a whole. This rate averaged a projected rate of less than 3 per cent for western Europe and higher than 3 per cent rate for the non-Soviet world outside the United States and western Europe.[2]

The Industry Division of the Economic Commission for Europe foresaw an increase of only $1\frac{1}{4}$ per cent per annum in western European energy requirements between 1953 and 1963.[3] P. H. Frankel, a leading authority on petroleum problems, considers that an increase in energy consumption of $2\frac{1}{2}$ per cent per annum is not unduly optimistic for the Organization for European Economic Co-operation countries during the period from 1955 to 1968.[4] Taking these estimates and other considerations into account, a reasonable assessment of the probable rate of increase in energy consumption of primary energy materials in the mature industrial economies might be of the order of 2 to $2\frac{1}{2}$ per cent per annum.

A second group of countries includes those economies currently

[2] President's Materials Policy Commission, Vol. I, *Resources for Freedom,* pp. 103 and 122.

[3] *Relationship Between Coal and Black Oils in the West European Fuel Market,* United Nations, E/ECE/191 (Geneva, 1954).

[4] P. H. Frankel, "The Role of Fuel Oils in Europe," a paper submitted to the Fourth World Petroleum Congress, Rome, June 1955.

subject to a rapid increase in industrialization. Many of the Latin American countries belong in this category, the U.S.S.R. certainly does, and possibly also certain other eastern European economies. This list is not meant to be all-inclusive. As the United Nations Paper on World Energy Requirements emphasizes,[5] 65 per cent of world energy consumption is accounted for by industry (including mining) and transport. If the relative importance of these activities — referred to here as "industry" — is increasing in an economy, the rate of increase in energy consumption will necessarily be high. Since the end of World War II the annual rate of increase of commerical energy consumption in Latin America has been 7½ per cent, and even if the shift from noncommercial to commercial sources is fully taken into account, the rate of increase of energy consumption from all sources has been above 5 per cent per annum. The percentage increase in the U.S.S.R. has been substantially higher.

There are two major questions that relate to projections of energy requirements for this second group of countries. To what extent is the currently rapid rate of industrialization institutionally related to a growth process that gives promise of being persistent and continuous? And, if it is so related, for how long a period is economic growth likely to be accompanied by an increasing relative importance of the industrial sector of the economy? We may hazard the estimate that for many countries in this category industrialization is an integral part of a growth process that by now has an institutional basis sufficient to assure its persistence. For others, however, it is possible that the current rapid rate of industrialization is the product of adventitious circumstances.

It has been the experience of most capitalist countries that increase in the relative importance of industry in the economy, whether measured in terms of employees or value of product, does not continue indefinitely at an undiminished rate. At some stage the industrial sector becomes relatively stable and further declines in primary production are to the benefit of services and other so-called tertiary activities. To the extent that this experience is relevant, the economies now undergoing rapid industrialization may experience a retardation in the rate of increase of their energy requirements. The

---

[5] Nathaniel B. Guyol, "World Energy Requirements in 1975 and 2000," United Nations, Geneva, 1955.

time this is likely to occur in a particular economy is obiously a matter of great uncertainty.

It seems fairly evident that projections of energy requirements for these rapidly industrializing countries, which may currently account for 20 to 25 per cent of world energy consumption, must be subject to a substantially greater degree of error than estimates for the first group. A figure of somewhat more than 5 per cent might be hazarded for the first half of the selected period, and somewhat less than 5 per cent for the latter half.

A third group of countries comprise the so-called underdeveloped or lesser developed areas, and include most of Asia and Africa and some parts of Latin America. This area accounts for perhaps 15 to 20 per cent of world energy consumption and presents the most difficult problem in energy projections. Per capita incomes and energy consumption throughout this part of the world have been low and relatively stagnant over long periods. However, the impetus to economic development is almost everywhere strong, and in many countries the conditions seem ripe for a fairly rapid expansion of national incomes. In these latter countries the increase in energy consumption could be very large. In other countries it is possible that per capita incomes and energy consumption will continue low. Any estimate of the rate of increase in energy requirements for this area as a whole can be little more than a guess, and, among guesses, a projected rate of 4 per cent is, perhaps, no worse than any other.

The prospective growth rates in different areas are estimated to produce an over-all rate of growth for the world as a whole of approximately 3 per cent a year. This would mean a doubling of requirements for primary energy materials by 1975 and a four- to fivefold increase by the year 2000. This is somewhat less than the growth rate of 3½ per cent in gross energy requirements envisaged by the author of the United Nations paper.[6] This divergence among estimates is

---

[6] There are no other projections that are precisely comparable to the UN projections in area covered and in time. The calculations of Putnam and McCabe on the basis of various assumptions concerning rates of population growth and per capita income, are interesting in that they show what continuous growth rates can do to magnitudes over long periods of time, but they are not put forward as projections of probable energy requirements. Palmer C. Putnam, *Energy in the Future* (New York, 1953); Louis C. McCabe, *Energy in the Service of Man,* UNESCO, N.S. 75, 1951.

much less important, however, than the fact that the information available unmistakably suggests to any informed observer that the rate of increase in world energy requirements is likely to be high and could be very high. (See Chart 1.)

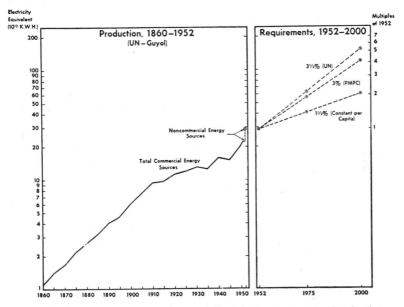

Chart 1. World Energy Production and Requirements (source: Production — UN Statistical Office; Requirements — Appendix Table A).

NOTE ON THE PROBLEM OF ENERGY MEASUREMENT

The analysis of energy requirements undertaken here follows the example of the UN paper in treating energy in terms of homogeneous units — megawatt hours, B.T.U.'s, bituminous coal equivalent — which are produced and consumed in the process of doing the world's work. This procedure is defensible in the light of the major purposes of this Conference. There is sufficient substitutability among mineral fuels including nuclear fuels, between heat and power, and among various forms of power to justify an over-all treatment of the energy problem.

Nevertheless, as the UN paper recognizes, to undertake this analysis in terms of interchangeable energy units is to neglect certain specific and important energy problems. There are no generally economical substitutes for coal in making metallurgical coke, or for coke in smelting iron ore. Supplies of black oil will be indispensable for certain parts of the world over the near future, and the conditions under which black oil will be available are not adequately indicated by a discussion of requirements and availabilities of energy in general. Electrical power is not substitutable for all forms of mechanical power, and, although heat can always be converted into power and vice-versa, the economic practicability of this conversion is a matter of importance. These problems are recognized, however, only to be neglected. We here treat energy in terms of homogeneous units while emphasizing that this procedure thrusts various significant problems firmly under the carpet.

There is the further difficulty that energy requirements can be stated either in terms of megawatt hours produced or megawatt hours consumed and there is no very stable or predictable relationship between these quantities. Requirements can be stated in terms of coal and oil, cubic feet of gas, and other appropriate units of production of energy materials. All these units can be converted into contained B.T.U.'s or megawatt hours, and the result stated in terms of units of energy that need to be produced in order to satisfy the demand.

Requirements can also be stated in terms of energy delivered to the point of consumption as converted to work. This is what the UN paper calls "useful energy," and in terms of a common unit it differs from megawatt hours produced by all the losses involved in producing, transporting, and converting energy materials into work. As a per cent of energy produced or consumed, these losses are the product of a large number of influences including the "mix" of energy materials, the extent of processing, increases in efficiency, changing difficulties of extracting energy materials, the average length of haul of energy materials or transmission of converted energy, and others. There is some evidence of a decline in energy consumed per dollar of output in countries of advanced technology. This trend, however, is in part the result of all the improvements in energy utilization in industry and elsewhere, and does not establish a necessary connection between megawatt hours produced and consumed on the one hand, and "useful energy" on the other. Requirements in this paper are stated in units of fuels produced and consumed, and not as "useful energy."

II. ECONOMIC GROWTH AND ENERGY CONSUMPTION

It has been emphasized that high per capita outputs are associated with high per capita consumption of energy, and that estimates of future requirements of energy depend upon estimates of prospective rates of economic growth. The purposes of this section are twofold: to examine the available data relevant to the relation between per capita real income and per capita energy consumption in various countries; and to consider various possible relationships between rates of economic growth and rates of increase in energy consumption.

ENERGY CONSUMPTION AND NATIONAL INCOMES

Chart 2 is concerned with the relationship between per capita incomes and per capita energy consumption in 42 countries in the year 1952. Despite substantial deficiencies in the data concerning both national income and energy consumption,[7] there is ample evidence of a rough but unmistakable positive correlation between per capita incomes and per capita energy consumption. Large differences in income are associated with large differences in energy intake, and we may take it for granted that no country at this stage of history can enjoy a high per capita income without becoming an extensive consumer of energy.

[7] The evidence supporting most of the noncommercial energy consumption estimates is fragmentary. Yet, noncommercial energy sources supply a significant, if not major, proportion of the total in many parts of the world. Lacking the necessary data, *minimal* estimates are made in most cases of noncommercial energy requirements for cooking only (excluding space heating requirements). This introduces a possibly serious understatement in many energy consumption estimates, with the largest proportional effect being felt in underdeveloped countries where the total is small. (A description of the derivation of the noncommercial energy consumption estimates is found on pp. 99–102 of "World Energy Supplies in Selected Years, 1929–1950," United Nations Statistical Papers J–1, New York, 1952.)

National income estimates for most of the countries with low per capita incomes are also at best fragmentary. There is reason to believe that in general per capita incomes are understated for underdeveloped areas. Thus, both per capita energy consumption and per capita incomes for countries represented on the left of the chart are probably somewhat higher than stated.

Despite this obvious relationship there are substantial differences in per capita energy consumption among countries with similar per capita incomes. Among countries where per capita income is less than $200 the relation between incomes and energy consumption is not particularly striking, and it is not clear that this apparent lack of

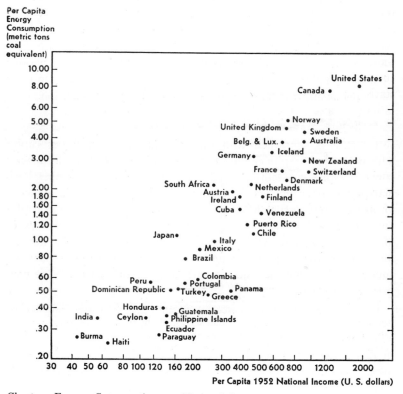

Chart 2. Energy Consumption vs. National Income, 1952 (source: Appendix Table B).

relationship is the result of inadequacies in the data. Predominantly agricultural economies can show great differences in per capita yields without great differences in energy consumption. Even among so-called developed countries, where the statistics are presumably more reliable, equal per capita incomes are associated with substantial differences in energy consumption. Denmark and Norway in 1952 had nearly equal per capita incomes ($725 and $714), yet per capita energy consumption in Norway was double that of Denmark (5.10 as against 2.77 metric tones of coal equivalent).

There are certain obvious reasons for these discrepancies including the extent of industrialization, the "product mix" of industry, the relative importance of energy-intensive processes in the industrial structure of different countries, climate, efficiency of energy utilization, and differences in energy costs. The effect on consumption of differences in energy cost is examined in the next section. Although the available data are not sufficiently reliable to justify an elaborate statistical analysis of the relative importance of these variables, certain observations are in order.

Transport, mining, energy production, and a number of manufacturing sectors are energy-intensive economic activities as compared with both agriculture and service activities. Consequently, per capita energy consumption will tend to vary with the importance of these activities in the economy. It has already been noted that 65 per cent of energy consumption world-wide is accounted for by industry (including mining) and transportation, although not more than one-fifth of the gainfully employed are engaged in these activities. Thus energy intensiveness is correlated with degree of industrialization, and, of course, the degree of industrialization by countries is highly correlated with per capita incomes.

It is interesting that the country having the highest proportion of net domestic product originating in agriculture, forestry, and fishing (Thailand, 57 per cent in 1950), and the highest rate of employment in this activity (88 per cent in 1937), also ranks among the very lowest consumers of energy on a per capita basis (.29 metric tons in 1949). It is also interesting to note that Japan, which had a relatively low per capita income ($165 in 1952), was a relatively large consumer of energy (1.07 metric tons in 1952). While industrialization is generally associated with high per capita incomes, it is inevitable that industrialization brings with it a high per capita energy consumption. However, there are certain countries such as Ireland and Finland, for example, that are not extensively industrialized but have relatively high rates of energy consumption. The reason for this appears to be relatively high per capita incomes and, in the case of Finland, an industrial structure that emphasizes energy-using processes.[8]

The extent of industrialization is difficult to assess quantitatively as an independent factor explaining differences in per capita energy consumption. There does, however, appear to be enough evidence of association of per capita energy consumption with extent of industrialization in countries enjoying similar per capita incomes to attribute some independent significance to this variable.

Table 1

Power Requirements for Selected Electro-process Products[a]

Product	Approximate K.W.H. required per ton of product
Titanium metal	40,000
Aluminum metal	18,000
95 per cent silicon metal	17,500
Electrolytic magnesium	16,000
35 per cent hydrogen peroxide (100 per cent basic)	16,000
Electrolytic manganese	10,200
Silicon carbide	8,600
70 per cent ferrotungsten	7,600
Sodium chlorate	5,200
Rayon	5,200
Phosphoric acid (via electric furnace)	3,900
Electrolytic zinc	3,400
Chlorine	3,000

[a] Source: President's Materials Policy Commission, Vol. III, p. 34.

It also makes a great deal of difference what kinds of industries are included in a country's industrial complex. Manufacturing industries exhibit a wide range of variation in energy input per employee, per ton of output and per dollar of value added. Table 1, above, illustrates the great differences in power consumption among various electro-process industries. Yet all these industries are highly energy-intensive, and any country whose industrial sector contains a high complement of these industries is bound to have a high per capita consumption of energy.

[8] In 1940, 57 per cent of the gainfully employed in Finland were engaged in primary activities; the figure for Ireland was 48 per cent. Per capita income in Finland in 1952 was $523, and in Ireland $384.

Canada, for example, is less highly industrialized than the United States and her per capita income is substantially lower. Yet Canada's energy consumption per head is nearly as high as that in the United States, and may be higher in a few years. The main reason for this is, of course, the high proportion of the Canadian industrial complex that is made up of electro-process industries, including aluminum which ranks about at the top of the list of major energy consumers per ton of product. Norway is another example of a country that, though not particularly highly industrialized, has a high per capita energy consumption because of the composition of her industrial activity. Since the electro-process industries are among the few that tend to be attracted to cheap power locations, it should be noted here that the juxtaposition of large sources of potentially cheap power and of raw materials required by electro-process industries, notably in Africa and South America, may produce very high rates of growth in power requirements in those areas.

Differences in climate obviously have a large influence on energy requirements for space heating (and in some small degree for space cooling). Furthermore, space heating accounts for a surprisingly large per cent of total energy requirements in cold climates. Although the available statistics do not permit an unambiguous determination, it is a fair guess that space heating, other than in industrial establishments, absorbs at least one-fifth of the total energy consumed in the United States. The figures are probably higher in some other countries. The high rates of consumption shown by Denmark, Canada, Finland, Iceland, Norway, Sweden, and Switzerland no doubt derive in part from this influence. Whatever the reason may be, it is a fact that a large part of the economically underdeveloped areas of the world lie in the tropics. Consequently, we would expect that the process of economic development in these parts of the world would not need to be fed by such large energy inputs as have been required in colder climates.

Finally, it is to be expected that there are substantial differences in the efficiency of energy utilization among countries. It is perhaps fair to assume that efficiencies for specific fuels are higher in developed than underdeveloped areas. If this is so, it would follow that energy inputs per unit of output tend to be higher in the latter than if the technologies of advanced countries were freely available.

An examination of these and other influences on per capita energy consumption supports the conclusion that while the relationship between economic growth and energy requirements can be fairly well determined for any particular country with its fixed climatic conditions, relatively stable structure of economic activities, and established efficiencies in energy use, this relationship on a world-wide basis becomes complex indeed. With this observation we pass to a more detailed consideration of the relation between economic growth and energy consumption.

TRENDS IN ENERGY CONSUMPTION AND NATIONAL INCOMES

It was suggested in Section I that in relating energy requirements to prospective rates of economic growth it might be useful to group the countries of the world into three categories. The first group comprises what might be called mature industrial economies including the United States, most of western Europe, and perhaps some other areas. These economies exhibit two characteristics that are relevant to probable rates of growth of energy requirements. In the first place, they are economies that have demonstrated a capacity for economic growth in terms both of increasing national income and of income per capita, and have developed institutions and customs that generate continuous economic growth. In the second place, the position of industrial activities in these countries has intended to become relatively stable in the short term, and to follow persistent trends over the longer run. Agricultural production will probably continue to decline in relative importance, but not at the rate that characterized the period of rapid industrialization. The manufacturing sector may continue to grow slowly in relation to other sectors, but probably not as rapidly as distribution and other services that constitute what is commonly known as tertiary production. Energy requirements in these economies tend to increase at about the rate of G.N.P. or more slowly.

Observation of long-term trends in national income and of institutional behavior that apparently assures on the average a relatively high rate of capital formation, a continuous flow of efficiency-increasing innovations, and a regular output of the administrative and technical capacities required to give direction to the process of production, entitles us to conclude that economic growth in these economies has become quasi-automatic. Rates of growth in these economies, of course, vary both because of differences in rates of population increase, and of differences in rates of increase in per capita productivity. The average annual rate of increase in G.N.P. in the United States during the last half-century has been about 3 per cent, and of per capita incomes about 2 per cent. Sweden in recent decades has shown a somewhat higher rate of economic growth of per capita income; most of the other countries in this category have shown somewhat lower rates.

The position of industry in these economies is also relatively stable. The per cent of the gainfully employed engaged in manufacture in the United States increased steadily until 1920, but declined somewhat between 1920 and 1940. The per cent is slightly higher since the end of the war, perhaps because of the continuation of a relatively high rate of armament production. The per cent employed in trade, finance, government, and private services rose rapidly.[9] The per cent of total employment accounted for in manufacture has been relatively stable in the United Kingdom for many decades, and the same is true of other mature industrial economies. In these countries, rates of increase in value of product per worker still tend to be higher in manufacture than in most other sectors of economic activity, but rates of increase in value of product for the manufacturing sector as a whole tend to be much lower than during the period of rapid industrialization.

For the countries here characterized as mature industrial economies the rate of increase in energy consumption has been slightly less than the rate of increase in G.N.P. In the United States the B.T.U. input per dollar of G.N.P. at 1939 prices declined from 300,000 in 1909 to 230,000 in 1952. Putnam's figures for the United Kingdom show a 50 per cent decline in 80 years, and for Japan a 20 per cent reduction in 15 years.[10] Obviously, shifts from energy-intensive activities to others, or vice-versa, within a manufacturing sector that is relatively stable over-all, may modify these trends substantially.

A second group of countries is clearly in mid-stream of a process of rapid industrialization. A number of Latin American countries belong in this category — notably Brazil, Colombia, Mexico, and Venezuela

[9] George J. Stigler, *Trends in Output and Employment,* National Bureau of Economic Research (New York, 1947).

[10] Putnam, *Energy in the Future.*

— as well as the U.S.S.R. and perhaps certain other countries in eastern Europe. These countries have either attained, or are in fair way toward attaining, an institutionalization of the process of economic growth. They are "over the hump" that separates the relatively stagnant underdeveloped areas from the technologically advanced, capital-intensive areas where increases in per capita income have become quasi-automatic. At the same time they are differentiated from the economies in the first category by the fact that industry (manufacture, mining, and transport) accounts for an increasing — in some cases a very rapidly increasing — per cent of total employment, mainly at the expense of agriculture.

National income is increasing rapidly in these countries because of a rapid increase in population, and a rapid increase of income per capita of the gainfully employed. But energy consumption could tend to increase more rapidly than G.N.P. mainly because of the increasing relative importance of transportation and the industrial sectors of these economies. The data on the rate of growth of commercial energy consumption tend, no doubt, to overstate the rate of growth of total energy consumption since there has been — and continues to be — a substantial shift in many of these countries from noncommercial to commercial sources of energy. For example, between 1925 and 1951, Argentina's dependence on firewood and other noncommercial sources decreased from 43 per cent to 26 per cent of total energy consumption, as per capita consumption increased by 35 per cent. It is also true that the rate of increase in energy requirements is substantially retarded by the increased efficiency of energy utilization. (See Chart 3.)

The third group of countries comprises most of the so-called underdeveloped areas of the world where per capita incomes are not only low but have not increased substantially over recent decades. It is usually a mistake to consider these areas as economically stagnant since frequently expanding enclaves of technologically advanced economic activity are to be found. But over most of the areas in question these exceptions remain enclaves that are not organically related to a growth process that can confidently be expected to produce for the economy as a whole a continuous increase in per capita incomes. This area in its entirety accounts for a small per cent of world

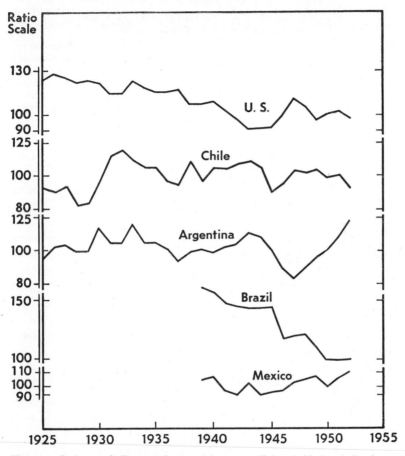

Chart 3. Indexes of Energy Consumption per Unit of National Product; 1950 = 100 (U. S. energy consumption — commercial energy only; others — total energy. Source: Appendix Table C).

energy requirements, and recent rates of increase in energy consumption have not been very large.

At the same time there is a strong determination on the part of the governments in most countries comprising these underdeveloped areas to bring about economic development, and a disposition on the part of economically advanced countries, for which there is little his-

Table 2

Energy Consumption and Income Originating in Industrial
Sectors in the United States, 1947[a]

Consuming Sector	Energy consumption (10^{12} B.T.U.)	Income originating (millions of dollars)	Energy input coefficient (10^3 B.T.U. per dollar of national income)
Agriculture, forestry, and fisheries	887	18,244	49
Mining and quarrying (including crude petroleum and natural gas)	1,114	4,776[d]	233
Transportation	8,640[b]	11,498	751
Railroad	3,782	6,294	601
Other (including pipelines)	4,812	5,204	925
Manufacturing	9,611[c]	58,132[c]	165
Energy processing	1,092	1,705[c]	640
Metals and metal products	3,515	11,050[c]	318
Chemicals and allied products	1,023	3,963	258
Stone, clay, and glass products	890	1,815[c]	490
Textile mill products	386	4,657	83
Paper and allied products	633	2,207	287
Other manufacturing	1,997	32,935	61
Domestic and commercial	9,504	(104,518)	(91)
All other	3,760		
Total domestically consumed	33,516	197,168	170
Exports	3,007		
Total supply available	36,523		

[a] Source: Energy consumption figures based on Table 4 of *Production, Consumption, and Uses of Fuels and Electric Energy in the United States in 1929, 1939 and 1947*, by W. H. Lyon and D. S. Colby, U. S. Bureau of Mines Report of Investigations 4805, U. S. Department of Interior, October 1951.

National income figures, modified as noted in footnote [d], taken from Table 13, pp. 176 and 177, of *National Income Supplement to the Survey of Current Business*, Office of Business Economics, U. S. Department of Commerce, 1954.

[b] Includes 46×10^{12} B.T.U. not allocated to sectors shown.

[c] Includes 75×10^{12} B.T.U. not allocated to sectors shown.

[d] Income originating in the mining and quarrying sector has been adjusted for understatements in the published figures (estimated at $585 million) resulting from vertical integrations of mineral and manufacturing corporations and the inclusion of the combined income in the manufacturing sector, as well as other factors. The essential basis for this adjustment is discussed in the 1951 Minerals Yearbook, pp. 8 and 9. Compensating downward adjustments have also been made in the corresponding components of the manufacturing sector.

torical precedent, to assist in this development. Consequently it would be a mistake to attempt to assess probable energy requirements for these countries by projecting past trends of energy consumption. It is probably also a mistake to assume, particularly for countries of high population density, that a growth process that has been institutionalized in economically advanced countries over decades can be accomplished here overnight. Certain currently underdeveloped areas may attain rapid rates of growth during the period under consideration and others may not. We may expect, with some confidence, that in those currently underdeveloped countries in which economic growth becomes possible, industrialization will bring about a rate of increase in energy requirements substantially more rapid than their growth in G.N.P.

In considering prospective energy requirements for countries at different stages of economic development we have focused attention upon two factors considered to be of paramount importance. The first factor has to do with the question whether an economy is so organized as to assure a rate of capital formation and of technological improvement, and an increase in administrative and professional competence such as to produce a legitimate expectation of sustained economic growth. The other factor has to do with the relative importance in a growing economy of energy-intensive economic activities. Table 2 attempts to put together for the United States data indicating energy inputs per dollar of income originating in various sectors of the economy.

III. CONDITIONS OF ENERGY USE

The preceding discussion has considered a number of the significant determinants of energy consumption. Now let us ask: What importance is to be attached to the availability and costs of energy in explaining the growth of national and per capita incomes and, in developing areas, to the rate of increase in energy consumption? To what extent have ample supplies of energy at low costs promoted economic development in some areas? To what extent has the high cost of energy in other areas been an effective deterrent to economic growth?

The available evidence seems to suggest that energy costs must be considered to be an important, but by no means a determining, factor in economic growth. Economic development in general, and the production and use of energy in particular, require large capital investment. Furthermore, for countries without extensive iron and steel and engineering industries, heavy foreign exchange commitments are involved in the development of energy-producing and energy-consuming industries. It seems clear that a reduction in energy costs will have a pronounced effect on economic growth only if access to capital and foreign funds can be assured at the same time.

The recent historical record is suggestive concerning the probable significance of nuclear energy, providing certain limitations are kept clearly in mind.

First, the historical record relates to the observed range of energy costs at different locations as determined by the use of conventional fuels. If the costs of nuclear energy fall within this range and may be said to have roughly the effect of reducing substantially the cost of energy in high-cost areas and moderating the upward movement of energy costs in areas in which they are now low, this record has some relevance to the probable consequences of the introduction of atomic energy. If at some stage, however, nuclear power is available in very large quantities at very low costs so that energy uses now impracticable become possible, such as the de-salting of sea water for purposes of irrigation, the views here expressed might have to be changed.

Secondly, the historical record is most directly relevant to the possible effects of atomic installations in reducing central station power costs; it has no particular relevance to various unconventional energy uses that nuclear power may make possible.

ENERGY TRANSPORTATION AND INTERNATIONAL ENERGY PRICES

The early development of industry close to sources of power was clearly no accident. But as the industrial revolution progressed a variety of influences weakened the hold of fuel wood, coal, and water power on the specific locations of the industrial nuclei of economic development. Transport became safer, faster, larger scale; markets developed at other places; communications became quicker; competing energies and energy sources were uncovered. Fuel and power locations, although still important, played a less dominant role in industrial development. With physical and institutional limits on the availability of volume energy for deficit areas overcome, emphasis shifted to comparative costs. Comparative international costs, in turn, depended on distance from energy resources, transportation technology and rates, and types of energy available on international markets.

Developments in energy transportation over the past century have been quite complex, but have operated to reduce differentials markedly. As shown in Appendix Table E, coal transport charges in 1871 were from one to four times the cost of coal at export point (Cardiff), depending on destination. Transport costs declined markedly during the next 30 years, and by 1902 were less than coal cost at origin to all except a few very distant points. The ratio of coal transport costs to coal cost at Cardiff thus declined by one-half to three-quarters. The major reasons were the replacement of sail, the use of larger and more efficient steam vessels, and a rise in the mine price of coal. During the next 20 years, coal transport charges as a fraction of coal cost at origin fell still further.

The expanded use of oil during the first half of the present century, with its high B.T.U. content per ton and much lower cost of shipment per ton-mile by tanker has tended still further to reduce average geographical differences in energy prices. Data for 1951 indicate that the cost of moving oil by sea was one-half to one-third the cost per B.T.U. of moving coal:[11]

	Dollars per million K.W.H. per mile	Mills per million B.T.U. per mile
Coal — ocean collier	0.27 to 0.45	0.08 to 0.13
Oil — ocean tanker	0.15	0.043

Transportation of oil and gas by pipeline has also reduced geographical differences. These price differences of energy have been further reduced by the discovery and development of energy materials at new locations, the most striking, of course, being Middle Eastern and South American oil. Finally, the tendency toward equalization of energy prices at different locations may recently have been accentuated by rising energy costs in certain countries where these costs have been traditionally low. Western European coal consumption has

[11] *Coal Age,* Nov. 1951.

been pressing upon resources, and the same thing has begun to be true of oil in the United States, as manifest by deeper wells and higher drilling costs.

The introduction of nuclear fuel, with its negligible fuel weight, will certainly reduce geographical price differences further and much more drastically, and thus strengthen a tendency that has been evident for the last century. The tie between industry and the location of energy materials is clearly becoming weaker.

The present international price differences in fuels are, of course, not insignificant as prices range from under $.10 to more than $1.00 per million B.T.U. If we rank countries according to increasing cost of fuel (cents per million B.T.U.), we find at the head of the list with the lowest fuel cost such countries as the Union of South Africa and parts of the United States. Among the countries having highest fuel costs are Japan and Brazil, and in the middle range are most of the European countries.[12]

SIGNIFICANCE OF COST DIFFERENCES

What importance for economic development should be attributed to these international price differences of energy materials? It should be stated at the outset that the price of energy is not always a good index of the conditions on which energy is available. Also, the existing data on energy prices and rates of consumption do not indicate clearly what the increased availability of energy might do to the process of economic development in the absence of price change. The price of energy in a particular area indicates the terms on which energy is available, at best, only in some long-run sense. At any particular time there may be an effective demand for double the quantities of energy that are in fact available at the going price. This is frequently the situation in growing areas where the unevenness of development may produce a situation in which an expansion of energy supply could increase national output by a multiple of the sum required to increase this supply.[13]

[12] The Schurr and Marshak study presents a detailed map of energy costs throughout the world as of 1937. Sam H. Schurr and Jacob Marshak, *Economic Aspects of Atomic Power* (Princeton, 1950).

[13] On Latin American experience cf. Adolpho Dorfman, "The Development of Electricity Production and Consumption as Related to the Process of Industrialization in the Latin American Countries," World Power Conference,

Furthermore, even if demand is fully satisfied at the going price it is possible that increased energy availability will set in motion a process of economic development even though the price of energy is not reduced. Finally, the existing data do not cover those situations where commercial fuels are not used at all because of high cost of fuel transport. In certain areas it is probable that present energy costs prohibit or deter an otherwise possible economic development. In such areas economic development might be stimulated if a source of power with low costs of fuel transport were to become available. Such possibilities should not be ignored.

Even when full account has been taken of these considerations it remains true that energy is available at some price in most areas. Furthermore, over time, price is likely to be a fair indication of the terms on which energy is available. If low-cost energy were essential to economic development, we would expect to find some association between the price of energy and the state of economic development. Plotting national income per capita against energy prices in fact indicates no significant correlation. Nor, indeed, should we expect to find in these price differences any major explanation of differences in the extent of economic development. In terms of additional cost for fuel and power to produce a pound of metal, an energy transport charge on fuel equivalent to 2 mills per K.W.H. would tend to raise aluminum and magnesium ingot prices by perhaps 10 per cent, other metal ingot prices by less, and finished metal prices by even smaller percentages. In addition, the effect of differences in energy cost on the prices of metals are substantially greater than for the prices of most other products.

The present price differences in fuels alone cannot explain differences in the degree of economic development of various countries. As already noted, there are some underdeveloped countries with low and some with high fuel costs. There are also some highly industrialized countries with low and some with high fuel costs. We also some-

---

Rio de Janeiro, July 1954: "Many instances could be cited when, owing to lack of electricity, new industries could not be established and the planned expansion of industrial concerns already in operation had to be restricted or postponed indefinitely. Severe rationing was imposed in many cities, both in industrial and home consumption and basic industries were impaired; as a consequence of demand exceeding supply, lines were overloaded, causing inconvenience in the service, such as low voltages, frequent interruptions, etc."

times find within a country differences in fuel costs and energy prices almost as wide as average cost differences from country to country. Within the United States we have areas where fuel prices are ten times those of the areas of lowest fuel prices. In Canada the differences are still greater.

Examination of efficiency gains in energy use also conveys some insight into this question of the significance of energy prices to economic development. While changes in the availability of energy materials and improvements in transport have tended to reduce energy costs in deficit areas, technological advances in the use of energy have reduced costs in all areas. The gains in efficiency in some industries have been remarkable. In producing electric power from coal, for example, fuel input in the United States has fallen from about 7 pounds per K.W.H. half a century ago to less than 1 pound today. In railroads, the decline has also been large — conversion to diesel power alone has reduced B.T.U.'s required to move a ton-mile to a mere 20 per cent or less of the amounts required by the steam locomotives that were replaced. The gains in efficiency of fuel utilization, that is, the decline in fuel required per unit of output by consuming industries, in steel making, in cement production, in chemical manufacture, in space heating, and in most uses, have been steady, although usually not as striking as in electric power generation or in the conversion to diesel locomotives. Barnett has found that commercial energy consumption per unit of national output in the United States declined at the rate of approximately 1 per cent per annum from World War I to 1947 (see Chart 3), and estimated this would continue for some years.[14] The Economic Commission for Europe indicates that efficiency in energy use in the United Kingdom increased at about the same rate during the period 1913–1947.[15] These gains in efficiency are equivalent to a reduction in the cost of energy to those areas that have had access to the relevant techniques. Granted such access, a reduction in cost through greater efficiency in use has the same potential effect on energy consumption and economic growth as the discovery of low-cost sources of energy materials or of innovations in energy production or transport.

[14] *Energy Uses and Supplies, 1939, 1947, 1965,* H. J. Barnett, U. S. Bureau of Mines, I.C. 7582, 1950.

[15] *Economic Survey of Europe in 1951,* Economic Commission for Europe, United Nations, E/ECE/140 (1952).

CAPITAL AND FOREIGN EXCHANGE REQUIREMENTS

The prices of energy materials in high-cost deficit areas have tended to decline over the last century or more, and the costs of energy use have declined in all areas. In many parts of the world, however, this decline in costs has not been accompanied by a rapid expansion in the rate of energy use. To explain why this is so would take us much further into an examination of the conditions of economic growth than we are prepared to venture in this discussion. There is, however, one obvious set of facts that bears directly on the answer. The high rates of energy consumption associated with high per capita income and rapid rates of economic growth establish requirements for capital investment and foreign exchange availability that not all countries are prepared to meet. Energy production by modern techniques is inevitably capital-intensive, which is one reason why an expansion of energy production in a country short of capital might not necessarily be accompanied by the development of industries that are heavy consumers of energy.

A recent study of the Economic Commission for Europe[16] indicates that ten cents per K.W.H. appears to be a representative figure for the investment required to provide a K.W.H. of new supply in certain European countries. Consider what is involved in increasing consumption by 250 million K.W.H. per year, which is roughly the output of a 70,000 K.W. plant operating at a 40 per cent plant factor. Investment in electric power, generation, transmission, and distribution facilities would be about $25 million. If fuel is produced locally, several additional million dollars of investment in fuel producing and fuel transport facilities may be required. In addition, investment is required in the consuming sector. As shown in Table 3, which is based on U. S. experience, this varies depending upon the industry which consumes the power, but tends to be several times as large as investment in the power and fuel industries.

A 70,000 K.W. installation represents an insignificant addition to the energy availability of large industrially advanced countries. The United States capacity is now well over 100 million K.W. If we con-

---

[16] *Recent Developments in the Electric Power Situation in Europe (1951–52)*, Economic Commission for Europe, United Nations E/ECE/160, E/ECE/EP/129 (1953), p. 29.

Table 3

Plant and Equipment Investment Required to Consume
250 Million K.W.H. in Certain Industries[a]

Census number and industry	Millions of 1947 dollars
21 Tobacco manufactures	310
22 Textile mill products	90
23 Apparel and related products	370
24 Lumber and related products, except furniture	300
25 Furniture and fixtures	290
29 Petroleum and coal products	270
32 Stone, clay and glass products	110
33 Primary metals industries	110
34 Fabricated metal industries	350

[a] Source: Appendix Table D.

sider the capital requirements involved in bringing the energy consumption of any of the south Asian countries up to say, one-fourth the per capita electric energy consumption of the United States, we get a figure at least two or three times the annual national income of these countries. Such a calculation suggests that an effective use of additional energy resources depends upon simultaneous increase in the rate of capital formation.

A shortage of capital is not the only factor limiting the expansion of energy producing and consuming facilities. There is a heavy foreign exchange component in most of the energy installations. This is particularly the case for countries without substantial iron and steel and engineering industries. The following table relating to five Latin American electricity projects shows that from one-third to two-thirds of the investment may well require foreign currencies.

Furthermore, if expansion of electric energy investment requires an increase in fuel importation, foreign exchange difficulties may be accentuated. In the case of countries deficient in energy materials a substantial per cent of foreign exchange requirements represents the importation of these materials. Argentina in 1952, according to Dorfman, had to import 65 per cent of its total commercial energy consumption, and Brazil and Chile 30 per cent. More than 10 per cent of the total value of imports of all three countries are represented by coal and oil.

On the other hand, low-cost nuclear energy could obviously reduce

Table 4

Expenditures for Selected Power Projects Financed with IBRD Loans[a]

Country and project	Total expenditure (thousands of U. S. dollars)	Foreign exchange required (per cent)
Brazil (Paulo Alfonso)	38,448	41
Colombia (Anchicaya Project)	13,296	36
Colombia (Lebrija Project)	6,898	41
Mexico (Program of the Federal Power Commission)	49,068	60
Mexico (Mexican Light & Power)	41,800	62
Uruguay (Program of the UTE)	36,567	72

[a] Source: Loan Agreements of the International Bank for Reconstruction and Development, as reported in Adolfo Dorfman, Table 7, p. 38.

substantially the annual foreign exchange requirements of countries now dependent on imported fuels. The capital requirements per K.W. for nuclear power installations, on the other hand, are high and the foreign exchange component might be large for most underdeveloped areas.

This brief examination of some of the obstacles to the expansion of energy production and use suggests that a reduction in energy prices, though important, can only lead to a large expansion in energy use in the presence of favorable conditions. The capital requirements for energy production, and for many forms of energy consumption, are large. In the case of those countries with very low rates of capital accumulation, some increase in these rates appears to be a precondition of a substantial expansion in energy use. Since the foreign exchange component of energy investment is high for most under-developed areas, the conditions on which capital is likely to be made available from abroad has an important bearing on the possibility of expanding energy use.

THE UNITED STATES, 1900–1950: A CASE STUDY IN THE USE OF ENERGY

An examination of energy price differences among countries and of the effects of technological changes on reducing the costs of energy use suggests that although the availability of energy at low costs may be a powerful stimulant to economic development, other conditions are necessary to large-scale expansion of energy use. In this connection a brief study of the experience of the United States during the half-century 1900–1950 may be illuminating. During these years energy costs were remarkably low relative to costs in other countries — perhaps as low as anywhere in the world. Furthermore, despite the great increase in output of coal, oil, and gas for domestic use and export, the real price of energy remained low. Under these favoring conditions the per capita use of energy in the United States increased rapidly — much more rapidly than in western Europe — and unmistakably facilitated the rapid increase in per capita productivity in this country. Energy consumption, it is true, increased somewhat less rapidly than real G.N.P. But, when account is taken of increased efficiency in energy use, it is probably fair to say that the effective use of energy increased faster than national output.

Undoubtedly the rapid expansion of energy supplies at low cost has much to do with explaining the economic growth of the United States during this period. However, an examination of the relation of energy costs to total costs indicates that in very few lines of economic activity were energy costs of great importance. Furthermore, both the rapid expansion of energy availability and of energy use required very large amounts of capital which were made available by a relatively high rate of capital formation. Finally, the ample supply of energy, and the terms on which it became available, were both cause and effect of the rapid technological process that characterized U. S. economic development.

U. S. ENERGY PRICES

The main features of the movement of U. S. energy prices during the last half-century seem to be these: coal prices were stable until World War I, achieved a new higher level in the twenties and thirties, and rose again to new higher levels in World War II and the aftermath period; oil prices followed this same general course, but with different amplitudes; natural gas prices, however, declined steadily until a decade ago, when they started upward; electricity prices have behaved like natural gas, except that recent years have been stable rather than upward.

When these prices are divided by the U. S. wholesale price index for all products (in order to remove the influence of general price movements), the series are markedly adjusted as shown in Chart 4. Both coal and oil prices when so expressed become much more stable — coal with a moderate upward trend. Natural gas and electricity (the latter not shown in Chart 4, but included in Appendix Table F) show steep downward trends. The average deflated price of all mineral fuels shows stability from 1900 to World War I, and then an abrupt 50 per cent rise to a level which has been stable for 35 years.[17]

During the whole of this period, U. S. energy prices were lower than in most of the world. A major reason was a fortunate physical endowment. America's coal reserves are large, high quality, easily accessible, in thick seams, and easily mined. The original U. S. oil and gas reserves also had economical characteristics. Gas had the additional feature that it was available in very large volume as the result of oil exploration, development, and production, but was almost a waste product due to disadvantageous location, when rather suddenly a great pipeline industry emerged to carry the gas to urban centers. It is only as "excess" supplies have been soaked up that economic pressure has led to rising prices. U. S. electricity prices have been lower than in most of the rest of the world because of low fuel costs and modern technology. Also public power projects — frequently in joint cost, multipurpose developments — aimed directly at lowering power costs and expanding power markets, have exploited efficient hydro sites.

Underlying all of the cost trends and pressing them downward (or retarding impulses toward increase) have been the plentiful supply of capital for new investment, and the low cost of capital. The prospect of over-all economic expansion prompted business investors to pour first hundreds of millions and then billions of dollars per annum into expanding capacity and improving efficiency. The fact of rapid general economic development provided the capital wherewithal

---

[17] It should be noted that the weighting system by which these average prices were calculated — each fuel price weighted by the B.T.U. importance of that fuel in each year — is relevant to a description of the long-term movement of average prices. Fixed year weighting systems, in which each fuel's price in each year is weighted by the quantity of the fuel in a single base year, would show different movements, depending upon the base year which is selected. The stable average energy prices (deflated) since 1920, shown in Chart 4, are a sensible approximation to actual experience.

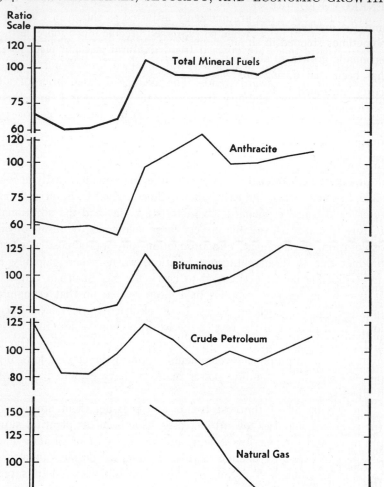

Chart 4. Relative Prices of Mineral Fuels in the United States; 1935–1939 = 100 (mineral fuels price at mine or well divided by wholesale price index for all products. Source: Appendix Table F).

and the markets for the flood of energy products. The government sometimes stepped in simultaneously to supply energy and facilitate economic growth to absorb it, as in the TVA area. One major result has been that during this whole period of economic growth energy costs continued to be low relative to the consumers' ability to pay.

In summary, energy costs in the United States have been low relative to the rest of the world and relative to income. They have been quite stable. The domestic supply has always been assured, the physical resources being present and the capital for expansion plentiful.

ENERGY CONSUMPTION

In response to many favorable factors, low energy prices among them, U. S. energy consumption expanded rapidly. Chart 5 shows changes in the total consumption of fuels and in the consumption of particular fuels. Electric energy consumption, not presented in Chart 5, but included in Appendix Table G, shows the most rapid expansion of all forms of energy. The rule of thumb in the United States is that electric power consumption doubles every ten years.

It would be an error to view the contrasting movements of the individual fuels as somewhat neutral substitutions of one form of B.T.U. for another. Much of the substitution is a reflection of the economic development process. Consider, for example, the great petrochemical industries and the varieties of new products which are concealed within minor B.T.U. movements on the chart; or the provision of water to arid lands; or the almost complete replacement of railroad motive power by Diesels and the revitalization of the railroads in a short 10 to 15 years.

Energy as a Component of Cost. If energy cost is a rather small fraction of aggregate cost of energy-using equipment, or of total cost of production, even large percentage variations in cost of energy may be converted to small total cost influences. Table 5 shows energy cost as a percentage of total manufacturing value added and of G.N.P. from 1899 to 1952, and Table 6 shows energy cost relative to value added in manufacturing in 1947 in specific industry groups.

Even small cost influences, however, can be important, for there are always business and technological decisions susceptible to even mild economic thrust. Moreover, increased energy use stimulated by a price advantage, by its nature, tends to invoke increase use of

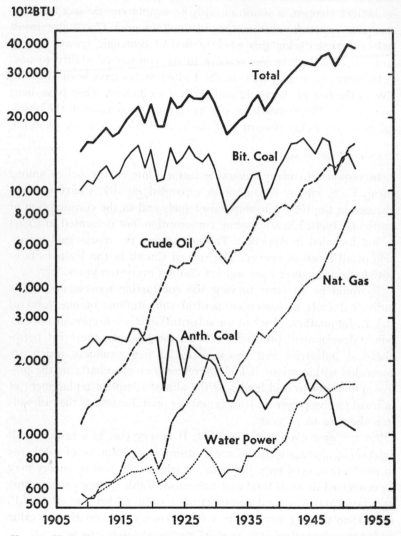

10¹²BTU

capital, innovation, and labor saving, and this can propagate impulse to further changes. Finally, in some cases such as transportation or, as Table 6 shows, in primary metals and stone, clay, and glass products, the energy component of total cost is quite high.

Table 5

Cost of Energy Consumed in Relation to Value Added in Manufacturing and to Gross National Product in the United States, 1899–1952[a]

	All Manufacturing			Total Economy		
Year	Cost of energy consumed	Value added	Energy cost as per cent of value added	Cost of energy consumed	Gross national product	Energy cost as per cent of G.N.P.
	(1)	(2)	(3)	(4)	(5)	(6)
1952	4.8	108.5	4.4	23.6[c]	346.1	6.8
1950	4.2	89.7	4.7	19.8	285.1	6.9
1947	3.3	74.4	4.5	15.3	232.2	6.6
1939	1.3	24.5	5.4	7.1	91.1	7.8
1929	1.6[b]	30.6	5.2	7.4	104.4	7.1
1919	1.4[b]	23.8	6.0	5.2	87.1	6.0
1909	.5[b]	8.2	6.2	1.7	33.1	5.1
1899	.2	4.6	4.5	.8	18.0	4.4

[a] Source: (1), (2) — U. S. Bureau of the Census, Censuses of Manufactures, and 1950 and 1952 Annual Surveys of Manufactures. (4) — Data supplied by Dr. Spencer based on U. S. Bureau of the Census and U. S. Bureau of Mines publications. (5) — 1929–1952 from 1954 *National Income Supplement to the Survey of Current Business*, U. S. Department of Commerce, 1954. 1909 and 1919 from U. S. Department of Commerce, as shown in the Economic Almanac, 1954, p. 490. 1899 estimated unofficially, based primarily on data in Simon Kuznets, *National Product Since 1869*, National Bureau of Economic Research (New York, 1946).
[b] Adjusted by Dr. V. E. Spencer, U. S. Bureau of the Census, to exclude duplication in published figures.
[c] Estimate based on data from U. S. Bureau of Mines, American Petroleum Institute, American Gas Association, and Edison Electric Institute.

Electricity. The oversimplification in viewing energy as simply B.T.U. may be particularly dangerous with respect to electric power. Increased consumption of electric power seems in a variety of ways to be more intimately bound up with economic development than increase in mineral fuel intake. It seems to a greater degree to relate to new products, new producing equipment, and new sources of materials, for example, the electro-process industries; it seems more closely tied to the whole process of innovation. The divisibility and easy control of electricity in very small amounts, furthermore, make it peculiarly well suited for appliances and other improved technology within the home, as handmaiden and handyman; and thereby it is heavily responsible for the liberation for other economic activity of housewives and for the almost complete disappearance (in the United States) of household servants. This view, however, is largely intuitive and, no doubt, a comparable case could be made for the special relation to innovation of motor fuels or other petroleum products.

Table 6

Cost of Energy in Manufacturing Industries in the United States, by Major Industry Group, 1947 [a]

Industry group	Value added by manufacture (millions of dollars)	Cost of fuels and purchased electric energy	
		Total (millions of dollars)	Per cent of value added
All manufacturing industries	74,426	3,332	4.5
Food and kindred products	9,025	279	3.1
Tobacco manufactures	641	6	0.9
Textile mill products	5,341	166	3.1
Apparel and related products	4,443	30	0.7
Lumber and products, except furniture	2,497	68	2.7
Furniture and fixtures	1,378	22	1.6
Paper and allied products	2,875	198	6.9
Printing and publishing industries	4,269	35	0.8
Chemicals and allied products	5,365	297	5.5
Petroleum and coal products	2,015	97	4.8
Rubber products	1,303	46	3.5
Leather and leather products	1,533	21	1.4
Stone, clay, and glass products	2,306	258	11.2
Primary metal industries	5,765	1,317	22.8
Fabricated metal products	4,921	111	2.3
Machinery (except electrical)	7,812	147	1.9
Electrical machinery	3,894	64	1.6
Transportation equipment	5,869	125	2.1
Instruments and related products	1,080	12	1.1
Miscellaneous manufactures	2,090	33	1.6

[a] Source: based on U. S. Bureau of the Census, *Census of Manufactures*, 1947, Vol. 1.

Regional Variations in Energy Costs. The United States is area-wise a large country of economically diverse regions, some of which are remote from fuel, and each settled at different times. Its fuel costs are quite variable among states and regions. For example, the average cost of fuel consumed by electric generating plants in 1953 varied from 8.7 cents per million B.T.U. for natural gas in Texas to $1.12 for fuel oil in Nevada.

An examination of the relationship between state per capita income and average costs of fuel in 1952 fails to show any inverse correlation between the variables (see Table H in Appendix). A relationship of any sort should really not be expected. The economic development process is a great deal more complicated than a description of an omnibus variable "per capita income" as a simple function of another omnibus variable "average energy price."

The Schurr and Marshak investigation of the effect of a cost reduction in central station power on a variety of power-intensive industries found that in a number of cases there could be significant impulse to change-over of technology in very specific industrial processes, and to change in certain plant locations.[18] But they also found that a host of other conditions and influences were operative, in the aggregate of greater weight than energy price alone. Barnett's inquiry into the probable economic effects of an assumed reduction of central station power costs in U. S. states with lower than average per capita income also concluded that the stimulating effect of lower power costs presupposed the presence of a number of other favorable factors.[19]

CONCLUSION

Low-cost energy appears in the United States, as elsewhere, to have been one of a number of elements facilitating economic growth. Particularly in the form of electricity, ample low-cost energy has had an obviously large influence on the location of certain leading industries, has had some effect on the structure of industry, and probably also therefore has influenced the rate of industrial growth generally. Thus, it is clear that ample availability of energy at nonprohibitive costs

---

[18] Schurr and Marshak, *Economic Aspects of Atomic Power.*

[19] Harold J. Barnett, "Atomic Energy in the United States Economy: A Consideration of Certain Industrial, Regional, and Economic Development Aspects," doctoral dissertation, Harvard University (Cambridge, Mass., 1953).

was an essential ingredient of U. S. economic progress. The main lesson of historical experience for countries in early stages of economic development, however, is that while energy is an essential factor, low-cost energy can exert its influence on economic growth only if other factors of growth, particularly adequate capital formation, are present.

IV. NUCLEAR POWER AND ENERGY REQUIREMENTS

The three preceding sections have concluded that:

World energy requirements may double by 1975 and quadruple by 2000, and could increase still more rapidly. The principal determinants will be the rate at which world output increases (by way of both population growth and the increase in per capita productivity), the extent of industrialization, changing efficiencies in energy production and utilization, and the climate of the areas in which economic development takes place.

While geographical differences in energy prices have been reduced over the last century by changes in the relative importance of particular energy materials, discovery of new sources, and improvements in transportation, these differences are still substantial.

Low-cost energy and ample supplies of energy are clearly stimulants to economic growth, while high-cost energy constitutes a deterrent. Energy costs, however, are only a relatively small fraction of the total costs of most economic activities, and energy supply is but one among many conditions necessary to economic development.

Energy production and consumption are capital-intensive activities and for most underdeveloped areas require large amounts of foreign exchange. Even low-cost energy will not promote economic growth in the absence of a satisfactory rate of capital formation and adequate access to foreign funds.

THE AVAILABILITY OF ENERGY FROM CONVENTIONAL FUELS

Before examining the possible consequences of the development of nuclear sources of power in the light of growing energy requirements, it will be useful to consider briefly some aspects of the availability of energy from conventional sources in relation to requirements. Enough is known about reserves of coal, oil, gas, and waterpower to be able to say with some confidence that any practicable increase in world requirements over the next half-century can be met from conventional energy sources *at some price*. But there would appear to be a real possibility, in these circumstances, that world energy prices under the impact of rapidly rising requirements would increase; that certain traditionally low-cost areas clearly face the prospect of rising costs; that the drain on oil resources, oil being the energy material that moves most easily in international trade, would be very large; and that existing geographical differences in energy prices would tend to persist.

The United States, which is predominantly an oil and gas economy, has traditionally enjoyed extremely low energy costs. Oil and gas together account for 62 per cent of U. S. energy consumption. There appears to be some reason to believe that future energy costs will be higher. The price of gas which now supplies 20 per cent of U. S. energy requirements has been rising for the last decade and will probably continue to rise. There is some evidence that the cost of discovering oil in the United States is increasing.[20] Although there are ample reserves of easily mined coal in the United States, the determination of wages and prices in the industry is such as to make it unlikely that coal will exercise an effective moderating influence on the price of other fuels. Hydroelectric power meets a very small fraction of U. S. energy requirements and unexploited low-cost power sites in the United States are limited.

However, the very large reserves of oil shale, which at present are convertible into petroleum products at costs not very much above those for the products of crude oil, will at some stage limit the upward movement of domestic oil prices. And, more immediately, increased imports of oil can exercise a restraining influence. The United States has become since the end of World War II a net importer of oil on a sizable scale — about a million barrels a day of a total consumption of 7½ million. Current policy regards imports as "supplementing but not replacing" domestic production, but this formula is unlikely to withstand a considerable increase in the cost and price of domestically produced oils. The Paley Commission foresaw a substantially increased dependence of the United States on external sources including the Middle East over the next quarter-century.[21]

[20] Report of the President's Materials Policy Commission, Vol. III, p. 5.
[21] Report of the President's Materials Policy Commission, Vol. III, pp. 9 and 10.

If conventional fuels continue to be the principal sources of energy, that dependence over a longer period would tend to become larger.

Whether the United States becomes a sizable importer of Middle Eastern oil may have some bearing on energy costs in western Europe. Like the United States, western Europe with its extensive coal reserves has traditionally been an area of ample and relatively low-cost energy supply. The area has been and still is predominantly a coal economy. In 1953, coal and lignite supplied nearly three-quarters of western Europe's energy requirements, but the situation was in process of rapid change. Between 1937 and 1953, when energy requirements of the area increased by 22.5 per cent, half of the increase was supplied by oil, 6 per cent by coal and lignite, and the remainder by hydro power.[22]

It seems generally agreed that the output of western European coal is unlikely to increase very much, and even present rates of output will probably be produced over time at rising costs. Hydroelectric potential in relation to the magnitude of prospective increases in energy requirements is distinctly limited. Consequently, if western Europe has to depend on conventional fuels to meet increasing energy requirements, the principal source must be oil. Although recent oil and gas discoveries in Europe are promising, the main dependence must be placed on the Middle East.

Middle Eastern crude oil prices for the last few years have been tied to the price of oil delivered from U. S. Gulf and Caribbean sources to the American eastern seaboard ports. If the United States becomes a large importer of Middle Eastern crude oil, the f.o.b. price Persian Gulf will probably continue to be determined by prices ruling on the eastern seaboard, the most distant large market the Middle East can profitably supply.[23]

Whether or not the United States becomes a significant importer of Middle Eastern oil, important competitors with western Europe for supplies from this source are likely to arise in the underdeveloped areas of Asia and Africa. The Middle East is the natural source of

[22] United Nations, E/ECE/191 (1954).

[23] Whether it would be possible to force the price of Middle Eastern crudes substantially below current levels (as suggested in a recent report of the Economic Commission for Europe, *The Price of Oil in Western Europe,* United Nations, E/ECE/205, 1955) is a complex question not discussed in this paper. It is sufficient to say that the difficulties are formidable.

supply for these territories and if income rises at anything like the 4 per cent per annum we have assumed for the underdeveloped areas, energy requirements before long will be large. Insofar as these requirements are met from conventional energy sources, the terms on which Middle Eastern oil is made available will, therefore, be important to presently underdeveloped areas as well as to western Europe and the United States.

Table 7 indicates that over the last twenty years the interregional movements of coal have almost everywhere declined, and the movement of oil has increased. North America and Europe have become

Table 7

Net Interregional Trade in Commercial Sources of Energy, 1929, 1937, and 1950[a]
(millions of metric tons coal equivalent)

Region	Year	Solid Fuels	Liquid Fuels	Total
North America	1929	2.0	0.1	2.1
	1937	−0.4	8.2	7.8
	1950	2.3	−61.1	−58.8
Europe	1929	21.0	−21.1	−0.1
	1937	16.7	−40.3	−23.6
	1950	10.5	−71.6	−61.1
Oceania	1929	—	−2.9	−2.9
	1937	0.1	−4.5	−4.4
	1950	−0.6	−10.1	−10.7
Others[b]	1929	−9.9	−2.3	−12.2
	1937	−4.9	−6.4	−11.3
	1950	−8.8	−20.3	−29.1
Africa	1929	−4.9	−3.1	−8.0
	1937	−5.0	−7.8	−12.8
	1950	0.7	−14.6	−13.9
Latin America	1929	−7.3	26.4	19.1
	1937	−6.2	38.0	31.8
	1950	−2.8	85.2	82.4
Asia	1929	−0.9	2.9	2.0
	1937	−0.3	12.8	12.5
	1950	−1.3	92.5	91.2

[a] Source: "World Energy Supplies in Selected Years, 1929–1950," United Nations Statistical Papers J-1, p. 38.

[b] The difference between imports and exports specifically accounted for; includes the trade of the U.S.S.R.

large net importers of oil and Latin America and Asia large net exporters. It seems probable that over the next few decades oil will be overwhelmingly the most important conventional fuel to move in international trade.

This brief and cursory survey is adequate to bring out certain probable developments in the relationship of conventional energy supplies to growing requirements. The trend of energy costs in the United States and western Europe is likely to be upward and, although oil imports may moderate this trend, they are not apt to reverse it. International and interregional energy movements, which are now predominantly in oil, will tend to become almost exclusively oil shipments. If the United States as well as western Europe and the developing areas of Asia and Africa are dependent on the Middle East for oil imports, the annual rate of consumption of Middle Eastern oil will within the next quarter-century become large even in relation to the immense reserves of the area. Finally, although increased trade in oil will have the effect of reducing still further geographical differences in energy costs, these differences will remain substantial as long as conventional fuels are the predominant source of energy.

THE POTENTIAL CONTRIBUTION OF NUCLEAR ENERGY

It is against this background that the role of nuclear energy in meeting energy requirements must be assessed. We have already emphasized that if, within the period under consideration here, the costs of nuclear power should fall substantially below the lowest costs now encountered in the use of conventional fuels, a range of possibilities might be opened up, to which the experience reviewed in this paper is not directly relevant. If, however, as seems probable, the costs of nuclear power fall within the relatively wide range between low-cost energy from conventional sources at certain locations and high-cost energy at others, and moves over time from the high side of the range toward the low side, the experience with conventional fuels is relevant.

Since the most striking economic aspect of nuclear power is the negligible cost of the movement of fuel, those areas stand to benefit where energy costs are now high because of remoteness from sources of conventional fuel. Many of the underdeveloped areas of the world now ripe for economic development and deficient in conventional fuels, are remote from current sources of supply. Providing capital and foreign exchange difficulties are overcome, nuclear energy can make an important contribution to the economic growth of these areas.

Nuclear power installations are, perhaps, more immediately practicable in the high-energy cost regions of capital-rich countries. It has been emphasized that energy cost differences within the United States and Canada, for example, are substantial. The availability of capital at low cost, and the absence of foreign exchange difficulties, would appear to make nuclear power plants at high-cost locations in these countries more feasible than in equally high-energy-cost underdeveloped areas where capital is less plentiful and foreign exchange is scarce. The high capital and low operating costs of nuclear power plants put a considerable premium on capital availability.

Beyond these high-cost areas, the role of nuclear power will presumably depend on two considerations: the extent of the increase in costs of energy from conventional sources; and the extent of decline in the cost of generating nuclear power. If nuclear power is subject to the same pattern of development as other new technologies, we may confidently expect that in the course of time it will be produced at costs lower than those that now seem feasible. There is also reason to believe, as we have seen, that costs and availability of energy from conventional sources are likely to become serious constraints. The prospects of this development are sufficiently pressing to have induced the United Kingdom to undertake a large nuclear power program.[24] A program of similar magnitude is now under way in the United States.

Even if nuclear power is produced within the period here under consideration at costs not lower than those now possible in efficient coal plants, the expansion of nuclear energy facilities can make an important contribution by forestalling an otherwise inevitable rise in the cost of energy from conventional fuel sources.

If nuclear power is considered from the limited point of view of an additional source of energy that may substantially reduce costs in currently high-cost areas and moderate a tendency toward rising costs

[24] Cf. "A Programme of Nuclear Power," Presented to Parliament by the Lord President of the Council and the Minister of Fuel and Power, Cmd. 9389, 1955, p. 1.: "The application that now appears practicable on a commercial scale is the use of nuclear fission as a source of heat to drive electric generating plant. This comes moreover at a time when the country's great and growing demand for energy, and especially electric power, is placing an increasing strain on our supplies of coal and makes the search for supplementary sources of energy a matter of urgency."

of energy from conventional sources, how is its potential contribution to economic development to be assessed?

Even though energy costs are not an overwhelmingly important fraction of total costs of industrial production, this contribution can be large, and the potential contribution is enormous. It clearly holds out the prospect of weakening further and drastically the connection of industrial expansion to particular sources of power. For underdeveloped areas, ready for economic development but deficient in conventional energy supplies, ample quantities of nuclear energy at lower costs can greatly facilitate the process of growth. And, for the world as a whole, the addition of a virtually limitless source of energy at competitive costs may with time become a factor of inestimable importance.

If full advantage of the potentialities of nuclear energy is to be taken, the technological development necessary to reduce the cost of nuclear power must be pushed, and means must be found to make this energy source available to the underdeveloped areas of the world. The technological developments are primarily, though not exclusively, the responsibility of the economically advanced industrial countries of the world. The provision of capital and foreign exchange necessary to the utilization of this new source of energy in underdeveloped areas is primarily, though not exclusively, the responsibility of underdeveloped areas themselves. Foreign loans and grants can help, but the overwhelming fraction of the very large capital investment required for the desired expansion of energy production and use, must necessarily come from domestic savings.

APPENDIX

Table A

Gross Energy Requirements Projections[a]
(10^{12} K.W.H. electricity equivalent)

Growth rate (per cent)	Available supply, 1952	Requirements projections	
		1975	2000
3½ (UN — Guyol)	29.0	64.0	151.2
3 (P.M.P.C.)	29.0	57.3	120.5
1½ (Constant per capita)	29.0	40.8	59.2

[a] Source: See text, Section 1; 1952 figure taken from N. B. Guyol.

Table B

Energy Consumption vs. National Income, 1952

Comparison of Per Capita National Income in U. S. Dollars and
Per Capita Energy Consumption from Commercial and
Noncommercial Sources for Selected Countries[a]

Country	Per capita national income (U. S. dollars)	Per capita energy consumption (metric tons coal equiv.)	Country	Per capita national income (U. S. dollars)	Per capita energy consumption (metric tons coal equiv.)
Australia	912[b]	3.82	Iceland	588	3.30
Austria	348	1.95	India	57[c]	.35
Belgium and			Ireland	384	1.81
Luxembourg	683	3.80	Italy	277	.98
Brazil	183	.78	Japan	165	1.07
Burma	43[b]	.27	Mexico	223	.88
Canada	1284	7.55	Netherlands	447	2.14
Ceylon	109	.35	New Zealand	921[b]	2.96
Chile	468	1.11	Norway	714	5.10
Colombia	219	.59	Panama	342	.52
Cuba	386	1.53	Paraguay	130	.28
Denmark	725	2.27	Peru	118	.57
Dominican			Philippines	143	.36
Republic	152	.51	Portugal	184	.56
Ecuador	144	.33	Puerto Rico	427	1.24
Finland	523	1.83	Sweden	914	4.37
France	677	2.59	Switzerland	972	2.57
Germany[d]	461	3.14	Turkey	168	.52
Greece	251	.48	South Africa	270[b]	2.12
Guatemala	162	.37	United Kingdom	715	4.58
Haiti	65[c]	.25	United States	1857	8.18
Honduras	137	.40	Venezuela	518	1.45

[a] Source: National income figures (except Brazil and Chile) supplied by W. R. Leonard, Director, United Nations Statistical Office, deflated by population figures from United Nations Statistical Yearbook. Figures for Brazil and Chile estimated independently based on United Nations data and official exchange rates, and *National and Per Capita Incomes, Seventy Countries, 1949*, United Nations Statistical Papers, E-1 (New York, 1950). Energy Consumption figures are the sum of two components: the first, commercial energy, from United Nations Statistical Yearbook; the second, noncommercial energy, derived from 1949 data appearing in "World Energy Supplies in Selected Years, 1929–1950," United Nations Statistical Papers, J-1.

[b] 1952–1953.

[c] 1951–1952.

[d] Federal Republic and West Berlin.

[317]

Table C

Indexes of Energy Consumption Per Unit of Real National Product,
Selected Countries[a]

Year	Argentina	Brazil	Chile	Mexico	United States
1952	121.1	100.2	93.5	110.1	97.4
1951	109.0	99.7	101.5	106.1	102.1
1950	100.0	100.0	100.0	100.0	100.0
1949	95.1	109.5	105.0	106.6	96.2
1948	88.2	119.1	103.6	104.7	105.5
1947	83.4	116.8	104.7	102.3	111.1
1946	89.0	115.0	96.5	96.6	99.1
1945	99.9	142.5	90.8	96.0	91.5
1944	110.4	142.2	107.1	94.1	91.1
1943	112.4	141.4	111.8	102.3	91.1
1942	105.3	143.8	109.2	94.4	97.4
1941	102.3	147.4	105.6	97.1	102.1
1940	99.2	157.8	106.5	106.7	108.9
1939	100.9	162.2	98.8	104.1	107.2
1938	99.0		110.6		107.2
1937	93.2		95.3		117.9
1936	101.3		98.5		116.2
1935	105.8		106.8		116.6
1934	105.5		107.1		120.4
1933	120.2		112.1		125.1
1932	105.3		119.5		115.7
1931	105.7		115.4		114.9
1930	116.1		96.7		123.8
1929	100.0		83.4		126.0
1928	99.7		82.5		124.7
1927	104.2		93.2		128.1
1926	102.3		89.9		131.5
1925	94.3		92.0		126.4

[a] Source: Indexes for Argentina, Brazil, Chile, and Mexico computed from data in Adolpho Dorfman, "The Development of Electricity Production and Consumption." (Estimates both of commercial and of noncommercial energy sources are included in these figures.) U. S. index derived from the ratio of gross mineral fuels and water power consumption (converted to B.T.U. equivalent) to G.N.P. in constant prices. (Only commercial energy sources are included in these figures.)

Table D

Capital Requirements to Consume the Output of a 70,000 K.W. Power Plant
(Yielding Approximately 250 Million K.W.H. Per Year
at 40 Percent Plant Factor)[a]

(All money figures are in millions of 1947 dollars,
except where noted otherwise)

Census industry group	1947 electric power consump- tion (10^9 K.W.H.)	1947 value added in manu- facturing	Value added per K.W.H. con- sumed (dollars)	Value added in consum- ing 250 mil. K.W.H.	Capital require- ments (excl. land) per dollar of value added	Total in- vestment in plant and equip- ment to consume 250 mil. K.W.H. per yr.
	(1)	(2)	(3)	(4)	(5)	(6)
21 Tobacco manu- factures	219	641	2.927	732	.424	310
22 Textile mill products	10,041	5,341	.532	133	.674	90
23 Apparel and re- lated products	850	4,443	5.227	1,307	.287	375
24 Lumber and re- lated products, except furniture	2,338	2,497	1.068	267	1.130	302
25 Furniture and fixtures	826	1,378	1.668	417	.687	286
29 Petroleum and coal products	6,498	2,015	.310	78	3.467	270
32 Stone, clay, and glass products	7,898	2,306	.292	73	1.520	111
33 Primary metals industries	40,645	5,765	.142	36	3.080	111
34 Fabricated metal industries	3,901	4,921	1.261	315	1.110	350

[a] Source: (1), (2) — 1947 U. S. Census of Manufactures. (3) — Ratio of (2) to (1). (4) — (3) × 250 million K.W.H. (5) — Adapted from R. Grosse, "Capital Requirements for the Expansion of Industrial Capacity," Bureau of the Budget, Office of Statistical Standards, 1953. In deriving these figures, capital coefficients for component industries of each two-digit Census industry group shown were aggregated on the basis of 1947 experience. It is necessary to point out, however, that the original capital coefficients have only limited applicability for the purpose to which they have here been put, and the aggregation procedures adopted were fairly rough. The resulting figures, therefore, are at best only of an approximate nature and may properly be used only to indicate the general order of magnitude of the desired quantities. (6) — Product of (4) and (5).

Table E

Coal Transportation Costs from Cardiff, England, to Selected Ports as Percentages of Cost of Coal at Cardiff, Selected Years, 1871–1933[a]

City	Distance from Cardiff (nautical miles)	Transportation cost as percentage of cost at Cardiff					Percentage comparison of transportation cost percentages			
		1871	1902	1904	1924	1933	1902/1871	1933/1871	1933/1904	1933/1924
Havre	377	83.07	34.18	35.29	13.81	23.11	41.15	27.82	65.49	167.32
Dieppe	412	83.07	35.55	35.29	13.56	22.33	42.79	26.88	63.28	164.70
Rouen	433	99.69	42.38	41.91	14.83	26.75	42.52	26.83	63.82	180.40
Bordeaux	540	91.38	32.81				35.22			
Antwerp	558	109.03	36.92	37.50	14.57	26.10	33.86	23.94	69.60	179.15
Bilbao	560	85.67	30.46	32.35	26.23	44.15	35.56	51.54	136.46	168.29
Hamburg	821	101.25	34.18				33.76			
Lisbon	873	103.84	36.92	39.71	26.23	41.16	35.55	39.64	103.67	156.90
Copenhagen	1,116			39.71	29.59	25.84			65.08	87.33
Gibraltar	1,153	114.23	42.38	44.85	24.33	35.97	37.10	31.49	80.19	147.82
Madeira	1,319			52.21	28.39	42.88			82.14	151.05
Stockholm	1,498	101.25	41.02				40.51			
Barcelona	1,664	205.09	55.37				27.00			
Cronstadt	1,776	98.65	41.02				41.58			
Marseilles	1,844	137.08	43.58				31.79			
Genoa	2,007	179.13	44.44	51.10	30.16	34.93	24.81	19.50	68.35	115.81
Palermo	2,065			50.00	33.20	44.15			88.30	132.97
Naples	2,132			48.53	28.72	36.62			75.46	127.53
Malta	2,133	150.57	35.55				23.61			
Cape de Verdes	2,408	155.76	58.11				37.31			
Piraeus	2,642	179.13	41.70	45.59	32.26	39.61	23.28	22.11	86.88	122.77
Trieste	2,806	192.11	45.80				23.84			
Venice	2,825	202.49	51.96	56.62	36.88	43.63	25.66	21.55	77.06	118.31
Sierra Leone	2,885	197.30	69.73				35.35			

Istanbul (Constantinople)	2,952			46.32	36.50	45.19	24.86	19.87	97.55	123.81
Alexandria	2,943	192.11	47.75	48.90	35.63	38.18	21.61	18.21	78.08	107.16
Port Said	3,082	202.49	43.75	46.69	33.96	36.88			78.98	108.58
Odessa	3,272	166.15	69.73				41.97			
St. Thomas	3,525	181.72	65.63				36.11			
Havana	4,025	207.68	69.73				33.57			
Jamaica	4,034	176.53	61.53				34.85			
Rio de Janeiro	5,027	259.61	92.29	78.31	38.88	51.81	35.55	19.96	66.16	133.27
Cape Town	5,998	223.26	128.52				57.57			
Montevideo	6,139	311.53	84.43	63.97	38.67	54.54	27.10	17.51	85.26	141.04
Buenos Aires	6,129	394.60	90.24	63.24	39.04	58.69	22.87	14.87	92.82	150.04
Bombay	6,154	269.99	82.03				30.38			
Singapore	11,574 / 8,132	267.39	98.44				36.82			
Valparaiso	8,869 / 7,588	311.53	98.44				31.60			
Iquique	9,623 / 6,830	379.02	85.45				22.55			
Aden	9,865 / 4,426	285.56	80.67	69.12	42.33	56.10	28.25	19.64	81.12	132.53
Colombo	10,330 / 6,515	249.22	86.14	72.79	42.71	57.65	34.56	23.13	79.20	134.50
Shanghai	10,466	446.52	136.04				30.47			
Yokohama	11,094	425.75	137.41				32.27			

Source: 1871 and 1902 — "The Growth and Direction of Our Foreign Trade in Coal During the Last Half Century" by D. A. Thomas, taken from the September 1903 issue of *Journal of the Royal Statistical Society*. The freight rates are from Appendix B, pages 67–69. For 1871 and 1902 the coal prices were taken from page 47. These are $9.63 and $10.53 respectively and are declared value of exported British coal. Since Appendix B does not give 1871 freight rates, the 1872 rates were used instead. The year 1871 was chosen because it is considered to reflect the earlier period more satisfactorily than 1872 or 1873 which is considered by Thomas (page 46) as being one in which prices were exceptionally high. 1904, 1924, and 1933 — freight and coal values are derived from the 1914, 1924, and 1934 issues of the *South Wales Coal Annual*. The prices for these years were assumed to equal 85 per cent of the price of large-colliery screened drys as given in the tables of each of the issues of the *Annual*. The following coal prices are used: 1871 — $9.63; 1902 — $10.53; 1904 — $11.33; 1924 — $23.23; 1933 — $16.04. Some of the rates in the Thomas publication are in francs. These were converted at 25 francs to the pound. Data not available for other years.

Table F[a]

Five-Year Averages of Relative Prices of Mineral Fuels[b] and Electric Power in the United States, 1900–1954

Period	All mineral fuels[c]	Bituminous and lignite coal	Anthracite coal	Crude petroleum	Natural gas	Electric power
1950–54	112.1	125.9	111.7[d]	113.1	72.9	36.7
1945–49	108.5	130.5	107.5	102.1	64.7	46.6
1940–44	96.4	113.6	102.1	92.1	81.4	69.4
1935–39	100.0	100.0	100.0	100.0	100.0	100.0
1930–34	94.7	93.2	129.6	89.4	141.2	132.5
1925–29	94.9	88.3	111.7	109.2	141.0	96.5
1920–24	107.4	119.7	96.8	123.3	159.1[e]	92.7
1915–19	66.1	78.9	56.1	97.4		88.2[f]
1910–14	60.8	74.6	61.3	81.3		152.6[g]
1905–09	60.7	77.3	60.5	82.4		184.4[h]
1900–04	68.1	85.3	63.6	123.5		236.0[i]

[a] Source: U. S. Bureau of Mines.

[b] Price at mine or well divided by wholesale price index for all products, expressed in index number form with 1935–39 = 100.

[c] Mine or well prices per million B.T.U.'s of all mineral fuels consumed in the United States. [d] 1950–53 only. [e] 1922–24 only. [f] 1917 only. [g] 1912 only. [h] 1907 only. [i] 1902 only.

Table G

Five-Year Averages of Mineral Fuels Consumption and Total Electric Power Production in the United States 1900–1953[a]

Period	Domestic mineral fuels apparent consumption[b] (10^{12} B.T.U.)	Electric power production[c] (10^{6} K.W.H.)
1950–53	34,792	449,814
1945–49	30,569	306,028
1940–44	27,139	233,685
1935–39	20,422	140,936
1930–34	17,784	107,285
1925–29	22,095	101,019
1920–24	19,189	63,636
1915–19	17,890	43,429[d]
1910–14	15,134	24,752[e]
1905–09	12,320	14,121[f]
1900–04	8,746	5,969[g]

[a] Source: U. S. Bureau of Mines and Federal Power Commission.

[b] "Apparent consumption" is defined as the sum of domestic production and imports less exports. It neglects all stock changes.

[c] Total public and industrial power production; excludes industrial and other power installations of less than 100 K.W. capacity.

[d] 1917 only. [e] 1912 only. [f] 1907 only. [g] 1902 only.

Table H

Central Power Station Average Fuel Cost and Per Capita Income, by States, 1952[a]

State	Average cost per million B.T.U. Rank	Cents	Per capita income Rank	Dollars
Vermont	1	57.00	30	1,362
Maine	2	37.57	31	1,358
Connecticut	3	37.20	3	2,071
Massachusetts	4	36.31	11	1,772
New Hampshire	5	36.17	25	1,555
Rhode Island	6	36.08	18	1,661
District of Columbia	7	35.00	2	2,135
New York	8	33.67	4	2,062
South Dakota	9	33.62	39	1,229
New Jersey	10	33.26	7	1,975
Washington	11	32.60	10	1,810
Oregon	12	32.40	14	1,712
Wisconsin	13	32.10	16	1,676
Maryland	14	32.02	12	1,754
North Carolina	15	31.70	44	1,058
Delaware	16	31.59	1	2,207
South Carolina	17	31.57	43	1,088
Florida	18	31.09	33	1,335
Michigan	19	30.72	9	1,830
Minnesota	20	30.24	27	1,502
Virginia	21	28.64	32	1,338
North Dakota	22	27.80	36	1,244
Iowa	23	27.07	24	1,573
Utah	24	26.25	28	1,459
Nebraska	25	25.57	23	1,584
Pennsylvania	26	24.58	13	1,734
Indiana	27	24.11	17	1,668
California	28	23.79	6	1,978
Illinois	29	23.52	5	1,988
Georgia	30	23.26	40	1,139
Ohio	31	22.91	8	1,872
Missouri	32	21.23	22	1,610
Tennessee	33	20.60	41	1,127
Kentucky	34	20.43	42	1,125
Montana	35	19.08	15	1,690
West Virginia	36	18.36	37	1,233
Alabama	37	18.16	45	999
Kansas	38	17.90	21	1,629
Arizona	39	17.71	26	1,503
New Mexico	40	17.65	34	1,331
Colorado	41	17.46	20	1,630
Wyoming	42	17.03	19	1,657
Arkansas	43	13.85	46	967
Mississippi	44	12.52	47	826
Oklahoma	45	9.38	35	1,293
Louisiana	46	9.21	38	1,230
Texas	47	9.07	29	1,457

[a] Source: *Steam-Electric Plant Fuel Consumption and Cost, 1952*, National Coal Association; *Survey of Current Business*, Aug. 1954.

PART IV

ANTITRUST POLICY

Introduction

Part IV brings together a number of papers on a subject that, after many years of study, continues to the author to remain baffling. How are such welfare conclusions as may be derived from an economist's analysis of monopoly and competition to be converted into appropriate public action via a sensible antitrust policy? First there is the question whether any welfare conclusions can in fact be derived, and second there is the question whether, if so, they can be converted into administratively applicable and judicially enforceable rules. A good deal of current discussion of the first question has utilized the promising phrase "workable" or "effective" competition. But, as my colleague Kingman Brewster has recently observed, a concept of workable competition is not enough; the standards must also be enforceable.

Despite a considerable literature on the subject, the notion of workable competition remains at best a protest. It is a protest, on the one hand, against the unqualified application of standards derived from the purely competitive model; it is also a protest against the operational irrelevance of the theory of monopolistic competition. The model gives us certain structural conditions of a properly defined market necessary to the maintenance of pure competition. The most important of these have to do with the number and size distribution of firms, of the conditions of entry and the absence of restrictive arrangements. If competition is to be "pure," however, in the sense that there is no recognition of interdependence among the firms, numbers have to be so large as to exclude most of the markets that make up American industry. And, if this impossible condition is relaxed, the question persists, how many firms, acting independently and with given conditions of entry, are necessary to make competition workable or effective? The proponents of a structural definition of workable competition are inclined to reply that there must be an "adequate" number of alternatives open to buyers and sellers, but this standard is somewhat less than precise.

The model also gives us tests of the competitive behavior of firms under equilibrium conditions. The most important of these have to do with cost-price relations, capacity-output relations, and the rate of profit. The empirical application of behavioral or performance tests is substantially more difficult than structural tests. Nevertheless persistent departures from competitive behavior can frequently be detected by examination of cost-price and profit data. We cannot, therefore, afford to abandon behavioral tests in favor of a purely structural conception of competition. Moreover, it is frequently impossible to form a judgment on those elements of market structure that have to do with the presence or absence of collusion without a study of the market behavior of the firms.

Given the available information on market structure and the behavior of firms, the primary focus of an evaluation of the effectiveness of competition is presumably on the extent or degree of market power possessed by individual firms or a number of firms acting in concert. Competition becomes unworkable if a firm or firms possess an "unreasonable" degree of market power. A major tenet of antitrust philosophy is that a policy of enforced competition is possible only if the rivalry of all firms in a market is such as to limit sharply the ability of each to earn more than competitive profit.

This ability obviously may not be sharply limited if there are economies of scale such as to reduce the number of firms in a market to a few or to produce a situation in which one or two large low-cost firms are confronted only by the competition of small high-cost rivals. American antitrust policy has always recognized that, owing to economies of scale, monopoly may be "thrust upon" a firm. There are those who contend that the only legitimate defense of a firm possessing a substantial degree of market power is a convincing demonstration of economies of scale.

If the workability of competition is to be judged by the tests of market structure and firm behavior so far mentioned, and if a departure from competition can be justified only by demonstrable economies of scale, it is obvious that, at best, workable competition is a variant of pure competition. All the standards of "workability" mentioned above are derived from the purely competitive model, and the only permissible defense of market power is the traditional defense of economies of size. A good deal of the writing on workable competition, however, has emphasized the limitations of these tests and has stressed the importance of innovation and the rate of technical improvement. Unfortunately the exponents of this view have never got much beyond the proposition that more progress is better than less. On the question whether a particular history of innovation is more or less than could be expected from a different, practically attainable, market structure or what the relation, if any, is between market structure and innovation, the record is relatively blank.

It is easy to see that dynamic elements in market rivalry can impinge on appropriate public policies for the enforcement of competition in two main ways. Continuous improvement in methods and products may be an important part of the competitive process through which the market power of the firms subject to this competition is limited. Secondly, if it is true that a considerable measure of relief from the continuous pressure of competition is necessary or conducive to innovation and improvement, the tests of market structure and enterprise behavior appropriate to a sensible antimonopoly policy may be substantially changed. These considerations, it is true, cut somewhat against each other. On the one hand, it is alleged that innovation limits market power; on the other hand, market power is held to be conducive to innovation. But if a time dimension is added to the analysis and competition is viewed as an historical process, there is no necessary incompatibility between them.

Schumpeter was the classic exponent of both positions. On innovation as a limiter of market power he held that the competition that counts is "the competition from the new commodity, the new technology, the new source of supply, the new type of organization (the largest scale unit of control, for instance) — competition which commands a decisive cost or quality advantage and which strikes not at the margin of the profits and their outputs of the existing firms but at their foundations and their very lives."

To the extent that this observation is true and important, it raises the possibility that the number of firms and conditions of entry may, at least in certain circumstances, limit market power less effectively than the product and process innovations of a few. Oligopoly may, under these circumstances, fall within a proper definition of workable competition.

Some degree of market power one the other hand — that is, some protection from a competitive forcing of prices toward short-run marginal costs — was regarded by Schumpeter as essential to successful innovations. This led him to reject pure competition and, implicitly the standards derived from it, as appropriate to the objectives of public policy in this area. Even if there are no important economies of scale and an approach to pure competition could therefore be plausibly considered to promote the static best use of resources in a particular market, Schumpeter would still object because considerations of growth may indicate the necessity of enterprises with substantial market power.

These ideas have colored a good deal of current writing on "the new competition" and have served to deck out with fresh plumage traditional defenses of the large firm. They have also reappeared in a number of recent antitrust decisions. If the performance of firms is "satisfactory," in some sense heavily oriented toward product and process improvement, why need we worry whether the structure of the market or even the behavior of the firm in this market conforms closely to standards derived from the static equilibrium of pure competition? Why indeed, unless it is that "satisfactory performance" is a concept far too slippery for any practical use to an antimonopoly policy.

Although little is known about the relation, if any, between the size of firms and the rate of innovation or about the effect of innovation in limiting market power, the suspicion remains that innovation is an important part of the competitive process. If so, this probably bears on the question whether a particular firm or group of firms possesses or does not possess an "unreasonable" degree of market power. Differences of opinion on the importance of this consideration go far to explain why the concept of workable competition has to date no objective meaning. Some emphasize the more precise, but perhaps irrelevant, tests derived from the competitive model; others stress the perhaps relevant, but certainly imprecise, standards of progressiveness and satisfactory performance.

It will be seen from the essays in Part IV that the author can hardly be called consistent in his treatment of these considerations. Chapters 15 and 16 represent attempts to inform lawyers on the economics of monopoly and competition. The essay on "Monopoly in Law and Economics" points out that substantial market power may exist in the absence of any conspiratorial or predatory conduct of a type that would justify antitrust action under existing law. The paper on "The Current Status of the Monopoly Problem in the United States," among other things, considers the possibility that, under certain circumstances, the behavior of firms may be aggressively competitive even though their numbers are few. Chapters 17 and 18 are semi-popular variations on the theme of efficiency versus market power. The concluding essay, on "Market Power and Business Conduct," represents the author's not altogether favorable reaction to the 1955 Report of the Attorney General's Committee on Antitrust Policy.

15

Monopoly in Law and Economics[1]

I

The term monopoly as used in the law is not a tool of analysis but a standard of evaluation. Not all trusts are held monopolistic but only "bad" trusts; not all restraints of trade are to be condemned but only "unreasonable" restraints. The law of monopoly has therefore been directed toward a development of public policy with respect to certain business practices. This policy has required, first, a distinction between the situations and practices which are to be approved as in the public interest and those which are to be disapproved, second, a classification of these situations as *either* competitive and consequently in the public interest *or* monopolistic and, if unregulated, contrary to the public interest, and, third, the devising and application of tests capable of demarcating the approved from the disapproved practices. But the devising of tests to distinguish monopoly from competition cannot be completely separated from the formulation of the concepts. It may be shown, on the contrary, that the difficulties of formulating tests of monopoly have definitely shaped the legal conception of monopoly.

Economics, on the other hand, has not quite decided whether its task is one of description and analysis or of evaluation and prescription, or both. With respect to the monopoly problem it is not altogether clear whether the work of economists should be oriented toward the formulation of public policy or toward the analysis of market situations. The trend, however, is definitely towards the latter. The further economics goes in this direction, the greater becomes the difference between legal and economic conceptions of the monopoly problem. Lawyers and economists are therefore rapidly ceasing to talk the same language.

Twenty years ago this was not the case. In 1915 there appeared in

[1] Reprinted from *The Yale Law Journal*, Vol. 47, No. 1, Nov. 1937.

the *Journal* an article on the trust problem which quoted the opinions of eminent economists on the significance of a contemporary "trust" decision.[2] The point the author was trying to make, flattering indeed to the study of economics, was "that in cases of this character no decision can be legally sound that is not fundamentally correct from an economic point of view."[3] The question posed to the economists was the import in terms of monopoly of the production by the International Harvester Company of 65 to 85 per cent of the national output of certain types of harvesting machinery.[4] While the answers may or may not have been helpful in the formulation of legal opinion, it is a point of peculiar interest that the economists conceived the problem in much the same way as the courts. It was not monopoly as an analytical concept but monopoly injurious to the public interest which colored their thinking. The economists' emphasis on free entry into the industry as characteristic of competition and restriction of entry as the *differentia specifica* of monopoly was in complete harmony with the judicial predilection. Monopoly was thought of as the antithesis of free competition, unregulated monopoly was always and necessarily a public evil, the nature of monopoly was to be found mainly in restrictions on trade, and its remedy was, in the Wilsonian phrase, "a fair field with no favor."

Since that time, particularly in recent years, economic thinking on the subject of monopoly has taken a radically different trend. Much more attention has been given to the shaping of the concept of monopoly as a tool of economic analysis rather than as a standard of evaluation in the judgment of public policy. Some of the consequences of this trend have been the focussing of attention on the problems of the individual firm rather than those of the industry, a recognition of monopoly elements in the practices of almost every firm, a recognition of the impossibility of using the fact of monopoly as a test of public policy, and a growing awareness of the necessity of making distinctions between market situations all of which have monopoly elements. The trend has led to a split between the approach to the monopoly problem in the law and economics which requires bridging by in-

[2] Friedman, "The Trust Problem in the Light of Some Recent Decisions" *Yale Law Journal,* 24 (1915).
[3] Friedman, p. 493.
[4] Friedman, pp. 502, 503.

terpretative work of a high order. The following pages are not concerned primarily with this task but rather with an economist's impression of the divergence between the present legal and economic concepts of monopoly.

II

The elements out of which both law and economics have built their ideas of monopoly are restriction of trade and control of the market. These elements are of course not independent. Restrictions of trade of various sorts are familiar devices for securing control of the market; control of the market may be used, as in predatory competition, to restrict trade and competition. Nevertheless, restraints of trade can exist without anything that the courts would be willing to call control of the market. And, control of the market, in the economic sense, can exist independently of any practice which the law would call a restraint of trade.

It is also important at this point to understand the content of several other basic concepts. The antithesis of the legal conception of monopoly is *free* competition, understood to be a situation in which the freedom of any individual or firm to engage in legitimate economic activity is not restrained by the state, by agreements between competitors or by the predatory practices of a rival. But free competition thus understood is quite compatible with the presence of monopoly elements in the *economic* sense of the word monopoly. For the antithesis of the economic conception of monopoly is not *free* but *pure* competition, understood to be a situation in which no seller or buyer has any control over the price of his product. Restriction of competition is the legal content of monopoly; control of the market is its economic substance. And these realities are by no means equivalent.

An illustration of the application of these concepts is presented by the facts of the Cream of Wheat case.[5] The Cream of Wheat Company bought purified middlings, a high-grade by-product of wheat, and, "without submitting them to any process or treatment, without adding anything to them, it puts up the middlings which it selects

[5] Great Atlantic and Pacific Tea Company v. Cream of Wheat Company, 227 Fed. 46 (1915).

in packages and offers its selection to the trade under the name of 'Cream of Wheat.' " [6] The court was unable to see either control of the market or restriction of trade in this practice. "The business of the defendant is not a monopoly, or even a quasi-monopoly. Really it is selling purified wheat middlings and its whole business covers only about 1 per cent of that product. It makes its own selection of what by-products of the middling process it will put up, and sells what it puts up under marks which tell the purchaser that these middlings are its own selection. It is open to Brown, Jones and Robinson to make their selections out of the 99 per cent of purified middlings and put them up and sell them; possibly one or more of them may prove to be better selectors than the defendant, or may persuade the public that they are." [7]

An economist, on the other hand, would be inclined to say that the product sold is not wheat middlings but Cream of Wheat, and that the Cream of Wheat Company exercises some monopolistic control of the market unless, and this is unlikely, the number and quantity of substitute products is such as to render the price independent of the quantity sold. He would add that it does not follow that the market control incident to such a monopoly position is contrary to public policy. Furthermore he would consider monopoly of the production of Cream of Wheat as perfectly compatible with competition on the part of actual or potential producers of substitute products.

The economists' emphasis is on control of the supply or price of a product. And "product" is defined in terms of consumer choice, for if consumers find that the goods sold by two competing dealers are different, they are different for purposes of market analysis regardless of what the scales or calipers say. Some control of the market exists whenever a seller can, by increasing or diminishing his sales, affect the price at which his product is sold. Since, outside the sphere of agricultural and a few other products, almost every seller is in this position, it is easy to see that if monopoly is identified with control of the market, monopolistic elements are practically omnipresent. This is the logical conclusion, it is submitted, where the emphasis is laid upon control of the market and the monopoly concept is considered as

[6] 227 Fed. 46, 47.
[7] 227 Fed. 46, 48.

a tool of analysis only, unrelated to public policy. But if monopoly is considered to be a standard of evaluation useful in the administration of public policy, then other considerations must be involved.

It is so used in the law. Although the history of the term's legal usage is filled with references to control of the market as evidence of monopoly, various factors, principally the difficulties of devising tests of the reasonableness of price and output controls, have focussed the attention of courts on another element, restriction of trade, as the decisive consideration. The development of this idea may be seen in the sources of the present law of monopoly and competition, which are, according to Jervey and Deák, to be found in "(A) the Statute against Monopolies and *D'Arcy v. Allein;* (B) the old English statutes against forestalling and engrossing; (C) the judicial adaptation of the ancient law on restraint of trade to the combination acting as a unit of controlled parts; and (D) the law of conspiracy as applied to the illegal end of suppression of competition, with particular reference to labor conspiracies insofar as they were seen as restraints on the market."[8]

It is clear from the Statute of Monopolies[9] and from contemporary definitions that monopoly meant *exclusion* of other producers or sellers by a dispensation from the sovereign granting *sole* rights to some person or persons.[10] Although *D'Arcy v. Allein*[11] declared the "inseparable incidents" of monopoly to be (1) the raising of the price of the product, (2) the deterioration of its quality, and (3) the "impoverishment of divers artificers and others" because of exclusion from their accustomed trades, a monopoly was considered to exist whether or not these "incidents" followed. It was not incumbent upon the courts to show that prices had actually been raised or quality of the product deteriorated in order to be able to hold that a

[8] Huger W. Jervey and Francis Deák, The Case of Monopoly v. Competition (mimeo., 1934).

[9] 21 Jac. I, c. 3 (1623).

[10] Coke defined monopoly in this way: "An institution, or allowance by the king, by his grant, commission, or otherwise, to any person or persons, bodies politique or corporate, of, or for the sole buying, selling, making, working, or using, of anything, whereby any person, or persons, bodies politique or corporate, are sought to be restrained of any freedom or liberty that they had before, or hindered in their lawful trade." Institutes, Vol. 3, No. 181.

[11] 11 Co. 84b, 74 Eng. Reprint 1131 (1602).

monopoly existed contrary to the common law.[12] Monopoly meant exclusion from a certain trade by legal dispensation and no examination of control of the market was necessary to establish this fact.

The injuries inflicted by forestalling, regrating, and engrossing were in the main conditioned and limited by an early and now obsolete system of distributing and marketing goods, principally foodstuffs. Laws were found necessary to prohibit the spreading of false reports as to the state of the market (regrating), to prohibit the purchase of victuals on the way to market for purposes of resale (forestalling), and to prohibit the cornering of the available supply of an article (engrossing).[13] It is true that engrossing in particular was an act undertaken to secure what an economist would call control of the market. But in the absence of a combination, of attempts to exclude competitors, or of other overt acts, it was difficult for the courts to find evidence of control of the market. There is no obvious answer to the question of how large a share of the available supply of an article an individual must purchase before he is guilty of engrossing. If, on the other hand, the engrossing were accomplished by a combination, particularly if the combination attempted to exclude competitors, the problem appeared to be more simple.[14] Conspiracy frequently accompanied engrossing in the early cases and was rarely absent in the later ones. In no engrossing case that has come before Anglo-Saxon courts in the last hundred and fifty years, so far as I am aware, has

[12] As a matter of fact it is quite possible that a monopoly dispensation would not give to its holder control of the market in the sense of ability to raise price or to lower the quality of the product. Whether it did or not would depend, in economic jargon, on the elasticity of demand for that product, and this in turn would be influenced by a number of factors including the existence of effective substitutes.

[13] See Jones, "Historical Development of The Law of Business Competition," *Yale Law Journal*, 35 (1926), 907 ff.

[14] "To gain a monopoly on a local market a common, organized action, in other words a cartel of the most powerful competitors, often became a necessity. The fact that competitors acted in agreement when engrossing the market is expressed in the English anti-monopolistic legislation by the significant term *conspiracy*. This word was first used in this connection in the Statute of 1353 [a Forestalling Statute, of 27 Edw. III], and reappears continually in the anti-monopolistic statutes. From here it passes over to the American anti-trust legislation, being thus a continuation of the old monopoly prohibitions." Pictrowski, Cartels and Trusts (1933), p. 148, quoted in Jervey and Deák.

a court undertaken to discover the existence of engrossing by examining the control of the engrosser over the price. What cases there are, and they have been few, have been complicated by the presence of combinations or conspiracies to restrain trade. The courts have found monopoly because of conspiracy and the exclusion of others from the market rather than control of the market. It is doubtful whether the act of engrossing itself, in the absence of a conspiracy to exclude competitors, would carry any monopoly connotation in the law. Consequently it seems doubtful whether the ancient law respecting engrossing, forestalling and regrating has made much of a contribution to present legal concepts of monopoly.

In a somewhat different status in this respect is the law on restraint of trade. The question of restraints originally came before the courts in cases involving the sale of a business in which, as an incident to the sale, the seller contracted not to compete with the buyer. Until sometime in the seventeenth century the courts uniformly held such contracts unenforceable, the basis of the rule being "that public policy demands from every man the free exercise of his trade in the public interest." [15] Did public policy demand the free exercise of trade because in the absence of such free exercise there would be a control of the market?

Restrictive covenants, if enforceable, certainly may lead to control of a local market, but control of the market is not dependent on the existence of such contracts. Doctors, lawyers, or tradesmen dealing in a particular type of article may be, and frequently were in the period in which restrictive covenants were unenforceable, the sole practitioners of their profession or trade in a given locality possessing a control of the local market. Yet this fact does not appear to have led to legislative or judicial concern. It appears more consistent with the early decisions to say that restrictive covenants were feared because one who contracted himself out of a livelihood might become a public charge.

The development in the seventeenth and eighteenth centuries of the doctrine of "reasonable restraints," as applied to restrictive covenants in connection with the sale of a business, does not seem to have involved any closer consideration of the monopoly problem. Although

[15] Cooke, "Legal Rule and Economic Function," *Economic Journal*, 46 (1936).

it is sometimes said,[16] or implied, that the reasonableness which concerned the courts in such contracts was understood not only in relation to the interests of the contracting parties but also to the public interest in prevention of control of the market, it is difficult to substantiate this view by an appeal to the decisions.[17] The application of the doctrine of reasonableness to the interests of the contracting parties is clear. The interest of the buyer was a property interest, that the value of the purchased business not be lessened by competition from the seller in the immediate vicinity, while that of the seller was not only a property interest, since he obtained through the sale the full value of the "good-will" of the business, but also an interest in safeguarding the possibility of continuing somewhere and at some time his trade or profession. The language of the courts indicates that the public interest was considered affected when the public was deprived by such a contract of a source of supply without justification, i.e., when such a deprivation was unnecessary to the protection of the private interests involved in the contract. This protection of the public interest was levelled primarily not against monopolistic control of the market but against the loss to the common weal of the services of a productive agent. There is no evidence that the courts examined the data relevant to the question whether such a contract might lead to control of the market. If any monopoly consideration was involved, it was monopoly in the sense of restriction of competition, not of control of the market.

If the test of reasonableness referred to the extent of competition or control of the market which would result from the restrictive contract, might we not have expected the courts to compare the market situation in the locality affected by the contract with the market situations in other localities? If the restrictive covenant reduced the number of possible competitors by one, this might have a very different effect on control of the market in a locality in which competitors were many from its effect in a locality in which only one remained. There is not much evidence, however, that the courts considered the easily available facts relative to extent of market control, and the cause seems to be that the "reasonableness" with which they

---

[16] See, e.g., Pope, "The Legal Aspects of Monopoly," *Harvard Law Review,* 20 (1907); Cooke, "Legal Rule and Economic Function."

[17] Mitchel v. Reynolds, 1 P. Wms. 181 (1711).

were concerned in cases involving restrictive covenants was rarely, if ever, related to the monopoly problem.

The gradual relaxation of the law on restrictive covenants is easily understood with reference to the interests of the contracting parties and requires no examination of the changes in the scope of market control. With the increase in economic opportunities incident to increasing division of labor the means of gaining a livelihood open to a seller of a business expanded, and the restrictions imposed on his activities by these covenants became less serious. On the other hand, with the growth of transportation facilities the area within which the competition of the seller might lessen the value of what he has sold had increased. For both these reasons the scope permitted restraints of trade of this sort has been enlarged.[18] Moreover, whether or not the establishment of a competing enterprise in a given locality was likely to affect the value of the business sold, and whether or not a limitation in trading in a given locality was likely to deprive a man of the means of earning his livelihood and the public of the fruit of his activity were questions to which common experience might be said to provide a tolerably satisfactory answer. The question whether the elimination of one unit of competition would result in control of the market, however, could hardly be answered without an examination of the number of competitors left in the restricted area and of the behavior of prices. To such an examination the courts were hesitant to proceed.

The application of the rule of reason to contracts between competitors designed solely to limit competition among themselves stands on different ground. It is frequently said that, as distinguished from restrictive covenants connected with the sale of a business, the interests of the contracting parties are here not at issue since such contracts will not be entered into unless there is prospect of gain to all from the limitation.[19] While this may or may not be true, if the rule of reason is to be applied to such cases, it must be applied on different grounds, or it must be a different rule than that used in the older cases of restraint of trade. For in this type of contract the public interest in the monopoly problem is paramount, and the question

---

[18] Handler, "Restraint of Trade," Encyclopedia of Social Sciences, 13 (1934).
[19] Cf. Pope, "The Legal Aspects of Monopoly"; Cooke, "Legal Rule and Economic Function."

of the private interests of the individual contractors is only secondary. The disposition of American courts has been, at least until very recently, to hold all contracts for division of territory, pooling, fixing of prices, common marketing control of supply, or which restrict the freedom of the contractors to compete in other ways, unenforceable and, since the Sherman Act, illegal. The opinions of the court in these cases constantly refer to monopoly in the sense of control of the market, but little examination of evidence pertinent to the question of market control is ever undertaken. The test of monopoly, or attempt of monopoly, is here restriction of competition. American courts have in this class of cases been willing to accept the contract itself as evidence of restriction and, consequently, of an attempt to monopolize, without inquiring further into the question of how great a control of the market is secured to the contracting parties.[20] The rule of reason enunciated with much fanfare by Chief Justice White purporting to provide a standard of judgment dividing those contractual restrictions which are in the public interest from those which are not has had, at least until the Appalachian Coal case[21] in 1933, a much narrower application than might have been expected.

The British courts, confronted with the same problem of applying a rule of reason to contracts between competitors resigned to limit competition, have returned a somewhat different answer. They have tended to accept every contract designed to limit competition among the contracting competitors as reasonable in the absence of intention or actual attempt to injure or destroy a competitor.[22] On the other

[20] In another class of cases, however, dealing principally with trade association activities, the Courts have drawn a distinction between limitation of competition and a regulation by business agreement of competitive methods. Nowhere is this distinction better expressed than by Justice Brandeis in Board of Trade of the City of Chicago et al. v. United States, 246 U. S. 231, at p. 239. "Every agreement concerning trade, every regulation of trade, restrains. To bind, to restrain, is of the very essence. The true test of legality is whether the restraint imposed is such as merely regulates and perhaps thereby promotes competition or whether it is such as may suppress or even destroy competition."

[21] Appalachian Coals, Inc. v. United States, 288 U. S. 344 (1933).

[22] See the dictum of Lord Parker in the Adelaide case: ". . . it is clear that the onus of showing that any contract is calculated to produce a monopoly or enhance prices to an unreasonable extent will be on the party alleging it, and that if once the court is satisfied that the restraint is reasonable as between the parties the onus will be no light one." Attorney-General of Australia v. Adelaide Steamship Co., 1913 A. C. 781, 796. Such a contract

hand, the trend of American opinion has been to regard all such contracts as unreasonable restraints of trade. In neither case has the rule of reason been given any intelligible content in terms of control of the market despite the frequency with which this phrase has graced judicial utterances.

Cases involving a union between competitors accomplished by amalgamation or fusion or merger have in this country most frequently involved the application of the rule of reason, and it is in these cases that the characteristic legal conception of monopoly is most evident. An amalgamation of competing firms may, and ordinarily does, take place for reasons other than to secure control of the price of the articles produced or sold by these firms. The courts could not, therefore, plausibly assume, as they did in the case of contracts to limit competition, that all amalgamations were prima facie evidence of an attempt to monopolize.

Since under the Sherman Act both the contract and the combination as an attempt to monopolize or restrain trade were illegal, some way had to be found of making the law on combinations equivalent to the law on contracts limiting competition. If monopoly had meant to the courts control of the market, some such equivalence might well have been found, although the problem would have been, and is, difficult. Yet the sources of evidence of control of the market are known: the behavior of prices and outputs, the relation of prices and costs, profits before and after the combination, share of the market controlled, the existence of business practices such as price discrimination, price stabilization and many others. The evidences of a control of the market established by combination would be found in the same sort of data as in control established by contract, and a rule of reason which set up as its standard control of the market would have yielded approximately the same results in both types of cases.

By monopoly, however, the courts did not mean control of the market but restriction of competition. While a contract between com-

---

may produce an "unreasonable" control of the market but the British courts have rarely found one. A contract which restricts competition by the destruction of a competitor's market is a different matter. Here there is an overt act, an obvious restraint of trade, partaking of the nature of conspiracy, that does not compel the courts to examine the behavior of prices and outputs which are the most obvious sources of information concerning control of the market.

petitors designed to limit competition carries the evidence on its face of an attempt to monopolize, a merger between competitors does not, so that the courts had perforce to enquire (1) into the intentions of the merging interests, and (2) into such acts of the merger as might indicate restriction of outside competition. If the intention behind a merger were control of the market it is unlikely that it would be communicated to the courts, and since the only evidences capable of indicating intention to control the market were ignored we may conclude that the courts found the presence of monopoly in other ways. If the manifestation of the intention to limit the competition of outsiders took the form of overt acts such as local price discrimination, espionage, or securing of railway rebates, the courts could find evidence of restrictions directly relevant to their conception of monopoly. As a matter of fact it is clear that this was the direction taken in the judicial application of the rule of reason. The size of the combination or its share of the total output of a product became important only when accompanied by predatory practices affecting the freedom of others to compete. In the words of one commentator, it had become clear by 1918 "that the Sherman Act had evolved from an anti-trust act into an act relating to the legal control of competitive methods." [23] Since monopoly meant restriction of competition rather than control of the market, this evolution was only logical.

The decision in the Standard Oil-Vacuum merger in 1931, it is true, gave somewhat more consideration to the problem of market control than has been usual in merger cases.[24] The court took into account (1) the merged concerns' share of sales of their various products in the *local* market, (2) the state of intercompany competition in the New England market, the number and size of companies, the area of their operations, and recent changes in the market position of the various companies, and (3) potential competition. Despite the advance, the dicta of Judge Kimbrough Stone in this case cannot be said to indicate a clear conception of monopoly in terms of market control. "Competition," he declares,

---

[23] McLaughlin, "Legal Control of Competitive Methods," *Iowa Law Review*, 21 (1936), 280.

[24] United States v. Standard Oil Co. of N. J., 47 F. (2d) 288 (C. C. A. 2d, 1931). For another realistic analysis of a market situation, see International Shoe Co. v. Federal Trade Commission, 29 F. (2d) 518 (C. C. A. 2d, 1931).

is the antithesis of monopoly. In a sense, any elimination of competition is a movement in the general direction of monopoly. But competition is, in its very essence, a contest for trade, and any progress or victory in such contest must lessen competition. . . . It is only when this lessening is with an unlawful purpose or by unlawful means, or when it proceeds to the point where it is or is threatening to become a menace to the public, that it is declared unlawful. . . . The point of danger is reached when monopoly is threatened.

We might now expect some indication of tests which the court will apply to determine when monopoly is threatened. But the opinion continues, "This threat of monopoly exists, irrespective of intent, whenever competition is lessened to the danger point." In other words monopoly is threatened when "competition is lessened to the danger point." Competition is lessened to the danger point when "monopoly is threatened." [25] Judge Stone in subsequent remarks appears to be able to get no farther forward with this idea and finally falls back on a dictum of Justice Holmes that "a combination in unreasonable restraint of trade imports an attempt to override normal market conditions." [26] Since nothing is more "normal" than monopolistic market conditions, this too does not get us very far.

This summary review of the law of monopoly must lead to the conclusion that whatever are considered to be the evils resulting from monopoly — enhancement of price, deterioration of product, or the like — a monopolistic situation, or an attempt to monopolize, is evidenced to the courts primarily, if not exclusively, by a limitation of the freedom to compete. The original meaning of monopoly, an exclusion of others from the market by a sovereign dispensation in favor of one seller, has continued to mean exclusion, in the broad sense of restriction of competition. Although "undue" or "unreasonable" control of the market is constantly inserted in judicial decisions as the meaning of monopoly, the data capable of indicating this control are almost universally ignored by the courts. In this country there has been a growing tendency in the law to declare every contract between competitors which restricts competition unenforceable and, since the Sherman Act, illegal, whatever the extent of the control made possible

[25] United States v. Standard Oil Co. of N. J., 47 F. (2d) 288, at 297 (C. C. A. 2d, 1931).
[26] American Column Co. v. United States, 257 U. S. 377 (1921).

by the contract.[27] In the case of mergers the monopoly or attempt to monopolize is discovered primarily in predatory practices designed to hamper the competition of outsiders and not in control of the market.

III

It has been noted above that the elements on which the idea of monopoly has been built both in law and in economics have been control of the market and restriction of competition. If in their development of the law of monopoly the courts have tended to give mere lip service to the former and to identify monopoly with restriction of competition, the principal reasons are probably the following:

(1) The courts have been faced with the necessity of devising and applying to particular situations a standard of evaluation relevant to a vague concept known as the public interest. The injury to numerous private interests, and consequently to the public interest, from predatory attacks on established business enterprises, or from other attempts to restrict competition, was much more direct than that which might possibly be inflicted on buyers or sellers by a control of the market exercised independently of any attempts to restrict competition.

(2) The formulation of a standard of monopoly or monopolizing contrary to the public interest required the selection of tests capable of distinguishing competitive from monopoly situations. If monopoly were conceived as control of the market, the tests must necessarily be

[27] There is no evidence that the courts in interpreting the Sherman Act and later antitrust legislation in the light of common law concepts of monopoly and restraint of trade were violating legislative intention or substituting their understanding of the monopoly problem for that of the Congress. On the contrary there is every reason to believe that the principal acts which the Sherman Act sought to prevent were the predatory practices of combinations which in many cases already enjoyed a commanding control of the market. The particular practices which received special legislative attention were railway rebating, local price-discrimination and price maintenance. The sponsors of the Act announced on many occasions that it was not designed to prevent combinations either of labor or capital, and in answer to the specific question whether an enterprise would be considered a monopoly if, because of superior skill, it alone received all the orders for a particular article, Senator Hoar replied, "The word 'monopoly' is a merely technical term which has a clear and legal significance, and it is this: it is the sole engrossing to a man's self *by means which prevent other men from engaging in fair competition with him." Congressional Record,* 21 (1890), 3152.

related to the behavior of prices, outputs and other variables indicative of control, an exceedingly difficult problem. If, on the other hand, monopoly is identified with restriction of competition, the devising of tests is comparatively simple.

(3) There is reason to believe that in an earlier period control of the market was much more dependent upon restriction of entry and other types of restriction of competition through predatory practices and harassing tactics than at present. The law of monopoly, though directed against restrictions of competition, may once have had more relevance to control of the market than it at present possesses.

(4) Before the Sherman Act, monopoly actions were brought, with but few exceptions, before the courts on the suit of private interests. These interests were more likely to be directly affected adversely by predatory practices or attempts at exclusion from the market than by control of prices.

Although these considerations may help to explain the almost complete preoccupation of the courts with restrictions on freedom of competition, it must be recognized that our modern law embraces an antiquated and inadequate conception of the monopoly problem. Attention and criticism have therefore centered around the following aspects of our public policy with respect to monopoly and competition: the tendency of the courts to find illegal every contract limiting competition among the contracting competitors regardless of the effect or probable effect of such a contract on control of the market; the tendency to judge the legality of a combination or merger primarily on the basis of its competitive practices without examination of the extent of its control of the market; the absence of a developed public policy with respect to unfair practices, in particular the unwillingness of the courts to extend the concept of unfair competition beyond injury to a competitor and to take account of the nature of the injury to the public.

The weakness of our public policy is not the result of judicial interpretation but of the inadequacy of legislation. It can only be corrected by legislation which will re-define the monopoly and trade-practice problem and provide tests by means of which market situations and business practices considered to be favorable to the public interest can be separated from those that are not. Since Congress has wrestled with this problem, off and on, for fifty years without conspicuous success, it does not appear likely that a ready-made solution can be found close at hand. Certainly economics has none to provide. Nevertheless, the economic approach, which is in some ways very different from the legal, can be utilized in the shaping of a more satisfactory public policy.

For its own purposes economics has found control of the market a much more useful approach to the concept of monopoly than restriction of competition. Some control of the market may be said to exist whenever the share of the sales or purchases made by any one seller or purchaser (or group of sellers or purchasers acting by means of an agreement) is sufficiently large to influence the price of the article sold. In a market from which control is completely absent every seller and buyer, acting independently, could increase or decrease his purchases or sales without appreciable effect on the price. Such markets, which may be said to be purely competitive in the sense of being completely devoid of any element of control over price, are comparatively rare. In most markets some sellers or buyers (or both) exercise some degree of control. Of course such control is perfectly compatible with the existence of some degree of competition. A seller with complete control of the market would be able to determine his price without regard for the actions of other sellers or the prices of other products; in other words, he would have no competition. No seller or buyer has such control. All markets, practically speaking, exhibit a fusion of monopoly and competitive elements.

It follows that if monopoly is identified with control of the market (a) it is impossible to separate markets into those that are competitive and those that are monopolistic; (b) a public policy which attempted to eliminate all positions of monopoly would confront a problem of impossible scope and complexity. It is, furthermore, by no means clear that the preservation of all the competitive elements and the suppression of all the monopolistic elements would be in the public interest, however conceived. Consequently, the existence of some control of the market is not likely to be in itself a good indication of the necessity or wisdom of applying preventative measures.

Having identified monopoly with control of the market, economics has proceeded further to an examination of certain typical monopoly situations. But the most that can be said of the results of monopoly investigations in economics is that they cast doubts on a number of traditional legal attitudes on the question of monopoly and restraint of trade, and that they emphasize a number of relevant considerations usually neglected by the interpreters of public policy. The significance of the existence of a relatively small number of buyers or sellers is a case in point. If the number of sellers (or buyers) is small enough to induce each seller, before changing his own selling policy, to take account of the probable effect of this change upon the policies of his rivals, the results of joint action by agreement, which might well be illegal, may be accomplished without collusion of any sort. It is quite obvious from the behavior of cigarette prices that the manufacturers of cigarettes are in something like this situation. No one can change his prices without an overwhelming probability that his rivals will immediately follow suit, and one result is that price changes are very infrequent. To produce many of the consequences of joint action no one seller has to have a preponderant share of the total output; if the number of sellers is relatively small, their individual share of the total output is of secondary importance.

Nor is control of the market to be inferred merely from the number of existing competitors. Potential competition must be considered. Indeed the dicta of many trust cases might be interpreted as indicating a judicial opinion that in the absence of legal restraints or of overt predatory acts against potential competitors, free entry to the market precludes any element of control. Free entry in this legal sense, however, is compatible under certain circumstances with a considerable degree of market control. The capital resources necessary to establish a new firm in an effective competitive position may be so large as to eliminate potential competition as a practical consideration. The fact that no new motor car company has been established in the last decade or that no new brand of cigarettes has been able since the war to capture a sizeable share of the market cannot be taken to indicate that no control of the market exists.

The legal significance attached to trade marks and trade names provides another example of the divergence between legal and economic conceptions of monopoly. Economics, primarily concerned with the fact of market control, has emphasized the control of price made possible by the exploitation of a mark or name. Extensive advertising expenditures may successfully differentiate in the minds of buyers the product of a given seller from those of his rivals. The more successful this differentiation the greater the control of the market it is possible for the seller to achieve, and, consequently, the more entrenched his monopoly position. But since there is no restriction of competition in the legal sense, the law, primarily concerned in trade mark and trade name cases with protection of intangible property interests, can see no element of monopoly. On the other hand, economic opinion does not proceed from the fact that there is a monopolistic significance in the use of a mark or name to the conclusion that this institution or practice is necessarily contrary to the public interest.[28]

It is fully consistent with the legal conception of the monopoly problem that the courts should enquire into the actual or probable results of agreements to restrain competition. But to do so would be to give up the traditional tests of monopolizing and to grapple with the problem of what is an unreasonable control of the market. The Appalachian Coals case[29] may indicate a tentative first step in this direction and somewhere between this and the Sugar Institute cases[30] is to be found the indistinctive dividing line between certain types of restrictions which are and are not at present considered to be in the public interest. The ways in which competition may be restrained or "regulated," however, are many, and if the courts are now willing to delve into the problems of market control they will have to rely more and more on economic analysis of the different types of control situations. The significance of market controls established through various kinds of open price quoting, basing-point and zone price systems, agreements as to price terms and the like, are not apparent without a study of data hitherto considered by the courts to be irrelevant to the monopoly problem.

On the other hand, if economics is to be put itself in a position to contribute to the formulation of public policy, it must conceive

[28] See Handler, "Unfair Competition," *Iowa Law Review*, 21 (1936), 185. For the views of an economist on these matters, see Chamberlin, *Monopolistic Competition* (1933), Appendix E.

[29] Appalachian Coals, Inc. v. United States, 288 U. S. 344 (1933).

[30] United States v. Sugar Institute, 297 U. S. 553 (1936), aff'g., 15 F. Supp. 817 (S. D. N. Y. 1934). For a thorough discussion of the problems, both legal and economic, raised by these cases, see Fly, "Observations on the Anti-Trust Laws, Economic Theory and the Sugar Institute Decisions," *Yale Law Journal*, 45 and 46 (1936).

the monopoly problem in a more extensive way than is at present customary. It is not enough to find evidence of the existence of market controls, nor is it sufficient to conduct purely analytical and descriptive studies of various types of control situations. While this is important, the formulation of public policy requires a distinction between situations and practices which are in the public interest and those that are not. And this requirement imposes the necessity of elaborating tests which can be applied by administrative bodies and by the courts. It is easy enough to present evidence of monopoly situations, which, to economics, is merely the absence of pure competition. The existence of price discrimination, of price rigidity, advertising expenditures, price leadership and other practices are sufficient to indicate the presence of monopoly elements. But these practices are hardly sufficient evidence of the presence or possibility of market controls adverse to the public interest. A further study of different types of industrial markets and business practices and of their effects on prices, outputs, investment and employment designed to indicate means of distingushing between socially desirable and undesirable situations and practices may or may not be fruitful. It is, in any case, the only way in which economics can contribute directly to the shaping of public policy. A simultaneous movement by legal and economic thinking away from entrenched positions might be conducive to progress on this front.

16

The Current Status of the Monopoly Problem
in the United States[1]

It is clearly an open question whether the people of the United States want competition and, if so, what kind of competition and in what areas. We apparently do not desire a competitive determination of farm prices and farm incomes. It is obvious from the Miller-Tydings Act and the fair trade laws now flourishing in forty-five states that we don't want price competition in a large section of retail trade. We have sought, and quite successfully, to "take wages out of competition." The action of the Texas Railroad Commission during the last few months in cutting back oil production by 750,000 barrels a day makes it clear that the "adjustment of supply to demand" in this area is not going to be accomplished exclusively by price competition. We don't want much disturbance of the channels of distribution from competitive sources and are apparently acquiescing in a reinterpretation of the Robinson-Patman Act "injury to competition" as injury to a competitor. Just recently I have become aware of the very cozy scheme worked out by the anthracite coal producers by means of which output is adjusted to sales.[2] Although, according to the producers, no consideration of price is allowed to intrude, John L. Lewis has indicated that the application of this system would be fine for the bituminous coal industry. One might extend considerably these examples of recent public action to soften the rigors of competition.

At the same time, and despite this course of events, we apparently do want competition in the industrial sector of the economy. The last ten years — particularly the last five — have witnessed the greatest flurry of antitrust activity since the passage of the Sherman Act. But the question can be raised, what kind of competition do we want?

[1] Reprinted from the *Harvard Law Review*, Vol. 62, No. 8, June 1949.
[2] *New York Times*, April 19, 1949, p. 20, col. 2.

I. THEORIES OF EFFECTIVE COMPETITION

After the recent decision in the Cement case,[3] the Universal Atlas Cement Company issued the following statement: "Universal Atlas Cement Company is abandoning on July 7 next the method of selling cement which it has used continuously for more than forty years; namely, sales in the market served by it at delivered prices as low as those quoted by any competitor."[4] The obvious implication of this announcement is that competition is being abandoned. On the other hand, quite a few people, including the Supreme Court of the United States, thought that what was being abandoned was a conspiracy to fix prices. Clearly competition means different things to different people.

There have always been at least two ways of looking at competition and of judging the effectiveness of competition in a particular market. In the first, competition is thought of as a type of market organization setting severe limits to the power or control exercised by the individual firm. This view stresses the limits, set principally by the number of his competitors, on the scope of action of a single seller or buyer. The other way of thinking about competition is in terms of the performance of firms in a market. Even pure competition — that plaything of economic theorists — can be thought of either in terms of market structure, large numbers of sellers and a standard product, or in terms of the performance which is supposed to result from these conditions, prices equal to marginal and to minimum average cost.

From the point of view of economic policy, competition is supposedly desirable, not as an end in itself, but for the results that are expected to follow from it.[5] These expected results may be paraphrased as efficient use of resources. Now under the technological and institutional conditions suited to pure competition —

_____

[3] FTC v. Cement Institute, 333 U. S. 683 (1948).
[4] *The U. S. Steel Quarterly,* Aug. 1948, p. 7; Machlup, *The Basing Point System* (1949), p. 82.
[5] On the other hand, an argument can be made on political grounds for competition conceived as a set of limits to the market position of firms, regardless of the relative efficiency of the business performance that results from this competition. Here we shall be concerned exclusively with the economic aspects of the problem.

imagining such conditions to be found — it is possible to show that a competitive organization of resources will produce the results desired from competition — an efficient use of these resources. But if technological and institutional conditions are not compatible with pure competition and, at the same time, are not deemed to be such as to justify a public utility regulation of the firms in question, there arises a problem of defining an acceptable kind of competition in terms of market structure such that it can normally be expected to be accompanied by the kind of performance considered acceptable in the use of resources. This is in fact the core of the difficulty of devising standards of public action in the antitrust field. None of the markets encountered meet the tests of pure competition; at the same time they fall short of a degree of monopoly justifying public utility regulation.[6] What is a suitable test of effective competition? Should it run in terms of market limitations on the scope of action of firms or in terms of standards of acceptable performance? Is there, necessarily, any incompatibility between these objectives? May not the conditions required of a competitive market structure be so defined as inevitably to produce desirable business performance?

Most of the recent literature on the subject of "workable competition" has stressed the conditions of market structure, the limitations on the market position or scope of action of firms, deemed necessary to the maintenance of effective competition.[7] Such com-

---

[6] A few of the principal conditions that may "justify" the imposition of a public utility type of regulation could be spelled out fairly adequately. Lacking, however, the time and space to do so, I here limit myself to assertion.

[7] J. M. Clark was, to the best of my knowledge, the first writer to use the term "workable competition." He defines workable competition to mean a "rivalry in selling goods in which each selling unit normally seeks maximum net revenue, under conditions such that the price or prices each seller can charge are effectively limited by the free option of the buyer to buy from a rival seller or sellers of what we think of as 'the same' product, necessitating an effort by each seller to equal or exceed the attractiveness of the others' offerings to a sufficient number of buyers to accomplish the end in view." Clark, "Toward a Concept of Workable Competition," *American Economic Review*, 30 (1940), 243.

Clair Wilcox defines workable competition as "the availability to buyers of genuine alternatives in policy among their sources of supply." Wilcox, *Competition and Monopoly in American Industry*, T.N.E.C. Monograph No. 21, 1940, p. 9.

George Stigler finds this conception "too loose." He prefers the following:

petition requires, to use the standard cliché, the availability to
buyers of an adequate number of alternative independent sources of
supply, and to sellers of an adequate number of independent customers. Workable competition is considered to require, principally, a
fairly large number of sellers and buyers, no one of whom occupies
a large share of the market, the absence of collusion among either
group, and the possibility of market entry by new firms.

There has also been, on the other hand, a good deal of discussion
of the kind of performance we should like to have from firms in
the industrial sector of the economy. Among the kinds of business
behavior emphasized as desirable have been the following: an un-
remitting pressure for product and process improvement, downward
adjustment of prices concomitant with substantial reductions in
costs, concentration of production in units of the most efficient size,
neither larger nor smaller than those required for low-cost operation,
an efficient adjustment of capacity to output, and the avoidance of
a waste of resources in selling activities.

The question now arises whether workable competition, in terms
of market structure, can be so defined that we may say, given
these conditions, it is likely that business performance will meet
the standards suggested above or, equally important, that if these
conditions are not present, acceptable standards of business performance are unlikely to be attained. Alternatively we may raise

---

"An industry is workably competitive when (1) there are a considerable
number of firms selling closely related products in each important market
area, (2) these firms are not in collusion, and (3) the long-run average cost
curve for a new firm is not materially higher than that for an established
firm." Stigler, "The Extent and Bases of Monopoly," *American Economic
Review*, Sup., June 1942.

Corwin Edwards has developed the idea of workable competition in greatest
detail. In addition to numbers of sellers and buyers, absence of collusion and
freedom of entry, he states a number of other conditions of which absence
of a dominant trader among the number of buyers and sellers seems to be
the most important. Edwards, *Maintaining Competition* (1949), pp. 9–10.

These writers clearly think of workable competition in terms of market
conditions imposing a set of limitations on the scope of action of the individual buyer or seller. These limitations prevent the exploitation of buyers by
sellers too few in number or in collusion with each other and prevent the
exploitation of sellers by buyers. There are an "adequate" number of alternatives from which to choose. Clark's conception of workable competition also
emphasizes these limitations, but it appears from his discussion that limitations
are not enough.

the question whether business behavior lends itself to formulation of standards of acceptable performance such that a judgment of the appropriateness of antitrust action can be made independently of what we have here called market conditions.

Without attempting, at this point, a direct answer to these questions, it seems useful to call attention to certain possibilities of conflict between competitive standards formulated in terms of market conditions and standards of acceptable business performance. Space limitations prevent more than a summary indication of these possibilities.

1. The most familiar and one of the most bothersome possibilities of conflict has to do with the economies of scale in relation to the number of sellers or buyers required for most efficient operations. Costs in relation to size of plant can, in most industries, be well enough estimated to form a judgment on the minimum scale required for efficiency. The main difficulties arise in judging the economies of scale involved in the management of multiplant properties, considering the functional complexity of management, and in disentangling the bargaining advantages of size from the advantages that pertain solely to the provisions of useful services. Is management a "technique for getting things done"[8] that carries with it significant economies of scale? The relation of size to the volume and quality of industrial research is another bothersome question that intrudes.

Enough has been said to indicate that a real possibility exists that the number of firms appropriate to efficiency, one aspect of desirable performance, may, in a number of industries, be too few to meet the market structure test of workable competition. Nor does it necessarily follow that, under these conditions, regulation of the public utility type is called for.

2. A second possibility of conflict exists when all the market conditions of workable competition are fulfilled but the behavior of the firms involved follows a routine and standard pattern unvaried by enterprise of any sort. Something like this seems to have characterized the system of retail distribution in the United States

[8] See "The Public Responsibilities of Big Business," address delivered by Eugene Holman, President of Standard Oil Co. of N. J., at the Economic Club of Detroit on November 8, 1948. See also Drucker, *The Concept of the Corporation* (1946); Edwards, *Maintaining Competition*, p. 116 n.

before the advent of chain stores and other mass distributors. In a case like this, does one judge the effectiveness of competition from the market structure point of view favorable to traditional distributors or from the business performance point of view favorable to the innovating large-scale mass distributor? [9]

3. Suppose, to take a third possibility of conflict, that the market conditions required for workable competition lead, in an industry characterized by large cyclical variations in sales and by high overhead costs, to cut-throat competition which in periods of depression destroys efficient business organizations which, under average conditions, could survive. This is the possibility, repeatedly emphasized by J. M. Clark, that apparently leads him to support a modified basing-point system in some industries having these characteristics.[10] Without passing judgment on the frequency and importance of such situations, it is sufficient to indicate that the standards-of-business-performance approach might lead to a modification of the conditions thought to be required for workable competition.

4. Fourth, one of the market conditions required for workable competition is the absence of collusion or agreement among the firms. But certain kinds of agreements clearly promote rather than restrain effective competition. The agreement among traders to regulate marketing practices on the Chicago Board of Trade was considered by no less an authority than Justice Brandeis to promote competition.[11] Agreements to standardize classifications of products and terms of sale are frequently necessary to permit buyer comparisons of prices quoted from different sources of supply. Under these and other circumstances the business performance that results from collusion must be considered to modify the application of standards drawn exclusively from market conditions.

5. Fifth, it is possible that certain restraints of trade or a degree of market control incompatible with the market structure standard of workable competition may facilitate the introduction of desirable product and process innovations. This is an argument most effec-

---

[9] Cf. Adelman, "The A & P Case: A Study in Applied Economic Theory," *Quarterly Journal of Economics*, 63 (1949).

[10] Most recently in Clark, "Law and Economics of Basing Points: Appraisals and Proposals," *American Economic Review*, 39 (1949).

[11] Board of Trade of the City of Chicago v. United States, 246 U. S. 231 (1918).

tively developed by J. A. Schumpeter.[12] His contention that the most effective kind of competition is that which derives from the introduction of new and improved products and from innovation in techniques of production has great merit. It is less clear, however, that industrial progressiveness stems mainly from firms of a size incompatible with the conditions of workable competition or necessitates arrangements among firms which violate these conditions. The relation of monopoly and competition to innovation is a relatively unknown area.

Other examples could be cited but perhaps enough has been said to indicate that antitrust action in a particular industry or industrial market may be thought appropriate on the basis of the business performance of firms in that market and inappropriate if judged by the presence or absence of the market conditions emphasized by the workable competition test.

II. LEGAL CRITERIA OF EFFECTIVE COMPETITION

A. BUSINESS PERFORMANCE AND MARKET STRUCTURE IN THE LEGAL DEFINITION OF MONOPOLY

What considerations influence the courts in their decisions on antitrust action? Is effective competition conceived to be a set of market conditions or is it judged in terms of effective business performance? Some twelve years ago, under the title of "Monopoly in Law and Economics," I published an article designed to show that legal and economic ideas of monopoly were growing further apart.[13] In referring back to this ancient document, I am reminded of a statement of Justice Holmes, "it ought always to be remembered that historic continuity with the past is not a duty, it is only a necessity."[14] Although it is not now a duty, I find it necessary to relate my present thinking on this question to what I thought earlier.

The argument of that article, simply stated, was that monopoly in the legal sense meant restrictive or abusive practices and, in the economic sense, control of the market; that the antithesis of legal

[12] Schumpeter, *Capitalism, Socialism, and Democracy* (2d ed. 1947), chs. 7, 8.
[13] *Yale Law Journal*, 47 (1937). Reprinted as Chapter 15 above.
[14] Holmes, "Learning and Science," in *Collected Legal Papers* (1920), p. 139.

monopoly was free competition, a state of affairs such that no actual or potential competitor was limited in his action either by agreement or the harassing tactics of large rivals, while the antithesis of economic monopoly was pure competition, a state of the market such that no buyer or seller could, by his own action, influence the price of the goods to be bought and sold. It was argued that one of the reasons for this dichotomy was that lawyers were concerned with tests that would stand up in a court, and that it was much easier to devise tests of restrictive practices than tests indicative of a substantial degree of market control.

I still think there was substantial merit in this distinction between legal and economic notions of monopoly, but, like many distinctions, it was much too sharply drawn. There is substantial evidence in the history of antitrust cases that although the precise holdings may not have been explicitly based on indications of the degree of market control and of what is here called business performance, such indications certainly influenced the judges' decisions.

But what about the recent active development of antitrust law? Do the courts tend to find evidence of violation in particular characteristics of market structure or in various kinds of business performance or both? My impression is:

1. That the courts have moved a substantial distance in the direction of accepting the presence or absence of the market conditions associated with the notion of workable competition as appropriate tests. On all four of the important desiderata, number of firms, share of the market, collusion, and the conditions of entry, previous doctrine has been altered or extended;

2. That standards of effective business performance, though imprecisely defined, still strongly influence the manner in which tests of monopoly relating to the structure of the market are applied. This is true of determinations of whether or not the antitrust laws have been violated, but it is even more true when the courts come to the fashioning of remedies.

Not only has the legal meaning of monopoly been extended but the courts have greatly expanded the scope of action embraced within the meaning of conspiracy. The legal status of actions both of large firms and of conspiracies with respect to the conditions of entry of new firms has been reinterpreted.

In the Aluminum case,[15] I interpret the court to hold (1) that Alcoa's share of the domestic consumption of aluminum ingot was such as to indicate a degree of market control equivalent to monopoly, and (2) that monopoly was not "thrust upon"[16] the company by forces lying outside its control but was actively and aggressively sought in ways that had the effect of excluding potential competitors.

Although this decision probably broke new legal ground, it is, from an economist's point of view, marred by what is at best some very dubious economics. The share of the market possessed by Alcoa was incorrectly measured, the degree of market control was identified with percentage share of the market, and the evidence concerning intent to exclude others is difficult to distinguish from ordinary, intelligent competitive action.

In measuring Alcoa's share of the market, the court excluded from the market substitute products and secondary aluminum ingot. Although the determination of what products to include in and what to exclude from a market presents a difficult problem, the existence of close substitutes in certain uses of aluminum is beyond question. With respect to secondary aluminum, the court's reasoning was ingenious but essentially incorrect. The argument was that since Alcoa's current production of primary ingot will at some future time be converted into secondary, the secondary, then coming onto the market, cannot be considered an independent source of supply. The question is whether a single producer of a product that will return to the market X years hence will, *because of that fact,* act differently with respect to current price and output than would a producer who is one of a larger number. If he does so, it can only be because he is willing to sacrifice a current profit by restricting output now in order to gain a problematical profit X years hence, which may be available because the supply of competitive scrap is not then so large as it would otherwise be. But the conditions that would make such action profitable are surely improbable.

Lawyers sometimes describe themselves as experts in relevance. Something more than logical relevance, however, is involved in a

[15] United States v. Aluminum Co. of Am., 148 F.2d 416 (2d Cir. 1945).
[16] 148 F. 2d 416, 429.

case of this sort. There is also the magnitude of the consideration that is declared to be relevant. It was, however, on the basis of the argument stated above that Judge Learned Hand decided that "Alcoa's control over the ingot market must be reckoned at over 90 per cent."[17] If sales of secondary ingot had been considered part of the market, Alcoa's share would have fallen to the mystical sixty to sixty-four per cent, where the existence of a monopoly becomes "doubtful."[18] Even if Alcoa's share of the market had been correctly measured, it would have been wrong to infer degree of market control directly from this share. If products excluded in defining the market are close substitutes, if the entry of new firms is relatively easy, if the supply of imports is elastic with respect to price changes, even a large percentage share of the market is compatible with a small degree of market control. On the other hand, even a small share of a particular market in the hands of an industrial giant may, under certain circumstances, be conducive to a high degree of market control.[19] Market share is an important condition relevant to workable competition, but in the absence of certain tests of performance it cannot be taken as a measure of market control.

With respect to one element of business performance the court was convinced that Alcoa's behavior indicated an intention to exclude potential rivals. The evidence was a tendency to build ahead of demand.

Nothing compelled it [Alcoa] to keep doubling and redoubling its capacity before others entered the field. It insists that it never excluded competitors; but we can think of no more effective exclusion than progressively to embrace each new opportunity as it opened, and to face every newcomer with new capacity already geared into a great organization, having the advantage of experience, trade connections and the elite of personnel.[20]

In this connection it is interesting to note that the leading economic authority on the aluminum industry found Alcoa's behavior to lead in exactly the opposite direction; that is, to a waiting for demand

---

[17] 148 F. 2d 416, 425.
[18] 148 F. 2d 416, 424.
[19] See Edwards, *Maintaining Competition*, p. 100.
[20] United States v. Aluminum Co. of Am., 148 F. 2d 416, 431 (2d Cir. 1945).

to develop before expanding capacity.[21] But, even if the court is correct, it would appear extremely difficult to distinguish between a progressive embracing "of each new opportunity" and what would ordinarily be considered desirable competitive performance.

Despite these observations, the decision in the Aluminum case represents a broadening of the legal meaning of monopoly in a direction favored by current views concerning workable competition. The Tobacco case[22] continued in this direction. The share of the market here was, in 1939, sixty-eight per cent of the production of small cigarettes by three firms, which the Court held were joined in a conspiracy. Such a market position carried with it the power to exclude potential rivals and was therefore illegal, said the Supreme Court, even in the absence of a demonstration of actual exclusion. The court's attitude toward the heavy advertising expenditures of the three firms was interesting but cryptic. On the one hand it was not "criticized as a business expense"; on the other the court thought that "such tremendous advertising, however, is also a widely published warning that these companies possess and know how to use a powerful offensive and defensive weapon against new competition." [23]

Both in this case and the Aluminum case it would seem that the decisions, based mainly on the market position of the companies, were at the same time influenced by the court's judgment on how the market position had been used. In other words, certain standards of business performance seem to have been involved.

The Columbia Steel case,[24] involving the acquisition of a small west coast plant by a subsidiary of United States Steel, produced one of the most careful examinations of the market position of a company to be found in the history of antitrust cases. Though the court here rejected a large share of the local market, with respect to certain products, as a ground for undoing the acquisition, it may well have been influenced by the spectacle of the Antitrust Division straining at the gnat of Columbia after swallowing the Geneva camel.

[21] Wallace, *Market Control of the Aluminum Industry* (1937), pp. 252, 259–260, 331.
[22] American Tobacco Co. v. United States, 328 U. S. 781 (1946).
[23] 328 U. S. 781 (1946).
[24] United States v. Columbia Steel Co., 334 U. S. 495 (1948).

The National Lead case[25] presented a situation in which the conditions of workable competition were violated both because of the fewness of sellers — four, with two accounting for ninety per cent of the sales — and because of collusive restraints. The court eliminated the restraints but refused to increase the number of sellers by ordering present sellers to divest themselves of part of their holdings. Apparently the majority of the judges were influenced by the finding of fact disclosing what they considered to be effective business performance in the industry:

From 1933 on there was active competition between [National Lead] and [DuPont] for customers. There has been a vast increase in sales; and repeated reductions in the price of titanium pigments have taken place and a very few increases.[26]

At another point the court says that the findings "disclose a vigorous, comparatively young, but comparatively large, world-wide industry, in which two great companies, National Lead and DuPont, now control approximately ninety-five per cent of the domestic production in approximately equal shares. . . . The findings show vigorous and apparently profitable competition on the part of each of the four producers, including an intimation that the smaller companies are gaining rather than losing ground." [27]

These and other recent cases concerning the legal meaning of monopoly appear to indicate that although the courts have moved some distance toward accepting certain of the market conditions associated with the notion of workable competition as standards of judgment — particularly share of the market and perhaps the number of firms — their application of these standards is strongly influenced by evidence relating to the character of business performance in these markets.

B. COLLUSION

When one turns to collusion, another of the elements of market structure emphasized in the literature on workable competition, interpreting the significance of recent legal actions presents a perplexing problem. The courts have certainly gone a long way in

[25] United States v. National Lead Co., 332 U. S. 319 (1947).
[26] 332 U. S. 319, 346–347.
[27] 332 U. S. 319, 347–348.

accepting various kinds of market behavior as evidence of a conspiracy among firms; so far, indeed, that it seems appropriate to
inquire whether market behavior rather than conspiracy has not
become the test of illegality.

Economists in recent years have speculated a good deal on the
possible courses of behavior of firms in markets in which the number of buyers and sellers is sufficiently few to make the rival firms
aware of their interdependence. Given merely the number of firms
any one of a wide variety of types of behavior is possible and an
explanation of a particular course of behavior becomes feasible
only after an examination of a number of other elements of the
market structure in which these firms operate. Among these conditions, high overhead costs, large cyclical variations in the volume
of sales, and immobility of resources are combined in a substantial
number of industrial markets. Given these conditions, together
with a small number of firms, some economists have contended that
such phenomena as price uniformity, price leadership and the relative inflexibility of prices to large variations in the national income,
are frequently compatible with the independent action of firms all
recognizing their interdependence.

Now independence of action is, by definition, the opposite of
collusion. But it may be impossible to determine from market behavior alone whether the firms are acting independently or together. At this point we may appropriately ask, what difference
does it make? With respect to the remedy to be applied it may
make considerable difference. If the behavior is really the result
of agreement, enjoining the agreement may, by securing independence of action, change the market behavior. But if the action of
firms is already independent, this remedy is useless.

A prime example is provided by the Tobacco case.[28] Both the
district court and the circuit court found from the record in this
case evidence of a price conspiracy among the three big producers
of cigarettes. Both bodies held that conspiracy does not require a
formal agreement or even a meeting together of the conspirators.
To the district court the essential condition was that "some character or manner of communication take place between them, sufficient to enable them to reach a definite, mutual understanding of

[28] American Tobacco Co. v. United States, 328 U. S. 781 (1946).

the common, unlawful objective or purpose to be thereafter accomplished, and that they will unite or combine their efforts to that end." [29]

The conception of conspiracy in the court of appeals was, perhaps, even broader than this: "The agreement may be shown by a concert of action, all the parties working together understandingly, with a single design for the accomplishment of a common purpose." [30]

When one turns to the record in the case, there is certainly some evidence of agreement among the firms.[31] The companies admittedly consulted with each other on the question of opening new leaf markets. It is probably a fact that the companies' systems of grading leaf tobacco required explicit understandings. But to suppose that ending such collusion or conspiracy as existed among the firms would produce a substantially different market behavior in the sale of cigarettes than that on which the charge of price conspiracy primarily rested is contrary both to logic and to the subsequent course of events in the industry.

There is certainly plenty of evidence that the business performance of the big tobacco companies did not meet reasonable standards of efficiency in the use of resources. Cigarette prices did not respond to substantial declines in leaf prices, it required the advent of ten-cent brands in the 1930's to bring about effective price competition; large resources were employed in what can only be regarded from the point of view of the community as wasteful advertising; the profits of the three companies were inordinately high. Nevertheless, this lamentable performance was and is quite compatible with independence of action on the part of the firms. Under these circumstances to bring a charge of conspiracy may have had the effect of enlarging the legal meaning of conspiracy. But it may also have had the effect of producing in some minds the illusion that eliminating the conspiracy will necessarily, in some sense, make competition work better.

---

[29] Transcript of Record, p. 6350, American Tobacco Co. v. United States, 328 U. S. 781 (1946).

[30] American Tobacco Co. v. United States, 147 F. 2d 93, 107 (6th Cir. 1944).

[31] I am indebted for an analysis of the record to the recent able Ph.D. thesis by my student, Warren Baum. See Baum, "Workable Competition in the Tobacco Industry" (unpublished, in the Harvard College Library, 1949).

The charge of collusion in the Cement case[32] was brought under Section 5 of the Federal Trade Commission Act[33] and the multiple basing-point system in use in that industry was found by the Supreme Court to be an "unfair method of competition." But there can be little doubt, after this decision, that a similar set of facts would justify a charge of conspiracy in violation of the Sherman Act. Whatever ingenuity economists have displayed in demonstrating that a basing-point system might emerge without collusion, there can be no doubt that in the cement industry, and probably in most industries in which this pricing system is used, collusion is involved. Furthermore, the collusive agreements ordinarily involved in an effective basing-point system are sufficiently central to the marketing practices of firms that elimination of the agreements may be expected to change substantially the character of the business performance in what were formerly basing-point industries.

Whether the business performance will be improved in any sense relevant to the concept of efficiency in the use of resources will depend on what alternative practices are adopted by the firms. The abolition of a basing-point system is in itself an approach toward workable competition as defined in terms of market conditions. By the performance test of competition, however, the elimination of basing-point systems is the beginning and not the end of the discussion.[34]

Considering these and other recent antitrust cases involving the charge of conspiracy or collusion,[35] it would seem that the courts have substantially enlarged the meaning of collusion or, at least,

[32] FTC v. Cement Institute, 333 U. S. 683 (1948).

[33] 38 Stat. 719–20 (1914), as amended, 52 Stat. 112 (1938), 15 U. S. C. §45 (b) (1946).

[34] "During the basic litigation, economic considerations are elbowed out or distorted by legalistic exigencies, both sides probably producing about equally bad or irrelevant or one-sided economics. Since serious and realistic consideration of the effects of an order cannot begin until after the order is issued, economic analysis is backward, though the heart of the legality in these cases is economic. This is unfortunate, but it seems to be the way our present system works." Clark, "The Law and Economics of Basing Points: Appraisals and Proposals, p. 431.

[35] See, e.g., United States v. Line Material Co., 333 U. S. 287 (1948); United States v. United States Gypsum Co., 333 U. S. 364 (1948); United States v. Masonite Corp., 316 U. S. 265 (1942); Interstate Circuit, Inc. v. United States, 306 U. S. 208 (1939).

the scope of the circumstances they are willing to accept as evidence of collusion. To this extent, the enforcement agencies find their task appreciably lightened. But included among the markets in which collusion may exist are some in which the abrogation of all agreements, existing and imagined, will constitute no progress toward effective competition judged either by standards of market structure or by standards of business performance. And there are others in which, while the abrogation of agreements may improve competition in the first sense, it will not necessarily do so in the second. It is now incumbent on us to look more closely at these alternative notions of competition.

III. CONCLUSION: OBJECTIVES OF ANTITRUST POLICY

The broad public policy question underlying these various theories of competition is what objective should an antimonopoly policy set for itself? Should it attempt to bring about a structure of industrial markets and a set of business practices such that the scope of action of individual firms is severely limited by the action of rival firms in the economy? Or should the objective be efficient use of economic resources, considering elements of market structure only when they can be shown to lead to ineffective business performance? It is the contention of this paper that neither objective can be set without regard to the other; that the tests both of workable competition and effective business performance have merits and demerits; and that these tests must be used to complement rather than to exclude each other.

In some ways the market structure tests are more precise and lend themselves more readily to administrative and judicial application. The number of buyers and sellers and the market-percentage share of each are roughly ascertainable facts, the chief difficulty being to know how much to include in a given market and what to exclude. The presence or absence of collusion, on the other hand, is sometimes difficult to discover and, the number of independent buyers or sellers considered necessary to the existence of an "adequate number of alternatives" is indeed a difficult question.

Stigler considers it necessary "that there [be] a considerable number of firms selling closely related products in each important market area. . . ."[36] A "considerable number" might mean a number large enough to eliminate recognition of interdependence. On the other hand, Edwards explicitly states that this is unnecessary.[37] The key question here is what is meant by the alternatives of which workable competition is supposed to require an "adequate number." I suggest that there is frequently no satisfactory way to assign meaning to this term without examining business performance in the market in question. The rapid expansion in the sale of titanium compounds with substantially and continually declining prices during the interwar period may have indicated that, under these circumstances, four sellers provide buyers with an adequate number of alternatives. At least the Supreme Court seemed to think so.[38] Eight or ten producers in a rapidly growing rayon industry which must meet the competition of substitute fabrics may be enough to provide buyers with adequate alternatives. Under other circumstances, this number might be too small. But whether the number is or is not sufficiently large can hardly be determined without looking at the business performance of the firms in question.

When one turns, however, to the problem of testing adequate business performance, it would have to be said that although it is probably possible to arrive at informed judgments, it is extremely difficult to devise tests that can be administered by a court of law. Among the tests mentioned in the literature are the following:[39]

1. Progressiveness: are the firms in the industry actively and effectively engaged in product and process innovation?

2. Cost-price relationships: are reductions in cost, whether due to

---

[36] Stigler, "The Extent and Bases of Monopoly," pp. 2–3.

[37] Edwards, *Maintaining Competition*, p. 9.

[38] See United States v. National Lead Co., 332 U. S. 319 (1947).

[39] Wallace, "Industrial Markets and Public Policy: Some Major Problems," *Public Policy:* 59 (1940), 99–100, includes among the issues involved in estimating the efficiency of business performance: (1) size of firms in relation to efficiency and economic progress and locational factors; (2) allocation of economic resources between industries, utilization of resources already invested, returns to owners; (3) the level of use of resources in the community as a whole; (4) severity of the business cycle; (5) progressiveness.

Professor Joe S. Bain in his three-volume work, *The Economics of the Pacific Coast Petroleum Industry* (1944, 1945, 1947), discusses standards of performance at three levels of industry operations, crude oil production, refining, and distribution. See particularly Volume III.

falling wages or material prices, technical improvements, discovery of new sources of supply, passed on promptly to buyers in the form of price reductions?

3. Capacity-output relationships: is investment excessive in relation to output?

4. The level of profits: are profits continually and substantially higher than in other industries exhibiting similar trends in sales, costs, innovations, etc.?

5. Selling expenditures: is competitive effort chiefly indicated by selling expenditures rather than by service and product improvements and price reductions?

No one familiar with the statistical and other material pertaining to the business performance of firms and industries would deny the extreme difficulty of constructing from this material a watertight case for or against the performance of particular firms in particular industries. Few, on the other hand, would deny that with respect to many industrial markets an informed judgment is possible. For example, it is possible from the record of the last two or three decades to determine that the performance of the automobile industry is relatively good, despite the existence of a small number of firms, while the performance of the construction industry is relatively bad. In any case, it is on the basis of just such industry data as we are now discussing that a decision even under the market structure test would have to be made whether the number of alternatives available to buyers or sellers in a particular industrial market is or is not "adequate."

A study of the performance of business firms in a particular industrial market may, of course, indicate the desirability of public action transcending the limits of antitrust policy. For example, one of the ways of improving the conditions of entry for new firms in the cigarette industry would be to change by legislation the present structure of excise taxes which is regressive with respect to the cheaper brands.[40] Professor Bain's study of the performance of firms in the Pacific coast petroleum industry led to a number of recommendations that lie outside the limits of antitrust action.[41]

[40] That is, the taxes do not increase with the base price of the cigarette as they would if the taxes were levied on an ad valorem basis.

[41] The two industry studies that have, in my opinion, gone furthest in an economic examination of the character of business performance are: Wallace,

But even within these limits considerations of efficiency in the use of resources cannot be neglected in judging the acceptability of the structure of and practices in particular industrial markets. The relative importance to be assigned to the objective of establishing appropriate market limitations on the scope of action of firms as against the objective of encouraging efficient performance in the use of economic resources no doubt presents serious difficulties. It seems probable that individual judgments will always be influenced to some extent by ideological considerations. There are those who are willing to sacrifice a lot in the way of performance to establish market structures which severely limit the power and scope of action of individual firms.[42] There are others to whom this seems less important. How much, in fact, would have to be sacrificed in the attainment of one objective to secure a given amount of progress towards the other is the heart of the public policy problem in the area of business organization. It is only necessary to indicate here that, in my opinion, the choice of one of these objectives, to the exclusion of the other, would make a substantial amount of difference in many industrial markets.

Finally, we must ask at what level of public action this question of the appropriate objectives for an antimonopoly policy should be considered. There are clearly three nonexclusive possibilities. The question can be raised at the level of legislation. Should the present antitrust laws be modified and, if so, how? As soon as this question is raised, it becomes obvious that a number of possible actions lying outside of traditional antitrust policy may, nevertheless, make an important contribution to an antimonopoly policy. Taxation discriminating against size and a series of measures favorable to the development of small firms may be mentioned as examples.

Secondly, the question can be discussed at the level of adjudication of cases brought under the antitrust laws. What are and what should be the legal tests of monopoly and restraint of trade? As we have seen, these tests have, in certain respects, been substantially

Market Control in the Aluminum Industry (1937), and Bain, *The Economics of the Pacific Coast Petroleum Industry.*

[42] See, e.g., forthcoming article by Lewis in the *American Economic Review:* "For competition to be effective or workable, or even acceptable, in any significant lasting sense, it must not only permit, *it must compel the results we want by the necessary and continuing operation of its processes.*"

broadened by recent antitrust decisions and the courts can, and no doubt will, extend present trends further.

Finally, and to my mind, the most important level within the framework of traditional antitrust policy, at which the question of appropriate standards and objectives can be discussed, is at the level of the enforcement agencies. These agencies have an enormous amount of discretion with respect to the kinds of cases that may be brought and the business areas within which to bring them. This fact is by implication frequently denied by representatives of the enforcement agencies who assert that, after all, they "have a statute to enforce." The statute, however, in the words of Chief Justice Hughes, is of the same order of generality as a constitutional provision.[43] Even if the Antitrust Division and the Federal Trade Commission enjoyed appropriations five times as large as they now have, they could not conceivably bring a tenth of the cases it would be possible to bring. Under these circumstances, it is a matter of considerable importance how and where they strike.

There has, in my opinion, been too much preoccupation in the enforcement agencies with the question what cases can be won and too little with the question what difference it makes.[44] The second question clearly involves a consideration of whether a different structure of the market and set of business practices, lying within the area subject to antitrust action, will be better, in some sense, than the existing structure and practices. At this point the alternative objectives of antitrust policy and how they should be related to each other, which has been the subject of this paper, can no longer be avoided.

[43] Appalachian Coals, Inc. v. United States, 288 U. S. 344, 360 (1933).

[44] But see the remarks of the present chief of the Antitrust Division, Herbert A. Bergson, Assistant Attorney General: "In selecting cases we analyze the effectiveness of the relief obtainable, the competitive positions in the particular industry, and our prospects in the courts. In this respect our decision is similar to that of any businessman who proposes to invest money — he wants to know what the return will be. In anti-trust enforcement that return should not be measured in dollars and cents, but in benefits to our economy and an American system of free enterprise." Bergson, "Current Problems in the Enforcement of the Anti-trust Laws," *Record of the N. Y. City Bar Association,* 4 (April 1949), 115.

17

The New Competition[1]

Many voices — including some unexpected ones — have recently made themselves heard in praise of the large business. Frederick Lewis Allen, in his recent book *The Big Change: America Transforms Itself* (New York, 1952), has looked upon the growth of giant enterprise and has found it good. A forthcoming study from the Brookings Institution, announced with considerable fanfare at a banquet in the Starlight Room of the Waldorf-Astoria, is described by Alfred P. Sloan, Jr., as a factual study that is hoped will "correct the more glaringly artificial and outmoded assumptions of the economic textbook and popular economic literature" concerning large corporations. David Lilienthal's *Big Business: A New Era* (New York, 1953), is an unqualified endorsement of the large firm as the primary source of economic growth and effective competition in the American economy. The recent report of the Business Advisory Council on Effective Competition seeks, among other things, a redefinition of competition that will recognize the innovating role of the large firm in the competitive process.

Behind these and other current discussions of bigness lie a number of academic studies that are increasingly cited in the popular literature. The statistical investigations of Morris Adelman at the Massachusetts Institute of Technology have at least raised doubts whether economic concentration has substantially increased in this country since the turn of the century, despite the growth of giant firms. The late Professor Schumpeter of Harvard has familiarized a generation of economists with the view that effective competition is essentially a process of "creative destruction," in which new products and processes, usually introduced by large firms, supplant old products and processes now become obsolete. Professor Galbraith, also at Harvard, has added to contemporary views on competition a doctrine of "countervailing power" that

[1] Reprinted from *The Yale Review*, Autumn 1953.

emphasizes the limits set by large buyers such as the A & P to the otherwise unchecked market power of large sellers.

A good deal of this recent writing on the role of the large firm in the competitive process leads towards a vigorous attack — either explicit or implicit — on current antitrust policy. Professor Schumpeter was fond of saying that he did not oppose a sensible antimonopoly policy. But he regarded antitrust policy in practice as a relatively senseless harassment of large firms by people with little understanding of the historical and potential contribution of large-scale enterprise to effective competition. Professor Galbraith is willing to grant that there is a limited utility in attempts to increase competition among sellers or buyers but finds that market power can usually be more effectively controlled by building an opposing power constellation rather than by reducing an existing one. To Lilienthal "trust-busting" is frankly an outworn doctrine. As the antitrust laws "are now construed, the very Bigness upon which we all now depend may be illegal." He proposes to replace the Sherman Law which negatively forbids "restraints of trade" with a positive law that fosters the "development of trade." The report of the Business Advisory Council on "Effective Competition" has no fault to find with the basic purpose of the Sherman Law but wants it interpreted in the light of a "rule of reason" that takes into account conditions now neglected in the enforcement of antitrust policy.

The criticism of antitrust policy tends to center on the allegation that this policy is an attack on "size as such." The enforcement agencies are pictured as engaged in a process of tearing down business structures essential to the growth, prosperity, and security of the United States. What is the truth of this charge that the antitrust laws as currently interpreted constitute an important attack on size as such?

It would have to be admitted by the critics of antitrust policy that, if the success of the attack on the large firm is to be judged by the number and importance of dissolutions or dismemberments actually accomplished, the results are meager indeed. During the last decade, when the attack on size was supposed to be at its height, there have been no more than five or six decisions that produced dismemberment of firms. Furthermore, none of the firms in question was large in comparison with such giants as U. S. Steel, Standard Oil of New Jersey, or General Motors. In 1945 the Pullman manufacturing properties were separated from the operation of Pullman services. Pullman Standard remained by far the largest producer of sleeping cars, though a new company controlled by the railroads took over the operation of the sleeping-car service. In 1948 a number of moving-picture producers were forced to dispose of distributing properties and theatres. None of these companies was large as size is now measured, nor was their share of the picture-producing market very extensive. The Court held, nevertheless, that integration produced an interdependence among producers for theatre outlets and an interdependence among theatre owners for films to be exhibited that smacked of collusion. In 1950 the owners of the controlling stock interests in the Aluminum Company of America and of Aluminum Ltd. of Canada were ordered to dispose of their stock interests in one or the other of these companies. These are the principal dissolutions that have been accomplished during the last ten years; they can hardly be said to add up to a massive change in the structure of American industry.

Furthermore, during this same period the Supreme Court handed down a number of decisions that ran quite in the other direction. Although Du Pont and National Lead were known to produce between them over 90 per cent of the national output of titanium pigments, the Court refused to accede to the request of the Department of Justice that these two companies be dissolved. When United States Steel, not only the largest steel company, but one of the largest corporations in any industry, acquired the Columbia Steel Company, the Court said this acquisition did not violate the antitrust laws. Although the Aluminum Company produced over 50 per cent of the country's output of aluminum ingot, Judge Knox did not find it necessary to accede to the request of the Department of Justice that the company be dismembered.

There are, of course, a number of important cases now before the courts in which the enforcement agencies are pressing for dissolution. Among them are cases against the A & P, American Telephone and Telegraph, Cellophane, International Business Machines, and Du Pont. It is possible to suppose that we are in the midst of an impressive attack on the large firm if attention is limited to the statements of certain judges, particularly dissenting judges, and to the abracadabra that accompanies the action of enforcement agencies. There is, however, a very long distance between what the Department of Justice asks for in its prayer for relief and what the courts will grant in the form of a remedy. And it must always be remembered that antitrust policy is not what various official or unofficial spokesmen think it might be, but what the majority of the Supreme Court says it is.

There is, however, a sense in which it is proper to say that anti-trust policy has been moving towards an attack on size as such. This is so despite the fact that every year since the war, as regularly as the migration of songbirds from the South, we are treated to a speech from the current head of the Antitrust Division piously disclaiming any concern with bigness as such. What he is talking about is the absolute size of firms measured in assets, number of employees, or in other possible ways. And, indeed, with the possible exception of the Du Pont case, it is probably correct to say that no action has been brought against a firm or combination merely because of its absolute economic size.

The critics, however, are talking about something else. They are concerned with cases that have been brought against firms that are *relatively* large; against firms, i.e., that are large in relation to the industries or markets in which they operate. According to the critics a firm that occupies a large share of the market may be found to be in violation of the antitrust laws even though its practices are as competitive as those of any smaller firm; in fact, the more competitive its practices the more guilty is it likely to be considered to be. This is a sense in which it is correct to say that current antitrust policy is an attack on size as such — and it pains Mr. Lilienthal and others deeply. He holds that "the doctrine of penalizing, prosecuting, hectoring and even dismembering a large business which, by research and managerial superiority, achieves competitive success (that is, wins a large share of the market) has serious consequences of a practical kind."

So, indeed, it has. But the practical consequences are not all, as Mr. Lilienthal supposes, injurious to effective competition. Any antimonopoly policy that attempts to set limits to the extension of market power may check the normal competitive expansion of a firm *in a particular market.* It does not follow, however, that the growth of the firm need be checked or that superior management or research possibilities need be frustrated for lack of appropriate "economic space." The firm still has an opportunity to expand into other markets and industries and, to the extent that it can do so effectively, it may not only realize the potentialities of superior management but contribute to the effectiveness of competition in those markets in which it expands. An attack on market power is not necessarily an attack on bigness.

There are strong reasons why the thrust of antitrust policy should be directed against market power. Furthermore, the share of the market occupied by a particular firm is one of the important bits of evidence bearing on the market power of that firm. It is not conclusive evidence and it must be carefully interpreted together with other types of evidence; but the enforcement agencies and the courts are fully justified in placing market share in a central position.

We have always looked to our competitive free-enterprise system to accomplish two different things. On the one hand, we have expected from it a set of powerful motivations, stimulations, and drives towards increased output, product improvement, cost reduction: in general, towards increased efficiency in the use of economic resources. On the other hand, we have expected from the competitive system a set of limitations to the growth of private economic power. The competitive system is supposed to be self-regulating in the sense that a continual striving for market advantage by all firms effectively sets limits to the market power of each.

Both of these objectives are important, and it is essential that public policy keep both in mind. My quarrel with the current worshipers of Big Business, both popular and academic, is that they have concentrated on one objective to the exclusion of the other. Their critique of current antitrust policy towards the large firm has included some important negative propositions but has almost completely neglected the central problem of market power that any effective antitrust policy must confront.

If we are to continue to rely on competition as the principal limiter of private economic power — rather than on public ownership or public utility regulation — we must center our attention on the position of firms in the various markets in which they operate. How and to what extent a particular firm is limited by a market in which it operates is difficult to judge. Yet a judgment must be made and such a judgment presupposes the formulation of applicable tests of permitted and nonpermitted power. The critics of antitrust policy have shown that the tests currently applied sometimes leave out relevant considerations. But they have made little or no contribution to the formulation of more acceptable tests. And some, including Lilienthal, in effect deny the existence of the problem.

Let us consider some of the more important points raised by the apostles of bigness. They emphasize first of all that, in judging the market share of a firm, products that are close substitutes for the articles produced by the firm in question must be taken into account. They insist, further, that the market power of a firm is limited not only by currently competing products but by the new products and processes that are likely to be introduced if any profit opportunity becomes available by reason of a monopoly price charged by existing firms. They also point out that the market power of a seller is limited not only by his rivals but by the bargaining power that may be exerted by big buyers. These are all important considerations. They all need to be taken into account in estimating the market power of large firms. It is true that they are frequently neglected not only by the enforcement agencies but by the courts.

Nevertheless, when these considerations have been fully evaluated, there remains a problem of market power that the protagonists of big business have either neglected or have not understood.

That commodities compete with other and physically different commodities, that a market must be understood to embrace all close substitutes, is a commonplace of textbook economics. Yet the courts and the enforcement agencies have sometimes neglected this obvious fact in attempting to estimate the market position of particular firms. Although copper, stainless steel, and other metals compete with aluminum in some uses, the Court, in the aluminum case, ignored this fact and stated resolutely, "Every product meets with competition of substitutes — this has no relevance for the existence of monopoly."

The Antitrust Division contends, in the Cellophane case now pending, that Du Pont's market position should be determined with reference solely to other producers of Cellophane. The defense holds, on the other hand, that Cellophane is in close and continuous competition with a variety of other wrapping materials. The same issue arises in the current suit against International Business Machines. Should the market for tabulating and calculating equipment be limited to mechanical and electronic calculators, or should all methods and devices for tabulating and bookkeeping be included?

The competition of substitutes is obviously an important consideration in judging the market power of a firm. There is even a sense in which it is true to say that all commodities compete with one another for the consumer's dollar. It does not follow, however, when due weight has been given to interproduct competition, that positions of market power are negligible in number and importance. All it means is that the dimensions of a market are frequently greater than those of a single product, and that this fact should be recognized in the application of antitrust policy.

The view is also advanced by the defenders of big business that product and process innovation is not only an important, but may be a sufficient, limitation to positions of market power. Lilienthal goes very far in this direction. The "new competition" he discovers in the American economy is largely a competition offered by new products and processes, which are chiefly the results of research in large units, public and private. To this "new competition" he attributes a tremendous growth in the productivity of the American economy during the last few decades.

In the first place, there is no evidence of any substantial increase in the *rate* of economic growth in the American economy. The growth rate of per capita output has been no higher during the last twenty-five years than it was in the previous quarter-century; nor is there any evidence that growth rates during the last half of the nineteenth century were any lower than during the first half of the twentieth. The economy has grown rapidly with relatively small firms *and* with relatively large firms. In the second place, the fact that research expenditures are highly concentrated in large firms does not mean that important product and process innovation is the product of large firms. This is something about which we know next to nothing. In the third place, although new products and new processes have dramatically displaced existing products and processes in certain areas, they have had relatively little effect in others.

The role of innovation in the competitive process has been discussed with more originality and cogency in the writings of the late Professor Schumpeter than in any others. "The competition that counts," he emphasized, "is the competition from the new commodity, the new technology, the new source of supply, the new type of organization (the largest scale unit of control for instance) — competition which commands a decisive cost or quality advantage and which strikes not at the margins of profit and their outputs of the existing firms, but at their foundations and their very lives. This kind of competition is as much more effective than the other as bombardment is in comparison with forcing a door, and so much more important that it becomes a matter of comparative indifference whether competition in the ordinary sense functions more or less promptly: the powerful lever that in the long run expands output and brings down prices is in any case made of other stuff."

Certainly it would have been rather foolish to have conducted an attack on a firm controlling a large share of the trade in carriages — if one had existed — at a time when the development of the motorcar was driving horse-drawn vehicles off the road. Market share is not always an indication of market power. There is a period in the development of most industries when the rate of innovation is such as to make the number of firms or their market shares irrelevant to a judgment on the effectiveness of competition. That is one of the reasons why it is unreasonable to conclude, because three or four firms produce from 70 to 80 per cent of the output in a particular industry, that competition is necessarily nonexistent. Competition may well be nonexistent, but a sensible antitrust policy will have to take other things into account than market shares.

To say that innovation is sufficient in certain situations to assure effective competition is not to say, however, that innovation may be relied upon to assure effective competition in all. Technological change is not something that spreads itself evenly over the economy, nor does it always work in the direction of increasing competition. Formidable positions of market power may persist in the most dynamic of economies, and the American economy is no exception.

Although Schumpeter assures us that what he is opposed to is not every antimonopoly policy but only certain kinds, he does not offer much guidance to a sensible policy. No more does Lilienthal. The critics have succeeded in pointing out a set of considerations relevant to the monopoly problem that have been relatively neglected. They have not, however, disposed of the problem itself.

Nor have the exponents of the theory of "countervailing power." It seems probable that in some situations the growth of large buyers has resulted not only in a wresting of monopoly profits away from large sellers but in passing on some of the advantages gained to ultimate consumers. It is possible that the A & P and other chain stores have fulfilled this function. Sears, Roebuck and the other mail-order houses may have done the same. Perhaps it is correct to say that, over the last three or four decades, mass distributors have, in general, accomplished this function, though what part of the price reductions brought about by these distributors is to be assigned to economies of large size and what to bargaining advantages it would be difficult indeed to determine.

To recognize, however, that under certain circumstances the power of large sellers may be checked by large buyers, not only to the advantage of these buyers but to the advantage of ultimate consumers, is not to conclude that in all circumstances this beneficial result will follow. It may well be that the predominant effect will be merely a division of potential monopoly profits between the large buyer and the large seller. Under what circumstances is this result likely to follow rather than the others and how do we tell whether market power is, or is not, adequately checked to the advantage of the consuming public? It is at this point that the proponents of countervailing power leave off the discussion.

In general it may be said that the recent literature extolling the virtues of bigness has offered some legitimate and telling criticism of current antitrust policy. It *is* true that interproduct competition tends to limit the market power of certain firms whose share of the sales of a particular product is large. Close substitutes should, therefore, be included in any proper calculation of that firm's share of the market. It *is* true that innovation in products and processes is of the essence of competition and that in certain industrial areas where the rate of innovation — and consequently of obsolescence —

is rapid, market share is essentially irrelevant to a judgment of market power. It is also true that market power is limited by rivals on the other side as well as by rivals on the same side of the market, though whether this rivalry offers the same advantage to consumers is open to question.

When, however, admitting the partial validity of the criticism, we ask the disciples of bigness to offer, from their superior insight, alternative and more realistic tests of permitted or nonpermitted positions of market power, we encounter a blank wall. Lilienthal, it is true, proposes a positive program, but it is couched in such general language that the reader has difficulty in determining whether, in fact, any substantial change from current practice would be accomplished. He suggests a "Basic Economic Law" containing "a broad declaration of public policy that the *prime* concern of Congress is not with competition, per se, nor with competitors, but with productivity and the promotion of an ethical and economic distribution of this productivity."

If, under this law, suit was brought against a company occupying a large share of a market "the legal test Bigness would have to face would thenceforth be whether the particular aspect of size challenged by the government does in fact *further the public interest.*" Until Lilienthal has specified his tests of public interest there is no way of knowing what he proposes is significantly different from what we now have. Under current antitrust policy, if a firm charged with monopolizing the market can effectively demonstrate not only that its practices are not predatory, but that costs of production and prices are likely to be lower than under an alternative market structure, there is little or no chance of its being found guilty of violating the antitrust laws. Under Lilienthal's proposed legislation the company would still apparently bear the burden of proof, and the sole question is whether his tests of "public interest" would be significantly different from those now applied in antitrust cases.

A similar charge of excessive vagueness must also be levied against the Business Advisory Council's contribution to the discussion of antitrust policy. Again the negative criticism is well directed, but the discussion ends abruptly at the point where positive tests of desirable competition or undesirable monopoly need to be considered. The council preaches the doctrine of "effective competition," but there are as many definitions of "effective" or "workable" competition as there are effective or working economists.

When all is said and done there is a problem of market power that is a proper concern of public policy. When the market is adequately defined, with full account taken of competition among products and of the position of buyers as well as sellers, there are strong reasons for supposing that a firm with a large share of the market will have a large degree of market power. The reasons are not conclusive; other considerations will need to be examined; and it does not follow, even though market power is demonstrated, that dissolution is the appropriate remedy. Nevertheless, the enforcement agencies and the courts are on the right track in emphasizing share of the market as a prima-facie indication of market power. This does not imply an attack on size as such. A firm whose position in a particular market is limited by public action is, and should be, free to expand in other markets as far as managerial qualifications and research potentialities permit. There remains, however, the question of market power, and nothing brought forward by the current defenders of big business has called into question either its existence or the need for a remedy.

18

Workable Competition Versus Workable Monopoly[1]

It has been approximately ten years since J. M. Clark introduced the phrase "workable competition." During that period, a lot of words have been shed without producing much in the way of illumination concerning usable standards relevant to an enlightened antitrust policy. One of the frequent reactions of students to my own attempts to discuss the meaning of the phrase "workable competition" is, "Professor, what you seem to be talking about is workable monopoly." And this reaction is certainly just in the sense that any practicable market structure or set of business practices is bound to include elements that an economist would call monopolistic.

In the phrase here under discussion, the word "workable" deserves at least as much attention as the word "competition." A competitive situation or a competitive standard should be workable in two senses: it must be practically attainable having regard to current technology and other factors conditioning the use of economic resources; it must also be compatible with currently accepted notions of what constitutes the public interest. With respect to the first condition, what needs to be emphasized is that there are some severe limitations, arising out of existing technology, spatial considerations, population distribution, and basic institutional conditions, to a rearrangement of market structure and business practices. What is practicable in the realm of antimonopoly policy must take these considerations into account. As a general rule, there seems to be small reason for attacking an existing situation, if no better set of market relationships can be put in its place.

To attempt to apply such a rule in the realm of antitrust policy will no doubt seem to many to confuse a violation of the law with the remedy. We are frequently told by the Antitrust Division that,

[1] Reprinted from *Business Practices Under Federal Anti-trust Laws*, 1951 Symposium of Section on Antitrust Law, New York State Bar Association.

after all, it has a statute to enforce, the implication being that violators have to be prosecuted come what may. But, for the really important current antitrust issues, the feasibility of a remedy seems a more promising guide to the selection of cases to be brought than the presence or absence of a supposed violation. In fact, the feasibility of a remedy should in many cases be a major consideration in determining whether a violation has taken place. Of what use is it to prosecute a case of parallel action as a conspiracy when successful prosecution leaves the market structure and practices exactly the same as before? Of what use is it to hold a set of requirements contracts to be a violation of the law when to do so merely substitutes integration through ownership for a much looser form of integration through long-term contract?

I am, of course, aware of the contention that antitrust cases are brought to establish new law as well as to provide a remedy in a particular situation. But I cannot refrain from asking, as a layman, how good is the law, in this area of business practices, that goes far towards divorcing the fact of violation from the possibility of remedy?

What we are concerned with in the main are not questions of crime and punishment but the devising of rules relating to market structure and business practices that will prevent the unhealthy, and facilitate the healthy, growth of the economy. It is a question of hygiene rather than of morals. Of course, the old-style conspiracy and the use of a wide variety of predatory practices are still with us; cases arise requiring punishment as well as remedy. Criminal action under the antitrust laws is still necessary, and grand jury proceedings are a useful device for gathering evidence. The questions I am concerned with are the currently important issues, the stuff of recent antitrust decisions: the problem of the firm that is large in relation to its market, questions of integration, parallel action, and the relation of price discrimination to competition and to monopoly. This is an area to which questions of crime and punishment and of violations divorceable from remedies seem singularly inappropriate.

I have pointed out that the notion of workable competition brings to the fore a consideration of practicable limitations to changes in business practices and market structure; in antitrust policy it

insists on the prime importance of an examination of possible remedies. It also raises questions concerning what the public wants and
expects to get from the market organization of economic resources.
The pure competition of the economic theorists is a concept divorced from time and space and independent of technological and
other considerations. But the standards of acceptable competition
or unacceptable monopoly applicable in particular cases tend to be
relative both to the basic conditions under which goods are produced and sold and to the development of ideas concerning the public interest and how it is to be served. Monopoly meant one thing
in the period when the flow of commodities to the annual fair or
market was subject to interruption by forestallers and engrossers;
it means something different under current conditions. Likewise,
one's view as to what constitutes an acceptably competitive structure of a market will vary depending on whether one considers the
maintenance of a large number of buyers and sellers, the prevention
of a certain degree of concentration of economic power, efficiency in
the use of resources or the preservation of conditions of economic
growth to be the primary objective of public policy in the area of
market structure and business practices.

The theologian depicted by Anatole France might fruitfully con-
template the pure concept of a "kick in the pants" until it ma-
terialized in the application of an actual shoe to an actual pair of
britches. A more mundane approach, however, will insist on an
examination of the thickness of the trousers, the structure of the
brogans, the degree of provocation, and various attendant psychological factors before assessing the social significance of the act in
question. Likewise, the mundane approach in the field of antitrust
policy will eschew "pure" concepts of competition and monopoly
and will concentrate attention on what practically can be done to
other market structures and business practices and what should be
done if currently acceptable standards of the public interest are to
be served.

One thing that antitrust policy is unlikely to be able to do is to
alter to any substantial degree the situation indicated by recent
data on economic concentration. If the hundred largest manufacturing companies were all broken up — and I think it will be agreed
that this would be an extensive dissolution program — a relatively

small number of corporations would still be found owning a substantial portion of all manufacturing assets. Economic concentration, like the automobile, seems to be here to stay. If the competitive ideal demands an economy exclusively composed of small-scale enterprise, the existing situation must be judged to be unfortunate. However, there seems no very good reason to limit the meaning of competition so narrowly.

Two elements that might appropriately be given consideration in formulating and applying public policy in the area here under consideration have to do with economic power and economic growth. Can the organization of economic resources in the fields of manufacture, mining, and distribution be effectively shaped towards a limitation of economic power compatible with growth and development? Let me say that I am primarily concerned here with one aspect of economic growth, innovation, and improvement in the use of economic resources. In the few minutes that remain to me I shall touch briefly on certain of the relations of economic power and innovation to antitrust policy.

With respect to the economic power of the large firm, antitrust policy has supposedly undergone during the last few years a remarkable change. From the doctrine of the Steel case[2] that "mere size" or "the existence of unexerted power" is not an offense, we have passed, via the decision of Justice Cardozo in the Swift case[3] that "size carries with it an opportunity for abuse that is not to be ignored when the opportunity is proved to have been utilized in the past," to the doctrine of the Aluminum[4] and Tobacco[5] cases that appears to assert that the mere existence of monopoly power, irrespective of its exercise, constitutes a violation.

The supposed change, however, on examination seems less substantial than is frequently asserted. After all, it is monopoly power, not power, or economic power, or market power that is condemned, and there remains the question of determining when power is to be considered monopolistic. In considering this question, Judge Hand in the Aluminum case laid great emphasis on the power to fix prices and the power to exclude competitors. This emphasis was

[2] 251 U. S. 417, at 451.
[3] 286 U. S. 106, at 116.
[4] 148 F. 2d 416.
[5] 328 U. S. 781.

followed by the Supreme Court in the Tobacco case[6] and by Judge Knox in his judgment concerning relief in the Aluminum case. According to Judge Knox,

In considering the matter of monopoly power, two ingredients are of outstanding significance: viz., the power to fix prices and the power to exclude competitors.[7]

This statement, however, merely pushes the argument one step backward. How is it to be determined when the power to fix prices or to exclude competitors exists? In considering the price question, Judge Hand pointed out the inconsistency between the holding that "all contracts fixing prices are unconditionally prohibited," and a holding that a single firm possessing equal or greater power to fix prices comes under the ban only conditionally; that is, if its power is abused. He sought to lessen this inconsistency by moving in the direction of an unconditional condemnation of power to fix prices wherever found.

There is, however, a fundamental difficulty in transferring the notion of price fixing from the realm of conspiracy and collusion to the sphere of action by the single firm. A price-fixing conspiracy is an agreement in accordance with which the participating firms sell at a price determined by the agreement or set by some agreed agency. Here the meaning of price fixing is unambiguous. What does price fixing mean, however, as applied to the action of a single firm? Outside the organized commodity exchanges almost every firm quotes or sets a price for its product and this price may continue unchanged for a longer or shorter period of time. There is nothing either in the process of price setting or in the behavior of prices themselves that permits the conclusion that certain prices are fixed and others not. If a price leader compels adherence by others to his price through retaliatory or predatory action, this might properly be called price fixing. The "fixing" in this case, however, lies in the overt action undertaken to maintain the price. I conclude that the concept of "price fixing" properly belongs in the

[6] 328 U. S. 781, 811. "The authorities support the view that the material consideration in determining whether a monopoly exists is not that prices are raised and that competition actually is excluded but that *power exists to raise prices or to exclude competition* when it is desired to do so."
[7] 91 F. Supp. 333.

category of old-style Sherman Act violations. Market power will certainly influence the behavior of prices but there is no breaking point between a non-monopolistic and a monopolistic degree of market power indicated by the ability to fix prices. Price fixing is an act which may or may not accompany monopoly power.

Likewise, the exclusion of competitors is a notion that has precise meaning only in terms of the deliberate action of a particular firm or firms directed against other firms. The old Standard Oil Company and the National Cash Register Company excluded competitors in no uncertain fashion. But to attempt to stretch this motion to cover the whole problem of entry of new firms is, I think, a mistake. Conditions of entry vary enormously among industries, and there is no point in the range between extremely easy and extremely difficult entry at which one can say, in the absence of overt acts, that competitors are excluded.

Price fixing and exclusion of competitors in the old-style Sherman Act sense were not only violations of law but also, and quite appropriately, bore a definite moral stigma. To use these terms in attempting to define limits to the permissible degree of market power, however, is not only confusing but introduces elements of moral judgment which are definitely not helpful in deciding issues that do not involve conspiratorial or predatory behavior.

What the courts appear to be reaching for, above and beyond the range of traditional Sherman Act violations, is a doctrine of permissible power. Some power there has to be, both because of inescapable limitations to the process of atomization and because power is needed to do the job the American public expects of its industrial machine. There is no reason, however, to tolerate positions of market power that can be lessened by appropriate antitrust action unless it can be shown that this lessening substantially interferes with the job to be done.

I have suggested above that an essential part of the job to be done is the promotion of economic growth. What American citizens have come to expect from their industry is a continual increase in per capita output. This is dependent, in the main, on improvement in the organization and administration of economic resources, technological innovation, and increasing quantities of capital per worker. A doctrine of permissible power must, therefore, be shaped with two objectives in mind: to limit power certainly, but also to preserve conditions propitious to growth. The problems of the large firm and of the relations of large firms in a market must be considered in the light of both of these objectives.

In determining the extent of permissible power that is consistent with the antitrust laws in a particular industry, the following factors are relevant: the number and strength of the firms in the market; their effective size from the standpoint of technological development, and from the standpoint of competition with substitute materials and foreign trade; national security interests in the maintenance of strong productive facilities, and maximum scientific research and development; together with the public interest in lowered costs and uninterrupted production.[8]

Whatever one thinks of the prospects of a workably competitive market for aluminum under the conditions of relief as laid down by Judge Knox, this judgment sets a new standard of judicial evaluation of market structure and business practice. Proper obeisance to the "power to fix prices" and "to exclude competitors" provides a legal blessing to what becomes a thoroughly objective examination not only of price behavior and conditions of entry but of other considerations relevant to market power and economic growth in the aluminum industry. There emerges a noteworthy contribution to the formulation of an acceptable standard of permissible power. Whether one chooses to call this standard workable competition or workable monopoly is to me a matter of no very great moment.

[8] United States v. Aluminum Company of America, 91 F. Supp. 333, at 339.

19

Market Power and Business Conduct: Some Comments on the Report of the Attorney General's Committee on Antitrust Policy[1]

The antitrust field is, perhaps, of all areas of discourse the one in which practitioners live best by taking in each other's washing. One shudders to think of what the position of an editor of an economic or legal journal in search of manuscripts must have been before the passage of the Sherman Law. John Stuart Mill tells us in his *Autobiography* that, at one stage in his youth, he was filled with anxiety lest all possible combinations of musical notes be exhausted and the world deprived of new compositions. Much more likely is it that all possible combinations of words on the subject of antitrust will be exhausted and our literature deprived of further new reflections on this subject. The Report before us makes a notable contribution in this direction.

It is difficult in judging this Report — and in fact any government report — to know how properly to assess the area of freedom open to the Committee. Any government report — and, as a frequent participant in such ventures, I speak from some experience — is a political product in at least two senses. The commissions responsible for such reports are usually established because it is judged to be politically expedient to do so. The expediency may consist of nothing more than a judgment that an act of "statesmanship" is currently required. There are also other reasons. Secondly, a government report is inevitably a group product and is usually an effort requiring the participation of a number of bureaus and departments. In this sense it necessitates an appeal to politics as "the art of the possible." In other words, government reports are written in an external and an internal political environment which circumscribe more or less seriously the area of freedom. Under

[1] Reprinted from *Papers and Proceedings,* American Economic Association, Vol. 46, 1956.

these circumstances it would be a mistake to expect in such a document a bold and original examination of antimonopoly policy. The Report before us does not, in this respect, disappoint our expectations.

On the other hand, if we push our analysis of the limitations surrounding such report writing too far, we are apt to fall into a frame of mind described in the French maxim, *"tout comprendre c'est tout pardonner."* To attain this level of benign objectivity is to ask too much of an economist or a lawyer commenting on the work of his professional colleagues.

"Give me a place to stand," said Archimedes, "and I will move the earth." Obviously, in addition to a place to stand Archimedes wanted a very long lever. The Attorney General's Committee had a relatively circumscribed place to stand and a rather short lever. Consequently this Report cannot be judged to have moved the earth. That would be to expect too much. On the other hand, in addition to a highly professional examination of antitrust cases and a competent discussion of workable versus pure competition, we might reasonably have expected a more illuminating consideration of the weakness and strength of antitrust policy than in fact we received.

The Commission described as its primary task "to mark out as clearly as possible the path antitrust has travelled and what it augurs for the future. "Our hope," the Report says, "is that from such clarification will emerge more practical guides for business seeking to comply with the antitrust laws and for Government officials charged with enforcing their prohibitions." [2]

In fact the Commission went somewhat further than this modest program would indicate. To its credit must be placed a forthright recommendation for repeal of federal price-maintenance legislation (the action which received most public attention); a perceptive and useful discussion of price discrimination and the Robinson-Patman Act; and, most important of all, a knowledgeable and effective defense of *per se* against a threatened encroachment of the rule of reason.

On the debit side, I would be inclined to put a tendency to con-

---

[2] *Report of the Attorney General's National Committee to study the Antitrust Laws* (Washington, March 1955), p. 4.

ceal a very real development of antitrust law toward increasing emphasis on market power at the expense of monopolizing and restraining practices in Sherman Act cases; a total failure to take advantage of an opportunity to suggest policy and clarify the law with respect to mergers; and a treatment of exemptions to the antitrust laws that can only be described as perfunctory.

I wish to limit myself in this short paper to some aspects of the issue of *per se* rules versus the rule of reason and to a few brief remarks on the significance of market power in antitrust policy, hoping that my colleagues on this program will illuminate other aspects of the Report of the Attorney General's Committee.

Eugene Rostow, while partially dissenting from the majority findings, nevertheless states that "the principal theme of the Report, on which we are unanimous, is that Congress and the Courts have developed a reasonably unified and consistent corpus of antitrust law, directed at protecting the economy against substantial and significant limitations on competitive conditions." [3] Certainly Dean Rostow, in making this statement, speaks for a much larger group than the membership of the Attorney General's Committee. But the accent should be on "developed." The law and policy as they now stand, elaborated and expressed in recent cases, are something rather different from the law and policy in 1920.

The Attorney General's Committee, it is true, denies that this is so. Their professionally deft and skillful exegesis discovers a uniform and consistent body of law from the Steel Case to date and, like the devil quoting scripture, the Report quotes a corroborative excerpt from almost every important decision. This, I submit, is a relatively easy thing to do. Pareto once remarked that the statements of Karl Marx are like bats; from one angle they resemble birds while from another view they look like mice. This observation is equally apropos with respect to antitrust decisions. It is possible for the skillful reader to buttress almost any preconceived notion of what the antitrust laws are about by judicious citation of chapter and verse.

On the other hand, when one asks the question whether the steel decision in 1920[4] or the United Shoe Machinery decision of 1918[5]

[3] *Report*, p. 388.
[4] U. S. v. U. S. Steel Corporation, 251 U. S. 417 (1920).
[5] U. S. v. United Shoe Machinery Co. of N. J., 247 U. S. 32 (1918).

would have been probable in 1955, I submit that an affirmative answer seems highly dubious. It seems to me even more doubtful whether the Alcoa case[6] or the Tobacco,[7] the second United Shoe Machinery[8] or the Standard Stations[9] would have been decided the way they were in fact decided by the courts of the 1920's. As I read the decisions there has been a substantial development of antitrust law in the direction of an expanding area of *per se* rules and of a greater emphasis on market power at the expense of illegal conduct or practices. This development is — or should be — of considerable interest to economists as well as to lawyers since it calls for the application of tools that are commonly supposed to be in economic tool kits.

PER SE RULES

When the appointment of the Attorney General's Committee was announced, there was considerable apprehension on the part of proponent's of rigorous antitrust enforcement, both inside and outside the Committee, that this opportunity would be seized by the opposition to recommend a substantial expansion of the rule of reason. There was much girding up of loins — which on the whole appears to have been successful. Even that notable dissenter Louis B. Schwartz is constrained to admit that, "The Majority Report . . . does not call for a general expansion of the 'rule of reason.' "[10] The word "admit" is used advisedly since there seems to be a disposition on the part of most of those whom I here refer to as proponents of rigorous antitrust policy to look the horse that brought them victory skeptically in the mouth. Mr. Schwartz finds that "some of (the Report's) specific proposals" and the heavy emphasis placed on "full economic investigation" look "in the direction of limitation of the scope of *per se*."[11] These doubts are perhaps to some extent justified by the rather complacent attitude of those whom I here call opponents of rigorous antitrust enforcement. This complacency seems largely to be associated with their approval of

[6] U. S. v. Aluminum Co. of America, 148 Fed. Ind. 416 (1945).
[7] American Tobacco Co. v. U. S., 328 U. S. 781 (1946).
[8] U. S. v. United Shoe Machinery Co., 110 F. Supp. 295 (1953).
[9] Standard Oil Co. of California v. U. S., 337 U. S. 293 (1948).
[10] *Report*, p. 391.
[11] *Report*, p. 391.

the "realistic" attitude of the Report, particularly evident in Chapter 7, toward economic considerations affecting monopoly and competition, with special reference to the definition of markets.

These attitudes of the proponents and opponents of "rigor" toward "full economic enquiry" and a careful examination of the extent of the relevant market are worthy of comment. Is it that those favoring a large scope for *per se* fear that "full economic investigation" would disclose a less serious limitation of competition than is commonly supposed? In part, of course, the difference between the "pros" and "antis" is based on procedural considerations. The application of *per se* rules is a relatively cheap and quick method of enforcing the law; an appeal to the rule of reason frequently involves the "big case" which drags on for years at great expense to all except the lawyers concerned. The presumption that a number of the Committee members favoring an expansion of the rule of reason are members of the antitrust bar is perhaps not unrelated to the legal paradise presented by rule of reason cases.

But there is obviously more to this division of opinion than procedural considerations. Those favoring a broad scope for *per se* clearly fear that full economic investigation would lead to substantive results less desirable from their point of view. Those favoring an expansion of the rule of reason obviously feel that full economic investigation will bring about an antitrust law closer to their hearts' desire. Is this so and, if so, why?

The rule of reason presumably requires an examination of the "effects" of an alleged violation in order to determine whether, in fact, a violation has occurred. But the "effects" of a particular course of conduct in an interdependent economy consisting of a large number of decision-making units can be very far-reaching indeed. Suppose a price-fixing agreement succeeds in raising the price of a particular commodity. Increased profits for the participating firms induce outsiders to enter this market. In other industries the apparent new profit opportunities lead to a redesign of products in the direction of the price fixing industry's market. Under the impact of these adaptations the price fixing scheme breaks down and the industry is found — under appropriate definitions of competition — to be much more competitive than it was before.

We would probably all admit that this is a possibility. In an economy such as ours a particular disturbance can be over- as well as undercompensated. Furthermore, the repercussions of this disturbance can continue for a long time and spread over a wide surface before they eventually sink into the embracing arms of long-run equilibrium.

How far is full investigation supposed to go before we are entitled to form a judgment on the "reasonableness" of a course of conduct in the application of antitrust policy. Must we not agree with Schumpeter that, since we are dealing with an economy in process of development, a judgment on the consequences of any particular part of it — say a combination of hitherto independent firms — can only be an historical judgment, as these consequences "unfold over decades," and a partial judgment, since these repercussions reverberate throughout an economy whose development is "organic?" [12]

An attempt to push enquiry into effects very far is clearly an invitation to non-enforcement. The dissenting members of the Attorney General's Committee are quite right in fearing the consequences of "full economic investigation." On the other hand, the rule of reason — even in its "most reasonable" application — has never, in fact, examined very far into the effects of a challenged course of business conduct. At most it has pursued economic investigation one or two steps beyond the point at which *per se* would have carried it. A combination that is not illegal *per se* becomes illegal under the rule of reason if it pursues certain practices regardless of what the effects of this combination plus practices might turn out to be over a substantial period of time. A trade-association program, though not illegal *per se,* becomes illegal under the rule of reason if investigation turns up one or two so-called restrictive elements. The difference between *per se* rules and the rule of reason is not a difference between de facto violation and violation dependent upon an assessment of ultimate consequences. At most it is a difference between a and a + b.

Lawyers are said to love rules and economists are certainly addicted to models. The proper use of both rules and models is a question that lies at the heart of a valid distinction between *per se* and rule of reason. *Per se* involves a conclusive presumption that a

[12] J. A. Schumpeter, *Capitalism, Socialism and Democracy* (New York, 1942), p. 83.

specified course of action is in violation of the law. It is a refusal to examine the effects. The application of such a rule makes economic sense when, and only when, the facts — i.e., the market situation or course of conduct complained of — permit a legitimate inference as to the effects. It is at this point that the economist with his models enters from the wings. Unless we want to climb with Schumpeter up and down the seamless web of history, we must become theorists and be prepared to generalize. We must be prepared to say, for example, that, given a price-fixing agreement, it is possible to infer the effects and unnecessary to conduct a further examination. Or we must be prepared to say either that all requirements contracts have certain undesirable effects or that certain kinds of requirements contracts under certain specified conditions have these effects. The difference between *per se* and the rule of reason is essentially a difference in the detail required of the model in order to permit an inference concerning effects. This question, what types of models permit what kinds of inferences, is one to which economists might be expected to give answers. I shall not attempt here, however, an assessment of the value of their contribution to date to antitrust policy.

The primary difficulty, of course, in inferring economic effects from market situations or business practices lies in the fact that a sensible antitrust policy has in mind two kinds of effects. On the one hand we expect from our competitive, free enterprise systems, a set of powerful motivations and drives toward increased output, product improvement, cost reduction; in general, toward increased efficiency in the use of resources. On the other hand, we expect from the competitive system a set of effective limitations to the growth of private economic power. Efficiency and power — the one to be embraced and the other rejected. Both these aims are important, and it is essential that public policy keep both in mind.

If efficiency were not a desideratum, along with limitation of market power, no rule of reason would be necessary. It would then be possible to entertain a conclusive presumption against size, or market share, or integration, or various types of business activity now in legal doubt without threatening the fundamental purposes of antitrust policy. The law could then consist exclusively of *per se* rules and, if the number of firms were larger, and the number of permitted practices smaller, than strictly necessary to the effective limitation of market power, no harm would be done. This is, in fact, the "limitist" solution to antitrust policy and, if limitation of market power is the sole objective, there is much to be said for it.

The fact that limitation of market power is not the sole objective does not, however, necessitate opening the door to full economic investigation of ultimate consequences. At most it prompts a limited enquiry into the economic justification, if any, of the alleged violation.[13] How far this enquiry needs to go depends, superficially, on what confidence the courts *do* have and, more profoundly, on what confidence the courts *should* have in the process of economic analysis and generalization.

The law holds firmly that a price-fixing agreement is illegal *per se* and the conduct complained of has been broadened to include any "tampering with prices." The economic rationale behind this *per se* rule is presumably that an agreement among competitors to sell at a fixed price expands market power without bringing any perceptible economies to the production and distribution of the commodity affected. As we have seen, a price-fixing agreement may, in fact, set off a chain of consequences leading ultimately to a market structure more competitive than before. There may also be real economies — a reduction of selling costs, for example — associated with the agreement. To defend a *per se* rule is not to deny that such beneficial results *may* occur; it is only to assert that this outcome is sufficiently infrequent not to be worth bothering about.

It would be useful if, at this point, economists could step forward with the assurance that exhaustive study of price agreements and their consequences had demonstrated that invariably, or in 95 per cent of the cases in a properly selected sample, such agreements limited competition and thus increased market power without compensatory advantages on the side of efficiency. Despite extensive study of price-fixing arrangements, I doubt whether any such assurance can be given. Nor, I think, is it necessary. The economics that is relevant to antitrust policy is, of necessity, an *a priori*,

[13] A phrase frequently used is "business justification," but of course this is a misnomer. Any kind of restrictive or monopolistic practice may have a business justification.

partial-equilibrium, *ceteris paribus*-and-all-that, kind of economics, but it seems to me sufficient for its purpose. At least I am prepared to hold to this view until the general-equilibrium, creative-competition, dynamic-growth, economics becomes a little more concrete and specific than, to date, it seems to have been able to do.

As I read the development of antitrust law over the last two decades, the courts have substantially expanded the area of business practices within which they are willing to entertain a conclusive presumption that the practice in question limits competition (increases market power) without accompanying economies that can legitimately be inferred. In the course of this development, the notion of what constitutes a price-fixing agreement has been somewhat expanded but it has not encompassed the phenomenon of parallel pricing without more. It has become clearer that the *per se* rule also embraces agreements to limit output and group boycotts, and it is a legitimate inference that any concert among competitors is in jeopardy in the absence of a prima-facie showing of efficiencies. The debatable area is, of course, that of trade-association practices, and it is right that this area continue debatable since the range of variation of practices is infinite and there are involved real possibilities of improvement of efficiency. But let me reassert that the existence of these possibilities does not justify an examination over time into ultimate consequences. It is a question of modifying to some small extent the framework of the model from which inferences are sought to be drawn.

The tying contract has clearly become illegal *per se* and, so far as I am aware, there is no case in which tying contracts have been struck down where it could be plausibly argued that efficient operations were sacrificed. On the other hand, requirements contracts have obviously led the courts to take a second look at some of the broader aspects of so-called exclusive dealing arrangements. The brief incursion of *per se* into the field of integration was marked by hasty disavowals, and the more extreme statements of the doctrine of "substantially" have tended to be softened. What seems to have been happening is that the courts have substantially moved forward the frontiers of *per se* but have retreated when it became obvious that a more complex model was required. This is as it should be. The law needs to be as flexible as American business practice, and as long as efficiency as well as the curbing of market power is a desideratum *per se* rules cannot be static.

The argument thus far concerning *per se* rules and the rule of reason may be summarized baldly as follows:

1. The demand for full investigation of the consequences of a market situation or a course of business conduct is a demand for non-enforcement of the antitrust laws.

2. Neither *per se* nor the rule of reason calls, in fact, for such an investigation. The justification for any kind of effective antitrust policy depends upon the possibility of valid inferences from relatively simple statements of fact.[14] At most the rule of reason requires a somewhat more detailed elaboration of the market situation and course of business conduct (here called the model) from which inferences are drawn.

3. The effects or consequences sought to be inferred from the statement of facts have to do, on the one hand, with market power (or limitation of competition) and on the other with efficiency (wrongly called business justification). The importance of efficiency as a desideratum inevitably condemns any purely "limitist" interpretation of antitrust policy.

4. The proper scope of *per se* embraces market situations and courses of conduct that prima facie limit competition (extend market power) with no prima-facie contribution to efficiency. An effective enforcement of antitrust policy will seek to extend this scope to its legitimate limits.

5. If there exists a prima-facie case for a contribution to the efficiency of economic operations the enquiry must be extended but only to those limits required for valid inference of probable effect.

MARKET POWER

I turn now to a brief examination of another issue raised by the Report of the Attorney General's Commission, the relevance of market power to the problem of antitrust enforcement. Although it is obvious that the "limitist" position pure and simple is untenable, it nevertheless remains true that "limitism" is an essential ingredient

[14] "Simple" facts, however, are not necessarily simply determined. Whether cellophane is or is not one among many products in a market for flexible wrapping materials might be considered a simple fact but the evidence and argument for and against added up to a sizeable record.

in any antitrust policy worthy of the name. If we are to continue to rely on the market rather than on the social conscience of corporate management to give us the kind of business performance we want, the structure of markets must be such as to enforce acceptable competitive behavior. In other words there must be limits to the permissible degree of market power.

One of the central questions facing public action in this area is whether an antitrust policy that relies exclusively or mainly on enquiries into how power was acquired (e.g., through merger or reinvestment of earnings), or whether it has been abused, can establish proper limits. A corollary question is whether current antitrust policy does, in fact, rely exclusively or mainly on such enquiries.

The Report of the Attorney General's Committee, speaking of Section 2 offenses, states that "Economic monopoly becomes illegal monopolization not only (1) if it was achieved or preserved by conduct violating Section 1 (i.e., through collusion, merger, etc.) but also (2) if it was, even by restrictions not prohibited by Section 1, deliberately obtained or maintained." [15]

"Economic monopoly" in this context is, of course, a phrase of specious accuracy. There are degrees of monopoly or market power and this fact is adequately recognized in recent antitrust decisions. The meaning of the phrase "deliberately obtained or maintained" is also, to say the least, subject to interpretation. The critical questions are how much market power and how obtained or maintained?

The Report, attempting to answer these questions by means of a careful examination of cases, manages to leave the impression that, however market power and conduct — or the relations between the two — are interpreted, antitrust policy on this issue has been substantially unchanged for the last three decades.[16] It would be impossible to document the case for another interpretation without an exegesis too prolonged for this paper. I can merely state it as my impression that the law of Section 2 has developed in at least two directions: market power or, if you prefer, economic monopoly, is recognized in situations that would rather easily have passed muster in 1920; and, the standards of what constitutes abuse of

---

[15] *Report*, p. 43.
[16] See, for example, the discussion in *Report*, p. 50.

power have been rather stringently tightened. Market power "without more" is still no violation. But the "more" is now less and the concept of power is more embracing that it was in the 1920's.

That market power is an elusive quantity requires no demonstration before this audience. It is not possible nor will it ever be possible, by calculating market shares, dividing price minus marginal cost by price, or other hocus pocus, to present an unambiguous measure of the degree of monopoly. Market power has many dimensions. Nevertheless it should be equally obvious that judgments concerning the extent of market power are made in the enforcement of the antitrust laws and must be made unless we are willing to scrap this legislation in favor of an altogether different approach.

Remedy proceedings involving dissolution, inevitably raise the question of market power. Whatever one may think of Judge Knox's conclusions in the Aluminum proceedings, there is no doubt that the central problem he grappled with was how much market power would Alcoa be likely to have in postwar markets.[17] A judgment concerning market power is of the essence of merger policy. A policy that forbade all mergers among competitors would be nonsensical. But, if some are to be permitted and others forbidden, the dividing line must turn on conceptions of market power. And, as I have emphasized, market power is an increasingly important ingredient in Section 2 cases. Since economists are suspected of having something important to say concerning the phenomenon of market power, it is well for us to recognize that judgments are going to be made and that, on the whole, it is probably desirable that these judgments be economically sophisticated.

If we view the problem of antitrust enforcement realistically, we shall probably have to admit that regardless of how much the concept and the methods of analyzing market power are refined, it is not going to make much difference in Sherman Act violation cases. Given a firm that has grown powerful in a market through reinvestment of earnings and whose practices are "honestly industrial" — whatever that means — judges are going to be extremely loathe to take action that involves the breaking up of an effectively functioning economic organization, and I suspect that economists would, in

[17] U. S. v. Aluminum Co. of America. 917 Fed. Supp. 333.

their place, behave in much the same fashion. On the other hand, if violation is found, for whatever reason, an economically sophisticated interpretation of market power can do much to shape a sensible remedy.

The most fruitful field for the application of a market power standard, however, is merger policy. And where, in Sherman Act cases, the existence of going concerns argues for the application of — at best — a relaxed standard of market power, there is every reason why, in Section 7 cases, the standard should be strict.

If I may sum up in a word my reaction to the Report of the Attorney General's National Committee to Study the Antitrust Laws, I would say that it is a deft, professional job of legal analysis that minimizes certain important recent developments of antitrust policy and ignores a real opportunity to contribute in areas where policy is still inchoate.

Index

Adelman, M. A., 17, 25, 28, 29, 30, 31, 41, 371
Addyston pipe case, 51
Africa, 242, 280, 287, 314
Agricultural Adjustment Act, 149
Agricultural implements: industry, 50; prices, 150
Agricultural Marketing Agreements Act, 149
Agriculture: commodities and prices, 110, 137, 141, 173; concentration in, 24, 25, 31, 39, 46; cyclic upswing of wages and prices, 171; and national income, 148; output, 132, 246, 258–259; raw materials, 85–88, 245, 248, 258–260, 264, 265, 270; surplus foodstuffs, 85–86. *See also* Foodstuffs
Alcoa. *See* Aluminum Company of America
Allen, Frederick Lewis, 371
Allied Chemical Co., 48
Aluminum, 237, 242, 261, 287
Aluminum Company of America, 94, 139, 359–360, 373; cases, 359, 361, 373, 376, 385, 392, 400
Amidon, Charles F., 212, 213
Andrews, P. W. S., quoted, 6
Antitrust cases, 334–335, 358–365 *passim*
Antitrust Division (U. S. Department of Justice), 134, 199, 361, 370, 377, 382
Antitrust laws, 35, 51, 141, 167, 204, 352–370 *passim*, 372, 387, 391, 397, 398; Report of Attorney General's National Committee to Study, 389–402
Antitrust policy, 2, 3, 5, 77, 171, 175, 176, 327–328, 366, 368–384 *passim*, 389–402; Schumpeter on, 91–100, 371, 372, 378, 379
Appalachian Coal case, 341, 349
Argentina, 259, 290, 300

Armament production, 237; German, 228
Asia, 242, 244, 280, 314
Assets, 17, 20, 57
Atomic energy. *See* Nuclear energy
Australia, 259
Austria, 267
Automobile industry, 49, 66–67, 94, 114, 115, 119, 180, 368
Automobiles, 150, 162

Bain, J. S., 367 n39, 368
Bakke, E. Wight, 217
Bargaining power, doctrine of equal, 213–215
Barnett, H. J., 298, 309
Basing-point system, 7, 140, 146–147, 151, 356, 365
Berge, Wendell, 74
Berle, A. A., 1, 19, 27
Bone Committee, 81
Boycotts, group, 397
Brand-consciousness, 157, 158
Brandeis, Louis, 356
Brazil, 289–290, 296, 300
Brewster, Kingman, 327
British Imperial Chemical Industries, 83
British Trades Disputes Act, *1906*, 213
Buffer-stock agreements, 273–275
Building materials: tables, 127, 128
Bureau of Mines, 241, 272
Burns, Arthur R., 8, 118
Business: competition, 218; cycle, 59, 109, 110, 132–133, 134, 159–167 *passim*, 174–178 *passim*, 182–195 *passim*; organization, 21–23; performance, 358–368 *passim*; practices, 95, 134, 194, 354, 383
Business Advisory Council on Effective Competition, 371
Buyers and sellers: in non-price com-

petition, 155–159; numbers, 173, 179, 348, 352, 354; and prices, 113, 137, 138, 142, 151, 156, 167, 178–179; "reasonableness" doctrine, 339

Canada: agriculture, 259; energy costs and prices, 287, 298, 315; large firms, 14, 38
Capacity-output relations, 328, 368
Capital, 159, 246, 294, 303, 310, 348
Capital goods prices, 110
Cassels, J. M., 59 n7
Cartels, 73–85; definition, 73–75; labor unions compared to, 202, 207; political aspects, 83–85; security aspects, 81–83; as trade barriers, 78–81. See also Commodity agreements
Cellophane case, 377
Cement case, 352, 365
Cement industry, 140
Census industry, 3, 5, 33
Chamberlain, Neil, 209 n17
Chamberlin, E., 2
Chemicals and drugs: tables, 127, 128
Chicago Board of Trade, 356
Chile, 300
Chromium ores: Balkans, 230
Cigarette industry, 51. See also Tobacco case
Clark, J. M., 353 n7, 356, 382
Clayton Act, 213
Climate: and energy requirements, 285, 287, 310
Coal, 141, 260, 264–267, 282, 298, 302–303, 310, 312, 313; anthracite industry, 50; Bituminous Coal Act, 149; bituminous coal industry, 148, 351; transportation costs, 295, 320–321; western European, 240, 312
Collective bargaining, 190, 203, 207–211 passim, 218
Collusion, 51, 328, 356, 362, 366
Colombia, 289–290
Columbia Steel Co. case, 361, 373
Combination, 337, 346. See also Mergers
Commerce, Dept. of, data, 29, 41
Commodity: agreements, 75; controls, 85–90; defined, 46; groups, 127;

postponable demand, 162; prices, 159; solutions, 274. See also Cartels
Competition: Chamberlin's view, 2; exclusion, 385, 386, 387; legal criteria, 359–362; limiting, 340–346, 375, 398; and monopoly, 44–54, 178–180; non-price aspects, 155–159; and price policies, 168–180; "pure," 328, 330, 352, 353, 358; types, 351–367; and unions, 198, 215; "workable," 177–180, 328–330, 351–367 passim, 381–385 passim
Competitive market "model," 2, 186, 327, 330, 398
Commons, John R., 21
Construction industries, 153, 154
Concentration: countries compared, 38–39; increase in, 23–32; measures of, 16–23, 31, 42; trends, 26–27, 28–35, 39–43, 44–54. See also Antitrust
Consumers, 157, 158, 159
Consumers' goods, 137, 138, 156, 161, 164
Copper, 225, 228, 229, 230, 237, 239, 261, 376
Conspiracy, 338, 364
Corporation: large, 15, 16, 17; and control, 45. See also Large firm
Cost of living, 172, 173
Cost-price relationship, 171–172, 176–177, 328, 354, 367–368. See also Price behavior
Costs, 110, 166, 174, 187, 303; in Keynesian analysis, 182; of raw materials, 225, 242–243; real: of fabrication, 256, of raw materials, 264, of minerals production, 261–262; and size of plant, 335; variable, 65. See also Energy, costs; Electricity, costs
Cotton textile industry, 148
"Countervailing power" theory, 379
Cox, Archibald, 216
Cream of Wheat case, 334–335
Crowder, W. F., 33
Currency convertibility, 260

D'Arcy v. Allein, 336
Deák, Francis, 336

Defense: and raw materials, 85, 88, 89, 224–225, 227, 233, 237–239; strategic areas, 226, 231, 233–234
Demand, 6, 169, 172, 193
Demand curve, 57, 115, 118
Denmark, 267, 285, 287
Depression, 51, 89, 161, 187–195, 244–245. *See also* Business, cycle
Dorfman, Adolfo, 300
Douglas, Paul, 203
Douglas, William O., 20–21, 216
Downswing. *See* Business, cycle
Dunlop, John T., 203
Du Pont Co., 74
Durable goods, 162–163, 254–255
Düsseldorf discussion, 82

Economic Commission for Europe, 298–299
Economic growth, 244–248, 269, 275–323 *passim*, 377, 385, 387; and energy, 277, 283–293, 297
Economic policy, 89–90, 117–119, 228, 235, 347, 352–353
Economic view of monopoly, 332–350 *passim*, 357, 359
Economic warfare, 77, 234–236
Economies of scale, 355
Efficiency, economic, 145–157 *passim*, 214, 298, 395, 398
Educational system, 169
Edwards, Corwin, 354 n7, 367
Electricity: costs, 163, 309; investment, 299–301; power consumption, 153, 305, 307–308; prices, 152, 302–303; substitutability, 282. *See also* Coal; Energy; Hydroelectricity; Power
Electro-process industries, 286, 287, 307
Employee, definition of, 216–217
Employers, 181, 191–194, 195, 197
Employment, 17, 24–25, 57, 89, 169, 170; rates of, 285, 289, 290; and wage-price problems, 115, 118, 140, 145–146, 151–154, 159–166, 176–177, 181–188, 189, 191–194
Employment Act of *1946*, 177
Energy: consumption, 277, 279–280, 282–288, 292, 296, 299, 302, 305,

306, 317, 318; costs, 285, 293, 295, 298, 299, 305–315 *passim;* prices, 296, 297–299, 301–303, 310; requirements, 266, 276–282 *passim*, 285, 287, 288, 291–293, 310, 312, 316; sources, 240, 265–268, 290, 297, 310–314; supply, 302, 310; use, 282, 285–305 *passim. See also* Electricity; Nuclear energy
Enforcement agencies, 370
Engels, Friedrich, 23
Engrossing, 337, 338
Entry, 327, 329, 333, 346, 348, 360
Excess capacity, 76–77
Export-Import Bank, 264
Exports, 78, 79, 85, 87–88, 89, 239–240, 243, 245–247, 257–258

Fabrication, 255; plant location, 151
Fair trade laws, 351
Farm: incomes, 190, 195; price supports, 190; products, 127, 128, 130. *See also* Agriculture
"Featherbedding," 206
Federal Reserve Board, 134
Federal Trade Commission, 1–2, 3, 16, 49, 150, 370; Report on Mergers, 27, 29
Federal Trade Commission Act, 365
Fellner, William, 202
Ferro-alloys, 228, 229
Finland, 285–286, 287
Firestone Co., 64, 68
Firms: and antitrust policy, 372–376; behavior of, 355, 363; compass of, 7, 21, 369; market power of, 352, 376, 377; number of, 327, 329, 355; size of, 16–23, 32, 52, 56–58, 66, 179, 355, 374. *See also* Large firms
Fishing industry, 86
Foodstuffs, 85–86, 127–130, 222, 255–260, 268, 270, 337
Foreign exchange requirements, 299–301
Foreign investment, 243, 248–249
Foreign trade, 87, 89
Ford Co., 64
Forest properties, 270–271
Forestalling, 337

Frankel, P. H., 278
Fuel, 127, 128, 294–300, 302, 309, 323

Galbraith, J. K., 111, 211, 371, 372
Garbarino, John, 204
Gas, 265, 266, 268, 295, 302–303, 310, 311
General Electric Co., International, 74
General Motors, 373
Germany: cartels, 85; price controls, 52; raw materials in World War II, 228–230, 235; wartime agreements with U. S., 81
Glass products, 307
Government: and buffer-stock agreements, 274; and full employment, 189; and limits on unions, 208, 210, 211; and pressure groups, 15, 194, 195; and price policy, 167, 273; and raw-material resources, 263–265, 270–272, 305; regulation: of cartels, 84, of control, 47; reports (general), 1–2, 389. See also Public policy; Public action
Great Britain: cartels, 83, 85; concentration in, 14, 38; court decisions on reasonableness, 341; and economic warfare, 235; energy problems, 267, 289, 290, 315; export coal costs, 295, 320–321; productivity, 256–257, 260; textile plants, 38; and unions, 212, 213
Grocery stores, 156
Gross National Product, 238, 254, 278, 289

Hand, Learned, 360, 385
Heating requirements, 266
Hides and leather products: tables, 127, 128
Holmes, Justice Oliver Wendell, 210, 212, 344, 357
Housefurnishing goods: tables, 127, 128
Houses, rate of use of, 162
Hughes, Charles Evans, 370
Humphrey, D. D., 112, 121
Hutcheson case, 199, 210, 215
Hydroelectricity, 265–267, 310, 311, 312

Iceland, 287
Ickes, Harold, 135
Ideology: of capitalism, 95; on market limitations, 369; of Schumpeter, 96
Imports, 87–88, 242, 255–260 passim, 267, 311, 360
Income, 37, 76, 87, 145, 148, 160, 163, 167, 169, 183, 191; and economic growth, 280, 283–285, 288, 290, 297–299, 309; and energy consumption, 283–293, 317; of power stations, 323
India, 14, 38
Industry Division of the Economic Commission for Europe, 278
Industrialization, 95, 244–248; and energy, 275–323 passim; and raw materials, 244–248, 255, 257, 269; growth rates, 264, 269, 280. See also Economic growth
Industries: and concentration, 14, 15, 24, 59; employment in, 25, 290; expansion of existing, 152; Marshallian competitive requirements, 6–7; in mature economies, 288–290, 297; self-government of, 208; in underdeveloped countries. See Underdeveloped countries
Inflation, 168, 169
Inflexibility. See Prices
Innovation, 92–94, 97–98, 179, 189, 329–330, 356, 357, 367, 377–379
Instability, 182. See also Prices
Insurance, 263
International Bank, 264
International Business Machines, 377
International Harvester Co., 63, 333
International Materials Conference, 237
Investment, 147–154, 205; foreign, 243, 248–249
Ireland, 285
Iron ore, 230, 239, 241, 243, 251, 264, 265, 282

Jackson, Robert, 134, 135
Japan, 38; energy problems, 238, 242, 245, 250, 257, 285, 289, 296
Jervey, Huger W., 336

Kerr, Clark, 204
Keynes, J. M., 106; analysis, 181–183
Knox, P. C., 373, 386, 400
Korean War, 253, 273
Labor: diversion from agriculture, 246, 248; division of, 340; market, 198–199, 215; relations, 208, 212; requirements for raw-material production, 230, 235; supply, 159, 197, 200, 201, 226, 255, 258. See also Collective bargaining; Employment; Unions
Labor-Management Conference, 1945, 217
Labor-Management Relations Act, 208, 211
Labor Statistics, Bureau of: data, 119–130 passim
Laidler, H. W., 49
Large firms: and antitrust actions, 371–381, 385; and cartels, 73–85, 89–90; and commodity agreements, 85–90; and concentration, 23–32, 36–39, 41–42; and declining competition, 44–54; defined, 16–18; influence on wages and prices, 182; and monopolies, 18–19, 32–35, 39–41; non-market aspects, 19–23; price and production policies, 55–72, 170–177; role of, 13–15; Schumpeter on, 91–101
Latin America, 229, 242, 244, 280
Latin-American Duperial Co., 74
Law: and collusion, 358–362; concept of monopoly, 334–350, 357–366
Leak, H., 37
Legislation: antitrust, see Antitrust laws; on government exploration for minerals, 271; on price fixing, 396; and self-interest doctrine, 210; and trade marks and trade names, 349. See also Public policy
Lester, Richard, 206, 217
Lewis, John L., 351
Lilienthal, David, 371–380 passim
Lumber, 270; industry, 171

McCabe, D. A., 211
McGowan, Lord, 73

Machlup, Fritz, 205
Maizels, A., 37
Management, 62, 208, 375; "prerogatives," 217–218
Manufacturing, 25, 31, 37, 38, 278, 286, 305. See also Industrialization
Market: analysis, 49, 60; competitive, 33–35, 170, 181; conditions, 353–362 passim; definitions of, 5, 21, 65, 68, 178, 381; limitations on firms' action, 369–376; "model," 2, 4–8, 186, 327, 330, 398; organization, 125, 137, 138, 352; shares, 51, 378, 379–380
Market control, 147, 166, 189, 334–349, 357, 359, 360
Market power, 92, 93, 328, 374–381 passim, 387–388, 391, 398, 399, 400; of labor unions, 196, 197–198, 200, 205, 206, 214
Market situation: and firms, 58, 61, 139, 171, 339, 398; and "workable competition," 178–180
Market structure, 48, 61, 65–70, 328–329, 352, 353, 354, 355, 358, 369, 383; oligopoly, 58–60; prices, 170–175 passim; tests, 366–368
Marshallian "model," 4–8
Marx, Karl, 23
Materials Policy Commission, President's, 222, 253, 256, 262, 263, 265, 268, 272, 274, 275, 278
Means, Gardiner, 9, 16, 25–26, 30, 33, 47, 52, 111, 121, 123
Mergers, 26, 30, 48, 51, 343, 399–401
Metals, 127, 128, 307; industry, 86; scrap, 230. See also specific entries
Mexico, 289–290
"Micro economics," 4
Middle East, 231–233, 312
Miller-Tydings Act, 351
Mills, F. C., 111, 121
Minerals, 86, 239–243, 260–265, 268, 271, 303, 304, 322; and economic growth, 247–250
Mining, 31, 47, 285, 385
Mond, Sir Alfred, 83
Monopolies, President's Message on, 135, 141
Monopolies, Statute of, 336

Monopoly: blended with competition, 174, 178; concepts of, 1–8, 332–333, 347–348; and concentration, 18–19, 32–43; degree of, 44–54, 110, 113, 196, 205, 399; economic versus legal definition, 332, 334–350, 357–366; and innovation, 356, 357; and labor unions, 176, 196–218 *passim;* legal tests of, 328, 336, 341–346, 369, 384; and prices, 53–54, 113, 141; problems, 5–8, 45, 147. See *also* Antitrust; Large firms
Monopoly Investigation. See Temporary National Economic Committee
Moore, H. L., 115
Multilateral contracts, 273, 274
Myrdal, Gunnar, 116

Nathan, Robert, 177, 184–187 *passim*
National Cash Register Company, 387
National Labor Relations Act, 203, 213, 216
National Lead case, 362
National Petroleum Council, 241
National Recovery Act, 141
National Resources Committee, 1, 33; Report, *1939*, 17
Near East, 242, 243, 244, 268
Norway, 212, 267, 285, 287
Nuclear energy, 276, 277, 294, 296, 300–301, 314–316
Nutter, G. Warren, 28, 33, 35–36 n38, 40, 41

O. P. A., 6
Oil, 141, 231–233, 239–242, 251, 265, 267, 282, 295, 302–303, 310–314
Oil company investment, 243
Oligopoly, 2, 5, 7, 58–60, 329
Organization for European Economic Cooperation, 278
Output: of census products, 32; data, 48–49; energy, 310, 342; expansion, 151, 153, 154, 258, 263; raw materials, 225, 227, 240; restrictions, 76, 149, 150, 354, 387, 397; and wages and prices, 162–187 *passim,* 216. See *also* Productivity
Ownership: relation to control, 3, 19–20, 45

Pakistan, 38
Paley Commission, 311–312
Patents, 81, 93
Per se, 390–398
Personnel, 97, 169
Petroleum, 50, 247, 260, 264–268, 272, 368. See *also* Oil
Pigou, A. C., 59 n8, 65, 94, 106
Population growth, 238, 254, 290, 310
Price, wholesale, 110, 119, 121, 124, 130, 159, 168, 189
Price behavior, 7, 8, 61, 115, 117, 142, 155, 167, 168–171, 189, 342; amplitude, 125–132, 161; "automatic" changes, 136; frequency of change, 119–125, 130–132, 161; geographical differences, 296; increases, 147, 159, 166, 169, 172, 184–186, 192–193, 261; reductions, 159, 160, 162–163, 177
Price fixing, 51, 155, 167, 348, 352, 385–387, 393, 396
Price flexibility, 182; defined, 109–111, 114–116; economic policy, 117–119; frequency and amplitude, 119–132; series, 110–113, 123, 125; statistical measures, 111–114
Price inflexibility, 52, 53–54, 109–110, 121, 124, 130, 141–142, 161–163, 178; defined, 105–106; measures of, 132, 160–161
Price policy: defined, 55–56; efficiency, 145–154; and employment, 138–167 *passim;* leadership, 50–51; and market structure, 56–61, 65–70, 171–177; raw materials, 273, 274; toward conspiracy, 363–364. See *also* Public policy
Price stability, 6, 53, 85, 142, 149, 168–170, 173–174, 184, 194–195; and market structure, 173–176
Price supports, 149, 150, 190, 273, 390
Price system, 109, 127, 137, 139, 144, 166, 170–173, 175, 176, 183
Price-wage relationship. See Wages
Private interests, 341, 346, 395
Product: costs, 158; definition, 33, 335; differentiation, 46; improvement, 354; markets, 65, 170, 198–

199, 215, 360; "mix," 285; prices, 110, 170, 335; standard, 352
Productivity, 189, 191, 238, 254, 256, 310; wartime, 81; peacetime, 225
Profits: and competition, 149, 150, 170, 178, 205, 328, 402; pooling, 202; as test, 368; and wages and prices, 188, 190, 194–195
Power, electric: capital requirements, table, 319; fuel costs and income, table, 323; projects, 303; requirements, table, 386; sources, 394. *See also* Electricity
Public action, 149, 211, 271, 351, 353, 368–369, 399. *See also* Antitrust
Public interest, 156, 333, 339, 340, 345; tests of, 380
Public policy: bases for formulating, 8–10; and collective bargaining, 208; and competition, 178, 329; in downswing, 188–189; on market power, 381; on monopoly, 35, 103, 332–333, 335, 336, 338, 341, 342, 346–350, 366–370; and price policy, 141–143, 175, 184; on prices, 70–72, 147, 149–151, 162–165, 167, 182, 191, 193–195; on raw materials, 269–272; in United Kingdom and Scandinavia, 212. *See also* Antitrust policy; Government; Price policy; Public action
Public utilities, 25, 27, 31, 47, 110, 353
Public Utilities Holding Company Act, 25
Pullman Co., 373

Rationing, of raw materials, 234–235
Raw materials: agricultural, *see* Agriculture; commodity agreements, 85–89; consumption, 250, 253, 257, 261; costs, 222, 225–226, 227, 240, 242, 261; and economic growth, 247–250, 254–259; and economic warfare, 234–236; Germany, 228–230, 235; minerals, *see* Minerals; prices, 86, 172, 174, 238, 240, 242, 250, 260, 274–275; requirements, 239–242, 252, 254–255; security, 226, 250–251; shortages, 235, 237–

238; sources and supplies, 225–228, 242–247, 250, 258–268; and technology, 269–272; terms of trade, 254–258
Rayon industry, 94, 367
Rearmament effort, 237–238. *See also* Raw materials
Reasonableness, doctrine of, 338–339, 340–342, 391, 393–394, 398
Regrating (definition), 337
Reinvestment of earnings, 399
Resources, economic, 76, 144, 147, 148, 151, 154, 167–168, 382, 385. *See also* Raw materials
Restraint of trade, 336, 338, 340, 356, 369
Restriction, public, 93, 148–149; by firms, 338, 340, 344, 357
Retail distribution, 25, 355
Reynolds, Lloyd, 205
Robinson, Joan, 1, 2, 65
Robinson-Patman Act, 351, 390
Rosenbluth, Gideon, 17, 37
Ross, Arthur, 203
Rostow, Eugene, 391
Rubber, synthetic, 241, 251

Sales: and prices, 154–159, 162–163, 174, 179; volume, 57
Says's law, 136
Scandinavia, 212, 260
Schumpeter, J. A., 8, 13, 20, 64 n12, 91–101 *passim,* 329–330, 357, 371, 372–379, 394
Schurr and Marshak investigation, 309
Schwartz, Louis B., 392
Scitovsky, T. de, 183 n4
Sears, Roebuck Co., 379
Security, 79, 81–83, 89, 250–252
Security and Exchange Commission, 29
Self-interest doctrine, 209–213, 216
Sellers. *See* Buyers and sellers
Selling expenditures, 368
Service markets, 170
Sherman Act, 341–346 *passim,* 351, 365, 372, 387
Shortages, 235–238, 254, 262
Sloan, Alfred P., 371

Smaller War Plants Corporation on Economic Concentration in World War II, Report of, 27
South America, 287. *See also* specific countries
Standard Oil Company, 49, 74, 94, 373, 387, 392
Standard Oil-Vacuum merger, 343
Static equilibrium assumptions, 59
Statistics of Income, 29
Steel, 237, 260, 264; alloy, 230; industry, 49–50, 67, 140, 146; prices, 118; stainless, 376; U. S. consumption, 261
Steel case, 385, 391
Steel wage settlement, *1949,* 186
Steel Workers' Organization Committee, 63
Stigler, George, 32, 35–36 n38, 353 n7, 366
Stockpiling, 251, 273
Stone, Kimbrough, 307, 343, 344
Strike losses, 191, 192
Substitution, 225, 232, 240, 269, 282, 305, 377. *See also* Synthetics
Sugar Act, 149
Sugar Institute, 49, 349
Supreme Court, U. S., 352, 373
Surplus production, 85, 88
Sweden, 267, 287
Swift case, 385
Switzerland, 267, 287
Synthetics, 240, 241, 251, 265, 267, 269

Taft-Hartley Act, 208, 211
Tanks, 228
Tariffs, protective, 76, 83, 263
Tatta Iron and Steel Works, 14, 38
Tax concessions, 263
Technical assistance programs, 264
Technology: and competition, 353, 382; development of, 250, 256, 265, 329, 378; in Far East and U. S., 38; in home, 308; and raw materials, 240–242, 244, 269–272
Temporary National Economic Committee, 1, 18, 134, 135, 138, 144, 164
Texas Railroad Commission, 351
Textiles, 38, 127, 128, 171, 241

Thailand, 285
Thorp, W. L., 33
Time differentials, 111
Tin, 228, 229
Tires, rubber, 68
Titanium, 242, 367
Timber, 260, 270
Tobacco case, 361, 363, 385, 386, 392
Trade: associations, 51; barriers, 78–81, 88; expansion, 25; restraints, 334, 342; terms of, 254–258; world, 87
Trade marks, 348–349
Trade unions. *See* Unions
"Transfer costs," 22
Transportation, 46, 278, 285, 294, 307; and control, 49; cost of, 295, 297; facilities, 340
Treaties, 263
Triffin, Robert, 5–6
Trucks, 150
Truman Committee (Special Senate Committee), 1
Tucker, Rufus C., 121
Tying contract, 397

Underdeveloped countries: energy requirements, 280; industrial growth of, 290–293; and raw materials, 244–248, 255
Unemployment, 152, 191, 193
Union of South Africa, 296
Unions: influence on prices, 181, 182, 204, 205, 216; influence on wages, 106, 168, 172, 181–182, 190–195, 203–206; limits to power of, 207–213 *passim;* market power of, 197, 203, 205; as monopolies, 176, 196–218 *passim;* rise of large, 15, 21; and steel wage settlement, 186. *See also* Labor
United Kingdom. *See* Great Britain
United Mine Workers, 216
United Nations Group of Experts, 193–194
United Nations Paper on World Energy Requirements, 279
United Shoe Machinery case, *1918,* 391, 392
United States: and cartels, 80, 83;

economy, 24, 38, 168–170, 189–190, 377; and energy, 238, 277, 278, 288, 302–310, 311–314; imports and exports, 87–89, 239, 261, 275; and international commodity regulation, 85–95; raw materials, 258–272 *passim. See also* Government; Law; Legislation; Productivity; Public Policy; Raw Materials

United States Steel Corporation, 14, 38, 48, 57, 62, 361, 373

Universal Atlas Cement Company, 352

U.S.S.R., 279, 290

Venezuela, 243, 247, 289–290

Wages: and employment, 115; increase in, 165; and overinvestment, 149; wage-price relationships, 9, 106, 110, 168–172, 174, 175–177, 182–195 *passim. See also* Unions

Wagner Act, 208, 213, 216

Webb-Pomerene law, 74

Western Alliance, 232

Western Europe: and energy, 267–268, 277, 278, 288, 295–296, 312; raw materials, 238, 240, 257

White, Edward Douglas, 341

Wholesale price. *See* Price, wholesale

Wilcox, Clair, 35 n38, 40, 353 n7

Williams, J. H., 181, 194, 195

Working conditions, 201, 206

World War I, 234, 236, 302

World War II, 302; economic warfare, 234, 235, 236; and raw materials, 227, 228, 253